The Solow Model of Economic Growth

In 1956, Solow proposed a neoclassical growth model in opposition or as an alternative to Keynesian growth models. The Solow model of economic growth provided foundations for models embedded in the new theory of economic growth, known as the theory of endogenous growth, such as the renowned growth models developed by Paul M. Romer and Robert E. Lucas in the 1980s and 1990s. The augmentations of the Solow model described in this book, excepting the Phelps golden rules of capital accumulation and the Mankiw-Romer-Weil and Nonneman-Vanhoudt models, were developed by the authors over the last two decades.

The book identifies six spheres of interest in modern macroeconomic theory: the impact of fiscal and monetary policy on growth; the effect of different returns to scale on production; the influence of mobility of factors of production among different countries on their development; the effect of population dynamics on growth; the periodicity of investment rates and their influence on growth; and the effect of exogenous shocks in the form of an epidemic. For each of these issues, the authors construct and analyse an appropriate growth model that focuses on the description of the specific macroeconomic problem.

This book not only continues the neoclassical tradition of thought in economics focused on quantitative economic change but also, and to a significant extent, discusses alternative approaches to certain questions of economic growth, utilizing conclusions that can be drawn from the Solow model. It is a useful tool in analysing contemporary issues related to growth.

Paweł Dykas is an Associate Professor at the Department of Mathematical Economics of the Jagiellonian University, Krakow, Poland.

Tomasz Tokarski is Full Professor of Economics at the Department of Mathematical Economics of the Jagiellonian University, Krakow, Poland.

Rafał Wisła is Professor of Economics at the Department of Economics and Innovation of the Jagiellonian University, Krakow, Poland.

Routledge Studies in Economic Theory, Method and Philosophy

False Feedback in Economics
The Case for Replication
Andrin Spescha

The Economics and Science of Measurement
A Study of Metrology
Albert N. Link

Teaching and Research Methods for Islamic Economics and Finance
Edited by Moh'd Ma'Sum Billah

The Art and Science of Econometrics
Ping Zong

Financial Market Analysis and Behaviour
The Adaptive Preference Hypothesis
Emil Dinga, Camelia Oprean-Stan, Cristina-Roxana Tănăsescu, Vasile Brătian, and Gabriela-Mariana Ionescu

Complexity Economics
Economic Governance, Science and Policy
Olivér Kovács

The Solow Model of Economic Growth
Application to Contemporary Macroeconomic Issues
Paweł Dykas, Tomasz Tokarski and Rafał Wisła

For more information about this series, please visit: www.routledge.com/Routledge-Studies-in-Economic-Theory-Method-and-Philosophy/book-series/RSEMTP

The Solow Model of Economic Growth

Application to Contemporary Macroeconomic Issues

Paweł Dykas,
Tomasz Tokarski and
Rafał Wisła

Routledge
Taylor & Francis Group
LONDON AND NEW YORK

First published 2023
by Routledge
4 Park Square, Milton Park, Abingdon, Oxon OX14 4RN

and by Routledge
605 Third Avenue, New York, NY 10158

Routledge is an imprint of the Taylor & Francis Group, an informa business

British Library Cataloguing-in-Publication Data
A catalogue record for this book is available from the British Library

Library of Congress Cataloging-in-Publication Data
A catalog record has been requested for this book

ISBN: 978-1-032-34775-2 (hbk)
ISBN: 978-1-032-34777-6 (pbk)
ISBN: 978-1-003-32379-2 (ebk)

DOI: 10.4324/9781003323792

Typeset in Times New Roman
by codeMantra

The open access license of the publication was funded by Ministry of Education and Science (Poland) under the Excellence in Science Programme (project ID: DNM/SP/548280/2022) and Jagiellonian University in Kraków.

To my wonderfull, darling Oleńka

ttokarski

Contents

Figures

Tables

Author Biographies

Paweł Dykas is an Associate Professor at the Department of Mathematical Economics of the Jagiellonian University in Krakow (Poland) and is also the author and co-author of over 50 academic publications such as *The Neoclassical Model of Economic Growth and Its Ability to Account for Demographic Forecasts* (2018), *Demographic Forecasts and Volatility of Investment Rates vs. Labour Productivity Trajectories* (2019) and *An Impact of the Variable Technological Progress Rate on the Trajectory of Labour Productivity* (2020). Recently, he has co-edited and contributed to *The Socioeconomic Impact of COVID-19 on Eastern European Countries* (Routledge, 2022). His main interests include the mathematical theory of economic growth, an analysis of the spatial diversity of economic development and an analysis of regional differences in the labour market.

Tomasz Tokarski is Full Professor of Economics at the Department of Mathematical Economics of the Jagiellonian University in Krakow (Poland) and is also the author and co-author of over 200 academic publications such as *Wybrane Modele Podażowych Czynników Wzrostu Gospodarczego* (Selected Supply Models of Economic Growth) (2005), *Ekonomia Matematyczna Modele Mikroekonomiczne* (Microeconomic models of Mathematical Economics) (2011), *Ekonomia Matematyczna Modele Makroekonomiczne* (Macroeconomic Models of Mathematical Economics) (2011) and extensive research and publications dealing with economic growth models and problems related to regional and local development. He is the Director of the Department of Mathematical Economics in the Institute of Economics, Finance and Management at the Jagiellonian University in Krakow. His main interests include gravitational growth models and the differentiation of spatial economic development in Europe.

Rafał Wisła is Professor of Economics at the Department of Economics and Innovation of the Jagiellonian University in Krakow (Poland) and is also the author and co-author of over 80 academic publications such as *Innovation in the Pharmaceutical and Medical Technology Industries of Poland* (2018), *Developmental Diversification of Contemporary Europe* (2016) and *Regional Patterns of Technology Accumulation in Central and Eastern Europe Countries* (2014). Recently, he has co-edited and contributed to *Economic Transformation in Poland and Ukraine* (Routledge, 2020) and *The Socioeconomic Impact of COVID-19 on Eastern European Countries*

(Routledge, 2022). He is the Head of the Department of Economics and Innovation in the Institute of Economics, Finance and Management at the Jagiellonian University in Krakow and also Doctoral Program Co-ordinator in Economics and Finance at Jagiellonian University (2019–2023). The issues that he deals with are the differentiation of spatial economic development in Europe and innovation activity from a regional perspective.

Introduction

Without the fundamental discoveries by Isaac Newton (the three universal laws of motion, the law of universal gravitation) and Albert Einstein (the theory of relativity), today's theoretical physics would be severely deficient. Its development was also greatly stimulated by the quantum theory (quantum mechanics) with its foundations laid by Albert Einstein, Max Planck, Werner Heisenberg and Erwin Schrödinger. The solution to numerous engineering and technical problems, the development and application of countless inventions that serve (with better or worse outcomes) both individuals and entire human societies would be impossible without advanced physics.

In macroeconomics, John M. Keynes and Robert M. Solow occupy similar positions as Newton, Einstein and Planck in physics. John M. Keynes was first to propose (in the 1930s) a coherent macroeconomic theory, and R. M. Solow (in the 1950s) laid foundations for the today's theory of economic growth. The macroeconomic theory proposed by Keynes can be described as a short-run and demand-side model while Solow developed a long-run and supply-side model.[1] The analyzes made by Keynes and Solow provided foundations for macroeconomic models that describe both short-run and long-run economic processes with increasing accuracy. The models result in improved quantification, better understanding and more correct forecasting of macroeconomic processes.

Economic growth was first addressed by the classical school of economy in the 18th century. However, that topic aroused the deepest interest in the 20th and 21st centuries when the phenomenon of increase in the value of output produced in an economy and the determinants of that increase became mathematically formalized.

Evsey D. Domar, an American economist who analyzed economic growth processes in the mid-20th century concluded that:

> In economic theory, growth has occupied an odd place: always seen around but seldom invited in. It has been either taken for granted or treated as an afterthought. In the meantime, we have cheerfully gone ahead discussing employment and investment, interest and profits, accumulation of capital, business cycles, and many other exciting problems

DOI: 10.4324/9781003323792-1

> which clearly demand the explicit use of the rate of growth, and which we have most ingeniously tried to solve in a theoretical wonderland...
>
> (Domar 1957, p. 16)

The Keynesian school pioneered in proposing formalized economic growth models, including principally the model developed by Roy F. Harrod (1939), Evsey D. Domar (1946) and (after the publication of the Solow growth model) the models created by Michał Kalecki (1963, 1996) and Nicholas Kaldor (1963). The Keynesian economic growth models were heavily influenced by the Great Depression in the 1930s. This explains why strong emphasis is placed in those models on discrepancies between demand-side and supply-side factors that determine economic growth. Considering that Keynesian economic growth models assume almost zero substitution of production factors (capital and labour) used in the production process, those models suggest that a free-market economy is exposed to an almost permanent risk of imbalance. The risk is posed by incomplete utilization of economy's output capacity, a deficiency that was relatively readily accepted by Keynesian macroeconomics that paid particular attention to this problem (Barro and Sala-i-Martin 1995, p. 10).

Solow proposed in 1956 a neoclassical growth model (referred to in this monograph as the Solow model) as an opposition (or alternative) to Keynesian growth models. The pioneering analyzes made by Solow were triggered by the following observation: "Harrod's writings, especially, were full of incompletely worked out claims that steady growth was in any case a very unstable sort of equilibrium", and:

> An expedition from Mars arriving on Earth, having read this literature [on Keynesian growth models] would have expected to find only the wreck-age of a capitalism that had shaken itself to pieces long ago. Economic history was indeed a record of fluctuations as well as of growth, but most business cycles seemed to be self-limiting.
>
> (Solow, 1988, pp. 307–308)

Thus, either the real economies somehow manage to function on the edge of no-control as suggested in the Keynesian growth models proposed by Harrod and Domar or those models are inadequate. Solow, writing about his early (i.e. dating back to the 1950s) work on neoclassical growth model, explains:

> That was the spirit in which I began tinkering with the theory of economic growth, trying to improve on the Harrod-Domar model (...). I know that even as a student I was drawn to the theory of production rather than to the formally almost identical theory of consumer choice. It seemed more down to earth. I know that it occurred to me very early, as a natural-born macroeconomist, that even if technology itself is not

> so very flexible (...) [and the economy can choose in the production process from] capital-intensive or labor-intensive or land-intensive goods.
> (Solow, 1988, p. 308)

Those observations inspired Solow to develop a neoclassical economic growth model. The model was eventually augmented to include e.g. an economy with two stocks of capital (the Mankiw-Romer-Weil model of 1992) and with any finite number *N* of capital stocks (the Nonneman-Vanhoudt model of 1996).

The Solow model of economic growth also provided foundations for models embedded in the new theory of economic growth (known as the theory of endogenous growth), such as the renowned growth models developed by Paul M. Romer (1986, 1990) and Robert E. Lucas (1988).

The importance of economic growth theory in today's macroeconomics is demonstrated by the number of Sveriges Riksbank Prizes in Economic Sciences in Memory of Alfred Nobel awarded in that field of study (R. Frisch, J. Tinbergen, S. Kuznets, J.R. Hicks, K.J. Arrow, G. Debreu, R.M. Solow, R.E. Lucas., W.D. Nordhaus or P.M. Romer).

Our book entitled *The Solow Model of Economic Growth: Application to Contemporary Macroeconomic Issues* also represents that area of research. The title not only indicates the topic of economic growth as the principal axis of our analyzes but also refers to the work of Robert M. Solow. The authors of this book base on broadly understood achievements of R.M. Solow and enter into debate with his thought. This book not only continues the neoclassical tradition of thought in economics focused on quantitative economic changes but also, and to a significant extent, discusses alternative approaches to certain questions of economic growth, utilizing conclusions that can be drawn from the Solow model.

The augmentations of the Solow model described in this monograph (except the Phelps capital accumulation model and the Mankiw-Romer-Weil and Nonneman-Vanhoudt models) were developed at the Department of Mathematical Economics, Jagiellonian University in Kraków, over the last two decades. The authors were supported in their work on those models by (in alphabetical order) Mgr. Mateusz Biernacki, Mgr. Monika Bolińska, Mgr. Olesia Chornenka, Dr. Katarzyna Filipowicz, Dr. Maciej Grodzicki, MEng. Oleksii Kelebaj, Mgr. Agata Luśtyk, Dr. Robert Syrek and Dr. Mariusz Trojak from the Jagiellonian University. Work on the gravity model of economic growth was also supported by Dr. Svitlana Chugaievska (Department of Math Analysis, Business Analytics and Statistics of Zhytomyr Ivan Franko State University, Ukraine) and by Dr. Tomasz Misiak (Faculty of Management, Rzeszów University of Technology, Poland).

The authors address in their discussion the following research topics: fiscal and monetary policy vs economic growth; economic growth at returns to scale conditions; bipolar growth models with investment flows; a gravity growth model, and the 2020+ pandemic vs economic growth, also in the context of Polish economy.

The book consists of ten chapters.

Chapter 1 is aimed to concisely describe selected scientific inspirations that led to the development of the Solow growth model in its versions proposed in 1956–1957. Particular attention is paid to the studies by Roy F. Harrod (1936, 1939), Evsey D. Domar (1946) and Nicholas Kaldor (1963).

Chapter 2 outlines the basic version of the Solow economic growth model that provides foundations for further discussions and proposed modifications. The chapter also describes selected special cases of the Solow model, such as the model with a power Cobb-Douglas production function (1928) and a CES (Constant Elasticity of Substitution) production function.

Chapter 3 describes generalizations of the Solow model i.e. the Mankiw-Romer-Weil model developed in 1992 and the Nonneman-Vanhoudt model proposed in 1996. The Mankiw-Romer-Weil growth model considers human capital accumulation in addition to physical capital accumulation. The Nonneman-Vanhoudt model describes an economy characterized by a finite number N of capital stocks.

Chapter 4 describes selected generalizations of the Mankiw-Romer-Weil model and a compilation of the Solow model with a Keynesian growth model proposed by Domar that consider the effect of both fiscal and monetary policy on long-run economic growth.

The neoclassical economic growth models base on a strong assumption of constant returns to scale. Chapter 5 questions that assumption to examine the long-run equilibrium in those models in the case of economy characterized by decreasing or increasing returns to scale.

The analysis in Chapter 6 covers bipolar models of economic growth describing two economies (conventionally termed a rich economy and a poor economy), and the effect of capital accumulation and investment flows on the dynamics of economic growth. Two models are proposed: a model with exogenous investment rates and a model wherein the assumption about the exogenous nature of investment rates and flows is cancelled.

The gravity model of economic growth described in Chapter 7 bases on the Solow model of economic growth. The Solow growth model assumes a closed and isolated economy while the gravity growth model also considers spatial interactions occurring in a set of (national or regional) economies. Since spatial interactions take place in the analyzed group of economies, the development of each of them also affects capital accumulation and growth rates in other economies. The concept of total and individual gravitational effects is introduced to describe spatial interactions in the gravity model of economic growth. The method used to quantify the force of individual gravitational effects bases on the field equations (employed in economic theory to analyze migration and foreign trade) that generalize Newton's law of universal gravitation.

Chapter 8 analyzes Solow equilibrium at alternative trajectories of the number of workers. It is assumed in the original Solow growth model that the number of workers rises at a constant growth rate, so that the value of that macroeconomic variable increases exponentially to infinity. We modify that assumption in our analyzes contained in Chapter 8, proposing two alternative versions. We assume in version 1 that an increase in the number of workers forms a logistic curve that approaches an asymptote. On the other hand, it is assumed in version 2 that if labour productivity rises, the growth rate of the number of workers drops from infinity to zero.

In Chapter 9, the Solow equilibrium is analyzed at sine-wave investment rates. The principal assumption underlying the discussion in Chapter 9 reads that the investment rate at each moment t is determined by a pre-defined sine wave. We also compare obtained solutions of the Solow model characterized by sine-wave investment rates with solutions of the original Solow model.

Chapter 10 is aimed to assess the effect of an epidemic on medium-term economic growth (i.e. over five years). The analysis is conducted using an epidemiological-economic model that combines the SIR (Susceptible – Infectious – Recovered) epidemiological model proposed by Kernack and McKendrick (1927) with a neoclassical model of economic growth proposed by Solow.

The authors wish to thank all who read previous versions of the proposed augmentations of the Solow growth model. We owe especial thanks to our colleagues from the research centres that closely cooperate with the Department of Mathematical Economics at the Jagiellonian University: the Faculty of Economics and Sociology at the University of Łódź, the Poznań University of Economics and Business and the Faculty of Economic Sciences and Management, Nicolaus Copernicus University in Toruń. Thus, the authors extend their thanks to (in alphabetical order): Prof. Adam Krawiec (Jagiellonian University), Prof. Eugeniusz Kwiatkowski (University of Łódź), Prof. Michał Majsterek (University of Łódź), Prof. Maciej Malaczewski (University of Łódź), Prof. Krzysztof Malaga (Poznań University of Economics and Business), Prof. Magdalena Osińska (Nicolaus Copernicus University in Toruń), Prof. Emil Panek (Poznań University of Economics and Business), Prof. Iwona Świeczewska (University of Łódź) and Prof. Zenon Wiśniewski (Nicolaus Copernicus University in Toruń). Our thanks are also due to Prof. Armen Edigarian and Dr. Piotr Kościelniak from the Institute of Mathematics at the Jagiellonian University for their verification of, and comments to, mathematically complex elements of the proposed economic growth models.

Naturally, the authors assume full responsibility for possible mistakes and deficiencies found in this study.

Note

1 Interestingly, concepts similar to Keynesian aggregated demand and Solow's determinants of long-run economic growth were almost simultaneously introduced by Michał Kalecki in Poland and Theodor W. Swan in Australia (hence the Solow model is also known in the literature on macroeconomics as the Solow-Swan model).

1 R. M. Solow's inspirations

1.1 Introduction

Economic growth was first addressed by the classical school of economy in the 18th century. In the years 1870–1945, studies were focused on effective allocation of limited resources, adopting a marginalist approach. Almost three decades after the Great Depression (1929–1933), discussions held among macroeconomists centred on the causes, effects and assessments of Keynesian responses to that series of events (Snowdon and Vane, 2000). The question why is economic growth spatially differentiated (analyzed both theoretically and empirically) became the leading research topic in economics of the second half of the 20th century. A majority of studies aimed to develop the theory of endogenous growth. However, they were preceded by an important event in the history of economic growth theories that occurred at the dawn of the second half of that century: the publication of two breakthrough papers by R.M. Solow (1956, 1957).

D. Romer (2012, p. 8) emphasized after almost 60 years that:

> The Solow model is the starting point for almost all analyses of growth. Even models that depart fundamentally from Solow's are often best understood through comparison with the Solow model. Thus understanding the model is essential to understanding theories of growth.

This is confirmed by the number of citations of both studies. It is almost impossible to review all responses to the concepts proposed by R.M. Solow (1956, 1957) that were published until today.

Hence, this chapter is aimed to concisely describe selected scientific inspirations that led to the development of the growth model in its versions proposed in 1956 and 1957. In his Nobel-prize lecture (Lecture to the memory of Alfred Nobel, December 8, 1987[2]), R.M. Solow emphasized: "(…) in the 1950s I was following a trail that had been marked out by Roy Harrod and by Evsey Domar (…)" (see also: Solow, 1988), and in Addendum (August, 2001), he added[3]:

> Another, much less prominent, line of thought may be worth mentioning. It goes back to the 1950s when Nicholas Kaldor tried to produce a

DOI: 10.4324/9781003323792-2

coherent growth model based entirely on relationships among rates of growth, conspicuously without any explicit function relating inputs and outputs.

1.2 Harrod's equilibrium

Harrod's equilibrium analysis was based on three assumptions (1936, p. 33; 1939, p. 14):

1. Saving is proportional to national income, $S_t = sY_t$; the level of a community's income is the most important determinant of its supply of saving,
2. Investment, the demand for saving, is proportional to the growth of national income, $I_t = g(Y_{t+1} - Y_t)$; the rate of increase of its income is an important determinant of its demand for saving, and
3. Saving equals investment, the demand for saving equals the supply of saving, $S_t = I_t$.

From this, one derives the "fundamental equation" of equilibrium:

$$\frac{Y_{t+1} - Y_t}{Y_t} \equiv \rho_\omega = \frac{s}{g},$$

in which ρ_ω is the "warranted" rate of growth. Put differently, national income follows the first-order difference equation $Y_t = \frac{s+g}{g} Y_{t-1}$, with $1 > g > s > 0$.

Harrod supplemented his formal analysis with speculations about the consequences of deviations of actual aggregate income from warranted aggregate income. Harrod said that such deviations were bound to occur because the warranted rate of growth usually differs from a "natural" rate of growth that is determined by changes in productivity and the labour force (Blume and Sargent, 2015, p. 350).

Harrod (1939) addressed the following issues:

1. the implications of the qualification that fixed-coefficients like the saving rate are not fixed exogenously but, instead, are determined by economic forces,
2. alternative senses and sources of instability,
3. some possible interactions between a multiplier (reflecting consumption decisions) and an accelerator (reflecting real investment decisions).

Harrod discussed these things in ways that readers today will find difficult to comprehend and appreciate, partly because of progress that the study of economic dynamics has made since 1939, partly because Harrod chose not to use or extend some lines of work preceding 1939 that would be more familiar to today's reader and partly because his analysis, done without benefit of a formal model, is hard to follow and the analytic categories differ from those we use today (Blume and Sargent, 2015, p. 351).

In the theory, for Harrod (and for Keynes), no distinction was drawn between capital goods and consumption goods. In measuring the increment of capital, the two were taken together; the increment consisted of total production less total consumption (Harrod, 1936, p. 18). Today we think of capital as a factor of production; consequently, the marginal product of capital is crucial to determining interest and wage rates, the distribution of output between capital owners and workers and so forth.

The parameter g describes for Harrod the demand for saving, not as we read it today, the inverse marginal or average product of capital. "It may be expected", Harrod (1936, p. 17) writes, "to vary as income grows and in different phases of the trade cycle; it may be somewhat dependent on the rate of interest". Similarly, "s is regarded as likely to vary with a change in the size of income" (Harrod, 1936, pp. 24–25).

Harrod is clear (Blume and Sargent, 2015, p. 351) that the "warranted" rate of growth is in fact the equilibrium growth rate of a model. If the key parameters s and g in fact vary with endogenous variables, then equilibrium is not yet determined until these additional relations are appended to the model. The easiest way to fill in the gaps, of course, is to read the Essay as a fixed-coefficients model, and this has become the tradition.

Harrod argues that sustainable growth is possible only if the "warranted growth rate" (G_W) equals the "natural growth rate" (G_N). The warranted growth rate results from the balance of savings and from the effect of realized investment outlays on economy's production capacity and is calculated as the quotient of savings rate $s \in (0;1)$ (proportion of savings in output) and the capital-output ratio $v_K = \frac{K}{Y}$ (where K is the stock of capital in the economy, and Y denotes output) which can be written as $G_W = \frac{s}{v_K}$ (Gandolfo, 1971, pp. 41–43). The natural growth rate G_N results from an increase in the number of workers and technological progress and is calculated as the total of growth rate of the number of workers $n > 0$ and growth rate of labour productivity $g > 0$ which can be written as $G_N = n + g$.

Harrod's economy achieves the state of long-run equilibrium when the warranted growth rate equals the natural growth rate which can be written as $\frac{s}{v} = g + n$.

The growth rate of the number of workers and the rate of technological progress are understood as exogenous variables in the Harrod model, while the capital-output ratio in Keynesian models is constant in time; hence, for Harrod's economy to achieve the state of long-run equilibrium, the savings rate must be $s = v_K(g + n)$. At an excessively high savings rate [i.e. $s > v_K(g + n)$], the warranted growth rate describing the supply capacity of the economy is greater than the natural growth rate. As a result, a fraction of the production potential available in the economy is unused because of too low effective demand. However, if $s < v_K(g + n)$, then $G_W < G_N$ and the situation is opposite. Harrod (1936, 1939) argues that the savings rate in a market economy changes spontaneously and the long-run equilibrium (without government intervention) is only possible by special coincidence, and deviations from that equilibrium can lead to secular stagnation.

1.3 Domar's equilibrium

Domar's analysis was based on five assumptions (1946, p. 137):

1 There is a constant general price level,
2 No lags are present,
3 Savings and investment refer to the income of the same period, both are net, i.e., over and above depreciation,
4 Depreciation is measured not with respect to historical costs, but to the cost of replacement of the depreciated asset by another one of the same productive capacity,
5 Productive capacity of an asset or of the whole economy is a measurable concept.

The central theme of the paper *Capital Expansion, Rate of Growth, and Employment* (Domar, 1946) is the rate of growth, a concept that has been little used in economic theory, and in which Domar had put much faith as an extremely useful instrument of economic analysis.

> One does not have to be a Keynesian to believe that employment is somehow dependent on national income, and that national income has something to do with investment. But as soon as investment comes in, growth cannot be left out, because for an individual firm investment may mean more capital and less labor, but for the economy as a whole (as a general case) investment means more capital and not less labor. If both are to be profitably employed, a growth of income must take place.
>
> (Domar, 1946, p. 147)

Domar (1957) argues that:

1 Demand on the product market $Y^d(t)$ in continuous time $t \in [0;+\infty)$ depends on exogenous net investment $I(t)$, in accordance with Keynes's multiplier formula $Y^d = \frac{1}{s}I$, where $s \in (0;1)$ is the marginal (= average) propensity to save which means that $1/s$ is the Keynesian investment multiplier.

2 Investments also produce effects on the side of aggregate supply in the economy, and the relationship between current net investment outlets and an increase in supply capacities of the economy[4] $\dot{Y}_s$ is described by the equation $\dot{Y}^S = \kappa I$, where $\kappa > 0$ denotes "potential social average investment productivity".[5]

It follows from assumption 1 that an increase in demand $\dot{Y}_d$ is described by the formula $\dot{Y}^d = \frac{\dot{I}}{s}$. The state of equilibrium in Domar's economy, defined as a situation where aggregate demand and aggregate supply are equal, leads to the conclusion that the following holds $\frac{\dot{I}}{s} = \kappa I$. This implies a growth rate of investment in the form $\frac{\dot{I}}{I} = \kappa s$ or $\frac{\dot{I}}{I} = \frac{s}{v_K}$ (it can also be demonstrated that if $\frac{\dot{I}}{I} = \kappa s = \frac{s}{v_K}$, then $\frac{\dot{Y}^d}{Y^d} = \frac{\dot{Y}^s}{Y^s} = \kappa s = \frac{s}{v_K}$, so that also aggregate demand and supply will rise at the rate $\kappa s = \frac{s}{v_K}$).

Domar's economy reaches the state of long-run equilibrium when the growth rate of investment equals ($\kappa s = \frac{s}{v_K}$). However, a question arises what will happen in that economy, if the actual growth rate of investment equals $\iota \neq \kappa s$? It can be demonstrated that if $\iota < \kappa s$, the analyzed economy will be characterized by a state of permanent surplus supply.

At constant ι, κ and s, that state of imbalance will become worse in time, and it will be almost impossible to rescue the economy from that condition. The reason is that if $\iota < \kappa s$ and $Y^s(t) > Y^d(t)$ at each time $t \in [0;+\infty)$, then investors realize that there are unused production capacities in the economy and will tend to reduce the actual growth rate of investment ι, thus increasing the difference between the rates κs and ι, and contributing to a growing imbalance on the output market (this phenomenon is known in economics as the Domar paradox). This leads to the conclusion that the Domar-model economy, like the previously analyzed the Harrod-model economy, is characterized by a knife-edge balance on the single possible growth path that can warrant macroeconomic equilibrium. Each departure from that path leads to the state of long-term, deepening disequilibrium.

> Harrod and Domar seemed to be answering a straightforward question: when is an economy capable of steady growth at a constant rate? They arrived by noticeably different routes, at a classically simple answer: the national saving rate (the fraction of income saved) has to be equal to the product of the capital-output ratio and the rate of growth of the (effective) labor force. Then and only then could the economy keep its stock of plant and equipment in balance with its supply of labor, so that steady growth could go on without the appearance of labor shortage on one side or labor surplus and growing unemployment on the other side. They were right about that general conclusion.
>
> (Solow, 1988, p. 307)

1.4 Kaldor's economic growth model

The production function in Kaldor's model[6] has the same characteristics as the production function in the Domar model. Also an increase in capital stock is defined similarly. The number of workers grows at the rate $n > 0$. The single (but principal) difference between Kaldor's model and earlier Keynesian economic growth models lies in that the savings rate is disaggregated, on an entire-economy scale, into savings rates from the total of wages and total of profits. Kaldor writes that domestic product (income) may be divided into the categories of wages W (including salaries) and profits Π (hence, $Y = W + \Pi$) and argues that "the important difference between [those categories lies] in the marginal propensities to consume (or save), wage-earners' marginal savings being small in relation to those of capitalists" (Kaldor, 1963, p. 83).

Thus, Kaldor assumes in his growth model that $s_W < s_\Pi$, where s_W and $s\Pi \in (0;1)$ denote the propensities to save out of wages and profits. That assumption also implies the equation of savings rate in the entire economy (Kaldor, 1963, p. 83; Blaug, 1990, p. 189):

$$s = s_W + \left(s_\Pi - s_W\right)\frac{\Pi}{Y}.$$

It can be demonstrated that equilibrium in Kaldor's economy is conditional on satisfying the inequality:

$$\frac{s_W}{v_K} \le n \le \frac{s_\Pi}{v_K} \tag{1.1}$$

or

$$0 \le \pi \le \frac{1}{v_K}, \tag{1.2}$$

where $\pi = \frac{\Pi}{K}$ is the profit rate in the entire economy (Allen, 1975, pp. 215–216).

Due to the relaxation of rigid assumptions about the savings rate in Kaldor's model (i.e. the disaggregation of that rate into savings from wages and from profits), the conditions for long-run equilibrium in Kaldor's economy (equations 1.1 and 1.2) reduce the edge-knife problem posed by prior Keynesian growth models. The conditions indicate that for Kaldor's economy to achieve the state of long-run equilibrium it is necessary and sufficient that the growth rate of the number of workers n is contained in a closed interval bounded from below by the quotient of savings rate from wages to the capital-output ratio and bounded from above by the proportion of savings rate from profit to capital-output ratio. Thus, if savings rates reach e.g. $s_\Pi = 66\%$, $s_W = 0\%$ (the case of zero savings from wages), and $n + g = 4\%$, the capital-output ratio will not exceed about 50/3 (Kaldor, 1963, p. 301; Allen, 1975, p. 217).

Assuming that the capital-output ratio in viable economies equals about 3–5, the probability of an economy encountering the knife-edge problem is relatively low. An analysis of the condition for equilibrium (equation 1.2) demonstrates that at a capital-output ratio of 3–5 the rate of profit that warrants equilibrium in Kaldor's economy may not exceed about 20%–33%, and if that value is exceeded, the model gets into a state of permanent imbalance, like the previously analyzed Keynesian growth models.

1.5 Principle of the original Solow economic growth model

The core version of the economic growth model proposed by R.M. Solow bases on the assumption that the manufacturing process of aggregate stream of goods (products and services) is described by the neoclassical production function written as:

$$Y(t) = F\left(K(t), L(t)\right), \tag{1.3}$$

where: $K \geq 0$ is the (physical) capital stock and $L \geq 0$ denotes the number of workers. It is assumed about that function that it is homogeneous of degree 1 and characterized by decreasing marginal productivities with respect to the stocks of capital and labour. It also meets the Inada conditions both with respect to K and L (the formal and mathematical properties of the production function (1.3) are discussed in detail in Chapter 2). In the Solow model, it is also assumed that the number of workers (L) is described by the exponential function:

$$L(t) = L_0 e^{nt}, \tag{1.4}$$

where $L_0 > 0$ is the number of workers $t \geq 0$ and $n > 0$ denotes the growth rate of the number of workers.

The assumption that the production function is homogeneous of degree 1 leads to a transformation of function (1.3) to its intensive form:

$$y(t) = f\left(k(t)\right), \tag{1.5}$$

where: $y = Y/L$ denotes labour productivity, and $k = K/L$ is the value of (physical) capital per worker. Function (1.5), in terms of macroeconomics, is an aggregate labour productivity function, that makes labour productivity y dependent on capital per worker k; one of its characteristics is that $f(0) = 0$, $\lim_{k \to +\infty} f(k) = +\infty$, $f'(k) > 0$ and $f''(k) < 0$.

R.M. Solow assumes that an increase in the capital stock (K) is calculated as the difference between investment and capital depreciation which can formally be written as:

$$\dot{K}(t) = sY(t) - \delta K(t), \tag{1.6}$$

where: $s \in (0;1)$ denotes the savings/investment rate, and $\delta \in (0;1)$ is the capital depreciation rate.

Additionally, investment is financed out of savings (being a fixed, equal s fraction of produced output Y).

The above assumption leads to the following differential equation (known as the Solow's equation):

$$\dot{k}(t) = sf\left(k(t)\right) - (\delta + n)k(t), \tag{1.7}$$

Equation (1.7) describes an increase in capital per worker as the difference between savings/investments per worker $sf(k)$ and capital decline per worker $(n + \delta)k$ that is caused both by capital depreciation (δk) and by an increase in the number of workers (nk).

The phase diagram of equation (1.7) is shown in Figure 1.1. The point k^* represents the stock of capital per worker in the Solow's long-run equilibrium, being the single non-trivial stable steady-state of Solow's equation.

Assuming also that the production function (1.3) is a Cobb-Douglas production function, we obtain a labour productivity function in the form:

$$y(t) = \left(k(t)\right)^{\alpha}, \tag{1.8}$$

then, capital per worker in the Solow's long-run equilibrium (calculated from equation (1.7)) is given by the formula:

$$k^* = \left(\frac{s}{\delta + n}\right)^{1/(1-\alpha)} \tag{1.9}$$

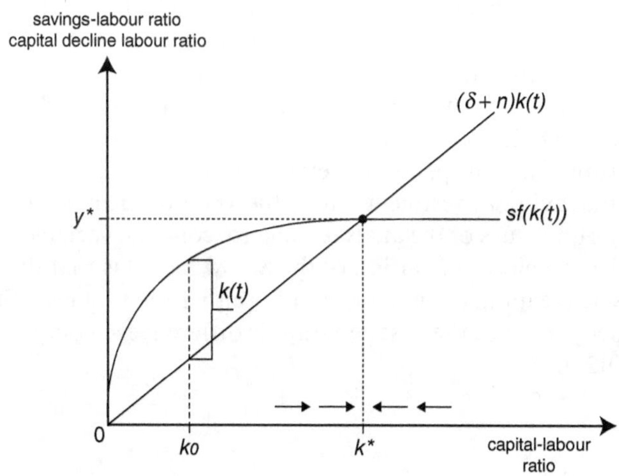

Figure 1.1 Phase diagram of differential equation (1.7).
Source: Aghion and Howitt (2009).

and labour productivity (substituting equation (1.9) to equation (1.8)) is given by:

$$y^* = \left(\frac{s}{\delta+n}\right)^{\alpha/(1-\alpha)} \tag{1.10}$$

It follows from equations (1.9) and (1.10) that the higher the savings/investment rate s or the lower the capital depreciation rate δ or the lower the growth rate of the number of workers n, the higher are the values of capital per worker k^* and labour productivity y^* in the long-run equilibrium of the core-version Solow model (see, e.g., Solow, 1956; Aghion and Howitt, 2009; Tokarski, 2009, 2011; Romer, 2012).

1.6 Conclusions

The discussion contained in this chapter, being an introductory section, can be summarized as follows:

First, the Harrod, Domar and Harrod–Domar models were influenced by the Great Depression in the 1930s. Those models propose their common general conclusion that the economy is exposed to the state of permanent imbalance, resulting among others from the assumption of almost zero substitution of capital and labour inputs in the production process. The models emphasize the role of government's activity in maintaining the economy on a growth path that guarantees the long-run macroeconomic equilibrium. The principal difference between Kaldor's model and earlier Keynesian economic growth models lies in that the savings rate is disaggregated, on an entire-economy scale, into savings rates from the total of wages and total of profits.

Second, the Solow model was developed in response to the Harrod and Domar models that describe economic reality with insufficient accuracy. Admittedly, economies undergo certain short-term fluctuations, but they tend to remain on a growth path that guarantees the long-run macroeconomic equilibrium. In that model, the long-run values of capital per worker and labour productivity are influenced among others by the savings/investment rate and the rate of capital decline per unit of effective labour. It can be concluded that the higher the savings/investment rate or the lower the decline rate, the higher are the long-run values of the analyzed macroeconomic variables.

Third, the principal conclusion of the Solow model is that the accumulation of physical capital cannot account for either the vast growth over time in output per person or the vast geographic differences in output per person (Romer, 2012, p. 8).

Notes

1 R.M. Solow, Prize Lecture (1987), https://www.nobelprize.org/prizes/economic-sciences/1987/solow/lecture/.

2 R.M. Solow, Prize Lecture (1987), https://www.nobelprize.org/prizes/economic-sciences/1987/solow/lecture/.

3 The form $\dot{x}(t) = \frac{dx}{dt}$ or $\dot{x} = \frac{dx}{dt}$ denotes a derivative of the variable x with respect to time t, i.e. (in terms of economics) an increase in the value of this variable at time t.

4 κ in the Domar model can also be treated as an inverse of the capital-output ratio v_K. The reason is that if the economy is characterized by a single-factor production function in the form $Y^S = \frac{K}{v_K}$, and an increase in the capital stock $\dot{K}$ equals net investments I, then $\dot{Y}^S = \frac{\dot{K}}{v_K} = \frac{I}{v_K}$, i.e. $\kappa = 1/v_K$.

5 A simplified version of the Kaldor's model is based on the study by Allen (1975, pp. 215–217). The complete Kaldor's model is described in his study (1963, pp. 93–144), see also: Blaug (1990, pp. 186–209).

2 The Solow model

2.1 Introduction

This chapter describes a basic version of the Solow economic growth model that provides foundations for the growth models characterized in the subsequent chapters of this monograph. The version is based on the publication by Romer (2012), Chapter 1 (see also Tokarski, 2009, 2011). Compared to the original version of the Solow model (as proposed in his article published in 1956), we will also consider the effect of capital depreciation and exogenous technological change/progress on the processes of equilibrium and economic growth.

This chapter also describes two special cases of the Solow model. These are the cases wherein the production function is a Cobb-Douglas power function (1928) or CES production function (*Constant Elasticity of Substitution* proposed in an article published by Arrow, Chenery, Minhas and Solow (1961)). A special version of the model will also be analyzed, known as the golden rules of capital accumulation proposed by Phelps (1961) that directly refer to the Solow model with the Cobb-Douglas production function.

2.2 The Solow model with a neoclassical production function

The Solow growth model in its basic version adopts the following assumptions about economy behaviour in a long run:

1. The production process is described by a neoclassical production function expressed by the formula:

   $$Y(t) = F\left(K(t), E(t)\right), \tag{2.1}$$

   where Y denotes the output (at the moment $t \in [0;+\infty)$, where the moment $t = 0$ is identical with the initial moment at which economy is analyzed), K refers to physical capital input,[1] E – to units of effective labour. The production function (2.1) makes the output Y depend on capital input

DOI: 10.4324/9781003323792-3

K and units of effective labour E. It is assumed that this function has the following properties (details can be found e.g. in Żółtowska (1997)):

i Its domain is defined as the set $[0;+\infty)^2$ and $F:[0;+\infty)^2 \to [0;+\infty)$.

ii Function F is differentiable at least twice in the set $(0;+\infty)^2$.

iii $\forall (K,E) \in [0;+\infty)^2 \; F(0,E) = F(K,0) = 0$, hence both capital inputs and units of effective labour are indispensable in the production process.

iv $\forall (K,E) \in [0;+\infty)^2 \; \lim_{K \to +\infty} F(K,E) = \lim_{K \to +\infty} F(K,E) = +\infty$, i.e. very large inputs of one of the production factors (at positive inputs of another production factor) correspond to a very large volume of output.

v The following inequalities are true: $\text{MPC} = \frac{\partial F}{\partial K} > 0$ and $\text{MPE} = \frac{\partial F}{\partial E} > 0$ for all $(K,E) \in (0;+\infty)^2$, where marginal product of capital (MPC) and marginal product of units of effective labour (MPE) are positive. Thus, an increase in capital inputs or in units of effective labour leads to an increase in output.[2]

vi. $\forall (K,E) \in (0;+\infty)^2 \; \frac{\partial \text{MPC}}{\partial K} = \frac{\partial^2 F}{\partial K^2} < 0 \wedge \frac{\partial \text{MPE}}{\partial E} = \frac{\partial^2 F}{\partial E^2} < 0$, i.e. with an increase in capital inputs or in units of effective labour, their marginal products fall. It follows from assumptions (v–vii) that the production function F is characterized by diminishing marginal productivities with respect to both K and E.

vii The Inada conditions are satisfied: $\forall E > 0 \; \lim_{K \to 0^+} \text{MPC} = +\infty$ and $\lim_{K \to +\infty} \text{MPC} = 0$ and $\forall K > 0 \; \lim_{E \to 0^+} \text{MPE} = +\infty$ and $\lim_{E \to +\infty} \text{MPE} = 0$. The Inada conditions together with assumption (vi) imply that when inputs of one of the production factors rise from 0 to $+\infty$ (at positive inputs of another production factor), the marginal product of that factor falls from $+\infty$ to 0.

viii The production function is homogeneous of degree 1, i.e.:

$$\forall (K,E) \in [0;+\infty)^2 \wedge \forall \varsigma > 0 \; F(\varsigma K, \varsigma E) = \varsigma F(K,E),$$

hence an increase in inputs of production factors by ς times leads to an increase in output by ς times. This property is known in macroeconomics as constant returns to scale.

A production function that satisfies assumptions (i–viii) is termed a neoclassical production function.

2 Capital accumulation is described by the following differential equation:

$$\dot{K}(t) = I(t) - \delta K(t), \tag{2.2}$$

where I denotes investments, and $\delta \in (0;1)$ represents the rate of capital depreciation (i.e. a percentage of capital that is consumed in the production process).

3 In a closed economy (like that analyzed by Solow), investments I are financed using savings S, hence:

$$I(t) = S(t), \tag{2.3a}$$

where savings represent a fraction of output that is not consumed. Consequently, consumption C can be described using the formula:

$$C(t) = Y(t) - S(t). \tag{2.3b}$$

4 Savings represent a constant fraction of output equal $s \in (0;1)$, i.e.:

$$S(t) = sY(t). \tag{2.4}$$

The rate s represents a percentage proportion of savings S (determining the amount of investment I) in the output Y. Therefore, that rate will be hereinafter referred to as the savings/investment rate (a proportion of savings/investment in output).

5 The units of effective labour E are calculated as a product of technology A and the number of workers L, hence:

$$E(t) = A(t)L(t). \tag{2.5}$$

6 The growth path[3] of technology is described by the function[4]:

$$A(t) = e^{gt}, \tag{2.6}$$

where $g > 0$ represents the rate of technological change[5] as defined by Harrod (or Harrodian rate of technological progress).[6]

7 The trajectory of the number of workers is expressed by the equation:

$$L(t) = e^{nt}, \tag{2.7}$$

where $n > 0$ denotes a rate of increase in the number of workers.

Let

$$y(t) = \frac{Y(t)}{L(t)}, \qquad 2.8a)$$

$$k(t) = \frac{K(t)}{L(t)}, \tag{2.8b}$$

and

$$p(t)=\frac{Y(t)}{K(t)}, \tag{2.8c}$$

denote, respectively, labour productivity (the output per worker), the capital-labour ratio (capital per worker) and capital productivity (the output per capital unit). Let:

$$y_E(t)=\frac{Y(t)}{E(t)} \tag{2.9a}$$

and

$$k_E(t)=\frac{K(t)}{E(t)} \tag{2.9b}$$

denote the output per unit of effective unit of labour (or effective labour) and capital per unit of effective labour. Then, we obtain from equations (2.5), (2.8a) and (2.9a):

$$y(t)=A(t)\,y_E(t),$$

and, considering equation (2.6), we get:

$$y(t)=e^{gt}y_E(t),$$

or, after taking logarithms of both sides (using a natural logarithm) and differentiating with respect to time t, we obtain:

$$\frac{\dot{y}(t)}{y(t)}=g+\frac{\dot{y}_E(t)}{y_E(t)}. \tag{2.10a}$$

By applying similar operations to equations (2.8b) and (2.9b), the following relation is obtained:

$$\frac{\dot{k}(t)}{k(t)}=g+\frac{\dot{k}_E(t)}{k_E(t)}. \tag{2.10b}$$

It follows from equations (2.10a,b) that if the output per unit of effective labour (capital per unit of effective labour) rises/falls, the productivity of labour (capital-labour ratio) rises at a growth rate greater/less than the rate of technological progress as defined by Harrod, that is g. If the output per unit of effective labour (capital per unit of effective labour) is constant in time, the growth rate of labour productivity (capital-labour ratio) equals the Harrodian rate of technological progress.

Considering property (viii), the production function (2.1) is homogeneous of degree 1; hence, for $\varsigma = 1/E$, we obtain:

$$y_E(t) = \frac{Y(t)}{E(t)} = F\left(\frac{K(t)}{E(t)}, 1\right) = F(k_E(t), 1),$$

or

$$y_E(t) = f(k_E(t)), \tag{2.11}$$

where $f(k_E) = F(k_E, 1)$. Function (2.11) is termed the production function in its intensive form. The function makes the output per unit of effective labour depend on capital inputs per unit of effective labour. Additionally, it follows directly from properties (i–viii) of the production function (2.1) that the production function in its intensive form (2.11) is characterized by the following properties:

a Its domain is defined as the set [0; +∞) and $f : [0; +\infty) \to [0; +\infty)$.
b Function f is differentiable at least twice in $(0; +\infty)$.
c $f(0) = 0$.
d $\lim_{k_E \to +\infty} f(k_E) = +\infty$.
e $f'(k_E) > 0 \wedge f''(k_E) < 0$. Hence, function (2.11) is characterized by diminishing marginal productivities of capital per unit of effective labour.

f $\lim_{k_E \to 0^+} f'(k_E) = +\infty$ and $\lim_{k_E \to +\infty} f'(k_E) = 0$. Consequently, function f satisfies the Inada conditions with respect to k_E.

Substituting equations (2.6 and 2.7) into (2.5), we obtain:

$$E(t) = e^{\lambda t}, \tag{2.12a}$$

where $\lambda = g + n > 0$. Taking logarithms on both sides of the above equation and differentiating after time t the resultant relation, we obtain:

$$\frac{\dot{E}(t)}{E(t)} = \lambda. \tag{2.12b}$$

It follows from equation (2.12b) that λ represents the rate of increase in units of effective labour (equal to the total of the Harrodian rate of technological progress g and the rate of increase in the number of workers n).

From relations (2.3a–2.4), we obtain:

$$I(t) = sY(t),$$

and it follows from the above relation and from equation (2.2) that:

$$\dot{K}(t) = sY(t) - \delta K(t). \tag{2.13}$$

Differentiating equation (2.9b) with respect to time t, we get:

$$\dot{k}_E(t) = \frac{\dot{K}(t)E(t) - K(t)\dot{E}(t)}{E^2(t)} = \frac{\dot{K}(t)}{E(t)} - k_E(t)\frac{\dot{E}(t)}{E(t)}. \tag{2.14}$$

Substituting relations (2.12b and 2.13) into the above equation, we obtain:

$$\dot{k}_E(t) = sy_E(t) - (\delta + \lambda)k_E(t). \tag{2.15}$$

Equation (2.15) is known as the Solow equation (see equation (1.7)). Its economic interpretation can be reduced to the statement that an increase in capital per unit of effective labour $\left(\dot{k}_E\right)$ equals the difference between savings/investment per unit of effective labour (i.e. sy_E) and the capital decline per unit of effective labour $\left((\delta+\lambda)k_E\right)$, and that decline results both from depreciation of capital (δk_E) and from an increase in units of effective labour (λk_E). Moreover, it follows from the Solow equation that if savings/investment per unit of effective labour are greater (less) than the capital decline per unit of effective labour, the stock of capital will rise (fall) in time. If $sy_E = \left((\delta+\lambda)k_E\right)$, then $\dot{k}_E = 0$ and the analyzed stock will not change.

Substituting function (2.11) into the Solow equation, we obtain the following ordinary differential equation:

$$\dot{k}_E(t) = sf\left(k_E(t)\right) - \mu k_E(t), \tag{2.16}$$

where $\mu = \delta + \lambda$.

Let us demonstrate now that differential equation (2.16) has two steady states, a trivial steady state (at $k_E = 0$) and a non-trivial steady state $\left(k_E^* > 0\right)$. We will also demonstrate that the non-trivial steady state k_E^* represents the point of long-run equilibrium in the Solow model.

A trivial steady state exists because if $k_E = 0$, both the right and the left side of differential equation (2.16) equals 0. The trivial steady state will be ignored in further discussion, because it is irrelevant for both economic and mathematical conclusions.

Note that if $k_E > 0$, then $\dot{k}_E > 0$ $\left(\dot{k}_E < 0\right)$ if and only if capital productivity (2.8c) that can also be expressed as $p(k_E) = \dfrac{f(k_E)}{k_E}$ is greater (less) than the quotient $\mu/s > 0$. Let us determine the properties of function $p(k_E)$ at k_E rising from 0 to $+\infty$. The properties of function f lead to the conclusion that[7]:

$$\lim_{k_E \to 0^+} p(k_E) = \lim_{k_E \to 0^+} \frac{f(k_E)}{k_E} \overset{H\left(\frac{0}{0}\right)}{=} \lim_{k_E \to 0^+} f'(k_E) = +\infty$$

this results from the first Inada condition,

$$\lim_{k_E \to +\infty} p(k_E) = \lim_{k_E \to +\infty} \frac{f(k_E)}{k_E} \overset{H\left(\frac{\infty}{\infty}\right)}{=} \lim_{k_E \to +\infty} f'(k_E) = 0$$

(in line with the second Inada condition) and[8]:

$$p'(k_E) = \frac{f'(k_E)k_E - f(k_E)}{k_E^2} = -\frac{\text{MPE}}{k_E^2} < 0.$$

Thus, if capital per unit of effective labour k_E rises from 0 to $+\infty$, capital productivity $p(k_E)$ falls from $+\infty$ to 0. It follows from the above relation, from the Darboux property of a continuous function and from differential equation (2.16) that there exists exactly one positive k_E^* such that:

$$\text{a} \ \forall k_E \in \left(0, k_E^*\right) \ p(k_E) > \frac{s}{\mu} \Rightarrow \forall t \in [0;+\infty) \ \dot{k}_E > 0,$$

$$\text{b} \ p\left(k_E^*\right) = \frac{s}{\mu} \Rightarrow \forall t \in [0;+\infty) \ \dot{k}_E = 0,$$

$$\text{c} \ \forall k_E \in \left(k_E^*, +\infty\right) \ p(k_E) < \frac{s}{\mu} \Rightarrow \forall t \in [0;+\infty) \ \dot{k}_E < 0.$$

Therefore, if the economy was characterized by capital per units of effective labour $k_E(0)$ less/greater than k_E^* at the moment $t = 0$, then fluctuations in that stock at each subsequent moment t will be positive/negative and the economy will approximate the stock k_E^* on the left/right side. If $k_E(0) = k_E^*$, then $k_E(t) = k_E^*$ at any moment $t > 0$. Hence, the stock k_E^* represents the stock of capital per unit of effective labour in the Solow's long-run equilibrium (or simply long-run stock of capital per unit of effective labour) such that[9]:

$$\forall k(0) > 0 \ \lim_{t \to +\infty} k_E(t) = k_E^*. \tag{2.17a}$$

It follows from the above relation and from the production function in its intensive form equation (2.11) that in a long run (i.e. at $t \to +\infty$), the output per unit of effective labour approaches y_E^* defined by the formula:

$$y_E^* = f\left(k_E^*\right). \tag{2.17b}$$

Under the conditions of Solow's long-run equilibrium, capital and output (both relative to a unit of effective labour) are constant. Hence, the capital-labour ratio k and labour productivity y rise as per equations (2.10a,b) at growth rates that equal the Harrodian rate of technological progress g. If the economy reaches point k_E^* on the left/right side, the growth rates y and k are greater/less than g.

It also follows from equation (2.16) and former substitutions ($\mu = \delta + g + n$) that the long-run stock k_E^* is an implicit function (e.g. of the rates s, δ and n) that solves the following equation:

$$\Phi\left(k_E^*, s, \delta, n\right) = p(k_E) - \frac{\delta + g + n}{s} = 0. \tag{2.18}$$

It follows from equation (2.18) and from the formulas for derivatives of an implicit function that:

$$\frac{\partial k_E^*}{\partial s} = -\frac{\frac{\partial \Phi}{\partial s}}{\frac{\partial \Phi}{\partial k_E^*}} = -\frac{\delta + g + n}{s^2 p'(k_E)} > 0,$$

$$\frac{\partial k_E^*}{\partial \delta} = -\frac{\frac{\partial \Phi}{\partial \delta}}{\frac{\partial \Phi}{\partial k_E^*}} = \frac{1}{s^2 p'(k_E)} < 0$$

and

$$\frac{\partial k_E^*}{\partial n} = -\frac{\frac{\partial \Phi}{\partial n}}{\frac{\partial \Phi}{\partial k_E^*}} = \frac{1}{s^2 p'(k_E)} < 0.$$

It can be concluded from the above relations that the higher the savings (investment) rate s or the less the capital depreciation rate δ or the growth rate of the number of workers n, the greater the long-run capital per unit of effective labour k_E^* in the Solow's equilibrium. This in turn implies that the long-term growth path of the capital-labour ratio $k^*(t)$ reaches a higher level (see e.g. Romer (2012), Chapter 1 or Tokarski (2011), Chapter 5).

Moreover, since for each $k_E > 0$ $f'(k_E) > 0$: $\frac{\partial y_E^*}{\partial s} > 0$ and $\frac{\partial y_E^*}{\partial \delta}, \frac{\partial y_E^*}{\partial n} < 0$. In terms of economics, the signs of the above partial derivatives lead to similar conclusions as the signs of partial derivatives k_E^*.

2.3 Special cases

Section 2.2 contains a description of the Solow growth model with a general, neoclassical production function. However, an analytical form of that function is not known, and hence neither a point of long-run equilibrium in the Solow model can be analytically determined nor equations can be found for growth paths followed by the analyzed macroeconomic variables to reach that equilibrium.

Therefore, special cases of the Solow model will be analyzed in Section 2.3, namely models with the Cobb-Douglas production function and with the CES production function. In the first of those cases, both the point of Solow's long-run equilibrium and the paths leading to that equilibrium can be determined. In the second case, a non-trivial steady state of the long-run equilibrium in the Solow model can be determined and its economic properties analyzed.

2.3.1 The Cobb-Douglas production function

The Cobb-Douglas production function is described by the following formula:

$$Y = F(K,L) = aK^{\alpha}L^{1-\alpha}, \tag{2.19}$$

where $a > 0$, and $\alpha \in (0;1)$.

Parameter a in the production function is known as the total factor productivity. The parameter obviously indicates how much output can be produced from certain amounts of capital input K and labour input L. Transforming equation (2.19), total factor productivity can also be described by the formula:

$$a = \frac{Y}{K^{\alpha}L^{1-\alpha}} = p^{\alpha}y^{1-\alpha},$$

hence, total factor productivity can be defined as a geometric weighted mean of capital productivity p and labour productivity y with weights equal (respectively) α and $1-\alpha$.

If $\varepsilon_K = \frac{\partial Y}{\partial K}\frac{K}{Y}$ and $\varepsilon_L = \frac{\partial Y}{\partial L}\frac{L}{Y}$ denote (respectively) the elasticity of output with respect to capital and the elasticity of output with respect to labour, it can be demonstrated that those elasticities equal α and $1-\alpha$.

The elasticities are also frequently identified with proportions of inputs of production factor in the output in studies into economics, e.g. in Clark's marginal theory of distribution. However, that approach is wrong, which can easily be demonstrated.

The main hypothesis of Clark's marginal theory of distribution can be reduced to the statement that under conditions of a competitive economy, each production factor receives a reward equal to its marginal product. An explanation: if the profit function (in real terms) of a typical manufacturer is described by the formula:

$$\pi(k,l) = f(k,l) - (w_k k + w_l l), \tag{2.20}$$

where $k, l \geq 0$ represents capital and labour inputs in an enterprise, f denotes a homogeneous production function of degree 1 (and the Cobb-Douglas production function represents its special case), w_k, $w_l > 0$ represent production factor prices, then the first-order conditions that must be met to maximize profit can be expressed by the following equations:

$$\frac{\partial f}{\partial k} = w_k \wedge \frac{\partial f}{\partial l} = w_l,$$

where $\partial f / \partial k$ and $\partial f / \partial l$ represent marginal products of production factors. Thus far, the reasoning is correct. However, a problem appears: if the production function f is homogeneous of degree 1, then the Hessian of the profit function is not negative-definite (and this is the second-order condition for the profit function π to be maximized).

Moreover, there is no combination of production factors $v = (k, l) \in (0, +\infty)^2$ that could maximize function (2.20). To demonstrate this, an indirect proof will be produced (see Tokarski and Zachorowska-Mazurkiewicz, 2016).

Assume, despite the above hypothesis, that a combination exists $\bar{v} = (\bar{k}, \bar{l}) \in (0, +\infty)^2$ such that the function $\pi(k, l)$ has a local extreme point. An open neighbourhood $z \subset (0, +\infty)^2$ of point $\bar{v}$ exists such that:

a $\forall v \in z \wedge \forall v \neq \bar{v}\ \pi(v) < \pi(\bar{v})$ for a local maximum

or

b $\forall v \in z \wedge \forall v \neq \bar{v}\ \pi(v) > \pi(\bar{v})$ for a local minimum.

Let us assume any circle $\kappa \subset z$ and a ray γ that starts at the origin of coordinate system and goes through point $\bar{v}$. Then, exactly two different points exist $v_1, v_2 \in \kappa \cap \gamma$ such that:

$$\pi(v_1), \pi(v_2) < \pi \tag{2.21a}$$

for a maximum, or

$$\pi(v_1), \pi(v_2) > \pi \tag{2.21b}$$

for a minimum. Let the point v_1 be located closer to the origin of coordinate system than v_2.

As both the production function $f(k, l)$ and the cost function $c(k, l) = w_k k + w_l l$ are homogeneous of degree 1 and $f(0, 0) = 0$ and $c(0, 0) = 0$, also the profit function (2.20) is characterized by homogeneity of degree 1 and by $\pi(0, 0) = 0$. Consequently, on each ray $x_1 = \zeta x_2$ (that starts in the origin of coordinate system and has a positive slope ζ), the values of function π rise (fall) from 0 to $+\infty$ ($-\infty$). Thus, also the following is true in particular:

a if $\pi(\bar{v})>0$, then $\pi(v_1)<\pi(\bar{v})<\pi(v_2)$,
b if $\pi(\bar{v})=0$, then $\pi(v_1)=\pi(\bar{v})=\pi(v_2)$,
or
c if $\pi(\bar{v})<0$, then $\pi(v_1)>\pi(\bar{v})>\pi(v_2)$,

which is inconsistent with inequalities (2.21ab).

This reasoning can be extended into any n-dimensional (for n = 3, 4, …), homogeneous production function and cost function of degree 1 (which is demonstrated in the study published by Tokarski and Zachorowska-Mazurkiewicz (2016)).

Hence, Clark's marginal theory of distribution is false (in the case of both bivariate and multivariate production functions with constant returns on scale), and parameters α and $1-\alpha$ in the Cobb-Douglas production function cannot be interpreted as participations of capital and labour in the output (the same is true for the parameters of bivariate and multivariate power production functions analyzed in this chapter).

It can be demonstrated that the Cobb-Douglas production function satisfies conditions (i–viii) applicable to the production function (2.1) with respect to K and L. This is because:

- Assumptions (i–ii) are satisfied directly as per equation (2.19).
- $\forall(K,L)\in[0,+\infty)^2\ F(0,L)=a0^{\alpha}L^{1-\alpha}=0$ and $F(K,0)=aK^{\alpha}0^{1-\alpha}=0$.
- $\forall(K,L)\in[0,+\infty)^2\ \lim_{K\to+\infty}F(K,L)=aL^{1-\alpha}\lim_{K\to+\infty}K^{\alpha}=+\infty$ and $\lim_{L\to+\infty}F(K,L)=aK^{\alpha}\lim_{L\to+\infty}L^{1-\alpha}=+\infty$.
- $\forall(K,L)\in[0,+\infty)^2\ \text{MPK}=\alpha aK^{\alpha-1}L^{1-\alpha}>0$ and $\text{MPL}=(1-\alpha)aK^{\alpha}L^{-\alpha}>0$.
- For all $(K, L)\in(0,+\infty)^2\ \frac{\partial\text{MPK}}{\partial K}=\alpha(\alpha-1)aK^{\alpha-2}L^{1-\alpha}<0$ and similar $\frac{\partial MPL}{\partial L}=-\alpha(\alpha-1)aK^{\alpha}L^{-\alpha-1}<0$.
- For K, $L>0$ $\lim_{K\to0^+}\text{MPK}=\alpha aL^{1-\alpha}\lim_{K\to0^+}K^{\alpha-1}=+\infty$, $\lim_{K\to+\infty}\text{MPK}=\alpha aL^{1-\alpha}\lim_{K\to+\infty}K^{\alpha-1}=0$, $\lim_{L\to0^+}\text{MPL}=(1-\alpha)aK^{\alpha}\lim_{L\to0^+}L^{1-\alpha}=+\infty$ and $\lim_{L\to+\infty}\text{MPL}=\lim_{L\to+\infty}\text{MPL}=(1-\alpha)aK^{\alpha}\lim_{L\to+\infty}L^{1-\alpha}=0$.
- $\forall K,L\geq0\wedge\varsigma>0\ F(\varsigma K,\varsigma L)=a(\varsigma K)^{a}(L)^{1-a}=\varsigma aK^{a}L^{1-a}=\varsigma F(K,L)$

Considering the Solow model with the Cobb-Douglas production function, we will replace relation (2.1) with the Cobb-Douglas function described by the formula:

$$Y(t) = (K(t))^{\alpha} (E(t))^{1-\alpha}, \tag{2.22}$$

assuming also that equations (2.2–2.7) are satisfied. According to relation (2.6), the total productivity of production factors in equation (2.22) equals $e^{(1-\alpha)gt}$. Consequently, we assume that the total productivity of production factors rises in time due to the effect of technical progress as defined by Harrod.

Dividing the sides of Cobb-Douglas function (2.22) by $E > 0$, we obtain the production function in its intensive form, described by the formula (symbols as in Section 2.2):

$$y_E(t) = (k_E(t))^{\alpha}. \tag{2.23}$$

Substituting relation (2.23) into the Solow equation (2.15), we obtain:

$$\dot{k}_E(t) = s(k_E(t))^{\alpha} - \mu k_E(t), \tag{2.24}$$

where $\mu = \delta + g + n$. Equation (2.24) is a Bernoulli differential equation. Its integral meeting the condition $k_E(0) = k_{E0} > 0$ (where k_{E0} denotes the stock of capital per unit of effective labour at the moment $t = 0$) determines the growth path of capital per unit of effective labour. Given that integral and using equation (2.23), we can determine the trajectory of output per unit of effective labour.

Ignoring the trivial solution ($k_E = 0$), the Bernoulli equations can be expressed as follows:

$$(k_E(t))^{-\alpha} \dot{k}_E(t) = s - \mu (k_E(t))^{1-\alpha}. \tag{2.25}$$

Bernoulli's substitution:

$$q(t) = (k_E(t))^{1-\alpha}, \tag{2.26a}$$

results in:

$$(k_E(t))^{-\alpha} \dot{k}_E(t) = \frac{\dot{q}(t)}{1-\alpha}. \tag{2.26b}$$

It follows from equation (2.25) and relation (2.26a,b) that:

$$\dot{q}(t) = (1-\alpha)s - (1-\alpha)\mu q(t). \tag{2.27}$$

The integral of equation (2.27) can be expressed by the formula:

$$q(t) = q_d(t) e^{-(1-\alpha)\mu t}, \tag{2.28a}$$

where q_d represents a complementary integral of integral q, hence:

$$\dot{q}(t)=\dot{q}_d(t)e^{-(1-\alpha)\mu t}-(1-\alpha)\mu q_d(t)e^{-(1-\alpha)\mu t}. \tag{2.28b}$$

It follows from relations (2.27) and (2.28ab) that:

$$\dot{q}_d(t)e^{-(1-\alpha)\mu t}=(1-\alpha)s \Rightarrow \dot{q}_d(t)=(1-\alpha)se^{(1-\alpha)\mu t},$$

hence:

$$q_d(t)=(1-\alpha)s\int e^{(1-\alpha)\mu t}dt=\frac{s}{\mu}e^{(1-\alpha)\mu t}+\phi, \tag{2.29}$$

where $\phi \in R$ represents the constant of integration. Substituting the complementary integral (2.29) into equation (2.28a):

$$q(t)=\left(\frac{s}{\mu}e^{(1-\alpha)\mu t}+\phi\right)e^{-(1-\alpha)\mu t}=\frac{s}{\mu}+\phi e^{-(1-\alpha)\mu t}. \tag{2.30}$$

Bernoulli substitution (2.26a) gives:

$$k_E(t)=\left(q(t)\right)^{1/(1-\alpha)},$$

and this together with equation (2.30) implies:

$$k_E(t)=\left(\frac{s}{\mu}+\phi e^{-(1-\alpha)\mu t}\right)^{1/(1-\alpha)}. \tag{2.31}$$

Equation (2.31) produces an infinite family of integrals of Bernoulli differential equation (2.24). To determine the trajectory of capital per unit of effective labour, the constant of integration ϕ must be selected so as to satisfy a Cauchy boundary condition $k_E(0)=k_{E0}$. Hence:

$$k_E(0)=\left(\frac{s}{\mu}+\phi\right)^{1/(1-\alpha)}=\left(\frac{s}{\delta+g+n}+\phi\right)^{1/(1-\alpha)}=k_{E0},$$

and consequently that constant is represented by $\bar{\phi}$ described using the formula:

$$\bar{\phi}=k_{E0}^{1-\alpha}-\frac{s}{\delta+g+n}. \tag{2.32}$$

Thus, the growth path of capital per unit of effective labour is expressed in this version of the Solow model by the formula:

$$k_E(t)=\left(\frac{s}{\delta+g+n}+\bar{\phi}e^{-(1-\alpha)\mu t}\right)^{1/(1-\alpha)}=\left(\frac{s}{\delta+g+n}+\bar{\phi}e^{-(1-\alpha)(\delta+g+n)t}\right)^{1/(1-\alpha)} \tag{2.33a}$$

while according to the equation of production function in its intensive form (2.23), the trajectory of output per unit of effective labour:

$$y_E(t)=\left(\frac{s}{\delta+g+n}+\bar{\phi}e^{-(1-\alpha)(\delta+g+n)t}\right)^{\alpha/(1-\alpha)}, \tag{2.33b}$$

where $\bar{\phi}$ describes relation (2.32). Given the growth paths of output and capital per unit of effective labour (i.e. y_E and k_E), and knowing that the labour productivity $y(t)$ equals $e^{gt}y_E(t)$ and the capital-labour ratio $k(t)=e^{gt}k_E(t)$, the trajectories of those macroeconomic variables can be determined.

However, let us return to the constant $\bar{\phi}$ described by equation (2.32). Note that it follows from equation (2.32) that if $k_{E0}>\left(\frac{s}{\delta+g+n}\right)^{1/(1-\alpha)}$ $\left(k_{E0}<\left(\frac{s}{\delta+g+n}\right)^{1/(1-\alpha)}\right)$, then $\bar{\phi}$ is negative (positive), while $k_{E0}=\left(\frac{s}{\delta+g+n}\right)^{1/(1-\alpha)}\rightarrow\bar{\phi}=0$. Initial capital per unit of effective labour $k_{E0}>\left(\frac{s}{\delta+g+n}\right)^{1/(1-\alpha)}$ $\left(k_{E0}<\left(\frac{s}{\delta+g+n}\right)^{1/(1-\alpha)}\right)$ will be termed high (low) k_{E0}.

Let us now differentiate time paths (2.33ab) with respect to time t. We see that:

$$\dot{k}_E(t)=-\bar{\phi}(\delta+g+n)\left(\frac{s}{\delta+g+n}+\bar{\phi}e^{-(1-\alpha)(\delta+g+n)t}\right)^{\frac{1}{(1-\alpha)}-1}e^{-(1-\alpha)(\delta+g+n)t}$$

and

$$\dot{y}_E(t)=-\bar{\phi}\alpha(\delta+g+n)\left(\frac{s}{\delta+g+n}+\bar{\phi}e^{-(1-\alpha)(\delta+g+n)t}\right)^{\frac{\alpha}{(1-\alpha)}-1}e^{-(1-\alpha)(\delta+g+n)t},$$

which implies that:

$$\operatorname{sgn}\dot{k}_E(t)=\operatorname{sgn}\dot{y}_E(t)=-\operatorname{sgn}\bar{\phi}. \tag{2.34}$$

A conclusion can be drawn from equation (2.34) and previous findings that if the economy was characterized by a high/low initial capital per unit of effective labour (i.e. $\bar{\phi}$ was positive/negative), then increases in capital an in output per unit of effective labour were negative/positive, and thus the values of those variables fell/rose. However, if:

$$k_{E0} = \left(\frac{s}{\delta+g+n}\right)^{1/(1-\alpha)},$$

then $\bar{\phi} = 0$ and the values of those variables did not change in time. It follows from the above statements and from relation (2.10ab) that at high/low initial values of capital per unit of effective labour, the growth rates of labour productivity $(\dot{y}/y)$ and of capital-labour ratio $(\dot{k}/k)$ were less/greater than the Harrodian rate of technological progress g. On the other hand, at $k_{E0} = \left(\frac{s}{\delta+g+n}\right)^{1/(1-\alpha)}$, the values of k_E and y_E did not change while $\frac{\dot{y}}{y} = \frac{\dot{k}}{k} = g$.

Let $k_E^* = \lim_{t\to+\infty} k_E(t)$ and $y_E^* = \lim_{t\to+\infty} y_E(t)$ denote the long-run stock of capital and output per unit of effective labour (that represent a special case of k_E^* and y_E^* from Section 2.2); then, using the relation (2.33a,b), we obtain:

$$k_E^* = \lim_{t\to+\infty} k_E(t) = \lim_{t\to+\infty}\left(\frac{s}{\delta+g+n} + \bar{\phi}e^{-(1-\alpha)(\delta+g+n)t}\right)^{1/(1-\alpha)} = \left(\frac{s}{\delta+g+n}\right)^{1/(1-\alpha)} \tag{2.35a}$$

and (similar):

$$y_E^* = \lim_{t\to+\infty} y_E(t) = \lim_{t\to+\infty}\left(\frac{s}{\delta+g+n} + \bar{\phi}e^{-(1-\alpha)(\delta+g+n)t}\right)^{\alpha/(1-\alpha)} = \left(\frac{s}{\delta+g+n}\right)^{\alpha/(1-\alpha)}. \tag{2.35b}$$

Because at $t \to +\infty$ $k_E(t) \to k_E^*$ and $y_E(t) \to y_E^*$, hence $\dot{k}_E(t),\ \dot{y}_E(t) \to 0$; then the growth rates of labour productivity and capital-labour ratio approach the rate of technological progress as defined by Harrod.

Moreover, it follows from equations (2.35a,b) that[10]:

$$\frac{\partial \ln k_E^*}{\partial s} = \frac{1}{(1-\alpha)s} > 0, \quad \frac{\partial \ln y_E^*}{\partial s} = \frac{\alpha}{(1-\alpha)s} > 0,$$

and

$$\frac{\partial \ln k_E^*}{\partial \delta} = \frac{\partial \ln k_E^*}{\partial n} = -\frac{1}{(1-\alpha)(\delta+g+n)} < 0,$$
$$\frac{\partial \ln y_E^*}{\partial \delta} = \frac{\partial \ln y_E^*}{\partial n} = -\frac{\alpha}{(1-\alpha)(\delta+g+n)} < 0.$$

It follows from the above relations that a high savings/investment rate or a low capital depreciation rate or a low growth rate of the number of workers are accompanied by high values of k_E^* and y_E^*, and (thus) by high levels of long-run growth paths of capital-labour ratio and labour productivity.

Differentiating equations (2.35a,b) with respect to α, we obtain:

$$\frac{\partial \ln k_E^*}{\partial \alpha} = \frac{\partial \ln y}{\partial \alpha} = \frac{1}{(1-\alpha)^2} \ln \frac{s}{\delta + g + n}$$

arriving at the conclusion that if $s > \delta + g + n$ ($s < \delta + g + n$), then $\frac{\partial \ln k_E^*}{\partial \alpha} = \frac{\partial \ln y_E^*}{\partial \alpha} > 0$ $\left(\frac{\partial \ln k_E^*}{\partial \alpha} = \frac{\partial \ln y_E^*}{\partial \alpha} < 0 \right)$ and a high elasticity α is accompanied by high (low) levels of long-run growth paths of labour productivity and capital-labour ratio.

2.3.2 The CES production function

The CES production function[11] is described by the formula (Arrow, Chenery, Minhas, and Solow (1961), see also e.g. Chiang (1994, pp. 426–430) or Tokarski (2009), Chapter 1, Section 1.4)[12]:

$$Y = F(K, L) = a\left(\alpha K^{-\sigma} + (1-\alpha) L^{-\sigma}\right)^{-1/\sigma}, \tag{2.36}$$

where $a > 0, \alpha \in (0;1), \sigma \in (0;+\infty)$. Y, K *i* L (like formerly) represent the output and capital and labour inputs. Parameter a represents the total productivity of production factors, because $F(1, 1) = a$. Parameter α has no direct economic interpretation[13] while parameter σ represents the elasticity of substitution between production factors, because that elasticity equals $1/(1+\sigma)$ (Chiang, 1994, p. 428). We will now demonstrate that the CES function satisfies most of the assumptions underlying the neoclassical production function (2.1).

i The set $(0;+\infty)^2$ represents the domain of CES function and $F: (0;+\infty)^2 \to (0;+\infty)$ which results directly from equation (2.36).
ii The CES function is freely differentiable in its domain.
iii The following is true:

$$\lim_{K \to 0^+} F(K, L) = \lim_{K \to 0^+} \frac{a}{\left(\frac{\alpha}{K^\sigma} + \frac{1-\alpha}{L^\sigma} \right)^{1/\sigma}} = 0$$

and

$$\lim_{L \to 0^+} F(K, L) = \lim_{L \to 0^+} \frac{a}{\left(\frac{\alpha}{K^\sigma} + \frac{1-\alpha}{L^\sigma} \right)^{1/\sigma}} = 0.$$

Consequently, property (iii) of the neoclassical production function is only asymptotically satisfied, because the domain of CES function $(0;+\infty)^2$ is contained in the domain of function (2.1), i.e. $[0;+\infty)^2$, and the point (0,0), where property (iii) of function (2.1) is satisfied, does not belong to the domain of CES function.

iv If $L > 0$, then

$$\lim_{K\to+\infty} F(K,L) = \lim_{K\to+\infty} \frac{a}{\left(\frac{\alpha}{K^\sigma}+\frac{1-\alpha}{L^\sigma}\right)^{1/\sigma}} = a\left(\frac{1-\alpha}{L^\sigma}\right)^{-1/\sigma} > 0$$

and for $K > 0$

$$\lim_{L\to+\infty} F(K,L) = \lim_{L\to+\infty} \frac{a}{\left(\frac{\alpha}{K^\sigma}+\frac{1-\alpha}{L^\sigma}\right)^{1/\sigma}} = a\left(\frac{\alpha}{K^\sigma}\right)^{-1/\sigma} > 0$$

Moreover:

$$\lim_{K\to+\infty\wedge L\to+\infty} F(K,L) = \lim_{K\to+\infty\wedge L\to+\infty} \frac{a}{\left(\frac{\alpha}{K^\sigma}+\frac{1-\alpha}{L^\sigma}\right)^{1/\sigma}} = +\infty.$$

Hence, property (iv) of function (2.1) in the case of CES production function is only partly satisfied.

v The marginal product of capital $(\partial F/\partial K)$ is described by the equation:

$$\frac{\partial F}{\partial K} = \frac{\alpha}{a^\sigma}\left(\frac{Y}{K}\right)^{1+\sigma} > 0 \;\forall K,L > 0.$$

The positive value of the marginal product of labour $(\partial F/\partial L)$ is similarly demonstrated:

$$\frac{\partial F}{\partial L} = \frac{1-\alpha}{a^\sigma}\left(\frac{Y}{L}\right)^{1+\sigma} > 0 \;\forall K,L > 0.$$

vi Second-order partial derivatives of the CES function are described by the equations:

$$\frac{\partial^2 F}{\partial K^2} = \frac{\alpha(1+\sigma)}{a^\sigma}\left(\frac{Y}{K}\right)^\sigma \cdot \frac{\frac{\partial F}{\partial K}K - F(K,L)}{K^2} \langle 0 \;\forall K,L \rangle 0$$

and

$$\frac{\partial^2 F}{\partial L^2} = \frac{(1-\alpha)(1+\sigma)}{a^\sigma}\left(\frac{Y}{L}\right)^\sigma \cdot \frac{\frac{\partial F}{\partial L}L - F(K,L)}{L^2} \langle 0 \;\forall K,L \rangle 0.$$

The partial derivative $\frac{\partial^2 F}{\partial K^2}$ is negative, because $\frac{\alpha(1+\sigma)}{a^\sigma}\left(\frac{Y}{K}\right)^\sigma > 0$, and $\frac{\alpha(1+\sigma)}{a^\sigma}\left(\frac{Y}{K}\right)^\sigma < 0$, because the CES production function (see property (viii)) is homogeneous of degree 1, hence the following is true (as per Euler's homogeneous function theorem):

$$\frac{\partial F}{\partial K}K + \frac{\partial F}{\partial L}L = F(K,L),$$

thus:

$$\frac{\partial F}{\partial K}K - F(K,L) = -\frac{\partial F}{\partial L}L < 0.$$

The negative value of the partial derivative $\partial^2 F/\partial L^2$ is similarly demonstrated.

(vii) The CES production function partly satisfies the Inada conditions. This is because:

$$\forall L > 0 \quad \lim_{K \to 0^+} \frac{\partial F}{\partial K} = \frac{\alpha}{a^\sigma} \lim_{K \to 0^+} \left(\frac{Y}{K}\right)^{1+\sigma} = \alpha a \lim_{K \to 0^+} \left(\frac{1}{\left(\alpha + (1-\alpha)\left(\frac{K}{L}\right)^\sigma\right)^{\frac{1}{\sigma}}} \right)^{1+\sigma} = \frac{a}{\alpha^{1/\sigma}},$$

$$\forall L > 0 \quad \lim_{K \to +\infty} \frac{\partial F}{\partial K} = \alpha a \lim_{K \to +\infty} \left(\frac{1}{\left(\alpha + (1-\alpha)\left(\frac{K}{L}\right)^\sigma\right)^{\frac{1}{\sigma}}} \right)^{1+\sigma} = 0.$$

Similarly:

$$\forall K > 0 \quad \lim_{L \to 0^+} \frac{\partial F}{\partial L} = \frac{1-\alpha}{a^\sigma} \lim_{L \to 0^+} \left(\frac{Y}{L}\right)^{1+\sigma} = (1-\alpha)a \lim_{L \to 0^+} \left(\frac{1}{\left(\alpha\left(\frac{L}{K}\right)^\sigma + (1-\alpha)\right)^{\frac{1}{\sigma}}} \right)^{1+\sigma}$$

$$= \frac{a}{(1-\alpha)^{1/\sigma}},$$

and

$$\forall K > 0 \ \lim_{L \to +\infty} \frac{\partial F}{\partial L} = (1-\alpha) a \lim_{L \to +\infty} \left(\frac{1}{\left(\alpha \left(\frac{L}{K} \right)^{\sigma} + (1-\alpha) \right)^{\frac{1}{\sigma}}} \right)^{1+\sigma} = 0.$$

vii $F(\varsigma K, \varsigma L) = \dfrac{a}{\left(\dfrac{\alpha}{(\varsigma K)^{\sigma}} + \dfrac{1-\alpha}{(\varsigma L)^{\sigma}} \right)^{1/\sigma}} = \dfrac{\varsigma a}{\left(\dfrac{\alpha}{K^{\sigma}} + \dfrac{1-\alpha}{L^{\sigma}} \right)^{1/\sigma}} = \varsigma F(K, L),$

hence the CES production function is homogeneous of degree 1 (characterized by constant returns to scale).

Note that at $\sigma \to 0^{+}$, the CES production function is convergent with the Cobb-Douglas function. This is because:

$$\begin{aligned}
\lim_{\sigma \to 0^{+}} \left(a \left(\alpha K^{-\sigma} + (1-\alpha) L^{-\sigma} \right)^{-1/\sigma} \right) &= a \lim_{\sigma \to 0^{+}} \exp\left(\ln\left(\alpha K^{-\sigma} + (1-\alpha) L^{-\sigma} \right)^{-1/\sigma} \right) \\
&= a \exp\left(-\lim_{\sigma \to 0^{+}} \frac{\ln\left(\alpha K^{-\sigma} + (1-\alpha) L^{-\sigma} \right)}{\sigma} \right)^{H\left(\frac{0}{0}\right)} \\
&= a \exp\left(-\lim_{\sigma \to 0^{+}} \frac{-\alpha K^{-\sigma} \ln K - (1-\alpha) L^{-\sigma} \ln L}{\alpha K^{-\sigma} + (1-\alpha) L^{-\sigma}} \right) \\
&= a \exp\left(\lim_{\sigma \to 0^{+}} \frac{\frac{\alpha}{K^{\sigma}} \ln K + \frac{1-\alpha}{L^{\sigma}} \ln L}{\frac{\alpha}{K^{\sigma}} + \frac{1-\alpha}{L^{\sigma}}} \right) \\
&= a \exp\left(\alpha \ln K + (1-\alpha) \ln L \right) = a K^{\alpha} L^{1-\alpha}
\end{aligned}$$

Let us consider now a special case of the Solow model wherein the production process is described by the CES production function expressed using the formula[14]:

$$Y(t) = \left(\alpha (K(t))^{-\sigma} + (1-\alpha)(L(t))^{-\sigma} \right)^{-1/\sigma}, \tag{2.37}$$

where the symbols have the meanings given above. We also assume that the remaining assumptions of the Solow model are satisfied. Dividing function

(2.37) by units of effective labour $E > 0$, we obtain the CES function in its intensive form described by the equation:

$$y_E(t) = f(k_E(t)) = \frac{1}{\left(\frac{\alpha}{(k_E(t))^\sigma} + 1 - \alpha\right)^{1/\sigma}}. \tag{2.38}$$

Substituting the production function in its intensive form equation (2.38) into the Solow equation (2.15), we obtain the following ordinary differential equation:

$$\dot{k}_E(t) = \frac{s}{\left(\frac{\alpha}{(k_E(t))^\sigma} + 1 - \alpha\right)^{1/\sigma}} - \mu k_E(t), \tag{2.39}$$

where $\mu = \delta + g + n$. This equation will be considered in the phase space $P = (0; +\infty)$. It follows from equation (2.39) that:

$$\dot{k}_E > 0 \Leftrightarrow k_E^\sigma < \frac{\left(\frac{s}{\mu}\right)^\sigma - \alpha}{1-\alpha} \left(\dot{k}_E < 0 \Leftrightarrow k_E^\sigma > \frac{\left(\frac{s}{\mu}\right)^\sigma - \alpha}{1-\alpha} \right)$$

i.e. (with an additional assumption that $\frac{s}{\mu} > \alpha^{1/\sigma}$) we arrive in this version of the Solow model at a non-trivial stable steady state that is represented by the stock of capital per unit of effective labour, expressed by the formula:

$$k_E^* = \left(\frac{\left(\frac{s}{\mu}\right)^\sigma - \alpha}{1-\alpha} \right)^{1/\sigma}. \tag{2.40a}$$

The steady state k_E^* represents a point of stable equilibrium, because if $k_E(0) \in \left(0; \left(\frac{\left(\frac{s}{\mu}\right)^\sigma - \alpha}{1-\alpha} \right)^{1/\sigma} \right)$, then at any moment $t > 0$ $\dot{k}_E(t) > 0$, and at

$k_E(0) \in \left(\left(\frac{\left(\frac{s}{\mu}\right)^{\sigma} - \alpha}{1-\alpha}\right)^{1/\sigma}; +\infty\right)$, we obtain $\dot{k}_E(t) < 0$. This leads to the conclusion that for any $k_E(0)$ at $t \to +\infty$, capital per unit of effective labour $k_E(t)$ approaches k_E^*, hence k_E^* described by formula (2.40a) determines the long-run output per unit of effective labour in this version of the Solow model.

It follows from equations (2.40a) and (2.38) that the long-run output per unit of effective labour is described by the equation[15]:

$$y_E^* = \left(\frac{\left(\frac{s}{\mu}\right)^{\sigma} - \alpha}{(1-\alpha)\left(\frac{s}{\mu}\right)^{\sigma}}\right)^{1/\sigma}, \tag{2.40b}$$

Differentiating equation (2.40a) over s, δ and n (keeping in mind that $\mu = \delta + g + n$), we obtain:

$$\frac{\partial k_E^*}{\partial s} = \frac{s^{\sigma-1}}{(1-\alpha)\mu^{\sigma}} \left(\frac{\left(\frac{s}{\mu}\right)^{\sigma} - \alpha}{1-\alpha}\right)^{\frac{1}{\sigma}-1} > 0 \Rightarrow \operatorname{sgn}\frac{\partial y_E^*}{\partial s} = \operatorname{sgn}\frac{\partial k_E^*}{\partial s} = 1$$

and

$$\frac{\partial k_E^*}{\partial \delta} = \frac{\partial k_E^*}{\partial n} = -\frac{s\sigma\mu^{\sigma-1}}{(1-\alpha)} \left(\frac{\left(\frac{s}{\mu}\right)^{\sigma} - \alpha}{1-\alpha}\right)^{\frac{1}{\sigma}-1}$$

$$> 0 \Rightarrow \operatorname{sgn}\frac{\partial y_E^*}{\partial \delta} = \operatorname{sgn}\frac{\partial y_E^*}{\partial n} = \operatorname{sgn}\frac{\partial k_E^*}{\partial \delta} = \operatorname{sgn}\frac{\partial k_E^*}{\partial n} = -1.$$

The signs of the above partial derivatives lead to the conclusion that the higher the rate s or the lower the rates δ and n, the greater the stock k_E^* and stream y_E^*, and (thus) the growth paths of labour productivity and capital-labour ratio reach higher levels (the conclusions are thus similar to those drawn from the versions of the Solow model discussed above).

2.4 Phelps' golden rules of capital accumulation

It follows from equations (2.3b) and (2.4) that consumption C in the Solow model at any moment $t \in [0;+\infty)$ can be described by the formula:

$$C(t) = Y(t) - S(t).$$

Dividing the above equation by units of effective labour $E > 0$, we arrive at the equation:

$$c_E(t) = (1-s)\, y_E(t),$$

where c_E represents consumption per unit of effective labour. Since in a long run (at $t \to +\infty$) $y_E(t) \to y_E^*$, hence $c_E(t) \to c_E^*$, where c_E^* is described by the equation:

$$c_E^* = (1-s)\, y_E^*. \tag{2.41}$$

An analysis of equation (2.41) demonstrates that if the savings/investment rate s rises, then (on the one hand) the proportion of consumption in output falls, i.e. $1-s$, and (on the other hand) the output per unit of effective labour in Solow equilibrium rises, hence y_E^*. Thus, consumption per unit of effective labour in a non-trivial steady state of the Solow model (i.e. at consumption per unit of effective labour equal c_E^*) can rise, fall or remain constant as a function of increase in the savings/investment rate s. As a result, the long-run consumption per worker $c = C/L$ will follow a growth path on a higher or lower level, or (in the case of constant c_E^*) the position of that path will not change.

Phelps' golden rule of accumulation is defined as a savings/investment rate s that leads to the maximum long-run consumption per unit of effective labour c_E^*, thus placing the economy on the highest long-run time path of consumption per worker.

It follows from equations (2.35b) and (2.41) that, assuming the Cobb-Douglas production function, consumption c_E^* can be described by the formula:

$$c_E^* = (1-s)\left(\frac{s}{\delta+g+n}\right)^{\alpha/(1-\alpha)}. \tag{2.42}$$

Hence, the determination of the golden rule of accumulation can be reduced to the maximization of the expression (2.42) with respect to $s \in (0;1)$.

First, note that:

$$\lim_{s \to 0^+} c_E^* = 0,$$

$$\lim_{s \to 1^-} c_E^* = 0$$

and

$$\forall s \in (0;1)\ c_E^* > 0,$$

hence, for each s in the interval (0, 1) $\operatorname{sgn}\frac{dc_E^*}{ds} = \operatorname{sgn} v'(s)$, where:

$$v(s) = \ln c_E^* = \ln(1-s) + \frac{\alpha}{1-\alpha}\ln s + \theta, \tag{2.43}$$

where $\theta = -\frac{\alpha}{1-\alpha}\ln(\delta + g + n) \in R$. Since it follows from equation (2.43) that:

$$v'(s) = -\frac{1}{1-s} + \frac{\alpha}{(1-\alpha)s} = \frac{\alpha - s}{(1-\alpha)(1-s)s},$$

if $s \in (0;\alpha)$, then $v'(s) > 0$ while at $s \in (\alpha;1)$ $v'(s) < 0$. This means that at a savings/investment rate $s = \alpha$, the function $v(s)$ and the long-run consumption per unit of effective labour c_E^* reach their maxima in the interval (0, 1).

This leads to the conclusion that the golden rule of capital accumulation is represented by a savings/investment rate s that equals the elasticity α of output Y with respect to capital inputs K.

2.5 Conclusions

The discussion contained in in this chapter can be summarized as follows:

I The assumptions listed below underlie the Solow growth model. The production process is described be a neoclassical production function that makes the volume of output depend on (physical) capital inputs and on units of effective labour (representing a product of available technology and the number of workers). The function is characterized e.g. by unconditional availability of each factor in the production process, diminishing marginal productivities and constant returns to scale. An increase in the stock of capital results from the difference between investment (financed from savings) and capital depreciation. Technology grows at the Harrodian rate of technological progress, and the number of workers increases at a constant growth rate. Consequently, units of effective labour rise at a growth rate obtained as the total of Harrodian rate of technological progress and growth rate of the number of workers.

II The assumptions adopted in the model lead to the Solow equation that describes an increase in capital per unit of effective labour. It follows from the Solow equation that the increase represents the difference between savings/investment per unit of effective labour and capital decline per unit of effective labour. The decline results from both capital depreciation and an increase in units of effective labour.

III The Solow equation has two steady states: a trivial and non-trivial one. In the non-trivial steady state (identical with the point of long-run equilibrium in the Solow model), capital per unit of effective labour rises with an increase in the savings/investment rate or with a reduction in capital depreciation rate and in the growth rate of the number of workers.

IV In a long-run Solow equilibrium, the labour productivity (output per worker) and capital-labour ratio (capital per worker) rise at a growth rate that equals the Harrodian rate of technological progress. The location of trajectories followed by those macroeconomic variables depends on the value of capital per unit of effective labour in the Solow long-run equilibrium. The greater/lower that capital value, the higher/lower the positions of long-run growth paths of labour productivity and capital-labour ratio.

V Those conclusions are also confirmed in special cases of the Solow model i.e. the model with the Cobb-Douglas production function and with the CES production function (proposed by Arrow, Chenery, Minhas and Solow).

VI Phelps' golden rule of accumulation is defined as a savings/investment rate that locates a Solow economy on the highest long-run growth path of consumption per worker. In the Solow model with the Cobb-Douglas production function, that rate equals the elasticity of output with respect to capital.

Notes

1 Physical capital inputs will also be referred to (simply) as capital inputs.

2 According to assumption 5, $E = AL$ (where A represents available technology and L denotes the number of workers), hence the marginal product of labour (MPL) can be expressed as:

$$\text{MPL} = \frac{\partial F}{\partial L} = \frac{\partial F}{\partial E}\frac{\partial E}{\partial L} = A \cdot \text{MPE},$$

i.e. according to assumption (v), we also obtain a positive MPL.

3 The growth path (time path or trajectory) of variable x is understood hereinafter as a specific function $x\,(t)$ that describes the values of that variable at subsequent moments $t \in [0;+\infty)$.

4 We implicitly assume that the initial stock of technology, i.e. A (0), equals 1. However, this assumption has no effect on the generality of further analyzes. A similar assumption is adopted for L (0) in equation (2.7).

5 Technical change can be defined (after Solow) as follows: "When we think about technical progress in the economist's abstract way it is only too natural to imagine a standard production diagram with inputs measured along the axes and a family of equal-output curves of the conventional shape, and to say that when

technical progress occurs, the family of equal-output curves shifts in such a way that more output can be produced from given inputs or the same output can be produced with fewer inputs" (Solow 1963, p. 48). See also Solow (1957).

6 I.e. the rate of such technological change that directly boosts the productivity of labour. More on that topic, see e.g. Allen (1975, p. 237) or Tokarski (2009, Chapter 1, Section 1.5).

7 Such expressions as $H\left(\frac{0}{0}\right)$ and $H\left(\frac{\infty}{\infty}\right)$ will denote indeterminate forms like 0/0 and ∞/∞, and will indicate that the authors use L'Hospital's rule.

8 $f'(k_E)k_E - f(k_E) = -\text{MPE} < 0$ results from the fact that output Y can be expressed as:

$$Y = f(k_E)E,$$

hence:

$$\begin{aligned}\text{MPE} &= \frac{\partial Y}{\partial E} = f'(k_E)\frac{\partial k_E}{\partial E}E + f(k_E) \\ &= -f'(k_E)\frac{K}{E^2}E + f(k_E) = -\left(f'(k_E)k_E - f(k_E)\right) > 0\end{aligned}.$$

9 An alternative proof of stability of the non-trivial steady state of the Solow equation can be found in the study published by Milo and Malaczewski (2005).

10 We use here the following property of a multivariate function. If the function $y = f(x)$, $x = (x_1, x_2, \ldots, x_n) \in R^n$, is (firstly) differentiable and (secondly) assumes positive values in the set $Z \subseteq R^n$, then for each $i = 1, 2, \ldots, n$: $\operatorname{sgn}\frac{\partial \ln y}{\partial x_i} = \operatorname{sgn}\frac{\partial y}{\partial x_i}$.

11 Section 2.3.2 is based on studies conducted by Tokarski (2008a, 2009) (Chapter 2, Section 2.5). The possible use of the CES production function in the Solow model is discussed e.g. by Klump and Preissler (2000), Klump, McAdam, and Willman (2011) and Sasaki (2017). See also Sulima (2011), who analyzes a Nonneman-Vanhoudt model (representing a generalization of the Solow model) with the CES production function.

12 Note that at $\sigma = 1$, the expression $\frac{1}{\left(\frac{\alpha}{K^\sigma} + \frac{1-\alpha}{L^\sigma}\right)^{1/\sigma}} = \frac{1}{\frac{\alpha}{K} + \frac{1-\alpha}{L}}$ in the CES production function represents a weighted harmonic mean of capital and labour inputs with weights equal α and $1 - \alpha$.

13 However, parameter α is identified with the proportion of capital inputs in the output in Clark's marginal theory of distribution.

14 Since we assume that technology is described by the equation $A(t) = e^{gt}$, we can also assume that the total productivity of production factors at the moment t = 0 equals 1, hence parameter a in the production function (2.37) also equals 1.

15 Since it follows from equation (2.38) that $\forall k_E > 0\ f'(k_E) = \alpha a k_E^{-\sigma-1}\left(\alpha k_E^{-\sigma} + 1 - \alpha\right)^{-\frac{1}{\sigma}-1} > 0$, $\operatorname{sgn}\frac{\partial k_E^*}{\partial s} = \operatorname{sgn}\frac{\partial y_E^*}{\partial s}$ and $\operatorname{sgn}\frac{\partial k_E^*}{\partial \mu} = \operatorname{sgn}\frac{\partial y_E^*}{\partial \mu}$.

3 Generalizations of the Solow model (the Mankiw-Romer-Weil and Nonneman-Vanhoudt models)

3.1 Introduction

This chapter describes generalizations of the Solow model, known in the literature, i.e. the Mankiw-Romer-Weil model developed in 1992 and the Nonneman-Vanhoudt model proposed in 1996. The Mankiw-Romer-Weil model considers human capital accumulation in addition to physical capital accumulation.[1] Therefore, that model is also known as a model of human capital accumulation. The Nonneman-Vanhoudt model is designed to analyze processes in an economy with a finite number of N stocks of capital (including various types of physical, human, social, etc. capital).

Our analysis of the Mankiw-Romer-Weil and Nonneman-Vanhoudt models (like the previous analysis of the Solow model) will begin with their purely general versions and then will proceed to special cases with the Cobb-Douglas and Constant Elasticity of Substitution (CES) production functions. We will also analyze the stability of non-trivial steady states of systems of differential equations that result from the assumptions adopted in the discussed growth models (see also Dykas, Sulima and Tokarski, 2008; Dykas, Edigarian and Tokarski, 2011; Sulima, 2011). We will find the golden rules of capital accumulation that (what will be demonstrated) represent simple generalizations of Phelps' golden rules of accumulation from the Solow model of economic growth.

3.2 The two-capital Mankiw-Romer-Weil model (a model of human capital accumulation)

3.2.1 The model with a neoclassical production function

The assumptions listed below underlie the economic growth model analyzed in this chapter.[2]

1 The production process is described by a neoclassical production function expressed by the formula:

$$Y(t) = F\big(K(t), H(t), E(t)\big), \tag{3.1}$$

DOI: 10.4324/9781003323792-4

where Y, K and E represent (like in the Solow model) the output, stock of physical capital and units of effective labour, respectively, and H denotes the total stock of human capital consisting of all workers in the economy. It is assumed that the production function (3.1), being a generalization of function (2.1), is characterized by the following properties[3]:

i Its domain is defined as the set $[0;+\infty)^3$ and $F:[0;+\infty)^3 \rightarrow [0;+\infty)$.

ii Function F is differentiable at least twice in the set $(0;+\infty)^3$.

iii For any $(K,H,E) \in [0;+\infty)^3$, the following is true:

iv $F(0,H,E)=F(K,0,E)=F(K,H,0)=0$.

v $\forall(K,H,E) \in (0;+\infty)^3 \lim\limits_{K\rightarrow+\infty} F(K,H,E)= \lim\limits_{H\rightarrow+\infty} F(K,H,E)=$

$\forall(K,H,E) \in (0;+\infty)^3$ ·

vi $\forall(K,H,E) \in (0;+\infty)^3 \frac{\partial F}{\partial K},\frac{\partial F}{\partial H},\frac{\partial F}{\partial E}>0$, where subsequent partial derivatives represent the marginal product of physical capital (MPK), marginal product of human capital and marginal product of units of effective labour (MPE).

vii $\forall(K,H,E) \in (0;+\infty)^3 \frac{\partial^2 F}{\partial K^2},\frac{\partial^2 F}{\partial H^2},\frac{\partial^2 F}{\partial E^2}<0$.

viii For any $(K,H,E) \in (0;+\infty)^3 \lim\limits_{K\rightarrow 0^+}\frac{\partial F}{\partial K}=\lim\limits_{H\rightarrow 0^+}\frac{\partial F}{\partial H}=\lim\limits_{E\rightarrow 0^+}\frac{\partial F}{\partial E}=+\infty$ and $\lim\limits_{K\rightarrow+\infty}\frac{\partial F}{\partial K}=\lim\limits_{H\rightarrow+\infty}\frac{\partial F}{\partial H}=\lim\limits_{E\rightarrow+\infty}\frac{\partial F}{\partial E}=0$ (we assume thus that the Inada conditions are satisfied).

ix $\forall(K,H,E) \in [0;+\infty)^3 \wedge \forall\varsigma>0 \quad F(\varsigma K,\varsigma H,\varsigma E)=\varsigma F(K,H,E)$.

2 An increase in the stock of physical/human capital equals the difference between investment $s_K Y/s_H Y$ in that capital and its depreciation $\delta_K K/\delta_H H$ (where s_K/s_H denotes the rate of investment in physical/human capital, and δ_K/δ_H represents the depreciation rate of that capital). It is assumed that the rates s_K, s_H, δ_K i δ_H belong to the interval (0,1) and that $s_K+s_H \in (0;1)$. Assumption 2 can be expressed using the following differential equations:

$$\dot{K}(t)=s_K Y(t)-\delta_K K(t) \tag{3.2a}$$

and

$$\dot{H}(t)=s_H Y(t)-\delta_H H(t). \tag{3.2b}$$

3 Units of effective labour change as per equation (2.12a), hence their growth rate λ equals the total of the Harrodian rate of technological progress (g) and the growth rate of the number of workers (n).

Like in the Solow model, let:

$$y(t)=\frac{Y(t)}{L(t)}, \tag{3.3a}$$

$$k(t)=\frac{K(t)}{L(t)} \tag{3.3b}$$

and

$$h(t)=\frac{H(t)}{L(t)}, \tag{3.3c}$$

denote, respectively, the output and the stocks of physical and human capital per worker, and let:

$$y_E(t)=\frac{Y(t)}{E(t)}, \tag{3.4a}$$

$$k_E(t)=\frac{K(t)}{E(t)} \tag{3.4b}$$

and

$$h_E(t)=\frac{H(t)}{E(t)}, \tag{3.4c}$$

denote the values given above per unit of effective labour. It follows from assumption 3 about units of effective labour and equations (3.3a–c) and (3.4a–c) that:

$$\frac{\dot{y}(t)}{y(t)}=g+\frac{\dot{y}_E(t)}{y_E(t)}, \tag{3.5a}$$

$$\frac{\dot{k}(t)}{k(t)}=g+\frac{\dot{k}_E(t)}{k_E(t)} \tag{3.5b}$$

and

$$\frac{\dot{h}(t)}{h(t)}=g+\frac{\dot{h}_E(t)}{h_E(t)}. \tag{3.5c}$$

It follows from equations (3.5a–c) that if the variables y_E, k_E, h_E rise/fall, then the growth rates y, k, h are greater/less than the Harrodian rate of technological progress g. When the analyzed macroeconomic variables expressed per unit of effective labour remain constant, the growth rates of labour productivity and of physical and human capital per worker equal the Harrodian rate of technological progress.

Dividing the production function (3.1) by units of effective labour $E > 0$ and using assumption (1) viii.), we obtain:

$$\frac{Y(t)}{E(t)}=F\left(\frac{K(t)}{E(t)},\frac{H(t)}{E(t)},1\right),$$

and this together with equations (3.4a–c) leads to the production function in its intensive form described by the formula:

$$y_E(t) = f(k_E(t), h_E(t)), \tag{3.6}$$

where $f(k_E, h_E) = F(k_E, h_E, 1)$.

Function (3.6) represents a simple generalization of function (2.11) known from the Solow model. Consequently, it is characterized by the following properties:

a Its domain is defined as the set $[0;+\infty)^2$ and $f:[0;+\infty)^2 \rightarrow [0;+\infty)$.

b The function is differentiable at least twice in the set $(0;+\infty)^2$.

c $\forall (k_E, h_E) \in [0;+\infty)^2 \;\; f(0;h_E) = f(k_E;0) = 0$.

d $\forall (k_E, h_E) \in (0;+\infty)^2 \;\; \lim\limits_{k_E \to +\infty} f(k_E, h_E) = \lim\limits_{h_E \to +\infty} f(k_E, h_E) = +\infty$.

e For each $(k_E, h_E) \in (0;+\infty)^2 \; \dfrac{\partial f}{\partial k_E}, \dfrac{\partial f}{\partial h_E} > 0$ and $\dfrac{\partial^2 f}{\partial k_E^2}, \dfrac{\partial^2 f}{\partial k_E^2} < 0$.

f For any $(k_E, h_E) \in (0;+\infty)^2$, the Inada conditions are satisfied, i.e.: $\lim\limits_{k_E \to 0^+} \dfrac{\partial f}{\partial k_E} = \lim\limits_{h_E \to 0^+} \dfrac{\partial f}{\partial h_E} = +\infty$ and $\lim\limits_{k_E \to +\infty} \dfrac{\partial f}{\partial k_E} = \lim\limits_{h_E \to +\infty} \dfrac{\partial f}{\partial h_E} = 0$.

Differentiating equations (3.4bc) after time t, we obtain:

$$\dot{k}_E(t) = \frac{\dot{K}(t)}{E(t)} - k_E(t)\frac{\dot{E}(t)}{E(t)} \;\wedge\; \dot{h}_E(t) = \frac{\dot{H}(t)}{E(t)} - h_E(t)\frac{\dot{E}(t)}{E(t)}.$$

From the above relation and equation (2.12b), we get:

$$\dot{k}_E(t) = \frac{\dot{K}(t)}{E(t)} - \lambda k_E(t) \wedge \dot{h}_E(t) = \frac{\dot{H}(t)}{E(t)} - \lambda h_E(t),$$

and considering equations (3.2ab), we arrive at the following system of differential equations:

$$\begin{cases} \dot{k}_E(t) = s_K y_E(t) - \mu_K k_E(t) \\ \dot{h}_E(t) = s_H y_E(t) - \mu_H h_E(t) \end{cases}, \tag{3.7}$$

where $\mu_K = \delta_K + g + n > 0$, $\mu_H = \delta_H + g + n > 0$ denotes the rate of physical/human capital decline per unit of effective labour. System of equations (3.7), also known as equations of motion of the Mankiw-Romer-Weil model, represents a simple generalization of the Solow equation (2.15). Thus, its economic interpretation can be reduced to the statement that an increase in the stock of physical/human capital per unit of effective labour equals the difference between investment in physical/human capital per unit of effective labour and capital decline that results from depreciation of physical/human capital and from an increase in units of effective labour.

Substituting the production function in its intensive form into system of differential equations (3.7), we get:

$$\begin{cases} \dot{k}_E(t) = s_K f(k_E(t), h_E(t)) - \mu_K k_E(t) \\ \dot{h}_E(t) = s_H f(k_E(t), h_E(t)) - \mu_H h_E(t) \end{cases} . \tag{3.8}$$

We will demonstrate now that system of differential equations (3.8) has two steady states: a trivial steady state (0, 0) and a non-trivial steady state in the phase space $P = (0;+\infty)^2$.

The existence of the trivial steady state results directly from property (*c*) of function (3.6). That point will be ignored in further analyzes (like in the case of the Solow model).

The non-trivial steady state solves the system of equations:

$$\begin{cases} \Phi_k(k_E, h_E, s_K, \mu_K) = 0 \\ \Phi_h(k_E, h_E, s_H, \mu_H) = 0 \end{cases} , \tag{3.9}$$

where:

$$\Phi_k(k_E, h_E, s_K, \mu_K) = p_K(k_E, h_E) - \frac{\mu_K}{s_K} = p_K(k_E, h_E) - \frac{\delta_K + g + n}{s_K}.$$

and

$$\Phi_h(k_E, h_E, s_H, \mu_H) = p_H(k_E, h_E) - \frac{\mu_H}{s_H} = p_H(k_E, h_E) - \frac{\delta_H + g + n}{s_H}$$

where the functions $p_K(k_E, h_E) = \frac{f(k_E, h_E)}{k_E}$, $p_H(k_E, h_E) = \frac{f(k_E, h_E)}{h_E}$ make (respectively) the productivity of physical capital p_K and productivity of human capital p_H depend on inputs of both physical capital k_E and human capital h_E per unit of effective labour.

The Jacobian determinant $|J|$ of system of equations (3.9) is defined by the formula:

$$|J| = \begin{vmatrix} \frac{\partial \Phi_k}{\partial k_E} & \frac{\partial \Phi_k}{\partial h_E} \\ \frac{\partial \Phi_h}{\partial k_E} & \frac{\partial \Phi_h}{\partial h_E} \end{vmatrix} = \begin{vmatrix} \partial p_K / \partial k_E & \partial p_K / \partial h_E \\ \partial p_H / \partial k_E & \partial p_H / \partial h_E \end{vmatrix} = \frac{\partial p_K}{\partial k_E}\frac{\partial p_H}{\partial h_E} - \frac{\partial p_K}{\partial h_E}\frac{\partial p_H}{\partial k_E} \tag{3.10}$$

Since:

$$\frac{\partial p_K}{\partial k_E}=\frac{\dfrac{\partial f}{\partial k_E}k_E-f(k_E,h_E)}{k_E^2},\quad \frac{\partial p_K}{\partial h_E}=\frac{\partial f/\partial h_E}{k_E}$$

and (similarly):

$$\frac{\partial p_H}{\partial h_E}=\frac{\dfrac{\partial f}{\partial h_E}h_E-f(k_E,h_E)}{h_E^2},\quad \frac{\partial p_H}{\partial k_E}=\frac{\partial f/\partial k_E}{h_E},$$

the Jacobian (3.10) satisfies the relation:

$$\forall(k_E,h_E)\in P\ \ |J|=\frac{\left(\dfrac{\partial f}{\partial k_E}k_E-f(k_E,h_E)\right)\left(\dfrac{\partial f}{\partial h_E}h_E-f(k_E,h_E)\right)}{k_E^2h_E^2}-\frac{\dfrac{\partial f}{\partial k_E}\dfrac{\partial f}{\partial h_E}}{k_Eh_E},$$

hence:

$$\forall(k_E,h_E)\in P\ \ |J|=f(k_E,h_E)\frac{f(k_E,h_E)-\dfrac{\partial f}{\partial k_E}k_E-\dfrac{\partial f}{\partial h_E}h_E}{k_E^2h_E^2}. \tag{3.11}$$

Considering that the production function (3.1) is homogeneous of degree 1 and given Euler's homogeneous function theorem, we conclude that for any $(K,H,E)\in(0;+\infty)^3$, the following is true:

$$F(K,H,E)=\frac{\partial F}{\partial K}K+\frac{\partial F}{\partial H}H+\frac{\partial F}{\partial E}E,$$

and this, divided by $E>0$, gives:

$$\forall(k_E,h_E)\in P\ \ f(k_E,h_E)=\frac{\partial F}{\partial K}k_E+\frac{\partial F}{\partial H}k_E+\frac{\partial F}{\partial E}. \tag{3.12}$$

Since[4] $\frac{\partial F}{\partial K}=\frac{\partial f}{\partial k_E}$ and $\frac{\partial F}{\partial H}=\frac{\partial f}{\partial h_E}$, equation (3.12) can be expressed as follows:

$$\forall(k_E,h_E)\in P\ \ f(k_E,h_E)=\frac{\partial f}{\partial k_E}k_E+\frac{\partial f}{\partial h_E}h_E+\frac{\partial F}{\partial E}.$$

We also know that $\frac{\partial F}{\partial E}>0$, hence[5]:

$$\forall(k_E,h_E)\in P\ \ f(k_E,h_E)>\frac{\partial f}{\partial k_E}k_E+\frac{\partial f}{\partial h_E}h_E \Rightarrow f(k_E,h_E)-\frac{\partial f}{\partial k_E}k_E-\frac{\partial f}{\partial h_E}h_E>0$$

and consequently the Jacobian determinant (3.11) is positive. As a result, there is a point $\kappa^* = \left(k_E^*, h_E^*\right) \epsilon F$ that solves system of equations (3.9). The point also represents the steady state of system of differential equations (3.8).

As the non-trivial steady state κ of the analyzed system of differential equations represents a special case of the non-trivial steady state of system of differential equations (3.40) known from the Nonneman-Vanhoudt model, and that steady state is Lyapunov asymptotically stable (Section 3.3.1), thus also the analyzed point κ is Lyapunov asymptotically stable.

Obviously, the growth rates of physical capital $\dot{k} / k$ and human capital $\dot{h} / h$ per worker (like in the Solow model) equal the Harrodian rate of technological progress g in steady state κ, as per equations (3.5bc). It follows from equation (3.6) that the long-run output per unit of effective labour equals $y_E^* = f\left(k_E^*, h_E^*\right)$, and the labour productivity rises at the growth rate $\dot{y} / y$ equal g as per equation (3.5a).

Moreover, since $\mu_K = \delta_K + g + n$ and $\mu_H = \delta_H + g + n$, it follows, from this relation and from system of equations (3.9), that the stocks k_E^* and h_E^* can be understood as certain implicit functions of investment rates s_K, s_H, of depreciation rates δ_K, δ_H and the growth rate of the number of workers n. Hence, the subsequent partial derivatives k_E^* and h_E^* with respect to those rates solve the following systems of equations:

$$\begin{bmatrix} \partial\Phi_k / \partial k_E & \partial\Phi_k / \partial h_E \\ \partial\Phi_h / \partial k_E & \partial\Phi_h / \partial h_E \end{bmatrix} \begin{bmatrix} \partial k_E^* / \partial s_K \\ \partial h_E^* / \partial s_K \end{bmatrix} = \begin{bmatrix} -\partial\Phi_k / \partial s_K \\ -\partial\Phi_h / \partial s_K \end{bmatrix}, \tag{3.13a}$$

$$\begin{bmatrix} \partial\Phi_k / \partial k_E & \partial\Phi_k / \partial h_E \\ \partial\Phi_h / \partial k_E & \partial\Phi_h / \partial h_E \end{bmatrix} \begin{bmatrix} \partial k_E^* / \partial s_H \\ \partial h_E^* / \partial s_H \end{bmatrix} = \begin{bmatrix} -\partial\Phi_k / \partial s_H \\ -\partial\Phi_h / \partial s_H \end{bmatrix}, \tag{3.13b}$$

$$\begin{bmatrix} \partial\Phi_k / \partial k_E & \partial\Phi_k / \partial h_E \\ \partial\Phi_h / \partial k_E & \partial\Phi_h / \partial h_E \end{bmatrix} \begin{bmatrix} \partial k_E^* / \partial \delta_K \\ \partial h_E^* / \partial \delta_K \end{bmatrix} = \begin{bmatrix} -\partial\Phi_k / \partial \delta_K \\ -\partial\Phi_h / \partial \delta_K \end{bmatrix} \tag{3.13c}$$

$$\begin{bmatrix} \partial\Phi_k / \partial k_E & \partial\Phi_k / \partial h_E \\ \partial\Phi_h / \partial k_E & \partial\Phi_h / \partial h_E \end{bmatrix} \begin{bmatrix} \partial k_E^* / \partial \delta_H \\ \partial h_E^* / \partial \delta_H \end{bmatrix} = \begin{bmatrix} -\partial\Phi_k / \partial \delta_H \\ -\partial\Phi_h / \partial \delta_H \end{bmatrix} \tag{3.13d}$$

and

$$\begin{bmatrix} \partial\Phi_k / \partial k_E & \partial\Phi_k / \partial h_E \\ \partial\Phi_h / \partial k_E & \partial\Phi_h / \partial h_E \end{bmatrix} \begin{bmatrix} \partial k_E^* / \partial n \\ \partial h_E^* / \partial n \end{bmatrix} = \begin{bmatrix} -\partial\Phi_k / \partial n \\ -\partial\Phi_h / \partial n \end{bmatrix}. \tag{3.13e}$$

It follows from equations (3.13abcde) that:

$$\frac{\partial k_E^*}{\partial s_K}=\frac{\begin{vmatrix}-\partial\Phi_k/\partial s_K & \partial\Phi_k/\partial h_E\\ -\partial\Phi_h/\partial s_K & \partial\Phi_h/\partial h_E\end{vmatrix}}{|J|}=\frac{\begin{vmatrix}-(\delta_K+g+n)/s_K^2 & \partial p_K/\partial h_E\\ 0 & \partial p_H/\partial h_E\end{vmatrix}}{|J|}$$

$$=-\frac{(\delta_K+g+n)\dfrac{\partial p_H}{\partial h_E}}{s_K^2|J|}=\frac{(\delta_K+g+n)\left(f(k_E,h_E)-\dfrac{\partial f}{\partial h_E}h_E\right)}{s_K^2h_E^2|J|}>0,$$

$$\frac{\partial h_E^*}{\partial s_K}=\frac{\begin{vmatrix}\partial\Phi_k/\partial k_E & -\partial\Phi_k/\partial s_K\\ \partial\Phi_h/\partial k_E & -\partial\Phi_h/\partial s_K\end{vmatrix}}{|J|}=\frac{\begin{vmatrix}\partial p_K/\partial k_E & -(\delta_K+g+n)/s_K^2\\ \partial p_H/\partial k_E & 0\end{vmatrix}}{|J|}$$

$$=\frac{(\delta_K+g+n)\dfrac{\partial p_H}{\partial k_E}}{s_K^2|J|}=\frac{(\delta_K+g+n)\dfrac{\partial f}{\partial k_E}}{s_K^2h_E|J|}>0.$$

$\dfrac{\partial k_E^*}{\partial s_H}>0$ by analogy with $\dfrac{\partial h_E^*}{\partial s_K}>0,$

$\dfrac{\partial h_E^*}{\partial s_H}>0$ similar to $\dfrac{\partial k_E^*}{\partial s_K}>0,$

$$\frac{\partial k_E^*}{\partial \delta_K}=\frac{\begin{vmatrix}-\partial\Phi_k/\partial \delta_K & \partial\Phi_k/\partial h_E\\ -\partial\Phi_h/\partial \delta_K & \partial\Phi_h/\partial h_E\end{vmatrix}}{|J|}=\frac{\begin{vmatrix}1/s_K & \partial p_K/\partial h_E\\ 0 & \partial p_H/\partial h_E\end{vmatrix}}{|J|}$$

$$=\frac{\partial p_H/\partial h_E}{s_K|J|}=-\frac{f(k_E,h_E)-\dfrac{\partial f}{\partial h_E}h_E}{s_K|J|}<0,$$

$$\frac{\partial h_E^*}{\partial \delta_K}=\frac{\begin{vmatrix}\partial\Phi_k/\partial k_E & -\partial\Phi_k/\partial \delta_K\\ \partial\Phi_h/\partial k_E & -\partial\Phi_h/\partial \delta_K\end{vmatrix}}{|J|}=\frac{\begin{vmatrix}\partial p_K/\partial k_E & 1/s_K\\ \partial p_H/\partial k_E & 0\end{vmatrix}}{|J|}$$

$$=-\frac{\dfrac{\partial p_H}{\partial k_E}}{s_K|J|}=-\frac{\dfrac{\partial f}{\partial k_E}}{s_Kh_E|J|}<0,$$

$\dfrac{\partial k_E^*}{\partial \delta_H}$ by analogy with $\dfrac{\partial h_E^*}{\partial \delta_K}<0,$

$$\frac{\partial h_E^*}{\partial \delta_H} \text{ similar to } \frac{\partial k_E^*}{\partial \delta_K} < 0,$$

$$\frac{\partial k_E^*}{\partial n} = \frac{\begin{vmatrix} -\partial \Phi_k / \partial n & \partial \Phi_k / \partial h_E \\ -\partial \Phi_h / \partial n & \partial \Phi_h / \partial h_E \end{vmatrix}}{|J|} = \frac{\begin{vmatrix} 1/s_K & \partial p_K / \partial h_E \\ 1/s_H & \partial p_H / \partial h_E \end{vmatrix}}{|J|}$$

$$= \frac{\dfrac{\partial p_H / \partial h_E}{s_K} - \dfrac{\partial p_K / \partial h_E}{s_H}}{|J|} = \frac{\dfrac{f(k_E, h_E) - \dfrac{\partial f}{\partial h_E} h_E}{s_K h_E^2} + \dfrac{\dfrac{\partial f}{\partial h_E}}{s_H k_E}}{|J|} < 0.$$

and (by analogy) $\frac{\partial h_E^*}{\partial n}$.

This leads to the conclusion that the higher the rates of investment in physical capital s_K or human capital s_H or the lower the depreciation rates of those stocks δ_K and δ_H or the lower the growth rate of the number of workers n, the greater the stocks k_E^* and h_E^* in the long-run Mankiw-Romer-Weil equilibrium, and (thus) the higher the levels reached by long-run growth paths of analyzed stocks of capital per worker.

Moreover, as the production function in its intensive form (3.6) has positive partial derivatives with respect to k_E^* and h_E^* due to property (*e*), the signs of partial derivatives y_E^* with respect to investment rates s_K, s_H, depreciation rates δ_K, δ_H and growth rate of the number of workers n are identical with the signs of partial derivatives k_E^* and h_E^*. Economic conclusions drawn from the signs of partial derivatives y_E^* with respect to s_K, s_H, δ_K, δ_H and n are similar to the conclusions drawn from the signs of partial derivatives k_E^* and h_E^*.

3.2.2 A model with the Cobb-Douglas production function

It is assumed in the original Mankiw-Romer-Weil model (i.e. a model with the Cobb-Douglas production function) that the production process is described by an extended Cobb-Douglas function expressed by the formula:

$$Y(t) = (K(t))^{\alpha_K} (H(t))^{\alpha_H} (E(t))^{1-\alpha_K-\alpha_H}, \tag{3.14}$$

where $\alpha_K, \alpha_H, (1-\alpha_K-\alpha_H) \in (0;1)$, and assumptions 2–3 underlying the model from Section 3.2.1 are satisfied. Parameters α_K and α_H in the production function (3.14), like parameter α in the original Cobb-Douglas production function, represent the elasticities of output Y with respect to the stock of physical capital K and human capital H.

As function (3.14) represents a simple generalization of the Cobb-Douglas function (2.19), it satisfies all the conditions applicable to the production function (3.1).

Dividing the production function (3.14) by $E > 0$, we get the production function in its intensive version expressed by the formula:

$$y_E(t) = (k_E(t))^{\alpha K} \, (h_E(t))^{\alpha H} . \tag{3.15}$$

Substituting relation (3.15) into (3.8), we obtain the following system of ordinary differential equations:

$$\begin{cases} \dot{k}_E(t) = s_K \, (k_E(t))^{\alpha K} \, (h_E(t))^{\alpha H} - \mu_K k_E(t) \\ \dot{h}_E(t) = s_H \, (k_E(t))^{\alpha K} \, (h_E(t))^{\alpha H} - \mu_H h_E(t) \end{cases} . \tag{3.16}$$

The non-trivial steady state (the trivial steady state is ignored) of system of differential equations (3.16), i.e. $\kappa \in P$, represents a solution of the system of equations described by the formula:

$$\begin{cases} k_E^{\alpha K - 1} h_E^{\alpha H} = \dfrac{\mu_K}{s_K} \\ k_E^{\alpha K} h_E^{\alpha H - 1} = \dfrac{\mu_H}{s_H} \end{cases} ,$$

that can also be expressed as a matrix:

$$\begin{bmatrix} -(1-\alpha_K) & \alpha_H \\ \alpha_K & -(1-\alpha_H) \end{bmatrix} \cdot \begin{bmatrix} \ln k_E \\ \ln h_E \end{bmatrix} = \begin{bmatrix} \ln(\mu_K / s_K) \\ \ln(\mu_H / s_H) \end{bmatrix} . \tag{3.17}$$

Using Cramer's rule, we find that the following equations are solved in point $\kappa = \left(k_E^*, h_E^*\right)$:

$$\ln k_E^* = \frac{\alpha_H \ln \dfrac{s_K}{\delta_K + g + n} + (1-\alpha_H) \ln \dfrac{s_H}{\delta_H + g + n}}{1 - \alpha_K - \alpha_H} \tag{3.18a}$$

and

$$\ln h_E^* = \frac{(1-\alpha_K) \ln \dfrac{s_K}{\delta_K + g + n} + \alpha_K \ln \dfrac{s_H}{\delta_H + g + n}}{1 - \alpha_K - \alpha_H} , \tag{3.18b}$$

because $\mu_K = \delta_K + g + n$ and $\mu_H = \delta_H + g + n$. Since it follows from equation (3.15) that:

$$\ln y_E(t) = \alpha_K \ln k_E(t) + \alpha_H \ln h_E(t),$$

then (in particular):

$$\ln y_E^* = \alpha_K \ln k_E^* + \alpha_H \ln h_E^*,$$

and this together with relations (3.18a,b) leads to:

$$\ln y_E^* = \frac{\alpha_K \ln \dfrac{s_K}{\delta_K + g + n} + \alpha_H \ln \dfrac{s_H}{\delta_H + g + n}}{1 - \alpha_{K - \alpha H}}. \tag{3.18c}$$

Equations (3.18a–c) lead to the following conclusions. First, partial logarithmic derivatives k_E^*, h_E^* and y_E^* with respect to investment rates s_K and s_H are positive, and hence the higher those rates, the higher levels are reached by long-run growth paths of the stocks of physical and human capital per worker and of labour productivity. Second, partial derivatives of the analyzed logarithms with respect to the depreciation rates of various stocks of capital and the growth rate of the number of workers are negative, and that leads to the conclusion that high values of rates δ_K, δ_H or n are accompanied by trajectories of k, h i y situated at low levels in a long term. Third, the signs of partial derivatives $\ln k_E^*$, $\ln h_E^*$ and $\ln y_E^*$ with respect to the elasticity α_K and α_H are ambiguous, because e.g.:

$$\frac{\partial \ln k_E^*}{\partial \alpha_K} = \frac{\alpha_H \ln \dfrac{s_K}{\delta_K + g + n} + (1 - \alpha_H) \ln \dfrac{s_H}{\delta_H + g + n}}{(1 - \alpha_K - \alpha_H)^2}.,$$

and

$$\frac{\partial \ln k_E^*}{\partial \alpha_H} = \frac{(1 - \alpha_K) \ln \dfrac{s_K}{\delta_K + g + n} + \alpha_K \ln \dfrac{s_H}{\delta_H + g + n}}{(1 - \alpha_K - \alpha_H)^2}.$$

3.2.3 A model with the CES production function

Let us consider now the Mankiw-Romer-Weil model of human capital accumulation with the CES production function.[6] We assume that the production process is described by a function that can be described as an extended

CES production function (2.37), expressed by the equation (with previous symbols preserved):

$$Y(t)=\left(\alpha_K\left(K(t)\right)^{-\sigma}+\alpha_H\left(H(t)\right)^{-\sigma}+(1-\alpha_H-\alpha_K)\left(E(t)\right)^{-\sigma}\right)^{-1/\sigma}, \qquad (3.19)$$

where α_K, α_H, $(1-\alpha_H-\alpha_K)\in(0;1)$, and $\sigma\in(0;1)$. Parameters α_K, α_H and σ are interpreted in terms of economics like parameters α and σ in function (2.36). Additionally, the production function (3.19) has similar properties as functions (2.36 and 2.37), because it represents its extension.

Dividing equation (3.19) by units of effective labour $E>0$, we get the relation:

$$y_E(t)=\left(\alpha_K\left(k_E(t)\right)^{-\sigma}+\alpha_H\left(h_E(t)\right)^{-\sigma}+1-\alpha_K-\alpha_H\right)^{-1/\sigma}. \qquad (3.20)$$

Substituting function (3.20) into the system of equations of motion in the Mankiw-Romer-Weil growth model, we obtain the system of differential equations:

$$\begin{cases}\dot{k}_E(t)=s_K\left(\alpha_K\left(k_E(t)\right)^{-\sigma}+\alpha_H\left(h_E(t)\right)^{-\sigma}+1-\alpha_K-\alpha_H\right)^{-1/\sigma}-\mu_K k_E(t)\\ \dot{h}_E(t)=s_H\left(\alpha_K\left(k_E(t)\right)^{-\sigma}+\alpha_H\left(h_E(t)\right)^{-\sigma}+1-\alpha_K-\alpha_H\right)^{-1/\sigma}-\mu_H h_E(t)\end{cases}. \qquad (3.21)$$

The system will be analyzed in the phase space $P=(0;+\infty)^2$.

Consequently, there exists a steady state $\kappa\in P$ of system of differential equations (3.21). First, let us demonstrate that system of differential equations (3.21) has exactly one steady state. The steady state $\kappa=\left(k_E^*,h_E^*\right)\in P$ represents a solution of the following system of equations:

$$\begin{cases}\Theta_k\left(k_E,h_E\right)=s_K\left(\alpha_K k_E^{-\sigma}+\alpha_H h_E^{-\sigma}+1-\alpha_K-\alpha_H\right)^{-1/\sigma}-\mu_K k_E=0\\ \Theta_h\left(k_E,h_E\right)=s_H\left(\alpha_K k_E^{-\sigma}+\alpha_H h_E^{-\sigma}+1-\alpha_K-\alpha_H\right)^{-1/\sigma}-\mu_H h_E=0\end{cases}, \qquad (3.22)$$

that can also be expressed as follows:

$$\begin{cases}\psi_k\left(q_k,q_h,\theta_K\right)=\alpha_H\dfrac{q_k}{q_h}+(1-\alpha_K-\alpha_H)q_k-\theta_K=0\\ \psi_h\left(q_k,q_h,\theta_H\right)=\alpha_K\dfrac{q_h}{q_k}+(1-\alpha_K-\alpha_H)q_h-\theta_H=0\end{cases}, \qquad (3.23)$$

where $\theta_K = \left(\frac{s_K}{\mu_K}\right)^\sigma - \alpha_K \in R$, $\theta_H = \left(\frac{s_H}{\mu_H}\right)^\sigma - \alpha_H \in R$, $q_k = k_E^\sigma > 0$ and $q_h = h_E^\sigma > 0$. The Jacobian determinant $|\bar{J}|$ of system of equations (3.23) is described by the relation:

$$|\bar{J}| = \begin{vmatrix} \partial\psi_k / \partial q_k & \partial\psi_k / \partial q_h \\ \partial\psi_h / \partial q_k & \partial\psi_h / \partial q_h \end{vmatrix} = \begin{vmatrix} \frac{\alpha_H}{q_h} + 1 - \alpha_K - \alpha_H & -\frac{\alpha_H q_k}{q_h^2} \\ -\frac{\alpha_K q_h}{q_k^2} & \frac{\alpha_K}{q_k} + 1 - \alpha_K - \alpha_H \end{vmatrix},$$

thus:

$$|\bar{J}| = (1 - \alpha_K - \alpha_H)\left(\frac{\alpha_K}{q_k} + \frac{\alpha_H}{q_h} + 1 - \alpha_K - \alpha_H\right) > 0,$$

hence, system of equations (3.23) has a solution.

Using the Grobman-Hartman theorem (Ombach, 1999, theorem 6.2.1), it can be demonstrated that the steady state is asymptotically stable.[7] For this purpose, we will show that all eigenvalues have real parts that are negative in the Jacobian matrix J of system of equations (3.23). The matrix is described in any point $(k_E, h_E) \subset P$ by the equation:

$$J(k_E, h_E) = \begin{bmatrix} \partial\Theta_k / \partial k_E & \partial\Theta_k / \partial h_E \\ \partial\Theta_h / \partial k_E & \partial\Theta_h / \partial h_E \end{bmatrix} = \begin{bmatrix} s_K mpk - \mu_K & s_K mph \\ s_H mpk & s_H mph - \mu_H \end{bmatrix}. \tag{3.24}$$

where $mpk = \frac{\partial y_E}{\partial k_E}$ and $mph = \frac{\partial y_E}{\partial h_E}$ denote (respectively) the MPK and of human capital per unit of effective labour (equal MPK and MPH). However, note that in the steady state κ (when $\Theta_k = \Theta_h = 0$), $s_K p_K = \mu_K$ and $s_H p_H = \mu_H$ (where $p_K = y_E/k_E$ and $p_H = y_E/k = h_E$ represent productivities of the physical and human capitals). Matrix (3.24) can be described in this point using the formula:

$$J(\kappa) = \begin{bmatrix} s_K(mpk - p_K) & s_K mph \\ s_H mpk & s_H(mph - p_H) \end{bmatrix}. \tag{3.25}$$

Eigenvalues of matrix (3.25) solve the equation: $\det(J(\kappa) - vI)$, where I denotes an identity matrix. Hence:

$$\det(J(\kappa) - vI) = \begin{bmatrix} s_K(mpk - p_K) - v & s_K mph \\ s_H mpk & s_H(mph - p_H) - v \end{bmatrix}.$$

Consequently, the sought eigenvalues υ represent a solution of the equation:

$$\left(s_K\left(mpk-p_K\right)-v\right)\left(s_H\left(mph-p_H\right)-v\right)-s_K s_K mpk\cdot mph=0,$$

which leads to the equation:

$$\begin{aligned} &v^2+\left(s_K\left(p_K-mpk\right)+s_H\left(p_H-mph\right)\right)v \\ &-s_K s_H\left(mpk\cdot p_H+mph\cdot p_K-p_K p_H\right)=0. \end{aligned} \tag{3.26}$$

The discriminant Δ of equation (3.26) is expressed by the formula:

$$\Delta=\left(s_K\left(p_K-mpk\right)+s_H\left(p_H-mph\right)\right)^2+4s_K s_K\left(mpk\cdot p_H+mph\cdot p_K-p_K p_H\right),$$

thus:

$$\Delta>\left(s_K\left(p_K-mpk\right)+s_H\left(p_H-mph\right)\right)^2+4s_K s_K\left(mpk\cdot p_H+mph\cdot p_K\right)>0.$$

Consequently, both eigenvalues of the Jacobian matrix (3.25) are real numbers. Moreover, the values satisfy the following relations as per Vieta's formulas[8]:

$$v_1+v_2=-\left(s_K\left(p_K-mpk\right)+s_H\left(p_H-mph\right)\right)<0$$

and

$$v_1 v_2=s_K s_H\left(mpk\cdot p_H+mph\cdot p_K-p_K p_H\right)>s_K s_H\left(mpk\cdot p_H+mph\cdot p_K\right)>0,$$

hence, the values are negative numbers. It follows from the above conclusion and from the Grobman-Hartman theorem that the steady state κ of the analyzed version of Mankiw-Romer-Weil model is asymptotically stable.

However, let us return to system of equations (3.23) that leads to the conclusion (substantiated by the former discussion) that certain implicit functions exist $q_k^*=q_k^*\left(\theta_K,\theta_H\right)$ and $q_h^*=q_h^*\left(\theta_K,\theta_H\right)$ that solve that system of equations. Moreover, derivatives of those functions (with respect to θ_K, θ_H) solve the following systems of equations:

$$\begin{bmatrix} \dfrac{\partial\psi_k}{\partial q_k} & \dfrac{\partial\psi_k}{\partial q_h} \\ \dfrac{\partial\psi_h}{\partial q_k} & \dfrac{\partial\psi_h}{\partial q_h} \end{bmatrix}\cdot\begin{bmatrix} \dfrac{\partial q_k^*}{\partial\theta_K} \\ \dfrac{\partial q_h^*}{\partial\theta_K} \end{bmatrix}=\begin{bmatrix} -\dfrac{\partial\psi_k}{\partial\theta_K} \\ -\dfrac{\partial\psi_h}{\partial\theta_K} \end{bmatrix} \tag{3.27a}$$

and

$$\begin{bmatrix} \frac{\partial \psi_k}{\partial q_k} & \frac{\partial \psi_k}{\partial q_h} \\ \frac{\partial \psi_h}{\partial q_k} & \frac{\partial \psi_h}{\partial q_h} \end{bmatrix} \cdot \begin{bmatrix} \frac{\partial q_k^*}{\partial \theta_H} \\ \frac{\partial q_h^*}{\partial \theta_H} \end{bmatrix} = \begin{bmatrix} -\frac{\partial \psi_k}{\partial \theta_H} \\ -\frac{\partial \psi_h}{\partial \theta_H} \end{bmatrix}. \tag{3.27b}$$

It follows from equation (3.27a) that:

$$\frac{\partial q_k^*}{\partial \theta_K} = \frac{\begin{vmatrix} -\partial \psi_k / \partial \theta_K & \partial \psi_k / \partial q_h \\ -\partial \psi_h / \partial \theta_K & \partial \psi_h / \partial q_h \end{vmatrix}}{|J|} = \frac{\begin{vmatrix} 1 & -\alpha_H \frac{q_k}{q_h^2} \\ 0 & \frac{\alpha_K}{q_k} \end{vmatrix}}{|J|} = \frac{\alpha_K}{q_k |J|} > 0 \tag{3.28a}$$

and

$$\frac{\partial q_h^*}{\partial \theta_K} = \frac{\begin{vmatrix} \partial \psi_k / \partial q_k & -\partial \psi_k / \partial \theta_K \\ \partial \psi_h / \partial q_k & -\partial \psi_h / \partial \theta_K \end{vmatrix}}{|J|} = \frac{\begin{vmatrix} \frac{\alpha_H}{q_h} & -1 \\ -\alpha_K \frac{q_h}{q_k^2} & 0 \end{vmatrix}}{|J|} = \frac{\alpha_K q_h}{q_k^2 |J|} > 0. \tag{3.28b}$$

It is demonstrated by analogy that:

$$\frac{\partial q_k^*}{\partial \theta_H} > 0 \tag{3.28c}$$

and

$$\frac{\partial q_h^*}{\partial \theta_H} > 0. \tag{3.28d}$$

It follows from substitutions $\theta_K = \left(\frac{s_K}{\delta_K + g + n} \right)^{\sigma} - \alpha_K$, $\theta_H = \left(\frac{s_H}{\delta_H + g + n} \right)^{\sigma} - \alpha_K$, $q_k = k_E^{\sigma}$ and $q_h = h_E^{\sigma}$ that:

$$\frac{\partial k_E}{\partial q_k} > 0 \wedge \frac{\partial h_E}{\partial q_h} > 0,$$

$$\frac{\partial \theta_K}{\partial s_K} > 0 \wedge \frac{\partial \theta_H}{\partial s_H} > 0.$$

and

$$\frac{\partial \theta_K}{\partial \delta_K} < 0 \wedge \frac{\partial \theta_H}{\partial \delta_H} < 0 \wedge \frac{\partial \theta_K}{\partial n}, \frac{\partial \theta_H}{\partial n} < 0,$$

and from the above results and equations (3.28a–d), we get:

$$\frac{\partial k_E^*}{\partial s_K} > 0 \wedge \frac{\partial h_E^*}{\partial s_H} > 0$$

and

$$\frac{\partial k_E^*}{\partial \delta_K} < 0 \quad \wedge \quad \frac{\partial h_E^*}{\partial \delta_H} < 0 \wedge \quad \frac{\partial k_E^*}{\partial n}, \frac{\partial h_E^*}{\partial n} < 0.$$

The above inequalities lead to similar conclusions in terms of economics as corresponding inequalities from the Mankiw-Romer-Weil model with a general production function or with the Cobb-Douglas production function.

3.2.4 Golden rules of accumulation in the Mankiw-Romer-Weil model

A single stock of capital was analyzed in the Solow model (the stock of physical capital) and hence only one investment rate was analyzed, namely the rate of investment in physical capital s. Two stocks of capital are considered in the Mankiw-Romer-Weil model (physical and human) and consequently two investment rates exist – the rate of investment in physical capital s_K and the rate of investment in human capital s_H. The golden rule of capital accumulation was defined in the Solow model as a rate of investment s that leads to a maximum consumption per unit of effective labour (the model from Section 2.4), while in the model analyzed in the current section, the golden rule of capital accumulation can be defined (by analogy) as a combination of the rates s_K and s_H that leads to a maximum value of consumption per unit of effective labour.

It follows from the assumptions underlying the Mankiw-Romer-Weil model that an s_K fraction of output in an economy is allocated to investment in physical capital, and an s_H fraction is allocated to investment in human capital. The fraction of output available for consumption equals $1 - s_K - s_H$. Hence, consumption at any time $t \in [0,+\infty)$ can be expressed using the formula (see also (2.3b) in Chapter 2):

$$C(t) = (1 - s_K - s_H)Y(t),$$

or, dividing the above equation by units of effective labour $E > 0$:

$$c_E(t) = (1 - s_K - s_H)\, y_E(t),$$

where c_E denotes (like in the model from Section 2.4) the consumption per unit of effective labour. Since in the Mankiw-Romer-Weil model $y_E(t) \to y_E^*$ (at $t \to +\infty$), then $c_E(t)$ approaches c_E^* described by the formula:

$$c_E^* = (1 - s_K - s_H)\, y_E^*. \tag{3.29}$$

Taking the long-term consumption per unit of effective labour c_E^* from the Mankiw-Romer-Weil model with the Cobb-Douglas production function (Section 3.2.2, equation (3.18c)), the relation (3.29) can be expressed as follows:

$$c_E^* = (1 - s_K - s_H)(s_K)^{\frac{\alpha_K}{1-\alpha_K-\alpha_H}} (s_H)^{\frac{\alpha_H}{1-\alpha_K-\alpha_H}} \Omega, \tag{3.30}$$

$$\text{where } \Omega = \frac{1}{(\delta_K + g + n)^{\frac{\alpha_K}{1-\alpha_K-\alpha_H}} (\delta_H + g + n)^{\frac{\alpha_H}{1-\alpha_K-\alpha_H}}} > 0$$

Since both investment rates s_K and s_H as well as their total must belong to the interval (0,1), determination of the golden rule of capital accumulation in the Mankiw-Romer-Weil model can be reduced to finding a combination of the rates s_K and s_H that maximizes function (3.30), i.e. leads to maximum values of that function within a right-angled triangle with vertices (0,0), (0,1), (1,0). On the legs of that triangle, we get:

$$\lim_{s_K \to 0^+} c_E^* = (s_H)^{\frac{\alpha_H}{1-\alpha_K-\alpha_H}} \Omega \lim_{s_K \to 0^+} \left((1 - s_K - s_H)(s_K)^{\frac{\alpha_K}{1-\alpha_K-\alpha_H}} \right) = 0,$$

$$\lim_{s_H \to 0^+} c_E^* = (s_K)^{\frac{\alpha_K}{1-\alpha_K-\alpha_H}} \Omega \lim_{s_H \to 0^+} \left((1 - s_K - s_H)(s_H)^{\frac{\alpha_H}{1-\alpha_K-\alpha_H}} (s_K)^{\frac{\alpha_K}{1-\alpha_K-\alpha_H}} \right) = 0,$$

and on the hypotenuse:

$$\lim_{(s_K+s_H) \to 1^-} c_E^* = \Omega \lim_{(s_K+s_H) \to 1^-} \left((1 - s_K - s_H)(s_K)^{\frac{\alpha_K}{1-\alpha_K-\alpha_H}} (s_H)^{\frac{\alpha_K}{1-\alpha_K-\alpha_H}} \right) = 0.$$

Function (3.30) assumes positive values inside the triangle. Its maximization is thus identical with the maximization of the following function:

$$v(s_K, s_H) = \ln c_E^* = \ln(1 - s_K - s_H) + \frac{\alpha_K}{1 - \alpha_K - \alpha_H} \ln s_K + \frac{\alpha_H}{1 - \alpha_K - \alpha_H} \ln s_H + \ln \Omega. \tag{3.31}$$

First-order conditions for the maximization of function (3.31) are described by the formulas:

$$\frac{\partial v}{\partial s_K} = -\frac{1}{1 - s_K - s_H} + \frac{\alpha_K}{(1 - \alpha_K - \alpha_H) s_K} = \frac{\alpha_K - (1 - \alpha_H) s_K - \alpha_K s_H}{(1 - \alpha_K - \alpha_H)(1 - s_K - s_H) s_K} = 0 \tag{3.32a}$$

and

$$\frac{\partial v}{\partial s_H} = -\frac{1}{1-s_K-s_H} + \frac{\alpha_H}{(1-\alpha_K-\alpha_H)s_H} = \frac{\alpha_H-(1-\alpha_K)s_H-\alpha_H s_K}{(1-\alpha_K-\alpha_H)(1-s_K-s_H)s_H} = 0, \tag{3.32b}$$

and second-order conditions are reduced to the requirement that the Hessian matrix:

$$\bar{H} = \begin{bmatrix} \partial^2 v / \partial s_K^2 & \partial v / (\partial s_K \partial s_H) \\ \partial v / (\partial s_K \partial s_H) & \partial^2 v / \partial s_H^2 \end{bmatrix}.$$

be negative-definite. The Hessian $\bar{H}$ can be described using the formula:

$$\bar{H} = \begin{bmatrix} -\left(\frac{1}{(1-s_K-s_H)^2} + \frac{\alpha_K}{(1-\alpha_K-\alpha_H)s_K^2}\right) & -\frac{1}{(1-s_K-s_H)^2} \\ -\frac{1}{(1-s_K-s_H)^2} & -\left(\frac{1}{(1-s_K-s_H)^2} + \frac{\alpha_H}{(1-\alpha_K-\alpha_H)s_H^2}\right) \end{bmatrix},$$

implying that its principal minors (m_1 and m_2) are expressed by the formulas:

$$m_1 = -\left(\frac{1}{(1-s_K-s_H)^2} + \frac{\alpha_K}{(1-\alpha_K-\alpha_H)s_K^2}\right) < 0.$$

and

$$m_2 = \det \bar{H} = \frac{1}{(1-s_K-s_H)^2}\left(\frac{\alpha_K}{(1-\alpha_K-\alpha_H)s_K^2} + \frac{\alpha_H}{(1-\alpha_K-\alpha_H)s_H^2}\right) + \frac{\alpha_K\alpha_H}{(1-\alpha_K-\alpha_H)^2 s_K^2 s_H^2} > 0.$$

Consequently, the Hessian $\bar{H}$ is negative-definite.

Transforming the first-order conditions, it can be demonstrated that the system of equations consisting of (3.32ab) has exactly one solution in point $(s_K, s_H) = (\alpha_K, \alpha_H)$. This means that the golden rule of capital accumulation in the Mankiw-Romer-Weil model is given by investment rates (in the stocks of capital distinguished in that model) that equal the elasticities of output with respect to those stocks. It is a simple generalization of Phelps' golden rules of capital accumulation from Section 2.4.

3.3 The multi-capital Nonneman-Vanhoudt model

3.3.1 The model with a neoclassical production function

The economic growth model analyzed in this section is based on the following assumptions about long-time processes in the economy[9]:

1 The value of output Y depends on N various stocks of capital K_1, K_2, ..., K_N and on units of effective labour E. The relations between capital inputs and the value of output are described by a neoclassical production function expressed by the formula:

$$Y(t) = F(\kappa(t), E(t)) = F(K_1(t), K_2(t), ..., K_N(t), E(t)), \tag{3.33}$$

where $\kappa = (K_1, K_2, ..., K_N) \in [0, +\infty)^N$ denotes a combination of inputs of various stocks of capital. It is assumed that function F, by analogy with the production functions (2.1) and (3.1), satisfies the following assumptions[10]:

i The domain of this function is defined as the set $[0,+\infty)^{N+1}$ and F: $[0,+\infty)^{N+1} \to [0,+\infty)$.

ii The production function (3.33) is differentiable at least twice in its domain.

iii $\forall \kappa \in [0,+\infty)^N \wedge \forall E \in [0,+\infty)$ it is true that:

$$F(0, K_2, ..., K_N, E) = F(K_1, 0, ..., K_N, E) = ... = F(K_1, K_2, ..., 0, E) \\ = F(K_1, K_2, ..., K_N, 0) = 0$$

iv In addition[11]:

$$\forall i \wedge \kappa \in (0,+\infty)^N \wedge E \in (0,+\infty) \lim_{K_i \to +\infty} F(\kappa, E) = \lim_{E \to +\infty} F(\kappa, E) = +\infty.$$

v The first partial derivatives of function (3.33) in the set $(0,+\infty)^{N+1}$ are positive, hence:

$$\forall i \ \mathrm{MPK}_i = \frac{\partial F}{\partial K_i} \wedge \mathrm{MPE} = \frac{\partial F}{\partial E} > 0,$$

where MPK_i is the marginal product of the ith stock of capital, and MPE (like previously) is the marginal product of units of effective labour.

vi $\forall i \wedge \kappa \in (0,+\infty)^N \wedge \forall E \in (0,+\infty) \ \frac{\partial^2 F}{\partial K_i^2} < 0 \wedge \frac{\partial^2 F}{\partial E^2} < 0$, i.e. function F is characterized by diminishing marginal productivities of each stock of capital and of units of effective labour.

vii The Inada conditions are satisfied, i.e.:

$$\forall i \wedge \kappa \in (0,+\infty)^N \wedge \forall E \in (0,+\infty) \quad \lim_{K_i \to 0^+} \mathrm{MPK}_i = \lim_{E \to 0^+} \mathrm{MPE} = +\infty$$

and

$$\forall i \wedge \kappa \in (0,+\infty)^N \wedge \forall E \in (0,+\infty) \quad \lim_{K_i \to +\infty} \text{MPK}_i = \lim_{E \to +\infty} \text{MPE} = 0$$

viii Constant returns to scale take place in the production process, hence:

$$\forall \kappa \in (0,+\infty)^N \wedge \forall E \in (0,+\infty) \wedge \forall \varsigma > 0 \quad F(\varsigma\kappa, \varsigma E) = \varsigma F(\kappa, E).$$

2 An increase in the ith stock of capital (for $I = 1, 2, \ldots, N$) is described by the following differential equation:

$$\dot{K}_i(t) = s_i Y(t) - \delta_i(t), \tag{3.34}$$

where s_i denotes the rate of investment in the ith stock of capital, and δ_i is the depreciation rate of that stock. It is assumed about the rates s_i and δ_i that $\forall i \; s_i, \delta_i \in (0,1)$ and $\sum_i s_i \in (0,1)$.

3 The trajectories of technology and of the number of workers are described like in the Solow model from Chapter 2. Thus, the growth path of units of effective labour is described by equation (2.12a).

It is clear that a model of economic growth with these parameters represents a multi-capital generalization of both the single-capital economic growth model proposed by Solow and the two-capital model proposed by Mankiw-Romer-Weil.

Let

$$y(t) = Y(t) / L(t) \tag{3.35a}$$

denote labour productivity and

$$\forall i \quad k_i(t) = K_i(t) / L(t) \tag{3.35b}$$

the stock of ith capital per worker. Let:

$$y_E(t) = Y(t) / E(t) \tag{3.36a}$$

denote the output per unit of effective labour, and

$$\forall i \quad k_{Ei}(t) = K_i(t) / E(t) \tag{3.36b}$$

ith capital per unit of effective labour. Let us also express by κ_E:

$$\kappa_E = (k_{E1}, k_{E2}, \ldots, k_{EN})$$

any combination of capital inputs per unit of effective labour in the set $[0,+\infty)^N$.

From equations (3.35ab), (3.36ab) and the assumption that units of effective labour rise at growth rate λ (representing the total of the Harrodian rate of technological progress g and the growth rate of the number of workers n), we get:

$$\frac{\dot{y}(t)}{y(t)} = g + \frac{\dot{y}_E(t)}{y_E(t)} \wedge \forall i \ \frac{\dot{k}_i(t)}{k_i(t)} = g + \frac{\dot{k}_{Ei}(t)}{k_{Ei}(t)}. \tag{3.37}$$

Equation (3.37) is interpreted in terms of economics by analogy with equations (3.5a–c).

From the assumption that the function F is homogeneous of degree 1 at $\varsigma = 1/E > 0$, we get the production function in its intensive form expressed by the formula:

$$y_E(t) = F\left(\frac{\kappa(t)}{E(t)},1\right) = f(\kappa_E(t)). \tag{3.38}$$

It follows from assumptions (i–viii) about the production function (3.33) that function (3.38) is characterized by the following properties:

a Its domain is defined as the set $[0,+\infty)^N$ and $f:[0,+\infty)^N \to [0,+\infty)$. Additionally, the analyzed function is differentiable at least twice in the set $(0,+\infty)^N$.

b $\forall \kappa_E \in [0,+\infty)^N \ f(0,k_{E2},\dots,k_{EN}) = f(k_{E1},0,\dots,k_{EN}) = \dots = f(k_{E1},k_{E2},\dots,0) = 0$.

c $\forall i \wedge \kappa_E \in (0,+\infty)^N \ \lim_{k_{Ei}\to+\infty} f(\kappa_E) = +\infty$.

d $\forall i \wedge \kappa_E \in (0,+\infty)^N \ mpk_{Ei} = \frac{\partial f}{\partial k_{Ei}} > 0 \wedge \frac{\partial^2 f}{\partial k_{Ei}^2} < 0$, where mpk_{Ei} denotes the marginal product of the ith stock of capital per unit of effective labour (equal MPK_i).

e $\forall i \wedge \kappa_E \in (0,+\infty)^N \ \lim_{k_{Ei}\to 0^+} mpk_{Ei} = +\infty \wedge \lim_{k_{Ei}\to+\infty} mpk_{Ei} = 0$.

f It follows from assumption (viii) and from Euler's homogeneous function theorem that:

$$\forall \kappa \in (0,+\infty)^N \wedge E \in (0,+\infty) \ \ Y = F(\kappa,E) = \sum\nolimits_i (\text{MPK}_i K_i) + \text{MPE} \cdot E.$$

Dividing the above equation by units of effective labour and considering that for each i (from 1 to N) $mpk_i = MPK_i$, we get:

$$\forall \kappa_E \in (0,+\infty)^N \quad y_E = f(\kappa_E) = \sum_i (mpk_i k_i) + \text{MPE}$$

hence (first)

$$\forall \kappa_E \in (0,+\infty)^N \quad f(\kappa_E) > \sum_i (mpk_i k_i)$$

and (second) for any $i = 1, 2, \ldots, N$ it is true that:

$$p_i > mpk_i.$$

Consequently, the productivity of the ith stock of capital ($p_i = Y/K_i = y_E/K_{Ei}$) is greater than the marginal product of that capital ($MPK_i = mpk_i$).

Differentiating equation (3.36b) after time $t \in [0,+\infty)$, we get:

$$\forall i \quad \dot{k}_{Ei}(t) = \frac{\dot{K}_i(t)}{E(t)} - \frac{\dot{E}(t)}{E(t)} k_{Ei}(t).$$

Considering that (as per assumption 3) $\dot{E}/E = \lambda$ and given equation (3.34), we obtain the relation:

$$\forall i \quad \dot{k}_{Ei}(t) = s_i y_E(t) - \mu_i k_{Ei}(t), \tag{3.39}$$

where $\mu_i = \delta_i + g + n$ denotes the rate of decline of the ith capital per unit of effective labour. System of differential equations (3.39) represents a generalization of system of equations of motion (3.7) from the Mankiw-Romer-Weil model. Therefore, each of these equations can be economically interpreted so that an increase in the ith stock of capital per unit of effective labour $(\dot{k}_{Ei})$ equals the difference between investment ($s_i y_E$) in that stock and its decline $(\mu_i k_{Ei})$, resulting both from depreciation of that stock of capital $(\delta_i k_{Ei})$ and from an increase in units of effective labour $((g+n)k_{Ei})$.

Substituting the production function in its intensive form (equation 3.38) into system of equations (3.39), we reduce it to the following system of differential equations:

$$\forall i \quad \dot{k}_{Ei}(t) = s_i f(\kappa_E(t)) - \mu_i k_{Ei}(t). \tag{3.40}$$

In phase space $P = [0,+\infty)^N$, system of equations (3.40) has both a trivial steady state (0, 0, …, 0) and a non-trivial steady state $\kappa_E^* = (k_{E1}^*, k_{E2}^*, \ldots, k_{EN}^*) \in (0,+\infty)^N$.

In phase space P, the non-trivial steady state of system of differential equations (3.40) represents a solution of the following system of equations:

$$\forall i \quad \psi_i\left(\kappa_E, s_i, \mu_i\right) = s_i p_i\left(\kappa_E\right) - \mu_i = 0. \tag{3.41}$$

The Jacobian $|\bar{J}|$ of system of equations (3.41) is defined by the relation:

$$|\bar{J}| = \begin{vmatrix} \partial\psi_1/\partial k_{E1} & \partial\psi_1/\partial k_{E2} & \dots & \partial\psi_1/\partial k_{EN} \\ \partial\psi_2/\partial k_{E1} & \partial\psi_2/\partial k_{E2} & \dots & \partial\psi_2/\partial k_{EN} \\ \vdots & \vdots & \ddots & \vdots \\ \partial\psi_N/\partial k_{E1} & \partial\psi_N/\partial k_{E2} & \dots & \partial\psi_N/\partial k_{EN} \end{vmatrix}.$$

The above Jacobian can also be expressed as follows, as per equation (3.41):

$$|\bar{J}| = \begin{vmatrix} s_1\partial p_1/\partial k_{E1} & s_1\partial p_1/\partial k_{E2} & \dots & s_1\partial p_1/\partial k_{EN} \\ s_2\partial p_2/\partial k_{E1} & s_2\partial p_2/\partial k_{E2} & \dots & s_2\partial p_2/\partial k_{EN} \\ \vdots & \vdots & \ddots & \vdots \\ s_N\partial p_N/\partial k_{E1} & s_N\partial p_N/\partial k_{E2} & \dots & s_N\partial p_N/\partial k_{EN} \end{vmatrix}. \tag{3.42}$$

The following is true for each $i = 1, 2, \dots, N$ in phase space P:

$$\frac{\partial p_i}{\partial k_{Ei}} = \frac{\partial}{\partial k_{Ei}}\left(\frac{f\left(\kappa_E\right)}{k_{Ei}}\right) = \frac{\frac{\partial f}{\partial k_{Ei}} k_{Ei} - f\left(\kappa_E\right)}{k_{Ei}^2} = \frac{mpk_i - p_i}{k_{Ei}} < 0 \tag{3.43a}$$

and

$$\forall j \neq i \quad \frac{\partial p_i}{\partial k_{Ej}} = \frac{\partial f/\partial k_{Ej}}{k_{Ei}} = \frac{mpk_j}{k_{Ei}} > 0. \tag{3.43b}$$

It follows from equations (3.43ab) that Jacobian (3.42) can be expressed as follows:

$$|\bar{J}| = \prod_i \left(\frac{s_i}{k_{Ei}}\right) \begin{vmatrix} mpk_1 - p_1 & mpk_2 & \dots & mpk_N \\ mpk_1 & mpk_2 - p_2 & \dots & mpk_N \\ \vdots & \vdots & \ddots & \vdots \\ mpk_1 & mpk_2 & \dots & mpk_N - p_N \end{vmatrix},$$

hence:

$$|J| = \prod_i \left(\frac{s_i}{k_{Ei}}\right) \begin{vmatrix} -p_1 & 0 & \cdots & p_N \\ 0 & -p_2 & \cdots & p_N \\ \vdots & \vdots & \ddots & \vdots \\ mpk_1 & mpk_2 & \cdots & mpk_N - p_N \end{vmatrix}$$

$$= \prod_i \left(\frac{s_i p_i}{k_{Ei}}\right) \begin{vmatrix} -1 & 0 & \cdots & 1 \\ 0 & -1 & \cdots & 1 \\ \vdots & \vdots & \ddots & \vdots \\ \frac{mpk_1}{p_1} & \frac{mpk_2}{p_2} & \cdots & \frac{mpk_N}{p_N} - 1 \end{vmatrix}$$

$$= (-1)^N \prod_i \left(\frac{s_i p_i}{k_{Ei}}\right) \begin{vmatrix} -1 & 0 & \cdots & 0 \\ 0 & -1 & \cdots & 0 \\ \vdots & \vdots & \ddots & \vdots \\ \frac{mpk_1}{p_1} & \frac{mpk_2}{p_2} & \cdots & 1 - \sum_i \frac{mpk_i}{p_i} \end{vmatrix}$$

thus:

$$|J| = (-1)^N \prod_i \left(\frac{s_i p_i}{k_{Ei}}\right) \left(1 - \sum_i \frac{mpk_i}{p_i}\right). \tag{3.44}$$

Given that for each $i = 1, 2, \ldots, N$ $\frac{mpk_i}{p_i} = \frac{\frac{\partial f}{\partial k_{Ei}} k_{Ei}}{f(\kappa_E)}$, and considering property (f) of the production function in its intensive form (2.38), it follows that $\sum_i \frac{mpk_i}{p_i} = \frac{\sum_i \frac{\partial f}{\partial k_{Ei}} k_{Ei}}{f(\kappa_E)} < 1$, and thus Jacobian (3.44) is positive/negative for an even/odd N in any point $\kappa_E \in P$. This means that system of differential equations (3.40) has a non-trivial steady state $\kappa_E^* \in P$ that solves system of equations (3.41).

It also follows from assumption (viii) about production function F and from property (d) of the production function in its intensive form f that the solution is unique.

We will now demonstrate that the point $\kappa_E^* \in P$ is Lyapunov asymptotically stable (proof given by Dykas, Edigarian and Tokarski (2011)).[12] The following function will be used for this purpose:

$$V(\kappa_E) = \sum_i \left(\rho_i \left(k_{Ei} - k_{Ei}^* \right)^2 \right), \tag{3.45}$$

where $\rho_i = \frac{\partial f / \partial k_{Ei}}{s_i} > 0$. Function (3.45) satisfies conditions (i–ii) applicable to the definition of a strong Lyapunov function.[13] To verify that function f is decreasing in its solution, it is enough to demonstrate that an open neighbourhood $\Pi \subset P$ of the steady state $\kappa_E^* \in \Pi$ exists such that the following inequality is true:

$$\forall \kappa_E \in \Pi \setminus \{\kappa_E^*\} \; \sum_i \left(\rho_i \left(s_i f(\kappa_E) - \mu_i k_{Ei} \right) \left(k_{Ei} - k_{Ei}^* \right) \right) < 0. \tag{3.46}$$

A Taylor series expansion of function f in the neighbourhood of point $\kappa_E^* \in \Pi$ leads to:

$$f(\kappa_E) = f(\kappa_E^*) + \sum_i \left(\frac{\partial f}{\partial k_{Ei}} \left(k_{Ei} - k_{Ei}^* \right) \right) + \varepsilon \left(\left\| \kappa_E - \kappa_E^* \right\| \right) \wedge \varepsilon \in o\left(\kappa_E - \kappa_E^* \right). \tag{3.47}$$

Thus, inequality (3.46) can be expressed as:

$$\left(\sum_i \rho_i s_i \left(k_{Ei} - k_{Ei}^* \right) \right) \left(\sum_i \frac{\partial f}{\partial k_{Ei}} (\kappa_E^*) \left(k_{Ei} - k_{Ei}^* \right) \right) - \sum_i \rho_i \mu_i \left(k_{Ei} - k_{Ei}^* \right)^2$$
$$+ \sum_i \rho_i s_i \left(k_{Ei} - k_{Ei}^* \right) \varepsilon \left(\left\| \kappa_E - \kappa_E^* \right\| \right) < 0.$$

It follows from the definiteness of function ε and from the relation: $\rho_i s_i = \frac{\partial f}{\partial k_{Ei}} (\kappa_E^*)$ that inequality (3.46) is satisfied if the following inequality is true:

$$\left(\sum_i \left(\rho_i s_i \left(k_{Ei} - k_{Ei}^* \right) \right) \right)^2 < \sum_i \left(\rho_i \mu_i \left(k_{Ei} - k_{Ei}^* \right)^2 \right) \tag{3.48}$$

It follows from property (*f*) of the production function in its intensive form (2.38) that: $\sum_i \frac{mpk_i}{p_i} < 1$, hence in the steady state $\kappa_E^* \in \Pi$ we get the inequality: $\sum_i \frac{\frac{\partial f}{\partial k_{Ei}}\left(\kappa_E^*\right)}{f\left(\kappa_E^*\right)} < 1$, and we obtain from it:

$$\sum_i \frac{\rho_i s_i^2}{\mu_i} < 1.$$

Using the above inequalities, we can determine the majorant for the left-hand side of inequality (3.48):

$$\left(\sum_i \rho_i s_i \left(k_{Ei} - k_{Ei}^*\right)\right)^2 = \sum_i \left(\frac{\rho_i s_i^2}{\mu_i} \frac{\mu_i}{s_i^2} \left(k_{Ei} - k_{Ei}^*\right)^2\right) < \sum_i \left(\frac{\rho_i s_i^2}{\mu_i} \left(\frac{\mu_i}{s_i^2}\right)^2 \left(k_{Ei} - k_{Ei}^*\right)^2\right)$$
$$= \sum_i \left(\rho_i \mu_i \left(k_{Ei} - k_{Ei}^*\right)^2\right)$$

We demonstrated that the function V realizes a strong Lyapunov function for problem (3.41), and this combined with the Lyapunov theorem implies the asymptotic stability of point $\kappa_E^* \in P$.

Let us proceed to the economic properties of point $\kappa_E^* \in P$. Since the point is characterized by Lyapunov asymptotic stability, it represents the point of stable long-run equilibrium in the Nonneman-Vanhoudt model. Moreover, since at $t \to +\infty$ the combination of capital inputs per unit of effective labour $\kappa_E(t) \to \kappa_E^*$, then $y_E(t) \to y_E^*$, where as per equation (3.38) we get:

$$y_E^* = f\left(k_E^*\right). \tag{3.49}$$

Since in the steady state of the Nonneman-Vanhoudt model $\dot{y}_E / y_E = 0$ and $\forall\, i = 1, 2, \ldots, N\ \dot{k}_{Ei} / k_{Ei} = 0$, it follows as per equation (3.37) that the growth rates of labour productivity $\dot{y} / y$ and of various stocks of capital per worker $\dot{k}_i / k_i$ equal the Harrodian rate of technological progress g.

Let us now return to system of equations (3.41). It follows from that system of equations that long-term stocks of various capitals per unit of effective labour in point $\kappa_E^* \in P$ represent implicit functions of the combination of $s = (s_1, s_2, \ldots, s_N)$ and $\mu = (\mu_1, \mu_2, \ldots, \mu_N)$. Hence:

$$\forall i \quad k_{Ei}^* = k_{Ei}^*(s, \mu). \tag{3.50}$$

Subsequent partial derivatives (for $i, j = 1, 2, \ldots, N$, where $i \neq j$) of function (3.50) solve the following systems of equations:

$$\begin{bmatrix} \partial\psi_1/\partial k_{E1} & \cdots & \partial\psi_1/\partial k_{Ei} & \cdots & \partial\psi_1/\partial k_{EN} \\ \vdots & \vdots & \vdots & \ddots & \vdots \\ \partial\psi_i/\partial k_{E1} & \cdots & \partial\psi_i/\partial k_{Ei} & \cdots & \partial\psi_i/\partial k_{EN} \\ \vdots & \ddots & \vdots & \ddots & \vdots \\ \partial\psi_N/\partial k_{E1} & \cdots & \partial\psi_N/\partial k_{Ei} & \cdots & \partial\psi_N/\partial k_{EN} \end{bmatrix} \cdot \begin{bmatrix} \partial\psi_1/\partial k_{E1}^* \\ \vdots \\ \partial\psi_i/\partial k_{Ei}^* \\ \vdots \\ \partial\psi_N/\partial k_{EN}^* \end{bmatrix} = \begin{bmatrix} -\partial\psi_1/\partial s_i \\ \vdots \\ -\partial\psi_i/\partial s_i \\ \vdots \\ -\partial\psi_N/\partial s_i \end{bmatrix}, \tag{3.51a}$$

$$\begin{bmatrix} \partial\psi_1/\partial k_{E1} & \cdots & \partial\psi_1/\partial k_{Ei} & \cdots & \partial\psi_1/\partial k_{EN} \\ \vdots & \vdots & \vdots & \ddots & \vdots \\ \partial\psi_i/\partial k_{E1} & \cdots & \partial\psi_i/\partial k_{Ei} & \cdots & \partial\psi_i/\partial k_{EN} \\ \vdots & \ddots & \vdots & \ddots & \vdots \\ \partial\psi_N/\partial k_{E1} & \cdots & \partial\psi_N/\partial k_{Ei} & \cdots & \partial\psi_N/\partial k_{EN} \end{bmatrix} \cdot \begin{bmatrix} \partial\psi_1/\partial k_{E1}^* \\ \vdots \\ \partial\psi_i/\partial k_{Ei}^* \\ \vdots \\ \partial\psi_N/\partial k_{EN}^* \end{bmatrix} = \begin{bmatrix} -\partial\psi_1/\partial s_j \\ \vdots \\ -\partial\psi_i/\partial s_j \\ \vdots \\ -\partial\psi_N/\partial s_j \end{bmatrix}, \tag{3.51b}$$

$$\begin{bmatrix} \partial\psi_1/\partial k_{E1} & \cdots & \partial\psi_1/\partial k_{Ei} & \cdots & \partial\psi_1/\partial k_{EN} \\ \vdots & \vdots & \vdots & \ddots & \vdots \\ \partial\psi_i/\partial k_{E1} & \cdots & \partial\psi_i/\partial k_{Ei} & \cdots & \partial\psi_i/\partial k_{EN} \\ \vdots & \ddots & \vdots & \ddots & \vdots \\ \partial\psi_N/\partial k_{E1} & \cdots & \partial\psi_N/\partial k_{Ei} & \cdots & \partial\psi_N/\partial k_{EN} \end{bmatrix} \cdot \begin{bmatrix} \partial\psi_1/\partial k_{E1}^* \\ \vdots \\ \partial\psi_i/\partial k_{Ei}^* \\ \vdots \\ \partial\psi_N/\partial k_{EN}^* \end{bmatrix} = \begin{bmatrix} -\partial\psi_1/\partial \mu_i \\ \vdots \\ -\partial\psi_i/\partial \mu_i \\ \vdots \\ -\partial\psi_N/\partial \mu_i \end{bmatrix} \tag{3.51c}$$

and

$$\begin{bmatrix} \partial\psi_1/\partial k_{E1} & \cdots & \partial\psi_1/\partial k_{Ei} & \cdots & \partial\psi_1/\partial k_{EN} \\ \vdots & \vdots & \vdots & \ddots & \vdots \\ \partial\psi_i/\partial k_{E1} & \cdots & \partial\psi_i/\partial k_{Ei} & \cdots & \partial\psi_i/\partial k_{EN} \\ \vdots & \ddots & \vdots & \ddots & \vdots \\ \partial\psi_N/\partial k_{E1} & \cdots & \partial\psi_N/\partial k_{Ei} & \cdots & \partial\psi_N/\partial k_{EN} \end{bmatrix} \cdot \begin{bmatrix} \partial\psi_1/\partial k_{E1}^* \\ \vdots \\ \partial\psi_i/\partial k_{Ei}^* \\ \vdots \\ \partial\psi_N/\partial k_{EN}^* \end{bmatrix} = \begin{bmatrix} -\partial\psi_1/\partial \mu_j \\ \vdots \\ -\partial\psi_i/\partial \mu_j \\ \vdots \\ -\partial\psi_N/\partial \mu_j \end{bmatrix}. \tag{3.51d}$$

It follows from equations (3.51a) and (3.44) that:

$$\frac{\partial k_{Ei}^*}{\partial s_i}=\frac{\begin{vmatrix} \partial\psi_1/\partial k_{E1} & \cdots & \partial\psi_1/\partial s_i & \cdots & \partial\psi_1/\partial k_{EN} \\ \vdots & \vdots & \vdots & \ddots & \vdots \\ \partial\psi_i/\partial k_{E1} & \cdots & \partial\psi_i/\partial s_i & \cdots & \partial\psi_i/\partial k_{EN} \\ \vdots & \ddots & \vdots & \ddots & \vdots \\ \partial\psi_N/\partial k_{E1} & \cdots & \partial\psi_N/\partial s_i & \cdots & \partial\psi_N/\partial k_{EN} \end{vmatrix}}{|J|}$$

$$=\frac{\begin{vmatrix} s_1\partial p_1/\partial k_{E1} & \cdots & 0 & \cdots & s_1\partial p_1/\partial k_{EN} \\ \vdots & \vdots & \vdots & \ddots & \vdots \\ s_i\partial p_i/\partial k_{E1} & \cdots & -1 & \cdots & s_i\partial p_i/\partial k_{EN} \\ \vdots & \ddots & \vdots & \ddots & \vdots \\ s_N\partial p_N/\partial k_{E1} & \cdots & 0 & \cdots & s_N\partial p_N/\partial k_{EN} \end{vmatrix}}{(-1)^N\left(\prod_l \frac{s_l p_l}{k_{El}}\right)\left(1-\sum_l \frac{mpk_l}{p_l}\right)}$$

$$=\frac{\begin{vmatrix} s_1\dfrac{mpk_1-p_1}{k_{E1}} & \cdots & 0 & \cdots & s_1\dfrac{mpk_N}{k_{E1}} \\ \vdots & \vdots & \vdots & \ddots & \vdots \\ s_i\dfrac{mpk_1}{k_{Ei}} & \cdots & -1 & \cdots & s_i\dfrac{mpk_N}{k_{Ei}} \\ \vdots & \ddots & \vdots & \ddots & \vdots \\ s_N\dfrac{mpk_1}{k_{EN}} & \cdots & 0 & \cdots & s_N\dfrac{mpk_N-p_N}{k_{EN}} \end{vmatrix}}{(-1)^N\left(\prod_l \frac{s_l p_l}{k_{El}}\right)\left(1-\sum_l \frac{mpk_l}{p_l}\right)}$$

$$=\frac{\left(\prod_l^{\neq i} \frac{s_l p_l}{k_{El}}\right)\begin{vmatrix} 1-\dfrac{mpk_1}{p_1} & \cdots & 0 & \cdots & -\dfrac{mpk_N}{k_{EN}} \\ \vdots & \vdots & \vdots & \ddots & \vdots \\ -\dfrac{mpk_1}{p_1} & \cdots & 1 & \cdots & -\dfrac{mpk_N}{k_{EN}} \\ \vdots & \ddots & \vdots & \ddots & \vdots \\ -\dfrac{mpk_1}{p_1} & \cdots & 0 & \cdots & 1-\dfrac{mpk_N}{k_{EN}} \end{vmatrix}}{\left(\prod_l \frac{s_l p_l}{k_{El}}\right)\left(1-\sum_l \frac{mpk_l}{p_l}\right)}$$

$$
= \frac{\begin{vmatrix} 1 & \cdots & 0 & \cdots & -1 \\ \vdots & \vdots & \vdots & \ddots & \vdots \\ 0 & \cdots & 1 & \cdots & -1 \\ \vdots & \ddots & \vdots & \ddots & \vdots \\ -\dfrac{mpk_1}{p_1} & \cdots & 0 & \cdots & 1-\dfrac{mpk_N}{k_{EN}} \end{vmatrix}}{\dfrac{s_i p_i}{k_{Ei}}\left(1-\sum_l \dfrac{mpk_l}{p_l}\right)}
$$

$$
= \frac{\begin{vmatrix} 1 & \cdots & 0 & \cdots & -1 \\ \vdots & \vdots & \vdots & \ddots & \vdots \\ 0 & \cdots & 1 & \cdots & -1 \\ \vdots & \ddots & \vdots & \ddots & \vdots \\ -\dfrac{mpk_1}{p_1} & \cdots & 0 & \cdots & 1-\sum_{l \neq i} \dfrac{mpk_l}{k_{El}} \end{vmatrix}}{\dfrac{s_i p_i}{k_{Ei}}\left(1-\sum_l \dfrac{mpk_l}{p_l}\right)}
$$

thus:

$$
\frac{\partial k_{Ei}^*}{\partial s_i} = \frac{1-\sum_{l \neq i} \dfrac{mpk_l}{k_{El}}}{\dfrac{s_i p_i}{k_{Ei}}\left(1-\sum_l \dfrac{mpk_l}{p_l}\right)} > 0 \qquad (3.52a)
$$

and by analogy:

$$
\frac{\partial k_{Ei}^*}{\partial s_j} = \frac{1-\sum_{l \neq j} \dfrac{mpk_l}{k_{El}}}{\dfrac{s_j p_j}{k_{Ei}}\left(1-\sum_l \dfrac{mpk_l}{p_l}\right)} > 0, \qquad (3.52b)
$$

and

$$\frac{\partial k_{Ei}^*}{\partial \mu_i} = \frac{\begin{vmatrix} \partial\psi_1/\partial k_{E1} & \cdots & \partial\psi_1/\partial\mu_i & \cdots & \partial\psi_1/\partial k_{EN} \\ \vdots & \vdots & \vdots & \ddots & \vdots \\ \partial\psi_i/\partial k_{E1} & \cdots & \partial\psi_i/\partial\mu_i & \cdots & \partial\psi_i/\partial k_{EN} \\ \vdots & \ddots & \vdots & \ddots & \vdots \\ \partial\psi_N/\partial k_{E1} & \cdots & \partial\psi_N/\partial\mu_i & \cdots & \partial\psi_N/\partial k_{EN} \end{vmatrix}}{|J|}$$

$$= \frac{\begin{vmatrix} 1-\frac{mpk_1}{p_1} & \cdots & 0 & \cdots & -\frac{mpk_N}{p_N} \\ \vdots & \vdots & \vdots & \ddots & \vdots \\ -\frac{mpk_1}{p_1} & \cdots & -1 & \cdots & -\frac{mpk_N}{p_N} \\ \vdots & \ddots & \vdots & \ddots & \vdots \\ -\frac{mpk_1}{p_1} & \cdots & 0 & \cdots & 1-\frac{mpk_N}{p_N} \end{vmatrix}}{\left(\prod_l \frac{s_l p_l}{k_{El}}\right)\left(1-\sum_l \frac{mpk_l}{p_l}\right)}$$

$$= \frac{\begin{vmatrix} 1 & \cdots & 0 & \cdots & -1 \\ \vdots & \vdots & \vdots & \ddots & \vdots \\ 0 & \cdots & -1 & \cdots & -1 \\ \vdots & \ddots & \vdots & \ddots & \vdots \\ -\frac{mpk_1}{p_1} & \cdots & 0 & \cdots & 1-\frac{mpk_N}{p_N} \end{vmatrix}}{\frac{s_i p_i}{k_{Ei}}\left(1-\sum_l \frac{mpk_l}{p_l}\right)}$$

$$= \frac{\begin{vmatrix} 1 & \cdots & 0 & \cdots & 0 \\ \vdots & \vdots & \vdots & \ddots & \vdots \\ 0 & \cdots & -1 & \cdots & 0 \\ \vdots & \ddots & \vdots & \ddots & \vdots \\ -\frac{mpk_1}{p_1} & \cdots & 0 & \cdots & 1-\sum_{l\neq i} \frac{mpk_l}{p_l} \end{vmatrix}}{\frac{s_i p_i}{k_{Ei}}\left(1-\sum_l \frac{mpk_l}{p_l}\right)}$$

hence:

$$\frac{\partial k_{Ei}^{*}}{\partial \mu_i} = \frac{1-\sum_{l\neq i}\frac{mpk_l}{p_l}}{\frac{s_i p_i}{k_{Ei}}\left(1-\sum_{l}\frac{mpk_l}{p_l}\right)} < 0 \tag{3.52c}$$

and similarly:

$$\frac{\partial k_{Ei}^{*}}{\partial \mu_j} = \frac{1-\sum_{l\neq j}\frac{mpk_l}{p_l}}{\frac{s_i p_i}{k_{Ei}}\left(1-\sum_{l}\frac{mpk_l}{p_l}\right)} < 0 \tag{3.52d}$$

It follows from relations (3.52ab) that the higher the rate of investment in the ith or in the jth stock of capital (where $i \neq j$), the higher values are achieved by k_{Ei}^{*} and the higher level is reached by the growth path of the ith stock of capital. Moreover, calculating exact differential of the production function in its intensive form (3.38), we get:

$$dy_E = \sum_{i} mpk_i dk_{Ei}, \tag{3.53}$$

and it can be concluded from this relation and from prior discussion that an increase in one of the investment rates s_i entails an increase in each of the stocks of capital per unit of effective labour in the combination κ_E^{*}. This causes, as per equation (3.53), an increase in y_E^{*} and labour productivity shifts to a long-term growth path situated on a higher level.

Since (for each $i = 1, 2, \ldots, N$) $\mu_i = \delta_i + g + n$, it follows from relations (3.52cd) that: $\forall i\ \frac{\partial k_{Ei}^{*}}{\partial \delta_i} < 0$, $\forall i, j \wedge j \neq i\ \frac{\partial k_{Ei}^{*}}{\partial \delta_j} < 0$ and $\forall i\ \frac{\partial k_{Ei}^{*}}{\partial n} < 0$. This implies as per equation (3.53) that $\forall i\ \frac{\partial y_E^{*}}{\partial \delta_i} < 0$ and $\frac{\partial y_E^{*}}{\partial n} < 0$. Hence, the higher the depreciation rates of various stocks of capital or the higher the growth rate of the number of workers, the lower the various stocks of capital and output (per unit of effective labour) in a long-run equilibrium of Nonneman-Vanhoudt, and also consequently the lower the levels of long-term trajectories of labour productivity and of various stocks of capital per worker.

These conclusions represent a generalization of similar conclusions drawn from the Solow and Mankiw-Romer-Weil models.

3.3.2 A model with the Cobb-Douglas production function

Like in the original model proposed by Nonneman and Vanhoudt, let us introduce an $N+1$-factor, extended Cobb-Douglas production function expressed by the formula:

$$Y(t)=\left(\prod_i (K_i(t))^{\alpha_i}\right)(E(t))^{1-\sum_i \alpha_i}, \tag{3.54}$$

where Y, K_1, K_2, …, K_N, E denote (like previously) the value of output and inputs of various stocks of capital and units of effective labour, and parameters α_i represent the elasticities of output with respect to various inputs of capital. It is assumed about these parameters that $\forall i\ \alpha_i \in (0,1)$ and $\sum_i \alpha_i \in (0,1)$. The production function (3.54) represents an extension of the production functions (2.19) and (3.14) and as such satisfies assumptions (i–viii) applicable to the production function (3.33).

Additionally, assumptions 2–3 underlying the model from Section 3.3.1 are regarded as satisfied.

Dividing the production function (3.54) by units of effective labour $E > 0$, we get:

$$y_E(t)=\prod_i (k_{Ei}(t))^{\alpha_i}. \tag{3.55}$$

Substituting equation (3.55) into system of differential equations (3.40), we arrive at differential equations:

$$\forall i\ \dot{k}_{Ei}(t)=s_i\prod_l (k_{El}(t))^{\alpha_l}-\mu_i k_{Ei}(t). \tag{3.56}$$

It is obvious that the system of differential equations has a trivial steady state that will be ignored in further analyzes.

The non-trivial steady state $\kappa_E^* \in P$ represents a solution of the following system of equations:

$$\forall i\ s_i k_{Ei}^{1-\alpha_i}\prod_{j\neq i} k_{Ej}^{-\alpha_j}=\frac{s_i}{\mu_i},$$

or

$$\begin{cases} (1-\alpha_1)\ln k_{E1} - \alpha_2 \ln k_{E2} - \ldots - \alpha_N \ln k_{EN} = \ln\left(\frac{s_1}{\mu_1}\right) \\ -\alpha_1 \ln k_{E1} + (1-\alpha_2)\ln k_{E1} - \ldots - \alpha_N \ln k_{EN} = \ln\left(\frac{s_2}{\mu_2}\right) \\ \vdots \\ -\alpha_1 \ln k_{E1} - \alpha_2 \ln k_{E2} - \ldots + (1-\alpha_1)\ln k_{EN} = \ln\left(\frac{s_N}{\mu_N}\right) \end{cases} . \tag{3.57}$$

Subtracting equation *N*th from *i*th equation (for $i = 1, 2, \ldots, N - 1$), we get:

$$\forall i \neq N \quad \ln k_{Ei} - \ln k_{EN} = \ln\left(\frac{s_i}{\mu_i}\right) - \ln\left(\frac{s_N}{\mu_N}\right),$$

hence:

$$\forall i \neq N \quad \ln k_{Ei} = \ln\left(\frac{s_i}{\mu_i}\right) - \ln\left(\frac{s_N}{\mu_N}\right) + \ln k_{EN} \tag{3.58}$$

Substituting equation (3.58) into the last equation in system (3.57), we get:

$$-\sum_{i \neq N}\left(\alpha_i \ln\left(\frac{s_i}{\mu_i}\right)\right) + \left(\sum_{i \neq N}\alpha_i\right)\ln\left(\frac{s_N}{\mu_N}\right) + \left(1-\sum_i \alpha_i\right)\ln k_{EN} = \ln\left(\frac{s_N}{\mu_N}\right),$$

results in:

$$\ln k_{EN} = \frac{\left(1-\sum_{i \neq N}\alpha_i\right)\ln\left(\frac{s_N}{\mu_N}\right) + \sum_{i \neq N}\left(\alpha_i \ln\left(\frac{s_i}{\mu_i}\right)\right)}{1-\sum_i \alpha_i}. \tag{3.59}$$

After several transformations, we obtain from equations (3.58 and 3.59):

$$\forall i \quad \ln k_{Ei}^* = \frac{\left(1-\sum_{j \neq i}\alpha_j\right)\ln\left(\frac{s_i}{\mu_i}\right) + \sum_{j \neq i}\left(\alpha_j \ln\left(\frac{s_j}{\mu_j}\right)\right)}{1-\sum_j \alpha_j}$$
$$= \frac{\left(1-\sum_{j \neq i}\alpha_j\right)\ln\left(\frac{s_i}{\delta_i + g + n}\right) + \sum_{j \neq i}\left(\alpha_j \ln\left(\frac{s_j}{\delta_j + g + n}\right)\right)}{1-\sum_j \alpha_j}. \tag{3.60}$$

Taking the logarithm of the production function in its intensive form (3.55), we get that for each $t \in [0,+\infty)$:

$$\ln y_E(t) = \sum_i \left(\alpha_i \ln k_{Ei}(t)\right),$$

and thus in particular at $t \to +\infty$:

$$\ln y_E^* = \sum_i \left(\alpha_i \ln k_{Ei}^*\right)$$

Substituting formula (3.60) into the above equation and performing some elementary transformation, we arrive at the relation:

$$\ln y_E^* = \frac{\sum_i \left(\alpha_i \ln\left(\frac{s_i}{\delta_i + g + n}\right)\right)}{1 - \sum_i \alpha_i}. \tag{3.61}$$

Equations (3.60 and 3.61) give various stocks of capital per unit of effective labour and the output per unit of effective labour in the Nonneman-Vanhoudt model with the Cobb-Douglas production function. An analysis of those equations clearly indicates that the signs of derivatives k_{Ei}^* and y_{Ei}^* with respect to investment rates s_i, depreciation rates δ_i and growth rate of the number of workers n are identical as in the model from Section 3.3.2.

3.3.3 A model with the CES production function

Another version of the Nonneman-Vanhoudt model to be analyzed in this chapter includes the CES production function expressed by the formula[14]:

$$Y(t) = \left(\sum_j \left(\alpha_j \left(K_j(t)\right)^{-\sigma}\right) + \left(1 - \sum_j \alpha_j\right)\left(E(t)\right)^{-\sigma}\right)^{-1/\sigma}, \tag{3.62}$$

where the variables Y, K_1, K_2, …, K_N and E have the same meanings as in the previously discussed versions of the Nonneman-Vanhoudt model, and the parameters α_1, α_2, …, α_N and σ are the same as in the CES function in the Solow or Mankiw-Romer-Weil model. Thus, it is assumed that each of the parameters α_j belongs to the interval (0,1), $\sum_j \alpha_j \in (0,1)$ and $\sigma \in (0,+\infty)$.

The remaining assumptions underlying the model analyzed here are identical with assumptions 2–3 underlying the model from Section 3.3.1.

Dividing both sides of the CES function (3.62) by $E > 0$, we obtain the production function in its intensive version expressed by the formula:

$$y_E(t) = f(\kappa_E) = \left(\sum_j \left(\alpha_j \left(k_{Ej}(t) \right)^{-\sigma} \right) + 1 - \sum_j \alpha_j \right)^{-1/\sigma}, \tag{3.63}$$

where $\kappa_E = (k_{E1}, k_{E2}, \ldots, k_{EN}) \in P = (0, +\infty)^N$ denotes a combination of inputs per unit of effective labour in phase space P. Substituting relation (3.63) into system of differential equations (3.39), we obtain the following form of that system of equations:

$$\forall j \quad \dot{k}_{Ej} = s_j \left(\sum_l \left(\alpha_l \left(k_{El}(t) \right)^{-\sigma} \right) + 1 - \sum_l \alpha_l \right)^{-1/\sigma} - \mu_j k_{Ej}(t). \tag{3.64}$$

We will demonstrate that (first) system of differential equations (3.64) has a steady state in phase space $P = (0, +\infty)^N$ and (second) that the steady state is asymptotically stable.

System of equations (3.64) can be reduced to a system of equations in the following form:

$$\forall j \quad \psi_j(\kappa_E, s_j, \mu_j) = s_j p_j(\kappa_E) - \mu_j, \tag{3.65}$$

where $\forall j \;\; p_j(\kappa_E) = f(\kappa_E) / k_{Ej}$ denotes the productivity of jth stock of capital. Since system of equations (3.65) represents a special case of system (3.41), its Jacobian is expressed by equation (3.44). This means that the Jacobian has a nonzero value for any $\kappa_E \in P$, and thus system of equations (3.65) has a solution. This leads to the conclusion that system of differential equations (3.64) has a non-trivial steady state $\kappa_E^* \in P$.

Jacobian matrix J of system of differential equations (3.64) is expressed by the formula:

$$J = \begin{bmatrix} s_1 \dfrac{\partial y_E}{\partial k_{E1}} - \mu_1 & s_2 \dfrac{\partial y_E}{\partial k_{E1}} & \cdots & s_N \dfrac{\partial y_E}{\partial k_{E1}} \\ s_1 \dfrac{\partial y_E}{\partial k_{E2}} & s_2 \dfrac{\partial y_E}{\partial k_{E2}} - \mu_2 & \cdots & s_N \dfrac{\partial y_E}{\partial k_{E2}} \\ \vdots & \vdots & \ddots & \vdots \\ s_1 \dfrac{\partial y_E}{\partial k_{EN}} & s_2 \dfrac{\partial y_E}{\partial k_{E1}} & \cdots & s_N \dfrac{\partial y_E}{\partial k_{EN}} - \mu_N \end{bmatrix}.$$

$$
= \begin{bmatrix} s_1 mpk_1 - \mu_1 & s_2 mpk_1 & \cdots & s_N mpk_1 \\ s_1 mpk_2 & s_2 mpk_2 - \mu_2 & \cdots & s_N mpk_2 \\ \vdots & \vdots & \ddots & \vdots \\ s_1 mpk_N & s_2 mpk_N & \cdots & s_N mpk_N - \mu_N \end{bmatrix}
$$

In the steady state κ_E^* for each $j = 1, 2, \ldots, N$, we get: $\mu_j = s_j p_j$, hence the matrix can be expressed by the formula:

$$
J = \begin{bmatrix} -s_1 (p_1 - mpk_1) & s_2 mpk_1 & \cdots & s_N mpk_1 \\ s_1 mpk_2 & -s_2 (p_2 - mpk_2) & \cdots & s_N mpk_2 \\ \vdots & \vdots & \ddots & \vdots \\ s_1 mpk_N & s_2 mpk_N & \cdots & -s_N (p_N - mpk_N) \end{bmatrix}. \tag{3.66}
$$

Eigenvalues υ of matrix (3.66) solve the equation:

$$
\det(J - vI) = 0,
$$

where I denotes an identity matrix. Since:

$$
\det(J - vI) = \begin{vmatrix} -s_1 (p_1 - mpk_1) - v & s_2 mpk_1 & \cdots & s_N mpk_1 \\ s_1 mpk_2 & -s_2 (p_2 - mpk_2) - v & \cdots & s_N mpk_2 \\ \vdots & \vdots & \ddots & \vdots \\ s_1 mpk_N & s_2 mpk_N & \cdots & -s_N (p_N - mpk_N) - v \end{vmatrix}.
$$

hence:

$$\det(J - vI) = (-1)^N \left(\prod_j \frac{s_j}{mpk_j} \right) \begin{vmatrix} \dfrac{p_1 + \frac{v}{s_1}}{mpk_1} - 1 & -1 & \cdots & -1 \\ -1 & \dfrac{p_2 + \frac{v}{s_2}}{mpk_2} - 1 & \cdots & -1 \\ \vdots & \vdots & \ddots & \vdots \\ -1 & -1 & \cdots & \dfrac{p_N + \frac{v}{s_N}}{mpk_N} - 1 \end{vmatrix}$$

$$= (-1)^N \left(\prod_j \frac{s_j}{mpk_j} \right) \begin{vmatrix} \dfrac{p_1 + \frac{v}{s_1}}{mpk_1} & 0 & \cdots & -1 \\ 0 & \dfrac{p_2 + \frac{v}{s_2}}{mpk_2} & \cdots & -1 \\ \vdots & \vdots & \ddots & \vdots \\ -\dfrac{p_N + \frac{v}{s_N}}{mpk_N} & -\dfrac{p_N + \frac{v}{s_N}}{mpk_N} & \cdots & \dfrac{p_N + \frac{v}{s_N}}{mpk_N} - 1 \end{vmatrix}$$

$$= (-1)^N \left(\prod_j \frac{s_j}{mpk_j} \right) \begin{vmatrix} 1 & 0 & \cdots & -\dfrac{mpk_1}{p_1 + \frac{v}{s_1}} \\ 0 & 1 & \cdots & -\dfrac{mpk_2}{p_2 + \frac{v}{s_2}} \\ \vdots & \vdots & \ddots & \vdots \\ -1 & -1 & \cdots & 1 - \dfrac{mpk_N}{p_N + \frac{v}{s_N}} \end{vmatrix}$$

thus:

$$\det(J - vI) = (-1)^N \left(\prod_j \frac{s_j}{p_j + \frac{v}{s_j}} \right) \left(1 - \sum_j \frac{mpk_j}{p_j + \frac{v}{s_j}} \right),$$

so that eigenvalues υ of Jacobian matrix (3.66) solve the solution:

$$(-1)^N \left(\prod_j \frac{s_j}{p_j + \frac{v}{s_j}} \right) \left(1 - \sum_j \frac{mpk_j}{p_j + \frac{v}{s_j}} \right) = 0. \tag{3.67}$$

We will demonstrate now that eigenvalues υ represent real numbers. An indirect proof will be provided for this purpose (see Dykas, Sulima and Tokarski (2008), see also Sulima (2011) and a similar proof for a gravity model of economic growth in the study by Mroczek, Tokarski and Trojak (2014)).

Equation (3.67) is true if and only if:

$$\sum_j \frac{1}{\frac{p_j}{mpk_j} + \frac{v}{s_j mpk_j}} = 1. \tag{3.68}$$

Let us assume then that the roots of equation (3.68) represent certain complex numbers in the form:

$$v = a + bi,$$

where $a, b \in R$ and $i = \sqrt{-1}$. Hence, equation (3.68) can be expressed by the formula:

$$\sum_j \frac{1}{\frac{p_j}{mpk_j} + \frac{a}{s_j mpk_j} + \frac{b}{s_j mpk_j} i} = 1. \tag{3.69}$$

As every complex number z satisfies the relation:

$$\frac{1}{z}=\frac{\overline{z}}{|z|^2},$$

where $\overline{z}=a-bi$ is a complex conjugate of z, so that we get as per quotation (3.69):

$$\sum_j \frac{\frac{p_j}{mpk_j}+\frac{a}{s_j mpk_j}-\frac{b}{s_j mpk_j}i}{\left(\frac{p_j}{mpk_j}+\frac{a}{s_j mpk_j}+\frac{b}{s_j mpk_j}i\right)^2+\left(\frac{b}{s_j mpk_j}\right)^2}=1,$$

so:

$$\sum_j \frac{\frac{p_j}{mpk_j}+\frac{a}{s_j mpk_j}}{\left(\frac{p_j}{mpk_j}+\frac{a}{s_j mpk_j}+\frac{b}{s_j mpk_j}i\right)^2+\left(\frac{b}{s_j mpk_j}\right)^2}-$$

$$bi\sum_j \frac{1/\left(s_j mpk_j\right)}{\left(\frac{p_j}{mpk_j}+\frac{a}{s_j mpk_j}+\frac{b}{s_j mpk_j}i\right)^2+\left(\frac{b}{s_j mpk_j}\right)^2}=1,$$

which leads to the conclusion that $b=0$. Hence, all eigenvalues υ of Jacobian matrix J are real numbers. Consequently, equation (3.69) can be expressed as follows:

$$\sum_j \frac{1}{\frac{p_j}{mpk_j}+\frac{a}{s_j mpk_j}}=1. \tag{3.70}$$

Another indirect proof will be provided to demonstrate that eigenvalues $\upsilon=a$ are negative. Let us now assume that $a\geq 0$. Then, as per (3.70):

$$\sum_j \frac{1}{\frac{p_j}{mpk_j}+\frac{a}{s_j mpk_j}}=\sum_j \frac{mpk_j}{p_j+\frac{a}{s_j}}\leq\sum_j \frac{mpk_j}{p_j}<1,$$

which is inconsistent with equation (3.70). This means that eigenvalues $\upsilon < 0$.

As per the Grobman-Hartman theorem, the steady state κ_E^* of system of differential equations (3.70) in the Nonneman-Vanhoudt model with the CES production function is asymptotically stable.

The partial derivatives of implicit functions $k_{Ej}^* = k_{Ej}^*(s,\mu)$, for subsequent $j = 1, 2, \ldots, N$, and $y_E^* = y_E^*(s,\mu)$ resulting from system of equations (3.65) behave identically as the corresponding partial derivatives of system of equations (3.41) – see relations (3.52a–d). Therefore, their interpretation in terms of economics is identical.

3.3.4 Golden rules of accumulation in the Nonneman-Vanhoudt model

The golden rules of capital accumulation are defined in the Nonneman-Vanhoudt model as a combination of investment rates $s = (s_1 s_1, \ldots, s_N) \in (0,1)^N$, where the sum of those investment rates also belongs to the interval (0,1) that leads to a maximum long-term consumption per unit of effective labour c_E^* (Dykas, Sulima and Tokarski 2008). That consumption value, like in the Solow or Mankiw-Romer-Weil model, can be expressed as follows:

$$c_E^* = \left(1 - \sum_i s_i\right) y_E^*.$$

Taking the long-run output per unit of effective labour from equation (3.61), i.e. from the original version of the Nonneman-Vanhoudt model with the Cobb-Douglas production function, we get:

$$c_E^* = \Omega\left(1 - \sum_i s_i\right)\prod_i s_i^{\frac{\alpha_i}{1-\sum_j \alpha_j}}, \tag{3.71}$$

where $\Omega = \prod_i \mu_i^{\frac{-\alpha_i}{1-\sum_j \alpha_j}} > 0$. It follows from equation (3.71) that:

$$\forall i \quad \lim_{s_i \to 0^+} c_E^* = \Omega \lim_{s_i \to 0^+}\left(\left(1 - \sum_i s_i\right)\prod_i s_i^{\frac{\alpha_i}{1-\sum_j \alpha_j}}\right) = 0,$$

$$\lim_{\sum_i s_i \to 1^-} c_E^* = \Omega \lim_{\sum_i s_i \to 1^-} \left(\left(1 - \sum_i s_i \right) \prod_i s_i^{\frac{\alpha_i}{1-\sum_j \alpha_j}} \right) = 0.$$

and

$$\forall s_i \in (0,1) \wedge \sum_i s_i \in (0,1) \quad c_E^*(s) > 0,$$

hence, the maximization of function $c_E^*(s)$ with respect to s (at limitations imposed on subsequent s_i) is identical with the maximization of function $v(s)$ expressed by the formula:

$$v(s) = \ln c_E^*(s) = \ln \Omega + \ln\left(1 - \sum_i s_i\right) + \frac{\sum_j (\alpha_j \ln s_j)}{1 - \sum_j \alpha_j}. \tag{3.72}$$

First-order conditions for the maximization of function (3.72) can be reduced to:

$$\forall i \quad \frac{\partial v}{\partial s_i} = -\frac{1}{1-\sum_i s_i} + \frac{\alpha_i}{\left(1-\sum_i \alpha_i\right) s_i} = \frac{\alpha_i \left(1-\sum_i s_i\right) - \left(1-\sum_i \alpha_i\right) s_i}{\left(1-\sum_i \alpha_i\right)\left(1-\sum_i s_i\right) s_i} = 0, \tag{3.73}$$

and the second-order condition is satisfied when the Hessian:

$$\bar{H} = \begin{bmatrix} \partial^2 v / \partial s_1^2 & \partial^2 v / (\partial s_1 \partial s_2) & \cdots & \partial^2 v / (\partial s_1 \partial s_N) \\ \partial^2 v / (\partial s_2 \partial s_1) & \partial^2 v / \partial s_2^2 & \cdots & \partial^2 v / (\partial s_2 \partial s_N) \\ \vdots & \vdots & \ddots & \vdots \\ \partial^2 v / (\partial s_N \partial s_1) & \partial^2 v / (\partial s_N \partial s_1) & \cdots & \partial^2 v / \partial s_N^2 \end{bmatrix} = \begin{bmatrix} -(a+b_1) & -a & \cdots & -a \\ -a & -(a+b_2) & \cdots & -a \\ \vdots & \vdots & \ddots & \\ -a & -a & \cdots & -(a+b_N) \end{bmatrix},$$

where $a = \dfrac{1}{\left(1-\sum_i s_i\right)^2} > 1$ and $\forall i \;\; b_i = \dfrac{\alpha_i}{\left(1-\sum_i \alpha_i\right) s_i^2} > 0$ is negative-definite at least in the point in which condition (3.73) is satisfied.

Subsequent principal minors m_i (for $i = 1, 2, \ldots, N$) of the Hessian $\bar{H}$ can be expressed as follows:

$$\forall i \quad m_i = \begin{vmatrix} -(a+b_1) & -a & \cdots & -a \\ -a & -(a+b_2) & \cdots & -a \\ \vdots & \vdots & \ddots & \vdots \\ -a & -a & \cdots & -(a+b_i) \end{vmatrix}$$

$$= (-1)^i \begin{vmatrix} -b_1 & 0 & \cdots & -b_i \\ 0 & -b_2 & \cdots & -b_i \\ \vdots & \vdots & \ddots & \vdots \\ a & a & \cdots & a+b_i \end{vmatrix}$$

$$= (-1)^i \prod_j b_j \begin{vmatrix} 1 & 0 & \cdots & -1 \\ 0 & 1 & \cdots & -1 \\ \vdots & \vdots & \ddots & \vdots \\ a/b_1 & a/b_2 & \cdots & a/b_i + 1 \end{vmatrix}$$

$$= (-1)^i \prod_j b_j \begin{vmatrix} 1 & 0 & \cdots & 0 \\ 0 & 1 & \cdots & 0 \\ \vdots & \vdots & \ddots & \vdots \\ a/b_1 & a/b_2 & \cdots & a\sum_j \left(\frac{1}{b_j}\right) + 1 \end{vmatrix},$$

therefore:

$$\forall i \quad m_i = (-1)^i \left(\prod_j b_j\right)\left(a\sum_j \left(\frac{1}{b_j}\right) + 1\right).$$

Since the expression $\left(\prod_j b_j\right)\left(a\sum_j\left(\frac{1}{b_j}\right)+1\right)$ is positive, the odd principal minors m_i of the Hessian $\bar{H}$ are negative, and the even principal minors are positive. Consequently, the Hessian is negative-definite, i.e. the second-order condition for the maximization of function $v(s)$ is satisfied.

First-order conditions (3.73) can be reduced to the following linear system of equations:

$$\forall i \quad \left(1-\sum_{j\neq i}\alpha_j\right)s_i+\alpha_i\sum_{j\neq i}s_j=\alpha_i. \tag{3.74}$$

Using Cramer's rule, we can demonstrate that system of equations (3.74) is solved by a combination of investment rates $s=(\alpha_1,\alpha_2,\ldots,\alpha_N)\in(0,1)^N$. Hence, Phelps' golden rule of accumulation in the Nonneman-Vanhoudt model is a combination of investment rates that equals the combination of output elasticities with respect to various inputs of capital. This rule represents a generalization of Phelps' golden rules from the Solow and Mankiw-Romer-Weil models.

3.4 Conclusions

The analyzes contained in this chapter can be summarized as follows:

I The Mankiw-Romer-Weil and Nonneman-Vanhoudt models represent natural generalizations of the neoclassical Solow growth model. The Mankiw-Romer-Weil model includes two types of capital, and the Nonneman-Vanhoudt model considers multiple capitals.

II Both models of economic growth discussed in this chapter (like the Solow model) assume that an increase in each of the analyzed stocks of capital equals the difference between investment in that stock and its depreciation, and units of effective labour rise at the growth rate that equals the sum of the Harrodian rate of technological progress and the growth rate of the number of workers.

III. Both the Mankiw-Romer-Weil and Nonneman-Vanhoudt models have a non-trivial steady state of a system of equations of motion and that state is Lyapunov asymptotically stable. In that state, labour productivity and various stocks of capital per worker rise at the Harrodian rate of technological progress.

IV In the point of long-run equilibrium of the analyzed growth models, the positions of growth paths of labour productivity and of various stocks of capital per worker depend on rates of investment in those stocks, their depreciation rates and the growth rate of the number of workers. The higher the investment rates or the lower the depreciation rates or the lower the growth rate of the number of workers, the higher levels are reached by those growth paths.

V The golden rules of capital accumulation in the Mankiw-Romer-Weil and Nonneman-Vanhoudt models are defined as combinations of investment rates corresponding to combinations of elasticities of output with respect to various inputs of capital.

Notes

1 The stock of human capital can be defined as "a general skill level, so that a worker with human capital $h(t)$ is the productive equivalent of two workers with $1/2h(t)$ each, or a half-time worker with $2h(t)$" (Lucas, 1988, p. 17). See also e.g. Becker (1975), Lucas (1990, 2010), Welfe (2000, 2009), Zienkowski (2003), Malaga (2004), Roszkowska (2005, 2013, 2014), Cichy and Malaga (2007), Cichy (2008) and Mroczek and Tokarski (2013).

2 This model represents a generalization of the Mankiw-Romer-Weil model. The original study published by Mankiw, Romer and Weil (1992) discusses a model with the Cobb-Douglas production function. Alternative versions of the Mankiw-Romer-Weil model can be found e.g. in the studies published by Zawadzki (2012, 2015), and its possible application in analyzes of regional growth is discussed by Malaga and Kliber (2007).

3 The economic interpretation of properties (i–viii) of the production function (3.1) is analogous to the interpretation of the corresponding properties of function (2.1).

4 This is because the output Y can be described using the formula: $Y = F(K,H,E) = f(k_E,h_E)E$ which implies that: $\frac{\partial F}{\partial K} = \frac{\partial f}{\partial k_E}\frac{\partial k_E}{\partial K}E = \frac{\partial f}{\partial k_E}$.

5 Then also $\forall (k_E,h_E) \in P \quad f(k_E,h_E) > \frac{\partial f}{\partial k_E}k_E \quad \wedge \quad f(k_E,h_E) > \frac{\partial f}{\partial h_E}h_E$.

6 This section is based on studies conducted by Tokarski (2008a, 2009) (Chapter 3, Section 3.4). See also Sulima (2011).

7 The asymptotic stability of steady states in Mankiw-Romer-Weil and Nonneman-Vanhoudt models with the CES production function needs to be demonstrated considering the properties of that function that fails to satisfy all conditions applicable to a neoclassical production function.

8 The inequalities are satisfied: $p_K > mpk \wedge p_H > mph$ because: $f(k_E,h_E) > \frac{\partial f}{\partial k_E}k_E \wedge f(k_E,h_E) > \frac{\partial f}{\partial h_E}h_E$, hence the expression $s_K(p_K - mpk) + s_H(p_H - mph)$ is positive.

9 This section is based on a study published by Dykas, Edigarian and Tokarski (2011), because the original article by Nonneman and Vanhoudt (1996) uses only an extended version of the Cobb-Douglas production function (the model known from Section 3.3.2) and fails to analyze the stability of the non-trivial steady state. See also Dykas, Sulima and Tokarski (2008).

10 The economic interpretation of properties (i–viii) of the production function (3.33) is obviously analogous to the interpretation of the corresponding properties of functions (2.1) and (3.1).

11 The expression $\forall i$ will hereinafter mean $\forall i = 1,2,...,N$. The expressions $\sum_i$ and $\prod_i$ will be read similarly.

12 Lyapunov stability is defined as follows (see Ombach, 1999, p. 214). Let us introduce an open set $\Omega \subset R^n$ and a function $f : \Omega \to R^n$, $f \in C^1(\Omega)$. The system $x' = f(x)$ generates a local flow $\varphi(t, x_0)$ and point $x_0 \in \Omega$ represents a steady state of φ. Then point x_0 is Lyapunov asymptotically stable if and only if:

- i A neighbourhood W of point x_0 exists such that $\forall x \in W : [0,+\infty) \subset I_x$, where $I_x = \{t \in R : (x,t) \in \Omega\}$ represents motion of point x.
- ii A neighbourhood U of point $x0$ exists and $\exists V \subset U$ such that $\forall x \in V\ \forall t \geq 0 : \varphi(t,x) \in U$.
- iii A neighbourhood Q of point $x0$ exists such that $\forall x \in Q : \varphi(t,x) \underset{t \to \infty}{\to} x_0$.

13 Let $E \subset \Omega$ denote a neighbourhood of the steady state $x0$, $V : E \to [0,+\infty)$, $V \in C^1(E)$. Function V is termed a strong Lyapunov function if and only if (see Ombach 1999, p. 227):

- i $\forall x \in E \setminus \{x_0\} : V(x) > 0$.
- ii $V(x) = 0 \Leftrightarrow x = x_0$.
- iii $\forall x \in E \setminus \{x_0\} : \dot{V}(x) < 0$.

14 See also Sulima 2011.

4 Fiscal and monetary policy vs economic growth

4.1 Introduction

Chapters 2 and 3 described both the single-capital, neoclassical Solow growth model and the two- and multi-capital Mankiw-Romer-Weil and Nonneman-Vanhoudt models. Those models did not address the effect of macroeconomic policy (i.e. fiscal and monetary policy) on the processes of long-run equilibrium and economic growth. Therefore, this chapter describes proposed generalizations of the Mankiw-Romer-Weil model and a compilation of the Solow model with a Keynesian growth model proposed by Domar (1946, 1957) that consider the effect of both fiscal and monetary policy on economic growth.

Section 4.2 describes models of economic growth that represent generalizations of the two-capital Mankiw-Romer-Weil growth model. Those models are based on the assumption that investments in physical and human capital are financed both from disposable income (income after taxes) of the private sector and from taxes collected by the government sector of the economy (Section 4.2.1); Section 4.2.2 describes a model with a separated capital of the government sector. The growth models described in Section 4.2 were proposed in the studies published by Tokarski (2000, 2005, Chapter 4) and Tokarski (2009, Chapter 7).

Section 4.3 contains a description of a Domar-Solow model. The economic growth model analyzed in that part of this monograph is termed a Domar-Solow model for two reasons. First, we will consider the effect of investment inputs in the economy on both the demand and the supply side of the economy, like in the original Domar model (the neoclassical Solow growth model does not include any analysis of the effect of investments on the value of aggregate demand in the economy). Second, the economic growth model analyzed there can be termed a Solow model, because (like in the Solow model) the production process is described using the neoclassical Cobb-Douglas production function, characterized by output elasticity of capital (an elastic capital-output ratio). The model was proposed by Tokarski (2009, Chapter 8).

An alternative approach to analyzing the effect of fiscal and monetary policy on the processes of long-run equilibrium and economic growth can be found in the following studies: Barro (1989, 1990, 1991), Grossman and Helpman (1991), Engen and Skinder (1992), Barro, Mankiw, and Sala-i-Martin (1995),

DOI: 10.4324/9781003323792-5

Kelly (1997), Aghion and Howitt (1998), Kneller, Bleaney, and Gemmell (1999), Welfe (2000, 2009), Folster and Henrekson (2001), Konopczyński (2004, 2005, 2006, 2009b, 2014, 2015), Krawiec (2005), Pietraszewski (2009), Dykas and Tokarski (2013), Malaga (2013) and Nowzosad and Wisła (2016).

4.2 Fiscal policy in a Mankiw-Romer-Weil model

4.2.1 The basic model

The following assumption underlies the discussion contained in this section:

1 Like in the original Mankiw-Romer-Weil model, the production process is described by a three-factor Cobb-Douglas production function expressed by the formula:

$$Y(t)=(K(t))^{\alpha K}(H(t))^{\alpha H}(E(t))^{1-\alpha K-\alpha H}, \tag{4.1}$$

where $Y,K,H,E \geq 0$ and $\alpha_K,\alpha_H,(\alpha_K+\alpha_H) \in (0,1)$ are read as in the model from Section 3.2.2.

2 At any moment $t \in [0; +\infty)$, increases in stocks of physical capital $\dot{K}$ and human capital $\dot{H}$ equal the differences between investments in those stocks (that is I_K and I_H) and their depreciation ($\delta_K K$ and $\delta_H H$). This means that the following differential equations are true:

$$\dot{K}(t)=I_K(t)-\delta_K K(t) \tag{4.2a}$$

and

$$\dot{H}(t)=I_H(t)-\delta_H H(t), \tag{4.2b}$$

where $\delta_K,\delta_H \in (0,1)$ denote depreciation rates of the analyzed stocks.

3 The stock of effective labour $E = AL$ rises at a growth rate that equals the total of Harrodian rate of technological progress $g>0$ and the growth rate of the number of workers $n > 0$. Hence, its trajectory is described by equation (2.12a).

4 The state collects (in the forms of taxes and increase in in public debt, etc.) a τth fraction of output, where $\tau \in (0; 1)$. The rate τ will hereinafter be termed the fiscalism index of the economy.[1]

5 A s_{KG}th fraction of output τY collected by the state is allocated to investment in physical capital, a s_{HG}th fraction τY represents investment of the government sector in human capital $s_{KG},s_{HG},(s_{KG}+s_{HG}) \in (0,1)$. This leads to the conclusion that the value of investment of the government sector in physical capital accumulation I_{KG} (understood as a sum of direct investment of the central budget, regional and local budget investment in social and economic infrastructure and investment transfers to the private sector) and human capital accumulation I_{HG} (defined as outlays of the government sector on public education, healthcare, etc.) is given by the formulas:

$$I_{KG}(t)=s_{KG}\tau Y(t) \tag{4.3a}$$

and

$$I_{HG}(t) = s_{HG}\tau Y(t). \tag{4.3b}$$

The variables s_{KG} and s_{HG} will hereinafter be termed investment rates of the government sector in the stocks of physical and human capital, because they represent a proportion in government budget revenues τY invested by the government sector in those stocks.

6 The private sector[2] invests an s_{KP}th fraction of income after taxes $(1-\tau)Y$ in the stock of physical capital, and s_{HP}th fraction of that income in human capital, and $s_{KP}, s_{HP}, (s_{KP}+s_{HP}) \in (0,1)$. Hence, investment in physical capital I_{KP} and human capital I_{HP} of that sector is described by the formulas:

$$I_{KP}(t) = s_{KP}(1-\tau)Y(t) \tag{4.4a}$$

and

$$I_{HP}(t) = s_{HP}(1-\tau)Y(t). \tag{4.4b}$$

7 Total investment outlays on physical capital I_K (human capital I_H) equal the total of outlays of the private sector I_{KP} (I_{HP}) and of the government sector I_{KG} (I_{HG}). Hence, the following equations are true:

$$I_K(t) = I_{KG}(t) + I_{KP}(t) \tag{4.5a}$$

and

$$I_H(t) = I_{HG}(t) + I_{HP}(t). \tag{4.5b}$$

From relations (4.3a,b), (4.4a,b) and (4.5a,b), we get:

$$I_K(t) = \left(s_{KG}\tau + s_{KP}(1-\tau)\right)Y(t)$$

and

$$I_H(t) = \left(s_{HG}\tau + s_{HP}(1-\tau)\right)Y(t).$$

It follows from the above equations and from equation (4.2ab) that the accumulation of various stocks of capital is described by the differential equations:

$$\dot{K}(t) = \left(s_{KG}\tau + s_{KP}(1-\tau)\right)Y(t) - \delta_K K(t) \tag{4.6a}$$

and

$$\dot{H}(t) = \left(s_{HG}\tau + s_{HP}(1-\tau)\right)Y(t) - \delta_H H(t). \tag{4.6b}$$

It follows from equations (4.6ab) that total investment rates (of the private sector and the government sector) in the stocks of physical and human capital equal, respectively, $s_{KG}\tau+s_{KP}(1-\tau)$ and $s_{HG}\tau+s_{HP}(1-\tau)$. Moreover, as assumptions 1–3 underlying the analyzed growth model are identical with the corresponding assumptions underlying the model from Section 3.2.2, the long-run output per unit of effective labour y_E^* can be expressed as follows as per equation (3.18c):

$$\ln y_E^* = \frac{\alpha_K \ln \frac{s_{KG}\tau+s_{KP}(1-\tau)}{\delta_K+g+n} + \alpha_H \ln \frac{s_{HG}\tau+s_{HP}(1-\tau)}{\delta_H+g+n}}{1-\alpha_K-\alpha_H}. \tag{4.7}$$

Equation (4.7) leads to the following conclusions:

- Since $\frac{\partial \ln y_E^*}{\partial s_{KP}}>0$, $\frac{\partial \ln y_E^*}{\partial s_{KG}}>0$, $\frac{\partial \ln y_E^*}{\partial s_{HP}}>0$ and $\frac{\partial \ln y_E^*}{\partial s_{HG}}>0$, the higher the investment rates of the private sector or the government sector in the stocks of physical or human capital, the higher the long-run output per unit of effective labour (and the higher level is reached by the long-run growth path of labour productivity).
- It follows from $\frac{\partial \ln y_E^*}{\partial \delta_K}<0$, $\frac{\partial \ln y_E^*}{\partial \delta_H}<0$ and $\frac{\partial \ln y_E^*}{\partial n}<0$ that (like in the original Mankiw-Romer-Weil model) high rates of capital depreciation or a high growth rate of the number of workers is accompanied by low values of y_E^* (and a low level of the trajectory of long-run output per worker).

Differentiating equation (4.7) with respect to the fiscalism index of the economy τ, we get:

$$\frac{\partial \ln y_E^*}{\partial \tau} = \frac{\alpha_K \frac{s_{KG}-s_{KP}}{s_{KG}\tau+s_{KP}(1-\tau)} + \alpha_H \frac{s_{HG}-s_{HP}}{s_{HG}\tau+s_{HP}(1-\tau)}}{1-\alpha_K-\alpha_H}. \tag{4.8}$$

The following nine cases have to be considered in an analysis of relation (4.8):

I $s_{KG}=s_{KP}$ and $s_{HG}=s_{HP}$, i.e. a case in which both analyzed sectors of the economy are characterized by equal investment rates in the stocks of physical and human capital;

II $s_{KG}>s_{KP}$ and $s_{HG}=s_{HP}$, i.e. a situation in which the government sector is characterized by a higher investment rare in physical capital and by the same rate of investment in human capital as the private sector;

III $s_{KG}<s_{KP}$ and $s_{HG}=s_{HP}$, i.e. a case opposite to case II;

IV $s_{KG}=s_{KP}$ and $s_{HG}>s_{HP}$, i.e. a situation in which the government sector has a higher (than the private sector) rate of investment in human capital and the same rate of investment in physical capital;

V $s_{KG}>s_{KP}$ and $s_{HG}>s_{HP}$, i.e. a case in which the government sector has both investment rates analyzed here greater than the private sector;

VI $s_{KG} < s_{KP}$ and $s_{HG} > s_{HP}$, i.e. the government sector has a higher rate of investment in human capital, and the private sector has a higher rate of investment in physical capital;

VII $s_{KG} = s_{KP}$ and $s_{HG} < s_{HP}$, i.e. a situation opposite to case IV;

VIII $s_{KG} > s_{KP}$ and $s_{HG} < s_{HP}$, i.e. the government sector has a higher rate of investment in physical capital, and the private sector has a higher rate of investment in human capital;

IX $s_{KG} < s_{KP}$ and $s_{HG} < s_{HP}$, i.e. the private sector is characterized by higher rates of investment in both stocks of capital considered in the Mankiw-Romer-Weil model.

If the first of the above cases is true, i.e. $s_{KG} = s_{KP}$ and $s_{HG} = s_{HP}$, partial derivative (4.8) equals zero, and this implies that at each fiscalism index τ the economy follows the same long-run growth path of labour productivity. This is because at $s_{KG} = s_{KP}$ and $s_{HG} = s_{HP}$ total investment rates in the entire economy (i.e. s_K and s_H) are independent of the fiscalism index τ.

In case II, i.e. when $s_{KG} > s_{KP}$ and $s_{HG} = s_{HP}$, partial derivative (4.8) can be expressed by:

$$\frac{\partial \ln y_E^*}{\partial \tau} = \frac{\alpha_K}{1-\alpha_K-\alpha_H} \cdot \frac{s_{KG}-s_{KP}}{s_{KG}\tau+s_{KP}(1-\tau)} > 0,$$

which implies that each increase in the fiscalism index of the economy τ leads to an increase in y_E^* and to the growth path of labour productivity situated at a higher level.

At $s_{KG} < s_{KP}$ and $s_{HG} = s_{HP}$, i.e. in case III, partial derivative (4.8) can be reduced to the relation:

$$\frac{\partial \ln y_E^*}{\partial \tau} = \frac{\alpha_K}{1-\alpha_K-\alpha_H} \cdot \frac{s_{KG}-s_{KP}}{s_{KG}\tau+s_{KP}(1-\tau)} < 0,$$

which means that an increase in the fiscalism index τ leads to a reduction in the output per unit of effective labour y_E^* in a Mankiw-Romer-Weil long-run equilibrium, and thus to a lower level of long-run growth path of labour productivity.

If case IV is true (i.e. when $s_{KG} = s_{KP}$ and $s_{HG} > s_{HP}$), the partial derivative $\frac{\partial \ln y_E^*}{\partial \tau}$ is described by the relation:

$$\frac{\partial \ln y_E^*}{\partial \tau} = \frac{\alpha_H}{1-\alpha_K-\alpha_H} \cdot \frac{s_{HG}-s_{HP}}{s_{HG}\tau+s_{HP}(1-\tau)} > 0;$$

and the conclusion is that under such circumstances, an increase in the fiscalism index of the economy leads to an increase in y_E^* and in a higher level of long-run path of economic growth.

In case V, i.e. when $s_{KG} > s_{KP}$ and $s_{HG} > s_{HP}$, partial derivative (4.8) assumes positive values and then each increase in τ moves a Mankiw-Romer-Weil economy onto a long-run growth path of labour productivity situated on a higher level.

If case VI is true, when $s_{KG} < s_{KP}$ and $s_{HG} > s_{HP}$, partial derivative (4.8) can be both positive and negative. Consequently, the derivative $\frac{\partial \ln y_E^*}{\partial \tau}$ can be expressed by the formula:

$$\frac{\partial \ln y_E^*}{\partial \tau} = \frac{\alpha_H (s_{HG} - s_{HP}) s_{KP} - \alpha_K (s_{KP} - s_{KG}) s_{HP} - (\alpha_K + \alpha_H)(s_{KP} - s_{KG})(s_{HG} - s_{HP})\tau}{(1 - \alpha_K - \alpha_H)(s_{HG}\tau + s_{HP}(1-\tau))(s_{KG}\tau + s_{KP}(1-\tau))}. \tag{4.9}$$

It follows from equation (4.9) that:

$$\frac{\partial \ln y_E^*}{\partial \tau} > 0 \Leftrightarrow \tau < \frac{\alpha_H (s_{HG} - s_{HP}) s_{KP} - \alpha_K (s_{KP} - s_{KG}) s_{HP}}{(\alpha_K + \alpha_H)(s_{KP} - s_{KG})(s_{HG} - s_{HP})}, \tag{4.10a}$$

$$\frac{\partial \ln y_E^*}{\partial \tau} = 0 \Leftrightarrow \tau = \frac{\alpha_H (s_{HG} - s_{HP}) s_{KP} - \alpha_K (s_{KP} - s_{KG}) s_{HP}}{(\alpha_K + \alpha_H)(s_{KP} - s_{KG})(s_{HG} - s_{HP})} \tag{4.10b}$$

and

$$\frac{\partial \ln y_E^*}{\partial \tau} \langle 0 \Leftrightarrow \tau \rangle \frac{\alpha_H (s_{HG} - s_{HP}) s_{KP} - \alpha_K (s_{KP} - s_{KG}) s_{HP}}{(\alpha_K + \alpha_H)(s_{KP} - s_{KG})(s_{HG} - s_{HP})}. \tag{4.10c}$$

Formulas (4.9) and (4.10a–c) lead to the following conclusions:

- If $\alpha_H (s_{HG} - s_{HP}) s_{KP} \leq \alpha_K (s_{KP} - s_{KG}) s_{HP}$, it follows from equation (4.9) that for each $\tau \in (0,1)$ the relation is true:

  $$\frac{\partial \ln y_E^*}{\partial \tau} \leq -\frac{(\alpha_K + \alpha_H)(s_{KP} - s_{KG})(s_{HG} - s_{HP})\tau}{(1 - \alpha_K - \alpha_H)(s_{HG}\tau + s_{HP}(1-\tau))(s_{KG}\tau + s_{KP}(1-\tau))} < 0$$

  i.e. each increase in the fiscalism index of the economy τ leads to a fall in y_E^* and to a lower level of the long-run growth path of labour productivity in a Mankiw-Romer-Weil economy.
- When:

  $$\alpha_H (s_{HG} - s_{HP}) s_{KP} > \alpha_K (s_{KP} - s_{KG}) s_{HP}$$

  and:
  $\alpha_H (s_{HG} - s_{HP}) s_{KP} < (\alpha_K + \alpha_H)(s_{KP} - s_{KG})(s_{HG} - s_{HP}) + \alpha_K (s_{KP} - s_{KG}) s_{HP}$, (first) at each fiscalism index of the economy $\tau \in \left(0; \frac{\alpha_H (s_{HG} - s_{HP}) s_{KP} - \alpha_K (s_{KP} - s_{KG}) s_{HP}}{(\alpha_K + \alpha_H)(s_{KP} - s_{KG})(s_{HG} - s_{HPKG})}\right)$ partial derivative (4.9) is positive, (second) at index $\bar{\tau} = \frac{\alpha_H (s_{HG} - s_{HP}) s_{KP} - \alpha_K (s_{KP} - s_{KG}) s_{HP}}{(\alpha_K + \alpha_H)(s_{KP} - s_{KG})(s_{HG} - s_{HPKG})}$ the derivative is zero and (third) for each $\tau \in \left(\frac{\alpha_H (s_{HG} - s_{HP}) s_{KP} - \alpha_K (s_{KP} - s_{KG}) s_{HP}}{(\alpha_K + \alpha_H)(s_{KP} - s_{KG})(s_{HG} - s_{HPKG})}, 1\right)$ the derivative $\frac{\partial \ln y_E^*}{\partial \tau}$ is negative. Then, an increase in the fiscalism index τ in the interval $\left(0, \frac{\alpha_H (s_{HG} - s_{HP}) s_{KP} - \alpha_K (s_{KP} - s_{KG}) s_{HP}}{(\alpha_K + \alpha_H)(s_{KP} - s_{KG})(s_{HG} - s_{HPKG})}\right)$ leads to a rise in y_E^* and the

economy climbs onto a long-run growth path of labour productivity on a higher level. At $\tau = \overline{\tau}$, the output per unit of effective labour y_E^* reaches it maximum with respect to the fiscalism index of the economy τ and the economy climbs onto the highest long-run growth path of labour productivity. If the fiscalism index of the economy exceeds the value of $\overline{\tau}$, an increase in that index entails a reduction in the value of variable y_E^* and the economy goes down to a lower growth path of the output per worker.

- This means that in the analyzed case, the optimum fiscalism index of the economy is $\overline{\tau}$ expressed by the formula:

$$\overline{\tau} = \frac{\alpha_H (s_{HG} - s_{HP}) s_{KP} - \alpha_K (s_{KP} - s_{KG}) s_{HP}}{(\alpha_K + \alpha_H)(s_{KP} - s_{KG})(s_{HG} - s_{HP})} \tag{4.11}$$

- And if:

$$\alpha_H (s_{HG} - s_{HP}) s_{KP} \geq (\alpha_K + \alpha_H)(s_{KP} - s_{KG})(s_{HG} - s_{HP}) + \alpha_K (s_{KP} - s_{KG}) s_{HP},$$

for each $\tau \in (0;1)$:

$$\alpha_H (s_{HG} - s_{HP}) s_{KP} - \alpha_K (s_{KP} - s_{KG}) s_{HP} - (\alpha_K + \alpha_H)(s_{KP} - s_{KG})(s_{HG} - s_{HP})\tau$$
$$> \alpha_H (s_{HG} - s_{HP}) s_{KP} - \alpha_K (s_{KP} - s_{KG}) s_{HP} - (\alpha_K + \alpha_H)(s_{KP} - s_{KG})(s_{HG} - s_{HP}) \geq 0$$

and this implies, as per equation (4.9), $\frac{\partial \ln y_E^*}{\partial \tau} > 0$, i.e. a high fiscalism index of the economy τ corres0.ponds to a high output per unit of effective labour y_E^* in the Mankiw-Romer-Weil long-run equilibrium and a to high level of the long-run growth path of labour productivity.

Equation (4.11) leads to the following conclusions:

- The optimum fiscalism index of the economy $\overline{\tau}$ depends on the elasticity α_K and α_H of output Y with respect to inputs of physical capital K and human capital H, investment rates s_{KG} and s_{HG} of the government sector of the economy and investment rates s_{KP} and s_{HP} of the private sector.
- Because at $s_{KG} < s_{KP}$, $s_{HG} > s_{HP}$, $\alpha_H (s_{HG} - s_{HP}) s_{KP} > \alpha_K (s_{KP} - s_{KG}) s_{HP}$ and

$$\alpha_H (s_{HG} - s_{HP}) s_{KP} < (\alpha_K + \alpha_H)(s_{KP} - s_{KG})(s_{HG} - s_{HP}) + \alpha_K (s_{KP} - s_{KG}) s_{HP},$$

it is true that:

$$\frac{\partial \overline{\tau}}{\partial \alpha_K} = -\alpha_H \frac{(s_{KP} - s_{KG}) s_{HP} + (s_{HG} - s_{HP}) s_{KP}}{(s_{KP} - s_{KG})(s_{HG} - s_{HP})(\alpha_K + \alpha_H)^2} < 0$$

then, the higher the elasticity α_K of output with respect to inputs of physical capital, the lower the optimum fiscalism index of the economy $\overline{\tau}$.

- As:

$$\frac{\partial \overline{\tau}}{\partial \alpha_H} = \alpha_K \frac{(s_{HG} - s_{HP}) s_{KP} + (s_{KP} - s_{KG}) s_{HP}}{(s_{KP} - s_{KG})(s_{HG} - s_{HP})(\alpha_K + \alpha_H)^2} > 0$$

it can be concluded that a high elasticity α_K of output with respect to inputs of human capital corresponds to a high optimum fiscalism index of the economy $\overline{\tau}$.

- Differentiating equation (4.11) with respect to investment rates s_{KG} and s_{HG} in the government sector, we get:

$$\frac{\partial \overline{\tau}}{\partial s_{KG}} = \frac{\alpha_H s_{KP}}{(\alpha_K + \alpha_H)(s_{KP} - s_{KG})^2} > 0$$

and

$$\frac{\partial \overline{\tau}}{\partial s_{HG}} = \frac{\alpha_K s_{HP}}{(\alpha_K + \alpha_H)(s_{HP} - s_{HP})^2} > 0.$$

It follows from the above inequalities that high investment rates in the government sector of the economy analyzed here are accompanied by a high optimum fiscalism index of the economy.

- It follows from:

$$\frac{\partial \overline{\tau}}{\partial s_{KP}} = -\frac{\alpha_H s_{KG}}{(\alpha_K + \alpha_H)(s_{KP} - s_{KG})^2} < 0$$

and

$$\frac{\partial \overline{\tau}}{\partial s_{HP}} = -\frac{\alpha_K s_{HP}}{(\alpha_K + \alpha_H)(s_{HG} - s_{HP})^2} < 0$$

that at high investment rates s_{KP} and s_{HP} in the private sector, the optimum fiscalism index of the economy $\overline{\tau}$ is low.

In case VII, i.e. at $s_{KG} = s_{KP}$ and $s_{HG} < s_{HP}$, the partial derivative $\frac{\partial \ln y_E^*}{\partial \tau}$ is expressed by the formula:

$$\frac{\partial \ln y_E^*}{\partial \tau} = \frac{\alpha_H}{1 - \alpha_K - \alpha_H} \cdot \frac{s_{HG} - s_{HP}}{\tau s_{HG} + (1-\tau) s_{HP}} < 0$$

which means that each increase in the fiscalism index of the economy translates into a reduction in y_E^* and a lower level of the long-run growth path of labour productivity.

In case VIII, i.e. at $s_{KG} > s_{KP}$ and $s_{HG} < s_{HP}$, partial derivative (4.8) can be expressed as:

$$\frac{\partial \ln y_E^*}{\partial \tau} = \frac{\alpha_K (s_{KG} - s_{KP}) s_{HP} - \alpha_H (s_{HP} - s_{HG}) s_{KP} - (\alpha_K + \alpha_H)(s_{KP} - s_{KG})(s_{HG} - s_{HP})\tau}{(1 - \alpha_K - \alpha_H)(s_{HG}\tau + s_{HP}(1-\tau))(s_{KG}\tau + s_{KP}(1-\tau))}. \tag{4.12}$$

Economic conclusions of equation (4.12) are analogous to those drawn from relation (4.9), because case VIII represents an opposite of case VI. Hence, the optimum fiscalism index is given by formula (4.11).

If case IX is true, i.e. $s_{KG} < s_{KP}$ and $s_{HG} < s_{HP}$, the following inequality is satisfied as per equation (4.8):

$$\frac{\partial \ln y_E^*}{\partial \tau} = \frac{\alpha_K}{1-\alpha_K-\alpha_H} \cdot \frac{s_{KG}-s_{KP}}{s_{KG}\tau+s_{KP}(1-\tau)} + \frac{\alpha_H}{1-\alpha_K-\alpha_H} \cdot \frac{s_{HG}-s_{HP}}{s_{HG}\tau+s_{HP}(1-\tau)} < 0$$

which means that under those circumstances, each increase in the fiscalism index of the economy τ leads to a reduction in the output per unit of effective labour y_E^* and brings long-run labour productivity to a lower path of economic growth.

This analysis of the long-run effectiveness or ineffectiveness of expansionary fiscal policy (consisting in an increase in fiscalism index of the economy τ) under conditions of varying ratios of investment rates in the government sector and private sector is summarized in Table 4.1.

The statement contained in Table 4.1 leads to the following conclusions:

- An expansionary fiscal policy of the state is effective (considering long-run economic growth) at each fiscalism index of the economy only if the private sector is characterized by a lower rate of investment in physical capital or human capital than the government sector, at the same or lower rate of investment in the other of the discussed factors of production. The reason is that if the government sector is characterized by higher rates of investment than the private sector (or by one rate greater than and the other equal to that characteristic of the private sector), each increase in the fiscalism index of the economy entails a rise in the rate (rates) of investment in the entire economy, and this in turn leads the economy onto growingly high economic growth paths. The conclusion is that under the analyzed conditions, the most advantageous fiscalism index (considering long-run economic growth) is $\tau = 1$.
- When the private sector is characterized by greater investment rates than the government sector (or by one of those rates being greater at the other equal), each increase in the fiscalism index of the economy reduces joint investment rates (or one of them) and brings the analyzed economy onto a lower path of economic growth. Therefore, the most advantageous fiscalism index of the economy in the described case is $\tau = 0$.

Table 4.1 Long-run effects of expansionary fiscal policy at various ratios between investment rates in the private sector and government sector

	$s_{HG} > s_H > s_{HP}$	$s_{HG} = s_H = s_{HP}$	$s_{HG} < s_H < s_{HP}$
$s_{KG} > s_K > s_{KP}$	Effective	Effective	An optimum fiscalism index exists[a]
$s_{KG} = s_K = s_{KP}$	Effective	Neutral	Ineffective
$s_{KG} < s_K < s_{KP}$	An optimum fiscalism index exists[a]	Ineffective	Ineffective

[a] If $\overline{\tau} \notin (0,1)$, the optimum fiscalism index equals 0% or 100%.

- If the rates of investment in the stocks of physical and human capital in the private sector and in the government sector are equal, fiscal policy has no effect on the level of long-run economic growth path.
- If the private sector is characterized by a greater rate of investment in one of the stocks of capital analyzed in the Mankiw-Romer-Weil model, while the government sector shows a greater rate of investment in the other stock of capital, a fiscalism index exists at which the economy reaches the highest path of economic growth. The index depends both on the rates of investment in the two stocks of capital in the private sector and in the government sector and on the elasticity of production function with respect to inputs of physical and human capital.

This discussion leads to the conclusion that an optimum fiscalism index of the economy τ^* is given in each of the cases considered above (except case I that is rather uninteresting in macroeconomic analyzes) by the formula:

$$\tau^* = \begin{cases} 0 & \text{in cases III, VII, IX or } \bar{\tau} \leq 0 \\ \dfrac{\alpha_H (s_{HG} - s_{HP}) s_{KP} - \alpha_K (s_{KP} - s_{KG}) s_{HP}}{(\alpha_K + \alpha_H)(s_{KP} - s_{KG})(s_{HG} - s_{HP})} & \text{in cases VI, VIII and } \bar{\tau} \in (0,1) \\ 1 & \text{in cases II, IV, V or } \bar{\tau} \geq 1 \end{cases}$$

If we additionally assume that the state can only set the fiscalism index of the economy at the level of $\tau \in [\tau_m;\tau_M] \subset (0;1)$, i.e. that the state can only set that index within the interval $[\tau_m; \tau_M]$ which is acceptable to the private sector of the economy, it must be concluded that a macroeconomic analysis of the effectiveness of fiscal policy makes sense only in the interval $[\tau_m; \tau_M]$. The following cases are possible under the above circumstances:

- If $\tau^* \in [0; \tau_m)$, the optimum fiscalism index of the economy contained within the interval $[\tau_m; \tau_M]$ equals the minimum, socially acceptable fiscalism index τ_m. Although the economy could reach a higher long-run growth path of labour productivity (corresponding to the fiscalism index of the economy τ^*), the above fiscalism index is insufficient to perform minimum functions of the state and the economy will remain on a growth path corresponding to a non-optimum fiscalism index τ_m.
- However, if $\tau^* \in [\tau_m; \tau_M]$, the state should choose the fiscalism index of the economy τ^*, because it is not only optimum for long-run economic growth but also acceptable to the private sector.
- If $\tau^* \in (\tau_M; 1]$, the state should choose a maximum socially acceptable fiscalism index of the economy τ_M, because then the output per unit of effective labour reaches its maximum y_E^* in the long-run equilibrium of the economy (in the interval $[\tau_m; \tau_M]$) and the Mankiw-Romer-Weil economy reaches the highest path of labour productivity in a long term.

4.2.2 A model with public capital

Section 4.2.1 discussed an economic growth model wherein the stocks of physical and human capital (and flows of investments in those stocks) were disaggregated into those financed by the private sector and those financed by the government sector of the economy. Section 4.2.2 contains an analysis of a growth model with two stocks of capital distinguished. Those stocks include (physical and human) capital that can be financed both by the private sector and the government sector and a stock of capital that is financed only by the government sector of the economy. That stock includes physical capital consisting of public social and economic infrastructure, public transport or aimed at environmental protection and human capital generated by state financing of basic research, elementary education, healthcare, etc.

The following assumptions underlie the analysis contained in this section:

1 The production process is described by a production function expressed by the formula:

$$Y(t)=(K(t))^{\alpha K}\,(P(t))^{\alpha P}\,(E(t))^{1-\alpha K-\alpha P}, \tag{4.13}$$

where Y, $E > 0$ have the same meanings as in the model from Section 4.2.1, $K > 0$ is the stock of capital that can be financed by both sectors of the economy, $P > 0$ is the stock of capital financed by the government sector. The parameters α_K and α_P represent elasticities of output with respect to the stocks of capital distinguished in this model. It is assumed about these parameters that $\alpha_K, \alpha_P, (\alpha_K+\alpha_P) \in (0,1)$. It can be concluded from equation (4.13) that both the government sector and the private sector benefit from accumulated capital that is financed only by the government sector (i.e. from capital accumulation P). The reason is that an increase in capital P entails a rise in capital productivity K, because that productivity is given by the formula:

$$\frac{Y(t)}{K(t)}=(K(t))^{\alpha K-1}\,(P(t))^{\alpha P}\,(E(t))^{1-\alpha K-\alpha P}.$$

2 Growths in capital financed by both sectors of the economy $\dot{K}$ and in capital financed only by the government sector $\dot{P}$ are described by the following differential equations:

$$\dot{K}(t)=I_K(t)-\delta_K K(t) \tag{4.14a}$$

and

$$\dot{P}(t)=I_P(t)-\delta_P P(t), \tag{4.14b}$$

where I_K denotes investments in capital K financed by both sectors of the economy, I_P represents investments financed by the government sector, and δ_K, $\delta_P \in (0,1)$ – depreciation rates of the discussed stocks of capital.

3 The state collects taxes using a fiscalism index $\tau \in (0,1)$. Thus, the state receives an income equal τY, and the private sector – an income given by $(1-\tau)Y$.
4 The public sector allocates an s_Pth fraction of its income τY to investments in capital *P*, s_{KG}th fraction to investments in capital *K*. We also assume that s_K, s_P, $(s_K + s_P) \in (0,1)$.
5 The private sector allocates to investments in capital *K* a fraction of its income $(1-\tau)Y$ equal $s_{KP} \in (0,1)$.
6 Units of effective labour are defined by a trajectory given by equation (2.12a).

It follows from assumptions 4–5 that total investments in stocks *K* and *P* are given by the formulas:

$$I_K(t) = (s_{KG}\tau + s_{KP}(1-\tau))Y(t)$$

and

$$I_P(t) = s_P \tau Y(t).$$

It follows from the above formulas and from equation (4.14ab) that the accumulation of various stocks of capital is described by the equations:

$$\dot{K}(t) = (s_{KG}\tau + s_{KP}(1-\tau))Y(t) - \delta_K K(t) \tag{4.15a}$$

and

$$\dot{P}(t) = s_P \tau Y(t) - \delta_P P(t) \tag{4.15b}$$

The growth model described by equations (4.13), (4.15a,b) and (2.12a) is mathematically characterized by the same properties as the original Mankiw-Romer-Weil model. Therefore, the long-run output per unit of effective labour is described by equation (3.18c). Hence, we get:

$$\ln y_E^* = \frac{\alpha_K \ln \frac{s_{KG}\tau + s_{KP}(1-\tau)}{\delta_K + g + n} + \alpha_P \ln \frac{s_P \tau}{\delta_P + g + n}}{1 - \alpha_K - \alpha_P}. \tag{4.16}$$

It follows from equation (4.16) that (like in the model from Section 4.2.1) the higher the rates of investment (made by both the government sector and the private sector) or the lower the depreciation rates of the analyzed stocks of capital, or the lower the growth rate of the number of workers, the greater the value of y_E^* and the higher the level of the long-run growth path of labour productivity.

Differentiating relation (4.16) with respect to the fiscalism index τ, we get:

$$\frac{\partial \ln y_E^*}{\partial \tau} = \frac{(\alpha_K + \alpha_P)(s_{KG} - s_{KP})\tau + \alpha_P s_{KP}}{(1 - \alpha_K - \alpha_P)\tau(s_{KG}\tau + s_{KP}(1-\tau))}. \tag{4.17}$$

When analyzing equation (4.17) in the context of expansionary fiscal policy, two cases must be considered. First, a case wherein the rate of investment by the government sector s_{KG} is not less than the rate of investment by the private sector s_{KP} and, second, a case wherein $s_{KG} < s_{KP}$.

In the first case, derivative (4.17) is positive, so that an increase in the fiscalism index of the economy entails a rise in y_E^* and brings the economy onto a higher long-run trajectory of labour productivity.

If $s_{KG} < s_{KP}$, it is true that:

$$\frac{\partial \ln y_E^*}{\partial \tau} > 0 \Leftrightarrow \tau < \frac{\alpha_P s_{KP}}{(\alpha_K + \alpha_P)(s_{KP} - s_{KG})},$$

and

$$\frac{\partial \ln y_E^*}{\partial \tau} \langle 0 \Leftrightarrow \tau \rangle \frac{\alpha_P s_{KP}}{(\alpha_K + \alpha_P)(s_{KP} - s_{KG})},$$

so that an optimum fiscalism index of the economy $\overline{\tau}$ is given by the formula:

$$\overline{\tau} = \frac{\alpha_P s_{KP}}{(\alpha_K + \alpha_P)(s_{KP} - s_{KG})}. \tag{4.18}$$

Importantly, the rate $\overline{\tau}$ does not need to belong to the interval (0, 1). Hence, an optimum fiscalism index can be expressed as:

$$\tau^* = \begin{cases} 0 & \text{if } \overline{\tau} \le 0 \\ \dfrac{\alpha_P s_{KP}}{(\alpha_K + \alpha_P)(s_{KP} - s_{KG})} & \text{if } \overline{\tau} \in (0,1) \\ 1 & \text{if } \overline{\tau} \ge 0 \end{cases}. \tag{4.19}$$

An analysis of equation (4.19) additionally assuming that $\overline{\tau} \in (0,1)$ leads to the following conclusions:

- Since $\frac{\partial \tau^*}{\partial \alpha_K} = -\frac{\alpha_P s_{KP}}{(\alpha_K + \alpha_P)^2 (s_{KP} - s_{KG})} < 0$, the higher the elasticity of output with respect to capital stock that can be financed by both sectors of the economy, the lower the optimum fiscalism index.
- And the higher the elasticity of output with respect to capital *P*, the higher the optimum fiscalism index, because $\frac{\partial \tau^*}{\partial \alpha_P} = \frac{\alpha_K s_{KP}}{(\alpha_K + \alpha_P)^2 (s_{KP} - s_{KG})} > 0$.
- Given that $\frac{\partial \tau^*}{\partial s_{KP}} = -\frac{\alpha_P s_{KG}}{(\alpha_K + \alpha_P)(s_{KP} - s_{KG})^2} < 0$, the greater the fraction of private sector's output allocated to investment, the lower the optimum fiscalism index.

- And the higher the rate of investment by the government sector in capital K, the higher the optimum fiscalism index of the economy, because $\frac{\partial \tau^*}{\partial s_{KG}} = \frac{\alpha_P s_{KP}}{(\alpha_K + \alpha_P)(s_{KP} - s_{KG})^2} > 0.$

Since the relations between τ^* described by equation (4.19) and the interval of socially acceptable fiscalism $[\tau_m, \tau_M]$ are analogous as between τ^* in the model from Section 4.2.1 and that interval, the state (when choosing a fiscalism index of the economy) should adopt similar criteria as indicated in Section 4.2.1. This means that (first) at $\tau^* < \tau_m$ the fiscalism index τ_m should be chosen, and (second) in the case of $\tau^* \tau[\tau_m, \tau_M]$, the state should choose the fiscalism index of the economy $\bar{\tau}$ given by equation (4.18), and (third) when $\tau^* > \tau_M$, the state should choose the maximum socially acceptable fiscalism index τ_M.

4.3 Monetary rules in a Domar-Solow model

The following assumptions underlie the model of monetary rules in a Domar-Solow economy:

1. The production process (like in the Solow model with the Cobb-Douglas production function) is described by a macroeconomic production function given by the formula:

$$Y^S(t) = (K(t))^\alpha \left(e^{gt} L(t)\right)^{1-\alpha}, \tag{4.20}$$

   where Y^S is the aggregate supply that could only be achieved using the full production capacity of the economy, K represents inputs of physical capital, L denotes inputs of labour, $g > 0$ is the Harrodian rate of technological progress, and $\alpha \in (0,1)$ is the elasticity of aggregate supply Y^S with respect to capital inputs K.
2. The value of aggregate demand Y^D in a Domar-Solow economy depends on the real interest rate r, the value of aggregate supply Y^S and the Keynesian multiplier of autonomous spending $m > 1$. The effect of that multiplier is analogous to its effect in the original Keynesian growth model proposed by Domar (1946, 1957). The influence of real interest rate on the value of aggregate demand Y^D results from its effect on consumer demand, investment demand and (through interest rate parity and the exchange rate fixing process) on net exports. It is also assumed that the elasticity of aggregate demand with respect to the real interest rate equals $-\beta$, where $\beta \in (0,1)$. The long-run effect of aggregate supply on the value of aggregate demand in the economy results from the fact that an increase in output entails a rise in demand in a long term due to a higher income from production factors. Thus, we assume in the below discussion that the aggregate demand rises with an increase in the aggregate supply, and its elasticity with respect to that supply amounts

to $\gamma \in (0,1)$. The fact that $\gamma < 1$ can be economically explained: if the aggregate demand depends on autonomous spending $a > 0$ as per equation $Y^D = a + cY$ (where the marginal propensity to consume c belongs to the interval (0;1)), then:

$$\frac{\dot{Y}^D}{Y^D} = \frac{c\dot{Y}}{a + cY} < \frac{\dot{Y}}{Y}.$$

Consequently, the function of aggregate demand can be expressed as follows in the economic growth model analyzed here:

$$Y^D(t) = m \cdot \left(Y^S(t)\right)^{\gamma} \cdot \left(r(t)\right)^{-\beta}. \tag{4.21}$$

3 An increase in the stock of capital $\dot{K}$ (like in the Solow model) represents the difference between investment I and capital depreciation δK, where the capital depreciation rate δ belongs to the interval (0,1). It is assumed about the investment function $I(r)$ that it is given by the formula $I(r) = I_0 r^{-\beta}$ (where $I_0 > 0$) which implies that $-\beta$ also represents the elasticity of investment with respect to the real interest rate. Thus, we implicitly assume that the sensitivity of investment I to fluctuations in the real interest rate r equals the sensitivity of other components of the aggregate demand Y^D to that macroeconomic quantity. The equation of increase in the stock of capital is expressed as:

$$\dot{K}(t) = I_0 \cdot \left(r(t)\right)^{-\beta} - \delta K(t). \tag{4.22}$$

4 The central bank follows three rules in its policy of real interest rates. First, the bank prevents the value of aggregate demand Y^D in the economy from exceeding the value of aggregate supply Y^S, because a surplus demand would exert inflationary pressure. Second, the central bank adapts the value of demand to the aggregate supply, to avoid unused production capacities in the stock of capital accumulated in the economy. Third, assuming that at time $t = 0$, the unemployment rate u equals the unemployment rate of equilibrium u^*, the central bank endeavours to maintain at any time $t \in [0; +\infty)$ an unemployment rate equal to the unemployment rate at time $t = 0$.[3] It follows from the first two rules indicated above that for any $t \in [0; +\infty)$:

$$Y^D(t) = Y^S(t), \tag{4.23}$$

the third rule leads to an equation of long-run growth rate of the number of workers:

$$\frac{\dot{L}(t)}{L(t)} = n, \tag{4.24}$$

where $n > 0$ represents the growth rate of the number of workers that equals the growth rate of labour supply that in a long term results principally from demographic factors. It follows from the above assumptions (about the rules of long-run monetary policy) that the central bank should maintain the real interest rates r at such a level that equations (4.23 and 4.24) are satisfied and the influence of those interest rates on the equilibrium in the Domar-Solow economy is exercised through the channels described by formulas (4.20–4.22).

The approach to achieving those objectives by modifications or the real rather than nominal interest rates can also be explained as follows. An approximate relation between the real (r) and nominal (R) interest rates is described by the identity: $r = R - \pi$, where π represents the inflation rate.[4] Let also the long-time inflation rate be given by the formula:

$$\pi(t) = \mu(t) - \frac{\dot{Y}(t)}{Y(t)} + h\frac{Y^D(t) - Y^S(t)}{Y^S(t)} \tag{4.25}$$

where μ denotes the growth rate of nominal money supply, and $h > 0$ is a coefficient describing the effect of relative output gap $\frac{Y^D - Y^S}{Y^S}$ on the inflation rate π. An assumption follows from relation (4.25) that the inflation rate can result from monetary factors $\left(\mu - \frac{\dot{Y}}{Y}\right)$ and from the inflationary pressure caused by the occurrence of output gap $\left(\frac{Y^D - Y^S}{Y^S}\right)$ in the economy. However, if the central bank manages to eliminate the output gap $\left(\frac{Y^D - Y^S}{Y^S} = 0\right)$, inflation will only be caused by monetary sources. Then, equation (4.25) can be reduced to the relation:

$$\pi(t) = \mu(t) - \frac{\dot{Y}(t)}{Y(t)}$$

and the real interest rate r is given by the formula:

$$r(t) = R(t) - \pi(t) = R(t) - \mu(t) + \frac{\dot{Y}(t)}{Y(t)}. \tag{4.26}$$

If we additionally assume that the central bank follows a policy of increase in nominal money supply (and not in interest rates) to achieve a long-run inflation target equal π^T, it must set a growth rate of nominal money supply μ at:

$$\mu(t) = \pi^T + \frac{\dot{Y}(t)}{Y(t)}.$$

This in turn reduces equation (4.26) to the relation:

$$r(t) = R(t) - \pi(t)$$

and then changes in nominal interest rates R (at an inflation target π^T) are identical with changes in real interest rates r.

Let Y represent the output produced in the economy that satisfies the equilibrium condition (4.23); then, the following relation is true:

$$Y(t) = Y^D(t) = Y^S(t). \tag{4.27}$$

It follows from equations (4.21) and (4.27) that:

$$Y(t) = m \cdot (Y(t))^{\gamma} \cdot (r(t))^{-\beta},$$

which leads to the formula:

$$r(t) = m^{1/\beta} (Y(t))^{\frac{\gamma-1}{\beta}}. \tag{4.28}$$

Equation (4.28) describes a time path of the real interest rate r and makes it depending, e.g., on the Keynesian multiplier m and the value of output Y. It follows from this equation that the real interest rate r (that brings a Domar-Solow economy in the state of equilibrium) is directly proportional to the Keynesian multiplier m and inversely proportional to the value of output Y.

Substituting the production function (4.20) into equation (4.28), and remembering that under equilibrium conditions $Y^S = Y$, we get:

$$r(t) = m^{1/\beta} (K(t))^{\frac{\alpha(\gamma-1)}{\beta}} \left(e^{gt} L(t)\right)^{\frac{(1-\alpha)(\gamma-1)}{\beta}},$$

which gives (taking the logarithm of both sides and differentiating with respect to time):

$$g_r(t) = -\frac{1-\gamma}{\beta}\left(\alpha G_K(t) + (1-\alpha)\left(g + \frac{\dot{L}(t)}{L(t)}\right)\right),$$

where $g_r = \dot{r}/r$ represents the growth rate of interest rate, and $G_K = \dot{K}/K$ is the growth rate of capital stock. Substituting the growth rate of the number of workers from equation (4.24) into the above equation, we arrive at the relation:

$$g_r(t) = -\frac{1-\gamma}{\beta}\left(\alpha G_K(t) + (1-\alpha)(g+n)\right). \tag{4.29}$$

Equation (4.29) makes the growth rate of real interest rate g_r depending on the growth rate of the stock of physical capital G_K, the growth rate of the number of workers n and the Harrodian rate of technological progress g.

Equation (4.22) can be expressed as:

$$G_K(t) + \delta = I_0 \frac{(r(t))^{-\beta}}{K(t)},$$

which leads to the formula:

$$\frac{\dot{G}_K(t)}{G_K(t)+\delta}=-\beta g_r(t)-G_K(t). \tag{4.30}$$

Since it follows from equation (4.29) that:

$$-\beta g_r(t)=(1-\gamma)\big(\alpha G_K(t)+(1-\alpha)(g+n)\big),$$

from the above relation and from equation (4.30), we arrive at the following differential equation (Riccati differential equation):

$$\dot{G}_K(t)=\big(G_K(t)+\delta\big)\big(\kappa_1-\kappa_2 G_K(t)\big), \tag{4.31}$$

where $\kappa_1=(1-\alpha)(1-\gamma)(g+n)>0$ and $\kappa_2=1-(1-\gamma)\alpha>0$. Since it follows from equation (4.22) that $G_K=\frac{\dot{K}}{K}>-\delta$, differential equation (4.31) is analyzed only at $G_K>-\delta$.

Relation (4.31) makes an increase in the growth rates of capital $\dot{G}_K$ depending on growth rates of that variable, i.e. G_K. Since $G_K>-\delta$, then $\operatorname{sgn}\dot{G}_K=\operatorname{sgn}(\kappa_1-\kappa_2 G_K)$. This means that if the growth rate of stock of capital belongs to the interval $\left(-\delta,\frac{\kappa_1}{\kappa_2}\right)$, then $\dot{G}_K>0$, and if $G_K>\frac{\kappa_1}{\kappa_2}$, then $\dot{G}_K<0$. It follows that the stable steady-state point of differential equation (4.31) is given by a growth rate $G_K^*=\frac{\kappa_1}{\kappa_2}$. That stable steady-state point can also be expressed as:

$$G_K^*=\frac{\kappa_1}{\kappa_2}=\frac{(1-\gamma)(1-\alpha)(g+n)}{1-\alpha(1-\gamma)}. \tag{4.32}$$

It follows from equation (4.32) that the long-run growth rate of capital G_K^* in the Domar-Solow model equilibrium is directly proportional to the rate of technological progress g (because $\frac{\partial G_K^*}{\partial g}=\frac{(1-\gamma)(1-\alpha)}{1-\alpha(1-\gamma)}>0$) and to the growth rate of the number of workers n (because $\frac{\partial G_K^*}{\partial n}=\frac{(1-\gamma)(1-\alpha)}{1-\alpha(1-\gamma)}>0$), and inversely proportional to the elasticity of output with respect to capital $\alpha\left(\frac{\partial G_K^*}{\partial \alpha}=-\gamma\frac{(1-\gamma)(g+n)}{(1-\alpha(1-\gamma))^2}<0\right)$ and to the elasticity of aggregate demand with respect to aggregate supply, i.e. the parameter $\gamma\left(\frac{\partial G_K^*}{\partial \gamma}=-\frac{(1-\gamma)(g+n)}{(1-\alpha+\alpha\gamma)^2}<0\right)$.

Taking the logarithm of both sides and differentiating with respect to time t the production function (4.20), we get:

$$G_Y(t)=\alpha G_K(t)+(1-\alpha)\left(g+\frac{\dot{L}(t)}{L(t)}\right),$$

where $G_Y = \dot{Y}/Y$ denotes the growth rate of output. Because, as per equation (4.24), $\frac{\dot{L}}{L} = n$, then the above equation can be expressed as:

$$G_Y(t) = \alpha G_K(t) + (1-\alpha)(g+n),$$

or at $t \to +\infty$:

$$G_Y^* = \lim_{t \to +\infty} G_Y(t) = \alpha G_K^* + (1-\alpha)(g+n). \tag{4.33}$$

Substituting the long-run growth rate of capital from (4.32) into equation (4.33), we arrive at the relation:

$$G_Y^* = \frac{(1-\alpha)(g+n)}{1-\alpha(1-\gamma)} \tag{4.34}$$

Equation (4.34) leads to the following conclusions. First, the long-run growth rate of output (like the long-run growth rate of stock of capital) depends on the Harrodian rate of technological progress g, on the growth rate of the number of workers n, on the elasticity of output with respect to capital (that is α) and on the elasticity of aggregate demand with respect to aggregate supply (that is γ). Second, high values of g and n correspond to a high long-run growth rate of output $\left(\frac{\partial G_Y^*}{\partial g} = \frac{\partial G_Y^*}{\partial n} = \frac{1-\alpha}{1-\alpha(1-\gamma)} > 0\right)$. Third, the higher the elasticities α and γ, the lower the rate G_Y^* $\left(\frac{\partial G_Y^*}{\partial \alpha} = -\frac{\gamma(g+n)}{(1-\alpha+\alpha\gamma)^2} < 0 \text{ and } \frac{\partial G_Y^*}{\partial \gamma} = -\frac{\alpha(1-\alpha)(g+n)}{(1-\alpha+\alpha\gamma)^2} < 0\right)$. Fourth, comparing the long-run growth rate of output (4.34) to the long-run growth rate of stock of capital (4.32) and with growth rates of output and capital (equal $g+n$) in the Solow model equilibrium, we conclude that the following inequalities are true:

$$\frac{(1-\gamma)(1-\alpha)(g+n)}{1-\alpha+\alpha\gamma} < \frac{(1-\alpha)(g+n)}{1-\alpha+\alpha\gamma} < g+n,$$

and it follows from them that the long-run growth rate of capital G_K^* in a Domar-Solow model is lower than the long-run growth rate of output G_Y^* in that economic growth model, which in turn is lower than the long-run growth rates of capital and output in the original Solow model.

Moreover, it follows from equation (4.29) that $\operatorname{sgn} \dot{g}(t) = -\operatorname{sgn} \dot{G}_K(t)$. Thus, if the growth rate of capital is greater/less than $\frac{(1-\gamma)(1-\alpha)(g+n)}{1-\alpha(1-\gamma)}$, the growth rates of interest rate at subsequent moments t are increasingly high. In a long term, the growth rate of interest rate g_r approaches g_r^* described by the formula:

$$g_r^* = \lim_{t \to +\infty} g_r(t) = -\frac{1-\alpha}{\beta}\left(\alpha G_K^* + (1-\alpha)(g+n)\right).$$

and this together with (4.32) leads to:

$$g_r^* = -\frac{(1-\gamma)(1-\alpha)(g+n)}{(1-\alpha(1-\gamma))\beta}. \tag{4.35}$$

It follows from equation (4.35) that the long-run growth rate of interest rate is directly proportional to the elasticities α, β and γ, because:

$$\frac{\partial g_r^*}{\partial \alpha} = \frac{\gamma(1-\alpha)(g+n)}{\beta(1-\alpha(1-\gamma))^2} > 0,$$

$$\frac{\partial g_r^*}{\partial \beta} = \frac{(1-\gamma)(1-\alpha)(g+n)}{(1-\alpha(1-\gamma))\beta^2} > 0$$

and

$$\frac{\partial g_r^*}{\partial \gamma} = \frac{(1-\alpha)(g+n)}{(1-\alpha(1-\gamma))^2\beta} > 0$$

and inversely proportional to the rate of technological progress g and the growth rate of the number of workers n, because:

$$\frac{\partial g_r^*}{\partial g} = \frac{\partial g_r^*}{\partial n} = -\frac{(1-\gamma)(1-\alpha)}{(1-\alpha(1-\gamma))\beta} < 0$$

4.4 Conclusions

The discussion contained in this chapter can be summarized as follows:

I The analyzes of the effect of fiscal policy on the process of long-run economic growth done in Section 4.2.1 (based on an extended Mankiw-Romer-Weil growth model) were based on the disaggregation of the rates of investment in physical and human capital stocks. That disaggregation meant that investments in those stocks of capital were divided into investment made by the private sector and investment made by the government sector. This type of extension of the Mankiw-Romer-Weil economic growth model makes possible an analysis of the effect of fiscalism index of the economy on the process of long-run economic growth.

II The discussion contained in that section leads to the conclusion that the higher the rates of investment in physical and human capital in both analyzed sectors of the economy, the higher (at a given fiscalism index of the economy) the path of long-run economic growth. However, the higher (lower) the fiscalism index of the economy, the stronger (weaker) influence is exerted on the location of that economic growth path by the rates of investment in the private sector (government sector).

III However, the favourable effect of a high fiscalism index of the economy on the location of that long-run economic growth path is possible only if the government sector is characterized by a rate of investment that is higher than that of the private sector in at least one of the stocks of capital considered in an extended Mankiw-Romer-Weil model, with an equal or greater rate of investment in the other stock of capital. If the private sector is characterized by higher investment rates (or by one investment rate higher than in the government sector and the other equal to that in the government sector), a low fiscalism index of the economy is more favourable to long-run economic growth.

IV If the private sector is characterized by a higher rate of investment in the stock of physical or human capital and the government sector is characterized by the second of the investment rates analyzed in Chapter 4, an optimum fiscalism index of the economy exists. That fiscalism index is described as an optimum because it enables the Mankiw-Romer-Weil economy to reach the highest long-run growth path of labour productivity. That index is directly proportional to the rates of investment in the government sector and inversely proportional to the rates of investment in the private sector. Moreover, an optimum fiscalism index of the economy also depends on the elasticity of output with respect to physical and human capital. If the government sector is characterized by a higher rate of investment in the stock of physical (human) capital than the private sector, the optimum fiscalism index of the economy is directly proportional to the elasticity of production with respect to inputs of physical (human) capital and inversely proportional to the elasticity of output with respect to inputs of human (physical) capital.

V The disaggregation of physical capital and human capital done in Section 4.2.2 into a stock of capital that can be financed either by the private sector or the government sector and a stock of capital that can only be financed by the government sector of the economy introduces a modification to the previous conclusions. Given the above assumption, if the government sector is characterized by a higher (than the private sector) rate of investment in the stock of capital financed by both sectors of the economy, an increase in the fiscalism index always brings the economy onto a higher path of economic growth. If the private sector is characterized by a higher rate of investment in that stock of capital, an optimum fiscalism index exists. Moreover, that index is directly proportional to the rate of investment made by the government sector in the stock of capital financed by both sectors and to the elasticity of output with respect to capital financed only by the government sector of the economy. Additionally, an optimum fiscalism index is inversely proportional to the rate of investment made by the private sector and to the elasticity of output with respect to capital financed by both analyzed economy sectors.

VI Since an optimum fiscalism index of the economy (in both models analyzed in this chapter) can assume any value, and microeconomic entities certainly accept fiscalism indexes contained within a definite, socially acceptable interval, the optimum fiscalism index does not need to be a value that the state can impose on the economy. If an optimum fiscalism index of the economy belongs to the interval of socially acceptable fiscalism, the state can choose optimum fiscalism by increasing or reducing the fiscalism index of the economy and bring the economy to the highest path of long-run economic growth. However, if an optimum fiscalism index of the economy is located below the lower (above the upper) socially acceptable limit, the state, aiming to bring the economy to the highest growth path of labour productivity in a long term, can only set a fiscalism index of the economy at the lower (upper) limit of the socially acceptable interval of fiscalism.

VII The larger the interval of socially acceptable fiscalism, i.e. the more freedom the state enjoys in setting the fiscalism index, the more probable is that the optimum fiscalism index will be contained in the socially acceptable interval. This in turn increases the probability that fiscal policy can bring the economy to the highest growth path in a long term.

VIII However, the state can place the optimum fiscalism index of the economy within the socially acceptable interval by changing its investment rates. A change in the combination of investment rates in the government sector together with setting an optimum fiscalism index of the economy within an interval acceptable to microeconomic entities will result in the economy being brought onto the highest available (given the rates of investment by microeconomic entities) path of economic growth.

IX In an analysis of the effect of monetary policy (real interest rates set by the central bank) on the equilibrium of long-run economic growth, a compilation of the Domar and Solow models provides a useful growth model. The reason is that a change in real interest rates should lead to a change in investment outlays in the economy. This will affect both the demand side of the economy (through Keynesian multiplier effects) and its supply side (by a change in the growth rate of the stock of physical capital). A compilation of the Domar growth model (effects of investments on demand and supply) with the Solow model (with its elastic capital-output ratio resulting from the Cobb-Douglas production function) enables us to determine a long-run equilibrium of the economy that is free from the problem of a unique growth path of investments that enables the economy to fully use its available production capacities (as is in the original Domar model).

X Moreover, that compilation is also useful when establishing long-run rules of monetary policy followed by the central bank and consisting in changes to the real interest rate. It follows from the Domar-Solow economic growth model analyzed in this chapter that the central bank can adapt the real interest rate to the growth rate of capital stock, aiming to fully use production capacities available in the economy. The growth rate of real interest rate under those conditions is a linear decreasing function of the growth rate of physical capital stock. The reason is that under the conditions of a high growth rate of capital, the central bank should reduce real interest rates at a tempo preventing a fall in the aggregate demand in the economy below the value of its aggregate supply. From this point of view, a rise in the real interest rate can only be reasonable if the growth rate of capital is very low, because under such circumstances maintaining a low value of the real interest rate entails the risk of expanding aggregate demand and consequently of short- or long-run inflationary pressure.

XI It also follows from the Domar-Solow model discussed in this chapter that if the central bank follows the described monetary rules, the growth rates of capital and output will reach in a long run (like in the neoclassical Solow, Mankiw-Romer-Weil and Nonneman-Vanhoudt growth models) a certain constant level determined to a significant extent by the exogenous Harrodian rate of technological progress and by the growth rate of the number of workers. Importantly, the long-run growth rates of those macroeconomic variables in Domar-Solow models are lower than the growth rates of those variables in neoclassical economic growth models. The reason is that the neoclassical models ignore limitations to demand (related to the process of economic growth) and analyze only a path of aggregate supply while "in the described reality, the theoretical assumption that output will reach its potential level is usually not satisfied" (Welfe, 2000, p. 64). A Domar-Solow model considers also limitations to demand in the process of economic growth and thus leads to a solution with long-run growth rates lower than in the neoclassical models.

Notes

1 The fiscalism index of the economy τ analyzed here can be formally expressed as:

$$\tau = \frac{T(t) + \dot{D}(t)}{Y(t)},$$

where T is the total of revenues from taxes, customs duties, etc., $\dot{D}$ denotes the present net increase in public debt, and Y denotes the output.

2 The private sector is understood as all households and enterprises (regardless of their ownership). The investment rate of that sector is defined as the ratio of its total investment outlays financed from own resources (not from subsidies or transfers from the government budget) to its disposable income (where taxes also include a net increase in public debt financed by households and enterprises). This means that investment financed by the private sector from subsidies or transfers from the government budget are included in investment of the government sector of the economy.

3 Certainly, if the initial unemployment rate u is greater of less than the unemployment rate of equilibrium u^*, certain adaptive mechanisms on the labour market must take place in a short and medium term, to make u equal u^*. However, those mechanisms can be subject to short- and medium-term rather than to long-run macroeconomic analyzes.

4 Precisely, the real interest rate should be expressed as: $r = \frac{1+R}{1+\pi} - 1 = \frac{R-\pi}{1+r}$. However, a simplified form of the real interest rate equation (as $r = R - \pi$) has no material effect on the below discussion.

5 Economic growth at returns to scale conditions

5.1 Introduction

We analyzed neoclassical economic growth models in the preceding chapters, assuming that the production process is characterized by constant returns to scale (i.e. when the production function is homogeneous of degree 1). In this chapter, we will depart from that assumption and analyze the long-run equilibrium in those models when the economy is affected by decreasing or increasing returns to scale (the degree of homogeneity of the production function will be higher or less than 1).

The subsequent sections of this chapter will contain analyzes of a single capital (Solow) model, a two-capital (Mankiw-Romer-Weil) model and a multiple-capital (Nonneman-Vanhoudt) model with a degree of homogeneity of the production function different from 1. We will also derive golden rules of capital accumulation under conditions of returns to scale in the production process.

The growth models described in this chapter were proposed in the studies by Tokarski (2007, 2008b, 2009, Chapter 9), Tokarski (2011, Chapter 7) and Dykas, Sulima, and Tokarski (2008).

5.2 Returns to scale in a single-capital (Solow) model

The following assumption about the economy underlies the discussion contained in this section:

1 The production process is described by a power (Cobb-Douglas) production function given by the formula:

$$Y(t)=\left(K(t)\right)^{\alpha}\left(E(t)\right)^{\Theta-\alpha}, \tag{5.1}$$

where Y, K, $E>0$ and $\alpha \in (0,1)$ are understood as in the Solow model from Section 2.3.1, and $\Theta \in (\alpha, 1+\alpha)$ is the degree of homogeneity of function (5.1). Hence, if that degree belongs to the interval $(\alpha,1)$, decreasing returns to scale are observed, and at $\Theta \in (1,1+\alpha)$, increasing

DOI: 10.4324/9781003323792-6

returns to scale take place. Importantly, given the production function analyzed here, (first) the elasticity of output with respect to labour inputs equals $\Theta-\alpha$ and (second) the production process is characterized by diminishing marginal productivities of both capital inputs and labour.

2 The process of capital accumulation is described by a differential equation like in the original Solow model:

$$\dot{K}(t)=sY(t)-\delta K(t), \tag{5.2}$$

where $s,\delta \in (0,1)$ denote (respectively) the savings/investment rate and the capital depreciation rate.

3 The trajectory of units of effective labour E is described by the equation:

$$E(t)=e^{(g+n)t}, \tag{5.3}$$

where $g,n>0$ are (respectively) the Harrodian rate of technological progress and the growth rate of the number of workers (thus, the trajectory of the number of workers is described by the equation $L(t)=e^{nt}$).

Let $y = Y/L$ denote labour productivity, and $k = K/L$ – capital-labour ratio. Let also $G_Y=\dot{Y}/Y$ and $G_K=\dot{K}/K$ denote the growth rates of output and capital, and $g_y=\dot{y}/y$ and $g_k=\dot{k}/k$ – the growth rates of labour productivity and capital-labour ratio. Since, as per assumption 3, the number of workers rises at the growth rate n, the growth rate of labour productivity (capital-labour ratio) equals the difference between the growth rate of product stream (capital stock) and the growth rate of the number of workers.

Substituting equation (5.3) into the production function (5.1), we get:

$$Y(t)=\left(K(t)\right)^{\alpha} e^{(\Theta-\alpha)(g+n)t}, \tag{5.4}$$

which gives (taking the logarithm of both sides and differentiating with respect to time t):

$$G_Y(t)=\alpha G_K(t)+(\Theta-\alpha)\mu, \tag{5.5}$$

where $\mu=g+n>0$ is the growth rate of units of effective labour. It follows from equation (5.5) that the growth rate of output equals the sum of growth rates of capital and units of effective labour weighted by the elasticities α and $\Theta-\alpha$.

Differential equation (5.2) can be expressed as:

$$G_K(t)=s\frac{Y(t)}{K(t)}-\delta \Rightarrow G_K(t)+\delta=s\frac{Y(t)}{K(t)},$$

which gives (taking the logarithm of both sides and differentiating with respect to time t):

$$\frac{\dot{G}_K(t)}{G_K(t)+\delta}=G_Y(t)-G_K(t),$$

or, multiplied by $G_K+\delta$ and considering equation (5.5):

$$\dot{G}_K(t)=\left(G_K(t)+\delta\right)\left((\Theta-\alpha)\mu-(1-\alpha)G_K(t)\right). \tag{5.6}$$

The differential equation makes an increase in the growth rate of capital depending on the growth rate of that variable. It is a Riccati differential equation like equation (4.31) and will be considered at $G_K>-\delta$. Therefore, $\operatorname{sgn}\dot{G}_K=\operatorname{sgn}\left((\Theta-\alpha)-(1-\alpha)G_K\right)$. Hence, for any $G_K\in\left(-\delta,\frac{(\Theta-\alpha)\mu}{1-\alpha}\right)$, we get $\dot{G}_K>0$, and if $G_K>\frac{(\Theta-\alpha)\mu}{1-\alpha}$, then $\dot{G}_K<0$. This leads to the conclusion that the stable steady-state point of differential equation (5.6) G_K^* is described by the formula:

$$G_K^*=\frac{(\Theta-\alpha)\mu}{1\quad\alpha}=\frac{(\Theta-\alpha)(g+n)}{1-\alpha}. \tag{5.7}$$

The rate G_K^* represents a long-run growth rate of the stock of capital in the growth model analyzed here. Equation (5.7) leads to the following economic conclusions. First, the long-run growth rate of capital depends on four factors: the Harrodian rate of technological progress g, the growth rate of the number of workers n, the elasticity α of output with respect to capital inputs and the degree of homogeneity of the production function Θ. Second, it follows from $\frac{\partial G_K^*}{\partial g}=\frac{\partial G_K^*}{\partial n}=\frac{\Theta-\alpha}{1-\alpha}>0$ that the higher the Harrodian rate of technological progress g or the growth rate of the number of workers n, the higher the long-run growth rate of capital G_K^*. Third, the direction of the effect that elasticity α exerts on the analyzed growth rate depends on the degree of homogeneity of the production function Θ. The reason is that $\frac{\partial G_K^*}{\partial\alpha}=\frac{(\Theta-1)(g+n)}{(1-\alpha)^2}$, hence if increasing/decreasing returns to scale take place, then the higher the elasticity α, the higher/lower the long-run growth rate of capital. Fourth, it follows from $\frac{\partial G_K^*}{\partial\Theta}=\frac{g+n}{1-\alpha}>0$ that the higher the degree of homogeneity of the production function, the higher the long-term growth rate of capital.

Using $G_Y^*=\lim_{t\to+\infty}G_Y(t)$ to designate the long-run growth rate of output and given equations (5.5) and (5.7), we can demonstrate that the long-run growth rate of output equals the long-run growth rate of capital, hence

$G_Y^* = \frac{(\Theta-\alpha)(g+n)}{1-\alpha} = G_K^*$. This means that the long-run growth rate of product stream equals the long-term growth rate of the capital stock.

Since at any moment $t \geq 0$, the growth rates of labour productivity (g_y) and capital-labour ratio (g_k) equal the differences between the growth rates of output (G_Y) and capital (G_K) and the growth rate of the number of workers (n), in the long-run equilibrium, we get particularly:

$$g_y^* = G_Y^* - n \wedge g_k^* = G_K^* - n,$$

where g_y^* and g_k^* denote the long-run growth rates of (respectively) labour productivity and capital-labour ratio. Substituting the long-run growth rates of output and capital equal $\frac{(\Theta-\alpha)(g+n)}{1-\alpha}$ into the above relations, we get:

$$g_y^* = g_k^* = \frac{(\Theta-\alpha)g+(\Theta-1)n}{1-\alpha}. \tag{5.8}$$

Equation (5.8) leads to the following conclusions. First, the long-run growth rates of labour productivity and capital-labour ratio in the growth model analyzed here depend on the same macroeconomic variables that determine the long-term growth rates of product stream and capital stock. Second, the higher the Harrodian rate of technological progress, the higher the long-run growth rates of output and capital per worker, because $\frac{\partial g_y^*}{\partial g} = \frac{\partial g_k^*}{\partial g} = \frac{\Theta-\alpha}{1-\alpha} > 0$. Third, it follows from $\frac{\partial g_y^*}{\partial n} = \frac{\partial g_k^*}{\partial n} = \frac{\Theta-1}{1-\alpha}$ that if decreasing/increasing returns to scale take place in the economy (i.e. Θ is different than 1), then the higher the long-run growth rate of the number of workers, the higher/lower the growth rates g_y^* and g_k^*. Fourth, under conditions of increasing (decreasing) returns to scale, a considerable elasticity of output with respect to capital α is accompanied by high (low) long-run growth rates of capital-labour ratio and labour productivity, because then $\frac{\partial g_y^*}{\partial \alpha} = \frac{\partial g_k^*}{\partial \alpha} = \frac{(\Theta-1)(g+n)}{(1-\alpha)^2} > 0$ $\left(\frac{\partial g_y^*}{\partial \alpha} = \frac{\partial g_k^*}{\partial \alpha} = \frac{(\Theta-1)(g+n)}{(1-\alpha)^2} < 0\right)$. Fifth, since partial derivatives $\frac{\partial g_y^*}{\partial \Theta} = \frac{\partial g_k^*}{\partial \Theta} = \frac{g+n}{1-\alpha}$ are positive, the higher the degree of homogeneity of the production function (5.1), the higher the analyzed growth rates.

A more general conclusion can be drawn: if increasing/decreasing returns to scale take place in the production process, both the long-run growth rates of capital and output (equal $\frac{(\Theta-\alpha)(g+n)}{1-\alpha}$) and capital-labour ratio (amounting to $\frac{(\Theta-\alpha)g+(\Theta-1)n}{1-\alpha}$) are greater/less than the corresponding growth rates in the original Solow model (equal $g+n$ in the case of $G_K^* = G_Y^*$ and n for $g_k^* = g_y^*$). Moreover, at increasing/decreasing returns to scale, a high growth rate of the number of workers raises/reduces the long-run rates of capital-labour ratio and labour productivity.

5.3 Returns to scale in a two-capital (Mankiw-Romer-Weil) model

In a two-capital (Mankiw-Romer-Weil) economic growth model with returns to scale, the following assumptions about economy are adopted:

1 Output is described by an extended production function given by the formula:

$$Y(t) = \left(K(t)\right)^{\alpha K} \left(H(t)\right)^{\alpha H} \left(E(t)\right)^{\Theta - \alpha K - \alpha H}, \tag{5.9}$$

where Y, K, H, E denote, like in the original Mankiw-Romer-Weil model described in Chapter 3, $\alpha_K, \alpha_H \in (0,1)$ the elasticity of output with respect to physical (α_K) and human (α_H) capital, and Θ is the degree of homogeneity of the production function (5.9). Since it is required that the production function (5.9) be characterized by diminishing marginal productivities of units of effective labour E, we assume that $(\Theta - \alpha_K - \alpha_H) \in (0,1)$. We thus assume that $\Theta \in (\alpha_K + \alpha_H, 1 + \alpha_K + \alpha_H)$. This means that if $\Theta \in (\alpha_K + \alpha_H, 1)$, decreasing returns to scale take place, and increasing returns to scale occur at $\Theta \in (1, 1 + \alpha_K + \alpha_H)$.

2 The processes of accumulation of physical and human capital are described by the differential equations:

$$\dot{K}(t) = s_K Y(t) - \delta_K K(t) \tag{5.10a}$$

and

$$\dot{H}(t) = s_H Y(t) - \delta_H H(t). \tag{5.10b}$$

The rates of investment s_K and s_H and depreciation rates δ_K and δ_H are economically interpreted like in the original Mankiw-Romer-Weil model. It is then assumed about those rates that s_K, s_H, $(s_K + s_H) \in (0,1)$ and $\delta_K, \delta_H \in (0,1)$.

3 The trajectory of units of effective labour is given by equation (5.3).

Let $G_Y = \dot{Y}/Y$, $G_K = \dot{K}/K$ and $G_H = \dot{H}/H$ represent growth rates of (respectively) the product stream and stocks of physical and human capital, and $g_y = \dot{y}/y$, $g_k = \dot{k}/k$ and $g_h = \dot{h}/h$ – the growth rates of those macroeconomic quantities per worker.

From the production function (5.9) and equation (5.3), we get:

$$Y(t) = \left(K(t)\right)^{\alpha K} \left(H(t)\right)^{\alpha H} e^{(\Theta - \alpha K - \alpha H)(g+n)t},$$

which gives, taking the logarithm of both sides and differentiating with respect to time $t \geq 0$:

$$G_Y(t) = \theta + \alpha_K G_K(t) + \alpha_H G_H(t), \tag{5.11}$$

where $\theta = (\Theta - \alpha_K - \alpha_H)(g+n) > 0$. Equation (5.11) makes the growth rate of product stream (G_Y) depending in the analyzed economic growth model e.g. on the growth rates of physical (G_K) and human (G_H) capital.

From equations (5.10a,b), ignoring trivial solutions $K(t) = H(t) = 0$, we directly get:

$$G_K(t) + \delta_K = s_K \frac{Y(t)}{K(t)} \tag{5.12a}$$

and

$$G_H(t) + \delta_H = s_H \frac{Y(t)}{H(t)}. \tag{5.12b}$$

The system consisting of equations (5.12a,b) is analyzed at $K, H > 0 \Rightarrow Y > 0$. It follows that at any moment $t \geq 0$: $G_K > -\delta_K$ and $G_H > -\delta_H$.

From equations (5.12a,b), taking the logarithm of both sides and differentiating with respect to time $t \geq 0$, we get:

$$\begin{cases} \dfrac{\dot{G}_K(t)}{G_K(t) + \delta_K} = G_Y(t) - G_K(t) \\ \dfrac{\dot{G}_H(t)}{G_H(t) + \delta_H} = G_Y(t) - G_H(t) \end{cases}.$$

Substituting relation (5.11) into the above system of equations, we obtain:

$$\begin{cases} \dfrac{\dot{G}_K(t)}{G_K(t) + \delta_K} = \theta - (1 - \alpha_K) G_K(t) + \alpha_H G_H(t) \\ \dfrac{\dot{G}_H(t)}{G_H(t) + \delta_H} = \theta + \alpha_K G_K(t) - (1 - \alpha_H) G_H(t) \end{cases}. \tag{5.13}$$

The system of differential equations (5.13) makes an increase in the growth rates of the stocks of physical ($\dot{G}_K$) and human ($\dot{G}_H$) capital depending on those growth rates (i.e. G_K and G_H).

It follows from the first equation in system (5.13) that at $G_K > -\delta_K$: $\dot{G}_K > 0$ $\left(\dot{G}_K < 0\right)$ if and only if $G_K < \frac{\theta + \alpha_H G_H}{1-\alpha_K}$ $\left(G_K > \frac{\theta + \alpha_H G_H}{1-\alpha_K}\right)$. The same applies to an increase in the growth rates of human capital. Consequently, a phase diagram of the system of differential equations assumes the form given in Figure 5.1.

It follows from the phase diagram of the analyzed system of differential equations that it has a stable point of long-run equilibrium $\left(G_K^*, G_H^*\right)$ that solves the following system of equations:

$$\begin{cases} 0 = \theta - (1-\alpha_K)G_K + \alpha_H G_H \\ 0 = \theta + \alpha_K G_K - (1-\alpha_H)G_H \end{cases}.$$

The system can also be expressed as a matrix:

$$\begin{bmatrix} 1-\alpha_K & -\alpha_H \\ -\alpha_K & 1-\alpha_K \end{bmatrix} \cdot \begin{bmatrix} G_K \\ G_H \end{bmatrix} = \begin{bmatrix} \theta \\ \theta \end{bmatrix}.$$

The point $\left(G_K^*, G_H^*\right)$ that solves the above system of equations determines the long-run growth rates of physical and human capital in the Mankiw-Romer-Weil equilibrium with returns to scale.

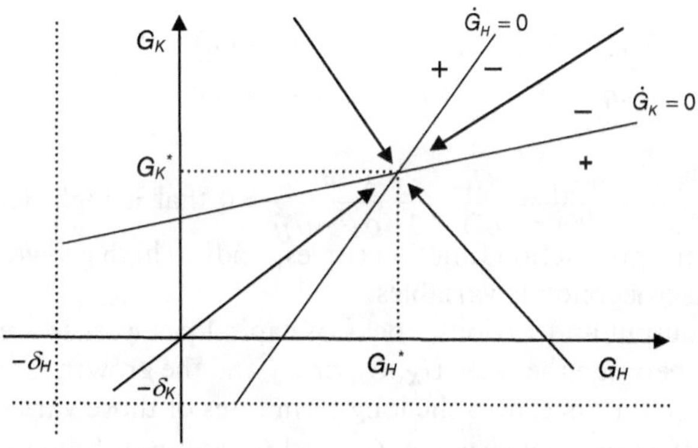

Figure 5.1 A phase diagram of system of differential equation (5.13).
Source: The author's own study.

Using the method of Cramer determinants, the long-term growth rates of physical G_K^* and human G_H^* capital can be described by the following formulas:

$$G_K^* = G_H^* = \frac{\theta}{1-\alpha_K-\alpha_H} = \frac{(\Theta-\alpha_K-\alpha_H)(g+n)}{1-\alpha_K-\alpha_H}. \tag{5.14}$$

It follows from the above formulas and from relation (5.11) that also the long-run growth rate of product stream G_Y^* equals in the analyzed economic growth model $\frac{(\Theta-\alpha_K-\alpha_H)(g+n)}{1-\alpha_K-\alpha_H}$. This leads to the following economic conclusions. First, the growth rates (5.14) represent a simple generalization of the growth rates (5.7) from the previously analyzed single-capital model with returns to scale. Second, the long-run growth rates of the stocks of capital and product stream depend on the Harrodian rate of technological progress (g), the growth rate of the number of workers (n), the elasticity (α_K and α_H) of the production function with respect to inputs of physical and human capital and the degree of homogeneity (Θ) of that function. Third, because:

$$\frac{\partial G_K^*}{\partial g} = \frac{\partial G_K^*}{\partial n} = \frac{\partial G_H^*}{\partial g} = \frac{\partial G_H^*}{\partial n} = \frac{\partial G_Y^*}{\partial g} = \frac{\partial G_Y^*}{\partial n} = \frac{\Theta-\alpha_K-\alpha_H}{1-\alpha_K-\alpha_H} > 0.$$

A high rate of technological progress or high growth rate of the number of workers is accompanied by high long-run growth rates of the analyzed macroeconomic variables. Fourth, if increasing (decreasing) returns to scale take place in the economy, then the higher the elasticities α_K and α_H, the higher (lower) the long-run growth rates G_K^*, G_H^* and G_Y^*, because:

$$\frac{\partial G_K^*}{\partial \alpha_K} = \frac{\partial G_H^*}{\partial \alpha_K} = \frac{\partial G_Y^*}{\partial \alpha_K} = \frac{\partial G_K^*}{\partial \alpha_H} = \frac{\partial G_H^*}{\partial \alpha_H} = \frac{\partial G_Y^*}{\partial \alpha_H} = \frac{(\Theta-1)(g+n)}{(1-\alpha_K-\alpha_H)^2} > 0,$$

$$\left(\frac{\partial G_K^*}{\partial \alpha_K} = \frac{\partial G_H^*}{\partial \alpha_K} = \frac{\partial G_Y^*}{\partial \alpha_K} = \frac{\partial G_K^*}{\partial \alpha_H} = \frac{\partial G_H^*}{\partial \alpha_H} = \frac{\partial G_Y^*}{\partial \alpha_H} = \frac{(\Theta-1)(g+n)}{(1-\alpha_K-\alpha_H)^2} < 0\right).$$

Fifth, it follows from $\frac{\partial G_K^*}{\partial \Theta} = \frac{\partial G_H^*}{\partial \Theta} = \frac{\partial G_Y^*}{\partial \Theta} = \frac{g+n}{1-\alpha_K-\alpha_H} > 0$ that a high degree of homogeneity of the production function corresponds to high growth rates of the analyzed macroeconomic variables.

The growth rates of output and various stocks of capital per worker are given by the differences between the rates G_K, G_H or G_Y and the growth rate of the number of workers n. Hence, also the long-term rates of those variables are given by the differences between G_K^*, G_H^* and G_Y^* and n. It follows, considering also equation (5.14), that:

$$g_k^* = g_h^* = g_y^* = \frac{(\Theta-\alpha_K-\alpha_H)g+(\Theta-1)n}{1-\alpha_K-\alpha_H}, \tag{5.15}$$

where g_k^*, g_h^* and g_y^* represent the long-run growth rates of (respectively) capital-labour ratio, human capital per worker and labour productivity. It follows from equation (5.15) that:

- The growth rates (5.15) represent a generalization of the growth rates (5.8) from the Solow model with returns to scale.
- The growth rates g_k^*, g_h^* and g_y^* are determined by the same macroeconomic variables as the growth rates G_K^*, G_H^* and G_Y^*.
- Since $\frac{\partial g_k^*}{\partial g}=\frac{\partial g_h^*}{\partial g}=\frac{\partial g_y^*}{\partial g}=\frac{\Theta-\alpha_K-\alpha_H}{1-\alpha_K-\alpha_H}>0$, the long-run growth rates of output and various stocks of capital per worker are directly proportional to the Harrodian rate of technological progress.
- It follows from $\frac{\partial g_k^*}{\partial n}=\frac{\partial g_h^*}{\partial n}=\frac{\partial g_y^*}{\partial n}=\frac{\Theta-1}{1-\alpha_K-\alpha_H}$ that if increasing/decreasing returns to scale take place in the production process, a high growth rate of the number of workers leads to high/low rates g_k^*, g_h^* and g_y^*.
- The higher the degree of homogeneity of the production function, the higher the analyzed growth rates, because $\frac{\partial g_k^*}{\partial \Theta}=\frac{\partial g_h^*}{\partial \Theta}=\frac{\partial g_y^*}{\partial \Theta}=\frac{g+n}{1-\alpha_K-\alpha_H}>0$.
- $\frac{\partial g_k^*}{\partial \alpha_K}=\frac{\partial g_h^*}{\partial \alpha_K}=\frac{\partial g_y^*}{\partial \alpha_K}=\frac{\partial g_k^*}{\partial \alpha_H}=\frac{\partial g_h^*}{\partial \alpha_H}=\frac{\partial g_y^*}{\partial \alpha_H}=\frac{(\Theta-1)(g+n)}{(1-\alpha_K-\alpha_H)^2}$, then under conditions of increasing/decreasing returns to scale, high elasticities α_K and α_H of the production function raise/reduce the long-run growth rates of output and various stocks of capital per worker.

5.4 Returns to scale in a multiple-capital (Nonneman-Vanhoudt) model

The following assumptions underlie this analysis of the effect of returns to scale on the long-run economic growth equilibrium in a multi-capital growth model:

1 The production process is described by the N + 1-factor production function given by the formula:

$$Y(t)=\left(\prod_i (K_i(t))^{\alpha_i}\right)(E(t))^{\Theta-\sum_i \alpha_i} \tag{5.16}$$

where Y, K_i and α_i (for $i = 1, 2, \ldots, N$) are interpreted like in the original Nonneman-Vanhoudt model, and Θ is the degree of homogeneity of the production function (5.16). It is assumed about the parameters α_i and Θ that each of the elasticities and their sum belong to the interval (0,1). The assumption that $\Theta\in\left(\sum_i \alpha_i, 1+\sum_i \alpha_i\right)$ is adopted to obtain a production function that is characterized by diminishing marginal productivities both for various stocks of capital and units of effective labour.

2 An increase in each stock of capital is described by the differential equations:

$$\forall i \quad \dot{K}_i(t) = s_i Y(t) - \delta_i K_i(t), \tag{5.17}$$

where s_i denotes the rates of investment in various stocks of capital, and δ_i – their depreciation rates. It is assumed about those rates (like previously) that $\forall i \quad s_i, \delta_i \in (0,1)$ and $\sum_i s_i \in (0,1)$.

3 The growth path of units of effective labour is described by equation (5.3).

Like previously, we ignore the trivial solution $\forall i \ K_i(t) = 0$. Let $y = Y/L$ represent labour productivity, $k_i = K_i/L$ – inputs of ith capital per worker, $G_Y = \dot{Y}/Y$ – the growth rate of output, $G_i = \dot{K}_i / K_i$ – the growth rates of various stocks of capital, $g_y = \dot{y}/y$ – the growth rate of labour productivity and $g_i = \dot{k}_i / k_i$ – the growth rates of various stocks of capital per worker (for all i).

From the production function (5.16), taking the logarithm of both sides and differentiating with respect to time $t \in [0,+\infty)$, we get:

$$G_Y(t) = \sum_i \alpha_i G_i(t) + \left(\Theta - \sum_i \alpha_i\right) \frac{\dot{E}(t)}{E(t)}$$

and from the above relation and equation (5.3), that leads to $\frac{\dot{E}}{E} = g + n$, we arrive at the formula:

$$G_Y(t) = \sum_i \alpha_i G_i(t) + \theta, \tag{5.18}$$

where $\theta = \left(\Theta - \sum_i \alpha_i\right)(g+n)$. Equation (5.18) makes the growth rate of output G_Y depending e.g. on the growth rates of various stocks of capital G_i and the growth rate of units of effective labour $g+n$.

From equations (5.17), we get:

$$\forall i \quad G_i(t) + \delta_i = s_i \frac{Y(t)}{K_i(t)},$$

which gives (taking the logarithm of both sides and differentiating with respect to time $t \in [0,+\infty)$):

$$\forall i \quad \frac{\dot{G}_i(t)}{G_i(t)+\delta_i} = G_Y(t) - G_i(t). \tag{5.19}$$

Equations (5.19) make an increase in the growth rates of various stocks of capital ($\dot{G}_i$) depending on those growth rates (G_i) and the growth rate of output G_Y. These equations are analyzed in the phase space $P = \{(G_1, G_2, \ldots G_N) \in R^N : \forall i \; G_i > -\delta\}$, because:

$$\forall i \; G_i + \delta_i = s_i \frac{Y}{K_i} > 0.$$

Let us substitute relation (5.18) into equations (5.19). We arrive then at the following system of differential equations:

$$\forall i \quad \frac{\dot{G}_i(t)}{G_i(t)+\delta_i} = \theta - (1-\alpha_i)G_i(t) + \sum_{j \neq i} G_j(t). \tag{5.20}$$

The system of differential equations (5.20) in the phase space P has exactly one steady state $\Gamma = (G_1^*, G_2^*, \ldots, G_N^*) \in P$. The reason is that Γ represents the solution of the following linear system of equations:

$$\forall i \quad (1-\alpha_i)G_i - \sum_{j \neq i} G_j = \theta. \tag{5.21}$$

It can easily be demonstrated that system of equations (5.21) is solved by point Γ in which for each i=1, 2, …, N:

$$G_i^* = \frac{\theta}{1-\sum_j \alpha_j} = \frac{\left(\Theta - \sum_j \alpha_j\right)(g+n)}{1-\sum_j \alpha_j}. \tag{5.22}$$

It follows from equations (5.18) and (5.22) that in the steady-state Γ the growth rate of output G_Y^* also equals $\frac{\left(\Theta - \sum_j \alpha_j\right)(g+n)}{1-\sum_j \alpha_j}$.

We will demonstrate in Section 5.5, analysing system of equations (5.30), that the steady state (5.22) is Lyapunov stable.

Since the steady state Γ is characterized by Lyapunov stability, the growth rates of various stocks of capital $G_1^*, G_2^*, \ldots, G_N^*$ corresponding to that point and the growth rate of product stream G_Y^* can be understood as growth rates of those macroeconomic quantities under conditions of long-run equilibrium in a multi-capital growth model with returns to scale. The following conclusions can be drawn from equation (5.22). First, the growth rates expressed by formulas (5.22) represent a generalization of the growth rates (5.7) from the single-capital model and the growth rates (5.14) from the two-capital model. Second, the long-run growth rates $G_1^*, G_2^*, \ldots, G_N^*$ and G_Y^* depend on the rate of technological progress g, the growth rate of the number of workers n, the elasticity α_i of the production function and the degree of homogeneity Θ of that function. Third, since $\frac{\partial G_Y^*}{\partial g} = \frac{\partial G_Y^*}{\partial n} = \frac{\Theta - \sum_j \alpha_j}{1 - \sum_j \alpha_j} > 0$, the higher the rate of technological progress or the growth rate of the number of workers, the higher the long-run growth rates analyzed here. Fourth, a high degree of homogeneity Θ corresponds to high values of $G_1^*, G_2^*, \ldots, G_N^*$ and G_Y^*, because $\frac{\partial G_Y^*}{\partial \Theta} = \frac{g+n}{1 - \sum_j \alpha_j} > 0$. Fifth, since for all i: $\frac{\partial G_Y^*}{\partial \alpha_i} = \frac{(\Theta - 1)(g+n)}{\left(1 - \sum_j \alpha_j\right)^2}$, if increasing/decreasing returns to scale take place in the production process, the growth rates analyzed here are directly/inversely proportional to the elasticities analyzed here.

Since the growth rates of various stocks of capital per worker g_i (labour productivity g_y) equal the differences between growth rates of those stocks G_i (product stream G_Y) and the growth rate of the number of workers n, the following equations are satisfied under conditions of long-run equilibrium:

$$g_y^* = g_1^* = g_2^* = \ldots = g_N^* = G_Y^* - n,$$

and it follows from the above relation and from equation (5.22) that:

$$g_y^* = g_1^* = g_2^* = \ldots = g_N^* = \frac{\left(\Theta - \sum_j \alpha_j\right) g + (\Theta - 1) n}{1 - \sum_j \alpha_j}. \tag{5.23}$$

It follows from equation (5.23) that:

- The growth rates (5.23) represent a generalization of analogous growth rates from the economic growth models previously analysed in Chapter 5.
- The long-run growth rates $g_y^* = g_1^* = g_2^* = \ldots = g_N^*$ depend on the same factors as the growth rates $G_1^*, G_2^*, \ldots, G_N^*$ and G_Y^*.

- It follows from $\frac{\partial g_y^*}{\partial g} = \frac{\Theta - \sum_j \alpha_j}{1 - \sum_j \alpha_j} > 0$ that the growth rates analyzed here are directly proportional to the Harrodian rate of technological progress.
- Since $\frac{\partial g_y^*}{\partial n} = \frac{\Theta - 1}{1 - \sum_j \alpha_j}$, under conditions of increasing/decreasing returns to scale, a high growth rate of the number of workers raises/reduces the long-run growth rates of various stocks of capital and product stream per worker.
- Additionally, under conditions of increasing/decreasing returns to scale, high elasticities α_i lead to high/low growth rates $g_y^* = g_1^* = g_2^* = \ldots = g_N^*$: The reason is that $i = 1, 2, \ldots, N$ we have: $\frac{\partial g_y^*}{\partial \alpha_i} = \frac{(\Theta - 1)(g + n)}{\left(1 - \sum_j \alpha_j\right)^2}$.

5.5 Golden rules of capital accumulation at returns to scale conditions

The golden rule of capital accumulation[1] was defined in Chapters 2 and 3 as a rate of investment (Chapter 2) or a combination of investment rates (Chapter 3) that leads to a maximum long-run consumption per unit of effective labour. This implicitly means that the investment rate or the combination of investment rates brings the economy onto the highest path of consumption per worker. The golden rule of capital accumulation will be defined in Section 5.5 in the same manner. However, it will be derived in a growth model with returns to scale and a finite number of N (N being a natural number) capital stocks. Certainly, at $N = 1$ that rule refers to a single-capital model from Section 5.2, at $N = 2$ – a two-capital model from Section 5.3, and at $N > 2$ – a multi-capital model from Section 5.4.

Let us derive auxiliary artificial variables described by:

$$\hat{y}(t) = \frac{Y(t)}{\exp\left(\frac{\left(\Theta - \sum_i \alpha_i\right)(g+n)}{1 - \sum_i \alpha_i} t\right)}, \tag{5.24a}$$

$$\hat{k}_i(t) = \frac{K_i(t)}{\exp\left(\frac{\left(\Theta - \sum_j \alpha_j\right)(g+n)}{1 - \sum_j \alpha_j} t\right)} \tag{5.24b}$$

and

$$\hat{c}(t)=\frac{C(t)}{\exp\left(\frac{\left(\Theta-\sum_i \alpha_i\right)(g+n)}{1-\sum_i \alpha_i}t\right)}, \tag{5.24c}$$

where C is the volume of consumption in the entire economy, and the remaining symbols have the same meanings as in the multiple-capital model from Section 5.4. It follows from equations (5.42a–c) that if output Y, various stocks of capital $K1$, $K2$, …, K_N and consumption C (in the entire economy) rise at a growth rate equal $\frac{\left(\Theta-\sum_i \alpha_i\right)(g+n)}{1-\sum_i \alpha_i}$ (i.e. a growth rate that equals the long-run equilibrium growth rate from the multiple-capital growth model described in Section 5.4), the artificial variables $\hat{y}$, $\hat{k}_1$, $\hat{k}_2$, …, $\hat{k}_N$ and $\hat{c}$ assume certain constant values.

Consumption C is defined in a closed economy as a non-invested fraction of production, and can be expressed as:

$$C(t)=\left(1-\sum_i s_i\right)Y(t), \tag{5.25}$$

where s_1, s_2, …, s_N denote rates of investment in various stocks of capital, and each of those rates and their sum belongs to the interval (0,1). It follows from equation (5.25) that at investment rates that are constant in time, the growth rates of production and consumption are equal. Hence (in particular), if production rises in a long run at the growth rate $\frac{\left(\Theta-\sum_i \alpha_i\right)(g+n)}{1-\sum_i \alpha_i}$, the growth rate of consumption also equals $\frac{\left(\Theta-\sum_i \alpha_i\right)(g+n)}{1-\sum_i \alpha_i}$.

Note that it follows from equations (5.25), (5.24a) and (5.24c) that:

$$\hat{c}(t)=\left(1-\sum_i s_i\right)\hat{y}(t). \tag{5.26}$$

It follows from equation (5.26) that if $\lim_{t\to+\infty}\hat{y}(t)=\hat{y}^*$, also $\lim_{t\to+\infty}\hat{c}(t)=\hat{c}^*$ given by the equation:

$$\hat{c}^* = \left(1-\sum_i s_i\right)\hat{y}^*. \tag{5.27}$$

An increase in $\hat{c}^*$ raises the long-run growth path of consumption per worker $c(t)$. Since consumption C (like output Y) rises in a long run at the growth rate equal $\frac{\left(\Theta-\sum_i \alpha_i\right)(g+n)}{1-\sum_i \alpha_i}$, the golden rule of capital accumulation should maximize $\hat{c}^*$ with respect to the combination of investment rates $(s_1,s_2,\dots,s_N)\in(0,1)^N$ at $\sum_i s_i \in (0,1)$.

The production function (5.16), divided by $\exp\left(\frac{\left(\Theta-\sum_j \alpha_j\right)(g+n)}{1-\sum_j \alpha_j}\right)$, can be expressed as:

$$\hat{y}(t)=\prod_i\left(\hat{k}_i(t)\right)^{\alpha_i}. \tag{5.28}$$

Differentiating both sides of equations (5.24b) with respect to time $t\in[0,+\infty)$, we get:

$$\forall i \quad \frac{d\hat{k}_i(t)}{dt} = \exp\left(\frac{\left(\Theta-\sum_j \alpha_j\right)(g+n)}{1-\sum_j \alpha_j}t\right)\frac{\dot{K}_i(t)-\frac{\left(\Theta-\sum_j \alpha_j\right)(g+n)}{1-\sum_j \alpha_j}K_i(t)}{2\exp\left(\frac{\frac{\left(\Theta-\sum_j \alpha_j\right)(g+n)}{1-\sum_j \alpha_j}t}{1-\sum_j \alpha_j}\right)} \quad \text{or}$$

$$= e^{\Phi t}\frac{\dot{K}_i(t)-\Phi K_i(t)}{e^{2\Phi t}} = \frac{\dot{K}_i(t)}{e^{\Phi t}}-\Phi\hat{k}_i(t), \tag{5.29}$$

where $\Phi = \frac{\left(\Theta - \sum_j \alpha_j\right)(g+n)}{1 - \sum_j \alpha_j} > 0$ denotes the long-run growth rates of product stream and various stocks of capital in the model from Section 5.4. Substituting relations (5.17) into differential equations (5.29), we arrive at the relation:

$$\forall i \quad \frac{d\hat{k}_i(t)}{dt} = s_i \hat{y}(t) - (\Phi + \delta_i)\hat{k}_i(t) = s_i \hat{y}(t) - \theta_i \hat{k}_i(t),$$

where for subsequent *is* $\theta_i = \Phi + \delta_i > 0$. Substituting function (5.28) into the above differential equations, we get:

$$\forall i \quad \frac{d\hat{k}_i(t)}{dt} = s_i \prod_j \left(\hat{k}_j(t)\right)^{\alpha_j} - \theta_i \hat{k}_i(t). \tag{5.30}$$

System of differential equations (5.30) has the same mathematical structure as system of equations (3.56) and that system (as we demonstrated in Chapter 3) is characterized by Lyapunov stability. Hence, also system of differential equations (5.30) has a non-trivial steady state that is Lyapunov asymptotically stable. Consequently, the steady state of system of differential equations (5.20), derived from system (equation 5.30), is also Lyapunov asymptotically stable.

Moreover, the steady state $\kappa = \left(\hat{k}_1, \hat{k}_2, \ldots, \hat{k}_N\right)$ is determined similarly to the steady state of system of equations (3.56). Hence:

$$\forall i \quad \ln \hat{k}_i^* = \frac{\left(1 - \sum_{j \neq i} \alpha_j\right) \ln \frac{s_i}{\theta_i} + \sum_{j \neq i} \left(\alpha_j \ln \frac{s_j}{\theta_j}\right)}{1 - \sum_j \alpha_j},$$

and it follows from this relation and equation (5.28) that the artificial variable $\hat{y}$ in the steady-state κ satisfies the relation:

$$\ln \hat{y}^* = \frac{\sum_i \left(\alpha_i \ln \frac{s_i}{\theta_i}\right)}{1 - \sum_i \alpha_i}. \tag{5.31}$$

It follows from equations (5.27) and (5.31) that the variable $\hat{c}^*$ in point κ satisfies the relation:

$$\ln \hat{c}^* = \ln\left(1 - \sum_i s_i\right) + \frac{\sum_i \left(\alpha_i \ln \frac{s_i}{\theta_i}\right)}{1 - \sum_i \alpha_i}. \tag{5.32}$$

The golden rule of capital accumulation in the analyzed model can be derived by maximizing $\hat{c}^*$ given by formula (5.32) with respect to the combination of investment rates $(s_1, s_2, \ldots, s_N) \in (0,1)^N$ at $\sum_i s_i \in (0,1)$. The problem is (mathematically) identical with maximizing function (3.71) with respect to that combination. Hence (like in the case of golden rules in the Nonneman-Vanhoudt equilibrium), the golden combination of investment rates is $(\alpha_1, \alpha_2, \ldots, \alpha_N)$, corresponding to the combination of elasticities of production function with respect to various capital inputs.

5.6 Conclusions

The discussion contained in this chapter can be summarized as follows:

- I The original neoclassical economic growth models (proposed by Solow, Mankiw, Romer, Weil and Nonneman, Vanhoudt) assume e.g. that the production process is described by a production function characterized by constant returns to scale. It follows from this assumption that basic macroeconomic variables (output and various stocks of capital) rise in the long-run equilibrium at a growth rate defined as the sum of Harrodian rate of technological progress and the growth rate of the number of workers. Those variables per worker rise at a growth rate that equals the Harrodian rate of technological progress.
- II In the models with returns to scale, the long-run growth rates (of product stream and capital stocks) equal (in the most general multiple-capital model) $\frac{\left(\Theta - \sum_j \alpha_j\right)(g+n)}{1 - \sum_j \alpha_j}$. In conclusion, if increasing/decreasing returns to scale take place in the economy, the rates are greater/less than the growth rates of those variables at constant returns to scale (equal $g+n$).
- III Also golden rules of capital accumulation determined in the models with returns to scale are consistent with the rules found in the Solow, Mankiw-Romer-Weil and Nonneman-Vanhoudt models.

Note

1 The model described here was proposed by Dykas, Sulima and Tokarski (2008).

6 Bipolar growth models with investment flows

6.1 Introduction

In the previous sections, we analyzed processes in a closed economy, understood as an economy unrelated to other economies. In that type of economy, investments may only be financed using domestic savings. We cancel that assumption in this chapter. It is aimed to analyze bipolar models of economic growth that are developed to study two economies, conventionally termed a rich economy and a poor economy. It is also assumed that those economies can invest their savings internally or abroad.

Section 6.2 describes a model with exogenous investment rates. The model was developed in a study published by Filipowicz and Tokarski (2015). In Section 6.3, we question the assumption about an exogenous nature of investment rates and flows. We modify this assumption in that model by the statement that the volumes of investment flows between the economies covered by our analysis depend on the ratio of capital productivities in those economies. According to our assumption, if capital productivity in one of the economies grows faster than in the other economy, investment inflow rises in the economy that is characterized by a faster growth of capital productivity and drops in the other analyzed economy. The model was proposed in a study published by Filipowicz, Wisła and Tokarski (2016).

In the theoretical growth models discussed in this chapter, neither trajectories of analyzed macroeconomic variables nor points of long-run equilibrium can be explicitly determined. Hence, Section 6.4 contains results of numerical simulations of values of major macroeconomic variables at calibrated parameters of the analyzed growth models.

Alternative approaches to the modelling of investment flow impact on the processes of long-run economic growth (both theoretical and empirical) can be found e.g. in the studies by Lucas (1990), Barro, Mankiw and Sala-i-Martin (1995), Borensztein, De Georgio and Lee (1995), Witkowska (1997), Markusen and Venables (1999), Welfe (2000, 2009), Carkovic and Levine (2002), Alfaro (2003), Alfaro, Chanda, Kalemli-Ozcan, and Sayek (2003), Moudatsou (2003), Latocha (2005), Aizenman, Jinjarak and Park (2011), Roman and Padureanu (2012), Ptaszyńska (2015) or Dinh, Vo, Vo and Nguyen (2019).

DOI: 10.4324/9781003323792-7

6.2 A model with exogenous investment flows

The following assumptions about processes taking place in the two types of economy underlie the analyzes done in Section 6.2:

1 The production process both in a rich economy (designated by the letter *R*) and in a poor economy (designated by *P*) is described by the Cobb-Douglas production function with external effects. Due to those effects, labour productivity y_R (y_P) in a rich (poor) economy is affected not only by the rate of capital per worker k_R (k_P) in that rich (poor) economy, but also by the value of that macroeconomic variable in the other analyzed economy. Hence, the labour productivity function in a rich economy can be expressed by the formula:

$$y_R(t)=(k_R(t))^{\alpha}(k_P(t))^{\beta}, \tag{6.1a}$$

and in a poor economy by:

$$y_P(t)=(k_P(t))^{\alpha}(k_R(t))^{\beta}, \tag{6.1b}$$

where it is assumed about parameters α and β that $\alpha,\beta,\alpha+\beta\in(0,1)$. α represents the elasticity of labour productivity in a rich (poor) economy with respect to capital per worker in that economy, β denotes the elasticity of that labour productivity in a rich (poor) economy with respect to capital per worker in a poor (rich) economy. We also assume that $\alpha>\beta$, which means that the level of labour productivity in a rich (poor) economy is more affected by capital per worker in that economy than by the value of that variable in a poor (rich) economy. The influence of capital per worker in a *P*-type (an *R*-type) economy on labour productivity in an *R*- type (a *P*- type) economy can be explained using three methods. First, it can result from gravity effects, like in the gravity growth model (see Chapter 7, Mroczek, Tokarski and Trojak (2014) or Filipowicz (2019)). Second, that influence can result from a process whereby a poor economy absorbs by imitation new technological developments, thus benefiting from a higher value of capital per worker in a rich economy. Third, the efficiency of processes in poor economies is favourably affected by well-developed infrastructure (e.g. transport) in rich economies while the efficiency of processes in rich economies is adversely affected by underdeveloped infrastructure in poor economies.[1]

2 An increase in capital in a rich economy is described by a differential equation:

$$\dot{K}_R(t)=s_{RD}Y_R(t)+s_{PF}Y_P(t)-\delta_K K_R(t), \tag{6.2a}$$

where K_R denotes the stock of capital in a rich economy Y_R (Y_P) represents the volume of production, i.e. output in a rich (poor) economy, s_{RD}

is the percentage of output produced in an R-type economy that is invested in that economy, s_{PF} is the percentage of output produced in a P economy and invested in an R-type economy, and $\delta_R \in (0,1)$ represents capital depreciation rate in an R-type economy. Similarly, it is assumed that:

$$\dot{K}_P(t) = s_{PD}Y_P(t) + s_{RF}Y_R(t) - \delta_P K_P(t), \tag{6.2b}$$

where the variables and parameters are understood like in equation (6.2a). It is assumed about investment proportions that $s_{RD}, s_{RF}, s_{PD}, s_{PF} \in (0,1)$ and $(s_{RD}+s_{RF}) \in (0,1)$ and $(s_{RD}+s_{RF}) \in (0,1)$. We also assume that $s_{RD} \geq s_{RF}$ $(s_{PD} \geq s_{PF})$, hence that domestic investments made by a rich (poor) economy are not less than investments made abroad by those economies.

3 The trajectory of the total number of workers (in both economies) is described by an exponential function given by the formula:

$$L(t) = e^{nt}, \tag{6.3}$$

where $n > 0$ is the growth rate of the number of workers (so that we implicitly assume that the total number of workers at moment $t = 0$ equals 1).

4 A rich (poor) economy absorbs a portion of total worker resources equal ω $(1-\omega)$, where $\omega \in (0,1)$. It follows from the above relation and from assumption 3 that the growth paths of the number of workers in a rich economy (L_R) and in a poor economy (L_P) are described by the equations:

$$L_R(t) = \omega e^{nt}, \tag{6.4a}$$

and

$$L_P(t) = (1-\omega)e^{nt}. \tag{6.4b}$$

Capital per worker in either of the economies can be expressed using the equation: $k_R = K_R/L_R$ and $k_P = K_P/L_P$. Differentiating k_R and k_P with respect to time, we get:

$$\dot{k}_R(t) = \frac{\dot{K}_R(t)L_R(t) - K_R(t)\dot{L}_R(t)}{\left(L_R(t)\right)^2} = \frac{\dot{K}_R(t)}{L_R(t)} - \frac{\dot{L}_R(t)}{L_R(t)}k_R(t)$$

and (by analogy):

$$\dot{k}_P(t) = \frac{\dot{K}_P(t)}{L_P(t)} - \frac{\dot{L}_P(t)}{L_P(t)}k_P(t).$$

Substituting relations (6.2a,b) and (6.4a,b) into the above equations and considering that:

$$\frac{\dot{L}(t)}{L(t)}=n\Rightarrow\frac{\dot{L}_R(t)}{L_R(t)}=\frac{\dot{L}_P(t)}{L_P(t)}=n$$

as per (6.3), we obtain the equation:

$$\dot{k}_R(t)=\frac{\omega s_{RD}y_R(t)L(t)+(1-\omega)s_{FP}y_P(t)L(t)-\delta_R k_R(t)L(t)}{\omega L(t)}-nk_R(t),$$

hence:

$$\dot{k}_R(t)=s_{RD}y_R(t)+\frac{1-\omega}{\omega}s_{PF}y_P(t)-\mu_R k_R(t) \tag{6.5a}$$

and (similarly):

$$\dot{k}_P(t)=s_{PD}y_P(t)+\frac{\omega}{1-\omega}s_{RF}y_R(t)-\mu_P k_P(t). \tag{6.5b}$$

where $\mu_i=\delta_i+n>0$ (for i = R, P) denote the rates of decline in capital per worker in the analyzed economies. Substituting labour productivity functions (6.1a,b) into relations (6.5a,b), we obtain the following system of differential equations:

$$\begin{cases}\dot{k}_R(t)=s_{RD}(k_R(t))^{\alpha}(k_P(t))^{\beta}+\frac{1-\omega}{\omega}s_{PF}(k_P(t))^{\alpha}(k_R(t))^{\beta}-\mu_R k_R(t)\\ \dot{k}_P(t)=s_{PD}(k_P(t))^{\alpha}(k_R(t))^{\beta}+\frac{\omega}{1-\omega}s_{RF}(k_R(t))^{\alpha}(k_P(t))^{\beta}-\mu_P k_P(t)\end{cases}. \tag{6.6}$$

System of differential equations (6.6) makes increases in stocks of capital per worker in a rich and poor economy depending on their values, on the combination of proportions of (domestic and foreign) investments in output, on the ratio by which labour resources are divided and on the rates of decline in capital per worker. The system is considered (ignoring a trivial solution) in phase space $P=(0,+\infty)^2$.

A non-trivial steady state of system of differential equations (6.6) represents the solution of the following system of equations:

$$\begin{cases}s_{RD}k_R^{\alpha-1}k_P^{\beta}+\frac{1-\omega}{\omega}s_{PF}k_R^{\beta-1}k_P^{\alpha}=\mu_R\\ s_{PD}k_R^{\beta}k_P^{\alpha-1}+\frac{\omega}{1-\omega}s_{RF}k_R^{\alpha}k_P^{\beta-1}=\mu_P\end{cases}.$$

Let us substitute: $k_R = uk_P$, where $u > 0$ denotes the value of capital per worker in a rich economy relative to the value of that variable in a poor economy (at any time $t \in [0,+\infty)$). The above system of equations can be then expressed as follows:

$$\begin{cases} k_P^{\alpha+\beta-1}\left(s_{RD}u^{\alpha-1}+\frac{1-\omega}{\omega}s_{PF}u^{\beta-1}\right)=\mu_R \\ k_P^{\alpha+\beta-1}\left(s_{PD}u^{\beta}+\frac{\omega}{1-\omega}s_{RF}u^{\alpha}\right)=\mu_P \end{cases}. \tag{6.7}$$

Dividing the first equation by the second equation in system (6.7), we get the relation:

$$\frac{s_{RD}u^{\alpha-1}+\frac{1-\omega}{\omega}s_{PF}u^{\beta-1}}{s_{PD}u^{\beta}+\frac{\omega}{1-\omega}s_{RF}u^{\alpha}}=\frac{\mu_R}{\mu_P},$$

that implies the equation:

$$\phi(u)=0, \tag{6.8}$$

where:

$$\phi(u)=a_1u^{\alpha-1}+a_2u^{\beta-1}-b_1u^{\beta}-b_2u^{\alpha},\ a_1=\mu_P s_{RD}>0,$$
$$a_2=\mu_P\frac{1-\omega}{\omega}s_{PF}>0,\ b_1=\mu_R s_{PD}>0, \text{ and } b_2=\mu_R\frac{\omega}{1-\omega}s_{RF}>0$$

Note that:

$$\lim_{u\to 0^+}\phi(u)=+\infty,$$
$$\lim_{u\to +\infty}\phi(u)=-\infty$$

and

$$\forall u>0\quad \phi'(u)=-(1-\alpha)a_1u^{\alpha-2}-(1-\beta)a_2u^{\beta-2}-\beta b_1u^{\beta-1}-\alpha b_2u^{\alpha-1}<0.$$

It follows from the above relations and from the Darboux property of a continuous function that equation (6.8) has exactly one solution $u^* > 0$ (because at u increasing from 0 to $+\infty$, the values of function $\phi(u)$ decrease from $+\infty$ to $-\infty$). Additionally, we get from the first equation in system (6.7):

$$k_P^*=\left(\frac{s_{RD}\left(u^*\right)^{\alpha-1}+\frac{1-\omega}{\omega}s_{PF}\left(u^*\right)^{\beta-1}}{\mu_R}\right)^{1/(1-\alpha-\beta)}, \tag{6.9a}$$

and this together with substitution $k_R = uk_P$ leads to:

$$k_R^* = u^* \left(\frac{s_{RD}\left(u^*\right)^{\alpha-1} + \frac{1-\omega}{\omega} s_{PF}\left(u^*\right)^{\beta-1}}{\mu_R} \right)^{1/(1-\alpha-\beta)} . \tag{6.9b}$$

Equations (6.9a,b) describe the combination of capitals per worker in a non-trivial steady state $\kappa = \left(k_R^*, k_P^*\right) \in P$ of system of differential equations (6.7).

A Jacobian matrix of system of differential equations (6.6) is expressed by the equation:

$$J = \begin{bmatrix} \alpha s_{RD} k_R^{\alpha-1} k_P^{\beta} + \beta \frac{1-\omega}{\omega} s_{PF} k_P^{\alpha} k_R^{\beta-1} - \mu_R & \beta s_{RD} k_R^{\alpha} k_P^{\beta-1} + \alpha \frac{1-\omega}{\omega} s_{PF} k_P^{\alpha-1} k_R^{\beta} \\ \beta s_{PD} k_P^{\alpha} k_R^{\beta-1} + \alpha \frac{\omega}{1-\omega} s_{RF} k_P^{\beta} k_R^{\alpha-1} & \alpha s_{PD} k_P^{\alpha-1} k_R^{\beta} + \beta \frac{\omega}{1-\omega} s_{RF} k_P^{\beta-1} k_R^{\alpha} - \mu_P \end{bmatrix}. \tag{6.10}$$

In the steady state, we get:

$$\mu_R = s_{RD} k_R^{\alpha-1} k_P^{\beta} + \frac{1-\omega}{\omega} s_{PF} k_R^{\beta-1} k_P^{\alpha}$$

and

$$\mu_P = s_{PD} k_R^{\beta} k_P^{\alpha-1} + \frac{\omega}{1-\omega} s_{RF} k_R^{\alpha} k_P^{\beta-1}.$$

Hence, Jacobian matrix (6.10) can be written as:

$$J^* = \begin{bmatrix} j_{11} & j_{12} \\ j_{21} & j_{22} \end{bmatrix}, \tag{6.11}$$

where:

$$j_{11} = -\frac{(1-\alpha) s_{RD} k_R^{\alpha} k_P^{\beta} + (1-\beta)\frac{1-\omega}{\omega} s_{PF} k_P^{\alpha} k_R^{\beta}}{k_R} < 0,$$

$$j_{12} = \frac{\beta s_{RD} k_R^{\alpha} k_P^{\beta} + \alpha \frac{1-\omega}{\omega} s_{PF} k_P^{\alpha} k_R^{\beta}}{k_P} > 0,$$

$$j_{21} = \frac{\beta s_{PD} k_P^{\alpha} k_R^{\beta} + \alpha \frac{\omega}{1-\omega} s_{RF} k_P^{\beta} k_R^{\alpha}}{k_R} > 0,$$

and

$$j_{22} = -\frac{(1-\alpha)s_{PD}k_P^{\alpha}k_R^{\beta} + (1-\beta)\frac{\omega}{1-\omega}s_{RF}k_P^{\beta}k_R^{\alpha}}{k_P} < 0.$$

The eigenvalues of Jacobian matrix J^* are given by the roots of the equation:

$$\lambda^2 - trJ^*\lambda + \det J^* = 0. \tag{6.12}$$

The discriminant Δ of equation (6.12) is described by the formula:

$$\Delta = tr^2J^* - 4\det J^* = (j_{11} - j_{22})^2 + 4j_{12}j_{21} > 0,$$

hence, both eigenvalues represent real numbers.

From Vieta's formulas, we conclude that the eigenvalues λ_1 and λ_2 are described by the formulas:

$$\lambda_1 + \lambda_2 = trJ^*$$

and

$$\lambda_1\lambda_2 = \det J^*.$$

We conclude that $trJ^* = j_{11} + j_{22} < 0$. Additionally, the relations are true:

$$j_{11}j_{22} = \frac{(1-\alpha)s_{RD}k_R^{\alpha}k_P^{\beta} + (1-\beta)\frac{1-\omega}{\omega}s_{PF}k_P^{\alpha}k_R^{\beta}}{k_R} \cdot \frac{(1-\alpha)s_{PD}k_P^{\alpha}k_R^{\beta} + (1-\beta)\frac{\omega}{1-\omega}s_{RF}k_P^{\beta}k_R^{\alpha}}{k_P}$$

$$= \frac{(1-\alpha)^2 s_{RD}s_{PD} + (1-\beta)^2 s_{PF}s_{RF}}{k_Rk_P}(k_Rk_P)^{\alpha+\beta}$$

$$+ \frac{(1-\alpha)(1-\beta)\left(\frac{\omega}{1-\omega}s_{RD}s_{RF}k_R^{2\alpha}k_P^{2\beta} + \frac{1-\omega}{\omega}s_{PD}s_{PF}k_R^{2\beta}k_P^{2\alpha}\right)}{k_Rk_P}$$

and

$$j_{12}j_{21} = \frac{\beta s_{RD}k_R^{\alpha}k_P^{\beta} + \alpha\frac{1-\omega}{\omega}s_{PF}k_P^{\alpha}k_R^{\beta}}{k_P} \cdot \frac{\beta s_{PD}k_P^{\alpha}k_R^{\beta} + \alpha\frac{\omega}{1-\omega}s_{RF}k_P^{\beta}k_R^{\alpha}}{k_R}$$

$$= \frac{\left(\alpha^2 s_{PF}s_{RF} + \beta^2 s_{RD}s_{PD}\right)(k_Rk_P)^{\alpha+\beta} + \alpha\beta\left(\frac{1-\omega}{\omega}s_{PF}s_{PD} + \frac{\omega}{1-\omega}s_{RD}s_{RF}\right)k_P^{2\alpha}k_R^{2\beta}}{k_Rk_P}$$

Since $\det J^* = j_{11}j_{22} - j_{12}j_{21}$, then:

$$\det J^* = \frac{(1-\alpha)^2 s_{RD}s_{PD} + (1-\beta)^2 s_{PF}s_{RF}}{k_R k_P}(k_R k_P)^{\alpha+\beta}$$
$$+\frac{(1-\alpha)(1-\beta)\left(\frac{\omega}{1-\omega}s_{RD}s_{RF}k_R^{2\alpha}k_P^{2\beta} + \frac{1-\omega}{\omega}s_{PD}s_{PF}k_R^{2\beta}k_P^{2\alpha}\right)}{k_R k_P}$$
$$-\frac{\left(\alpha^2 s_{PF}s_{RF} + \beta^2 s_{RD}s_{PD}\right)(k_R k_P)^{\alpha+\beta} + \alpha\beta\left(\frac{\omega}{1-\omega}s_{RD}s_{RF} + \frac{1-\omega}{\omega}s_{PF}s_{PD}\right)k_P^{2\alpha}k_R^{2\beta}}{k_R k_P}$$

results in:

$$\det J^* = \frac{(1-\alpha-\beta)(1-\alpha+\beta)(s_{RD}s_{PD} + s_{PF}s_{RF})(k_R k_P)^{\alpha+\beta}}{k_P k_R}$$
$$+\frac{(1-\alpha-\beta)\left(\frac{\omega}{1-\omega}s_{RD}s_{RF}k_R^{2\alpha}k_P^{2\beta} + \frac{1-\omega}{\omega}s_{PD}s_{PF}k_P^{2\alpha}k_R^{2\beta}\right)}{k_P k_R} > 0.$$

As the total of eigenvalues is negative, and their product is positive, both eigenvalues represent negative real numbers. As per the Grobman-Hartman theorem, system of differential equations (6.7) is asymptotically stable in a sufficiently close neighbourhood of steady state $\left(k_R^*, k_P^*\right)$.

$u^* = k_R^* / k_P^*$ solving equation (6.8) describes the value of capital per worker in a rich economy relative to capital per worker in a poor economy in the long-run equilibrium in the growth model analyzed here. If $u^* = 1$, then convergence in capital per worker occurs between a poor economy and a rich economy. If $u^* = 0$, capital per worker in a poor economy k_P (at certain moment $\bar{t} > 0$) reaches the value of capital per worker k_R in a rich economy, to eventually exceed that value continually while $\lim_{t\to+\infty}\frac{k_R(t)}{k_P(t)} = 0$. However, at $u^* \to +\infty$ and $t \to +\infty$, the ratio k_R/k_P approaches $+\infty$. Hence, at $u^* = 1$ there is convergence in capital per worker while at $u^* \to +\infty$ $\left(u^* = 0\right)$ a divergence process takes place in which a poor economy catches up and then overtakes a rich economy.

It follows from equation (6.8) that the long-run ratio of capitals per worker u^* can be written as:

$$u^* = u^*\left(a_1(s_{RD}, \delta_P, n), a_2(s_{PF}, \omega, \delta_P, n), b_1(s_{PD}, \delta_R, n), b_2(s_{RF}, \omega, \delta_R, n)\right). \quad (6.13)$$

Equation (6.13) leads to the following conclusions:

- The long-run ratio of stocks of capital per worker in rich and poor economies depends e.g. on the rates of their internal, domestic investment

(s_{RD} and s_{PD}), rates of investment abroad (s_{RF} and s_{PF}) rates of capital depreciation in a rich economy and in a poor economy (δ_R and δ_P), the percentage ω of total worker resources that is absorbed by a rich economy and the growth rate of the number of workers (n) in both types of economy.

- Since[2]:

$$\frac{\partial u^*}{\partial s_{RD}} = -\frac{\frac{\partial \phi}{\partial s_{RD}}}{\frac{\partial \phi}{\partial u}} = -\frac{\frac{\partial \phi}{\partial a_1} \cdot \frac{\partial a_1}{\partial s_{RD}}}{\frac{\partial \phi}{\partial u}} = -\frac{u^{\alpha-1}\mu_P}{\frac{\partial \phi}{\partial u}} > 0,$$

so that the greater fraction of output produced in a rich economy is invested in that economy, the greater is the long-run ratio k_R^* / k_P^*.

- It follows from:

$$\frac{\partial u^*}{\partial s_{PD}} = -\frac{\frac{\partial \phi}{\partial s_{PD}}}{\frac{\partial \phi}{\partial u}} = -\frac{\frac{\partial \phi}{\partial b_1} \cdot \frac{\partial b_1}{\partial s_{PD}}}{\frac{\partial \phi}{\partial u}} = \frac{u^{\beta}\mu_R}{\frac{\partial \phi}{\partial u}} < 0$$

that a high rate of domestic investment in a poor economy corresponds to a low long-run ratio k_R^* / k_P^*.

- The inequality:

$$\frac{\partial u^*}{\partial \omega} = -\frac{\frac{\partial \phi}{\partial a_2} \cdot \frac{\partial a_2}{\partial \omega} + \frac{\partial \phi}{\partial b_2} \cdot \frac{\partial b_2}{\partial \omega}}{\frac{\partial \phi}{\partial u}} = \frac{\frac{u^{\beta-1}\mu_P s_{PF}}{\omega^2} + \frac{u^{\alpha}\mu_R s_{RF}}{(1-\omega)^2}}{\frac{\partial \phi}{\partial u}} < 0,$$

implies that a high percentage ω of people working in a rich economy (considering people working in both types of economy) corresponds to a low ratio of long-run stocks of capital per worker k_R^* and k_P^*.

- A high rate of capital depreciation in a rich economy reduces the long-run ratio k_R^* / k_P^*. The reason is that:

$$\frac{\partial u^*}{\partial \delta_R} = -\frac{\frac{\partial \phi}{\partial b_1} \cdot \frac{\partial b_1}{\partial \delta_R} + \frac{\partial \phi}{\partial b_2} \cdot \frac{\partial b_2}{\partial \delta_R}}{\frac{\partial \phi}{\partial u}} = \frac{u^{\beta} s_{PD} + u^{\alpha} \frac{\omega}{1-\omega} s_{RF}}{\frac{\partial \phi}{\partial u}} < 0.$$

- The effect of δ_P on the ratio of u^* is opposite. This is because:

$$\frac{\partial u^*}{\partial \delta_P} = -\frac{\frac{\partial \phi}{\partial a_1}\cdot\frac{\partial a_1}{\partial \delta_P}+\frac{\partial \phi}{\partial a_2}\cdot\frac{\partial a_2}{\partial \delta_P}}{\frac{\partial \phi}{\partial u}} = -\frac{u^{\alpha-1}s_{RD}+u^{\beta-1}\frac{1-\omega}{\omega}s_{PF}}{\frac{\partial \phi}{\partial u}} > 0.$$

- Since:

$$\frac{\partial u^*}{\partial n} = -\frac{\frac{\partial \phi}{\partial a_1}\cdot\frac{\partial a_1}{\partial n}+\frac{\partial \phi}{\partial a_2}\cdot\frac{\partial a_2}{\partial n}+\frac{\partial \phi}{\partial b_1}\cdot\frac{\partial b_1}{\partial n}+\frac{\partial \phi}{\partial b_2}\cdot\frac{\partial b_2}{\partial n}}{\frac{\partial \phi}{\partial u}}$$

$$= \frac{u^{\alpha-1}s_{RD}+u^{\beta-1}\frac{1-\omega}{\omega}s_{PF}-\left(u^{\beta}s_{PD}+u^{\alpha}\frac{\omega}{1-\omega}s_{RF}\right)}{-\frac{\partial \phi}{\partial u}},$$

  the direction of effect of the growth rate of the number of workers n on the ratio of u^* is not obvious (because the partial derivative $\frac{\partial u^*}{\partial n}$ can be both positive, negative and equal 0).

Let us use $v = y_R/y_P$ to denote (at any time $t \geq 0$) the ratio of labour productivities in rich economies and in poor economies at subsequent moments t. Then, it follows from equations (6.1a,b) that:

$$v(t) = \frac{y_R(t)}{y_P(t)} = \frac{(k_R(t))^{\alpha}(k_P(t))^{\beta}}{(k_P(t))^{\alpha}(k_R(t))^{\beta}} = \left(\frac{k_R(t)}{k_P(t)}\right)^{\alpha-\beta},$$

hence $v(t) = (u(t))^{\alpha-\beta}$, or:

$$v^* = (u^*)^{\alpha-\beta},$$

where $v^* = y_R^* / y_P^*$ denotes the ratio of labour productivities in an R economy and a P economy in a long run. Since $\alpha > \beta$, then $\operatorname{sgn}\frac{\partial u^*}{\partial x} = \operatorname{sgn}\frac{\partial v^*}{\partial x}$ (where x denotes any independent variable that determines u^*). This means that the direction of effect exerted by the several exogenous variables on the v^* ratio of labour productivities in a long-run equilibrium in the economic growth model analyzed here is identical to the direction of effect exerted by those variables on the u^* ratio of capitals per worker.

6.3 A model with investment flows conditional on capital productivity

In the model analyzed in Section 6.2, we assumed that investment flows (between an R-type economy and a P-type economy) are exogenous. Hence, investment flows were independent of capital productivity in both types of economy. We cancel this assumption in the model described in Section 6.3 and propose that those flows from one type of economy to the other type of economy (i.e. from economy i to economy j) are directly proportional to the ratio of capital productivity in economy j to capital productivity in economy i. Hence, the following assumptions are adopted in the model analyzed here:

1 Production processes in both types of economy are described by equations (6.1a,b).
2 Increases in the stocks of capital per worker (in rich and poor economies) are described by differential equations in the form[3]:

$$\dot{k}_R(t) = s_{RD}(t)\,y_R(t) + s_{PF}(t)\frac{1-\omega}{\omega}y_P(t) - \mu_R k_R(t) \tag{6.14a}$$

and

$$\dot{k}_P(t) = s_{PD}(t)\,y_P(t) + s_{RF}(t)\frac{\omega}{1-\omega}y_R(t) - \mu_P k_P(t), \tag{6.14b}$$

where the variables k_R, k_P, y_R, $y_P > 0$, parameters[4] $\mu_R = \delta_R + n > 0$, $\mu_P = \delta_P + n > 0$ and $\omega \in (0,1)$ are read like in the model from Section 6.2. The trajectories of investment rates (s_{RD}, s_{RF}, s_{PD} and s_{PF}) are described by equations derived from assumptions 3–4.
3 Total savings rates in rich (poor) economies equal $s_R \in (0,1)\left(s_P \in (0,1)\right)$. Savings achieved in those economies are invested both internally and abroad. Domestic investments of rich (poor) economies equal a $1-\ell_R$ $(1-\ell_P)$ fraction of their savings and their investments abroad equal a $\ell_R\,(\ell_P)$ fraction.
4 The proportion of national savings invested abroad ℓ_R (in rich economies) depends on domestic capital productivity ($p_R = y_R/k_R$), and capital productivity abroad ($p_P = y_P/k_P$). Moreover, we assume that the higher the ratio of capital productivity in a poor economy (p_P) to capital productivity in a rich economy (p_R), the larger fraction of domestic savings achieved in the rich economy will be invested in a poor economy. Hence, we assume that:

$$\ell_R(t) = \frac{\gamma_R}{1+\exp\left(-\frac{p_P(t)}{p_R(t)}\right)}, \tag{6.15a}$$

where $\gamma_K \in (0,1)$. It follows from equation (6.15a) that:

i $\lim_{\frac{p_P}{p_R}\to 0^+} \ell_R = \frac{\gamma_R}{2}$, and if capital productivity in a poor economy was extremely low (compared to capital productivity in a rich economy), the rich economy would be ready to invest in the poor economy a ℓ_R fraction of its savings equal $\gamma_R/2$.

ii $\lim_{\frac{p_P}{p_R}\to +\infty} \ell_R = \gamma_R$, i.e. if the ratio p_P/p_R was very high, the R-type economy would invest in the P-type economy a fraction of its savings equal γ_R.

iii Since: $\frac{d\ell_R}{d(p_p/p_R)} = \frac{\gamma_R \frac{p_p}{p_R}\exp\left(-\frac{p_p}{p_R}\right)}{\left(1+\exp\left(-\frac{p_p}{p_R}\right)\right)^2} > 0$ (for any $\frac{p_P}{p_R} > 0$), the greater the ratio of capital productivity in a P-type economy to the value of that variable in an R-type economy, the greater fraction of national savings achieved in the rich economy is invested in the poor economy.

It is assumed that the trajectory ℓ_P is described by an equation similar to (6.15a), i.e.:

$$\ell_P(t) = \frac{\gamma_P}{1+\exp\left(-\frac{p_R(t)}{p_p(t)}\right)}, \tag{6.15b}$$

where the parameter $\gamma_P \in (0,1)$ is interpreted in terms of economics like the parameter γ_R in equation (6.15a). Obviously, function (6.15b) is characterized by similar (economic and mathematical) properties as function (6.15a).

5 The trajectories of numbers of workers in rich and poor economies are described by equations (6.3) and (6.4a,b).

The quotients of capital productivities can be written as:

$$\frac{p_R(t)}{p_p(t)} = \frac{y_R(t)/k_R(t)}{y_P(t)/k_P(t)} = \frac{y_R(t)/y_P(t)}{k_R(t)/k_P(t)},$$

and it follows from the above relation and from equation (6.1a,b) that:

$$\frac{p_R(t)}{p_p(t)} = \left(\frac{k_R(t)}{k_P(t)}\right)^{\alpha-\beta-1}. \tag{6.16}$$

Equation (6.16) makes the ratio of capital productivity in a rich economy to capital productivity in a poor economy (p_R/p_P) conditional on the relationship between capital-labour ratios (k_R/k_P).

Substituting relation (6.16) into equations (6.15a,b), we obtain:

$$\ell_R(t)=\frac{\gamma_R}{1+\exp\left(-\left(\frac{k_R(t)}{k_P(t)}\right)^{\alpha-\beta-1}\right)}=\frac{\gamma_R}{1+\exp\left(-\left(u(t)\right)^{\alpha-\beta-1}\right)} \tag{6.17a}$$

and

$$\ell_P(t)=\frac{\gamma_P}{1+\exp\left(-\left(\frac{k_R(t)}{k_P(t)}\right)^{-(1-\alpha+\beta)}\right)}=\frac{\gamma_P}{1+\exp\left(-\left(u(t)\right)^{-(1-\alpha+\beta)}\right)}, \tag{6.17b}$$

where the quotient $u = k_R/k_P > 0$ represents the relationship between capital-labour ratios in a rich economy and in a poor economy.

The following system of differential equations is obtained from relations (6.1a,b), (6.17a,b) and (6.14a,b):

$$\begin{cases} \dot{k}_R(t)=s_R\left(1-\ell_R(t)\right)\left(k_R(t)\right)^{\alpha}\left(k_P(t)\right)^{\beta} \\ +s_P\frac{1-\omega}{\omega}\ell_P(t)\left(k_P(t)\right)^{\alpha}\left(k_R(t)\right)^{\beta}-\mu_R k_R(t) \\ \\ \dot{k}_P(t)=s_P\left(1-\ell_P(t)\right)\left(k_P(t)\right)^{\alpha}\left(k_R(t)\right)^{\beta} \\ +s_R\frac{\omega}{1-\omega}\ell_R(t)\left(k_R(t)\right)^{\alpha}\left(k_P(t)\right)^{\beta}-\mu_P k_P(t) \end{cases}. \tag{6.18}$$

Let us demonstrate now that system of differential equations (6.18) has exactly one non-trivial steady state in the phase space $P=(0,+\infty)^2$. In the non-trivial steady state, the following holds: $\dot{k}_R=\dot{k}_P=0$ and $k_P>0$. It follows from the above relations and from formula (6.18) that the following system of equations is satisfied in that state:

$$\begin{cases} s_R\left(1-\ell_R(u)\right)k_R^{\alpha}k_P^{\beta}+s_P\frac{1-\omega}{\omega}\ell_P(u)k_P^{\alpha}k_R^{\beta}=\mu_R k_R \\ s_P\left(1-\ell_P(u)\right)k_P^{\alpha}k_R^{\beta}+s_R\frac{\omega}{1-\omega}\ell_R(u)k_R^{\alpha}k_P^{\beta}=\mu_P k_P \end{cases},$$

that, substituting $u = k_R/k_P$, can also be written as:

$$\begin{cases} \left(s_R\left(1-\ell_R(u)\right)u^\alpha + s_P\dfrac{1-\omega}{\omega}\ell_P(u)u^\beta\right)k_P^{\alpha+\beta} = \mu_R k_R \\ \left(s_P\left(1-\ell_P(u)\right)u^\beta + s_R\dfrac{\omega}{1-\omega}\ell_R(u)u^\alpha\right)k_P^{\alpha+\beta} = \mu_P k_P \end{cases},$$

Dividing the first by the second of the above equations, we get:

$$\frac{s_R\left(1-\ell_R(u)\right)u^\alpha + \dfrac{(1-\omega)s_P}{\omega}\ell_P(u)u^\beta}{s_P\left(1-\ell_P(u)\right)u^\beta + \dfrac{\omega s_R}{1-\omega}\ell_R(u)u^\alpha} = \frac{\mu_R}{\mu_P}u,$$

and performing some elementary transformation, we arrive at the equation:

$$\left(\frac{s_P}{\mu_P}\left(1-\ell_P(u)\right)u^\beta + \frac{\omega s_R}{(1-\omega)\mu_P}\ell_R(u)u^\alpha - \frac{s_R}{\mu_R}\left(1-\ell_R(u)\right)u^{\alpha-1} - \frac{(1-\omega)s_P}{\omega\mu_R}\ell_P(u)u^{\beta-1}\right)u = 0,$$

that (considering our search for $u > 0$) gives:

$$\varphi(u) = 0, \tag{6.19}$$

where:

$$\begin{aligned} \varphi(u) = {} & \frac{s_P}{\mu_P}\left(1-\ell_P(u)\right)u^\beta + \frac{\omega s_R}{(1-\omega)\mu_P}\ell_R(u)u^\alpha \\ & - \frac{s_R}{\mu_R}\left(1-\ell_R(u)\right)u^{\alpha-1} - \frac{(1-\omega)s_P}{\omega\mu_R}\ell_P(u)u^{\beta-1}. \end{aligned} \tag{6.20}$$

The function $\varphi(u)$ is described by equation (6.20) and characterized by the following properties:

i Equations (6.17a,b) lead to the conclusion that $\ell_R(0) = \dfrac{\gamma_R}{2}$ and $\lim\limits_{u\to 0^+}\ell_P(u) = \lim\limits_{u\to 0^+}\dfrac{\gamma_P}{1+\exp\left(-\dfrac{1}{u^{1-\alpha+\beta}}\right)} = \gamma_P$, and consequently: $\lim\limits_{u\to 0^+}\varphi(u) = -\infty$;

ii because $\lim\limits_{u\to+\infty}\ell_R(u) = \gamma_R$ and $\lim\limits_{u\to+\infty}\ell_P(u) = \dfrac{\gamma_P}{2}$, so $\lim\limits_{u\to+\infty}\varphi(u) = +\infty$;

iii since:

$$\ell'_R(u) = \frac{(1-\alpha+\beta)\gamma_R u^{\alpha-\beta}\exp\left(-u^{1-\alpha+\beta}\right)}{\left(1+\exp\left(-u^{1-\alpha+\beta}\right)\right)^2} > 0,$$

$$\ell'_P(u) = -\frac{(1-\alpha+\beta)\gamma_P u^{\alpha-\beta-2}\exp\left(-u^{-(1-\alpha+\beta)}\right)}{\left(1+\exp\left(-u^{-(1-\alpha+\beta)}\right)\right)^2} < 0,$$

and

$$\varphi'(u) = \frac{s_P}{\mu_P}\left[\beta\left(1-\ell_P(u)-\ell'_P(u)u\right)\right]u^{\beta-1} + \frac{\omega s_R}{(1-\omega)\mu_P}\left[\ell'_R(u)u+\alpha\ell_R(u)\right]u^{\alpha-1}$$
$$+\frac{s_R}{\mu_R}\left[\ell'_R(u)u+(1-\alpha)\left(1-\ell_R(u)\right)\right]u^{\alpha-2} + \frac{(1-\omega)s_P}{\omega\mu_R}\left[(1-\beta)\ell_P(u)-\ell'_P(u)u\right]u^{\beta-2}$$

Then $\forall u > 0 \quad \varphi'(u) > 0$.

It follows that if the ratio $u = k_R/k_P$ increases from 0 to $+\infty$, the values of function $\varphi(u)$ increase from $-\infty$ to $+\infty$. It follows from the above relations and from the Darboux property that exactly one $u^* > 0$ exists such that solves equation (6.19).

A Jacobian matrix of system of differential equations (6.18) is expressed by the equation:

$$J = \begin{bmatrix} \partial\phi_R/\partial k_R & \partial\phi_R/\partial k_P \\ \partial\phi_P/\partial k_R & \partial\phi_P/\partial k_P \end{bmatrix} \tag{6.21}$$

where:

$$\frac{\partial\phi_R}{\partial k_R} = s_R\left[\alpha\left(1-\ell_R(k_R/k_P)\right)k_P - \frac{d\ell_R}{d(k_R/k_P)}k_R\right]k_R^{\alpha-1}k_P^{\beta-1}$$
$$+\frac{s_P(1-\omega)}{\omega}\left[\beta\ell_P(k_R/k_P)k_P + \frac{d\ell_P}{d(k_R/k_P)}k_R\right]k_P^{\alpha-1}k_R^{\beta-1} - \mu_R$$

$$\frac{\partial\phi_R}{\partial k_P} = s_R\left[\beta\left(1-\ell_R(k_R/k_P)\right)k_P + \frac{d\ell_R}{d(k_R/k_P)}k_R\right]k_R^{\alpha}k_P^{\beta-2}$$
$$+\frac{s_P(1-\omega)}{\omega}\left[\alpha\ell_P(k_R/k_P)k_P - \frac{d\ell_P}{d(k_R/k_P)}k_R\right]k_P^{\alpha-2}k_R^{\beta}$$

$$\frac{\partial\phi_P}{\partial k_R} = s_P\left[\beta\left(1-\ell_P(k_R/k_P)\right)k_P - \frac{d\ell_P}{d(k_R/k_P)}k_R\right]k_P^{\alpha-1}k_R^{\beta-1}$$
$$+\frac{s_R\omega}{1-\omega}\left[\alpha\ell_R(k_R/k_P)k_P + \frac{d\ell_R}{d(k_R/k_P)}k_R\right]k_R^{\alpha-1}k_P^{\beta-1}$$

and

$$\frac{\partial \phi_P}{\partial k_P} = s_P \left[\alpha \left(1 - \ell_P (k_R / k_P)\right) k_P + \frac{d\ell_P}{d(k_R / k_P)} k_R \right] k_P^{\alpha-2} k_R^{\beta} + \frac{s_R \omega}{1-\omega} \left[\beta \ell_R (k_R / k_P) k_P - \frac{d\ell_R}{d(k_R / k_P)} k_R \right] k_R^{\alpha} k_P^{\beta-2} - \mu_P.$$

In the steady state, we get:

$$\mu_R = s_R \left(1 - \ell_R (k_R / k_P)\right) k_R^{\alpha-1} k_P^{\beta} + \frac{(1-\omega) s_P}{\omega} \ell_P (k_R / k_P) k_P^{\alpha} k_R^{\beta-1}$$

and

$$\mu_P = s_P \left(1 - \ell_P (k_R / k_P)\right) k_P^{\alpha-1} k_R^{\beta} + \frac{\omega s_R}{1-\omega} \ell_R (k_R / k_P) k_R^{\alpha} k_P^{\beta-1}.$$

Hence, a Jacobian matrix in a steady state of the analyzed system of differential equations can be written as:

$$J^* = \begin{bmatrix} j_{11} & j_{12} \\ j_{21} & j_{22} \end{bmatrix}, \tag{6.22}$$

where[5]:

$$j_{11} = -s_R \left[(1-\alpha)\left(1 - \ell_R\left(\frac{k_R}{k_P}\right)\right) k_P + \frac{d\ell_R}{d\left(\frac{k_R}{k_P}\right)} k_R \right] k_R^{\alpha-1} k_P^{\beta-1} - \frac{s_P(1-\omega)}{\omega} \left[(1-\beta)\ell_P\left(\frac{k_R}{k_P}\right) k_P - \frac{d\ell_P}{d\left(\frac{k_R}{k_P}\right)} k_R \right] k_P^{\alpha-1} k_R^{\beta-1} < 0$$

$$j_{21} = s_R \left[\beta\left(1 - \ell_R\left(\frac{k_R}{k_P}\right)\right) k_P + \frac{d\ell_R}{d\left(\frac{k_R}{k_P}\right)} k_R \right] k_R^{\alpha} k_P^{\beta-2} + \frac{s_P(1-\omega)}{\omega} \left[\alpha\ell_P\left(\frac{k_R}{k_P}\right) k_P - \frac{d\ell_P}{d\left(\frac{k_R}{k_P}\right)} k_R \right] k_P^{\alpha-2} k_R^{\beta} > 0$$

$$j_{12} = s_P \left[\beta \left(1 - \ell_P \left(\frac{k_R}{k_P} \right) \right) k_P - \frac{d\ell_P}{d\left(\frac{k_R}{k_P} \right)} k_R \right] k_P^{\alpha-1} k_R^{\beta-1}$$

$$+ \frac{s_R \omega}{1-\omega} \left[\alpha \ell_R \left(\frac{k_R}{k_P} \right) k_P + \frac{d\ell_R}{d\left(\frac{k_R}{k_P} \right)} k_R \right] k_R^{\alpha-1} k_P^{\beta-1} > 0$$

and

$$j_{22} = -s_P \left[(1-\alpha) \left(1 - \ell_P \left(\frac{k_R}{k_P} \right) \right) k_P - \frac{d\ell_P}{d\left(\frac{k_R}{k_P} \right)} k_R \right] k_P^{\alpha-2} k_R^{\beta}$$

$$- \frac{s_R \omega}{1-\omega} \left[(1-\beta) \ell_R \left(\frac{k_R}{k_P} \right) k_P + \frac{d\ell_R}{d\left(\frac{k_R}{k_P} \right)} k_R \right] k_R^{\alpha} k_R^{\beta-2} < 0$$

Eigenvalues of matrix J^* solve the equation:

$$\lambda^2 - trJ^* \lambda + \det J^* = 0 \tag{6.23}$$

The discriminant Δ of equation (6.23) is expressed by the formula:

$$\Delta = tr^2 J^* - 4 \det J^* = (j_{11} - j_{22})^2 + 4 j_{12} j_{21} > 0,$$

and this leads to the conclusion that both eigenvalues of the analyzed matrix represent real numbers.

We will demonstrate now that the total of eigenvalues ($\lambda 1$ and $\lambda 2$) is negative, and their product is positive. From Vieta's formulas, we get:

$$\lambda_1 + \lambda_2 = trJ^* = j_{11} + j_{22} < 0,$$

and

$$\lambda_1 \lambda_2 = \det J^* = j_{11} j_{22} - j_{12} j_{21}.$$

It can be demonstrated, following a series of complex transformations that will not be included here, that:

$$j_{11} j_{22} = q_1 s_R s_P k_R^{\alpha+\beta-1} k_P^{\alpha+\beta-3} + q_2 s_R^2 \frac{\omega}{1-\omega} k_R^{2\alpha-1} k_P^{2\beta-3} + q_3 s_P^2 \frac{1-\omega}{\omega} k_R^{2\beta-1} k_P^{2\alpha-3}, \tag{6.24a}$$

where:

$$q_1 = \left[(1-\alpha)\left(1-\ell_R\left(\frac{k_R}{k_P}\right)\right)k_P + \frac{d\ell_R}{d\left(\frac{k_R}{k_P}\right)}k_R\right]\cdot\left[(1-\alpha)\left(1-\ell_P\left(\frac{k_R}{k_P}\right)\right)k_P + \frac{d\ell_P}{d\left(\frac{k_R}{k_P}\right)}k_R\right]$$

$$+\left[(1-\beta)\,\ell_P\left(\frac{k_R}{k_P}\right)k_P - \frac{d\ell_P}{d\left(\frac{k_R}{k_P}\right)}k_P\right]\cdot\left[(1-\beta)\,\ell_R\left(\frac{k_R}{k_P}\right)k_P + \frac{d\ell_R}{d\left(\frac{k_R}{k_P}\right)}k_R\right]$$

$$q_2 = \left[(1-\alpha)\left(1-\ell_R\left(\frac{k_R}{k_P}\right)\right)k_P + \frac{d\ell_R}{d\left(\frac{k_R}{k_P}\right)}k_R\right]\cdot\left[(1-\beta)\,\ell_R\left(\frac{k_R}{k_P}\right)k_P + \frac{d\ell_R}{d\left(\frac{k_R}{k_P}\right)}k_R\right]$$

and

$$q_3 = \left[(1-\beta)\,\ell_P\left(\frac{k_R}{k_P}\right)k_P - \frac{d\ell_P}{d\left(\frac{k_R}{k_P}\right)}k_R\right]\cdot\left[(1-\alpha)\left(1-\ell_P\left(\frac{k_R}{k_P}\right)\right)k_P - \frac{d\ell_P}{d\left(\frac{k_R}{k_P}\right)}k_R\right],$$

and

$$j_{12}j_{21} = r_1 s_R s_P k_R^{\alpha+\beta-1}k_P^{\alpha+\beta-3} + r_2 s_R^2\frac{\omega}{1-\omega}k_R^{2\alpha-1}k_P^{2\beta-3} + r_3 s_P^2\frac{1-\omega}{\omega}k_R^{2\beta-1}k_P^{2\alpha-3}, \tag{6.24b}$$

where:

$$r_1 = \left[\beta\left(1-\ell_R\left(\frac{k_R}{k_P}\right)\right)k_P + \frac{d\ell_R}{d\left(\frac{k_R}{k_P}\right)}k_R\right]\cdot\left[\beta\left(1-\ell_P\left(\frac{k_R}{k_P}\right)\right)k_P - \frac{d\ell_P}{d\left(\frac{k_R}{k_P}\right)}k_R\right]$$

$$+\left[\alpha\ell_P\left(\frac{k_R}{k_P}\right)k_P - \frac{d\ell_P}{d\left(\frac{k_R}{k_P}\right)}k_R\right]\cdot\left[\alpha\ell_R\left(\frac{k_R}{k_P}\right)k_P + \frac{d\ell_R}{d\left(\frac{k_R}{k_P}\right)}k_R\right]$$

$$r_2 = \left[\beta\left(1-\ell_R\left(\frac{k_R}{k_P}\right)\right)k_P + \frac{d\ell_R}{d\left(\frac{k_R}{k_P}\right)}k_R\right]\cdot\left[\alpha\ell_R\left(\frac{k_R}{k_P}\right)k_P + \frac{d\ell_R}{d\left(\frac{k_R}{k_P}\right)}k_R\right]$$

and

$$r_3 = \left[\alpha\ell_P\left(\frac{k_R}{k_P}\right)k_P - \frac{d\ell_P}{d\left(\frac{k_R}{k_P}\right)}k_R\right]\cdot\left[\beta\left(1-\ell_P\left(\frac{k_R}{k_P}\right)\right)k_P - \frac{d\ell_P}{d\left(\frac{k_R}{k_P}\right)}k_R\right].$$

Because $1-\alpha > \beta$ and $1-\beta > \alpha$, we get:

$$q_1 > \left[\beta\left(1-\ell_R\left(\frac{k_R}{k_P}\right)\right)k_P + \frac{d\ell_R}{d\left(\frac{k_R}{k_P}\right)}k_R\right]\cdot\left[\beta\left(1-\ell_P\left(\frac{k_R}{k_P}\right)\right)k_P - \frac{d\ell_P}{d\left(\frac{k_R}{k_P}\right)}k_R\right]$$
$$+\left[\alpha\ell_P\left(\frac{k_R}{k_P}\right)k_P + \frac{d\ell_P}{d\left(\frac{k_R}{k_P}\right)}k_R\right]\cdot\left[\alpha\ell_R\left(\frac{k_R}{k_P}\right)k_P - \frac{d\ell_R}{d\left(\frac{k_R}{k_P}\right)}k_R\right] = r_1,$$

$$q_2 > \left[\beta\left(1-\ell_R\left(\frac{k_R}{k_P}\right)\right)k_P + \frac{d\ell_R}{d\left(\frac{k_R}{k_P}\right)}k_R\right]\cdot\left[\alpha\ell_R\left(\frac{k_R}{k_P}\right)k_P + \frac{d\ell_R}{d\left(\frac{k_R}{k_P}\right)}k_R\right] = r_2$$

and

$$q_3 > \left[\alpha\ell_P\left(\frac{k_R}{k_P}\right)k_P - \frac{d\ell_P}{d\left(\frac{k_R}{k_P}\right)}k_R\right]\cdot\left[\beta\left(1-\ell_P\left(\frac{k_R}{k_P}\right)\right)k_P - \frac{d\ell_P}{d\left(\frac{k_R}{k_P}\right)}k_R\right] = r_3.$$

From the statement that for each i = 1, 2, 3 $q_i > r_i$ and from equations (6.24a,b), it follows that $\det J^* > 0$. Hence, both eigenvalues of the analyzed Jacobian matrix represent negative real numbers. Consequently (as per the Grobman-Hartman theorem), system of differential equations (6.18) is asymptotically stable in its steady state.

6.4 Numerical simulations of economy growth trajectories

6.4.1 Exogenous investment flows

To perform simulations of growth paths in the model from Section 6.2, we assume e.g. that the ratio of elasticities of labour productivity functions (6.1a,b), i.e. α and β, can be expressed as 10:1 (i.e. the stock of domestic capital per worker has an effect on domestic flow of labour productivity that is ten times stronger than the effect of stock of foreign capital per worker). [6] Then, the functions (in a discrete time $t = 0, 1, \ldots$) can be written as:

$$y_{Rt} = k_{Rt}^{10\beta} k_{Pt}^{\beta}, \tag{6.25a}$$

and

$$y_{Pt} = k_{Pt}^{10\beta} k_{Rt}^{\beta}, \tag{6.25b}$$

Parameter β is calibrated so that at a ratio of capital per worker in a rich economy to capital per worker in a poor economy equal 5:1, the ratio of labour productivities equals 3:1. This leads to the conclusion that as per equations (6.25a,b):

$$\frac{y_{Rt}}{y_{Pt}} = \left(\frac{k_{Rt}}{k_{Pt}}\right)^{9\beta},$$

which gives:

$$3 = 5^{9\beta},$$

thus:

$$\beta = \frac{\ln 3}{9 \ln 5} \approx 0.07585 \;\Rightarrow\; \alpha = 10\beta \approx 0.7585.$$

Given the adopted assumptions (about the elasticities α and β), the labour productivity functions can be written as:

$$y_{Rt} = k_{Rt}^{0.7585} k_{Pt}^{0.07585} \tag{6.26a}$$

and

$$y_{Pt} = k_{Pt}^{0.7585} k_{Rt}^{0.07585}, \tag{6.26b}$$

The capital depreciation rate, both in a rich economy and in a poor economy, is calibrated at the level of 7% (hence, $\delta_R = \delta_P = 0.07$, and the growth rate of the number of workers at n = 0.005. Then, $\mu_R = \mu_P = 0.075$ and an approximation of system of differential equations (6.6) is given by the following system of differential equations:

$$\begin{cases} \Delta k_{Rt} = s_{RD} k_{Rt-1}^{0.7585} k_{Pt-1}^{0.07585} + \dfrac{1-\omega}{\omega} s_{PF} k_{Pt-1}^{0.7585} k_{Rt-1}^{0.07585} - 0.075 k_{Rt-1} \\ \Delta k_{Pt} = s_{PD} k_{Pt-1}^{0.7585} k_{Rt-1}^{0.07585} + \dfrac{\omega}{1-\omega} s_{RF} k_{Rt-1}^{0.7585} k_{Pt-1}^{0.07585} - 0.075 k_{Pt-1} \end{cases},$$

or:

$$\begin{cases} k_{Rt} = s_{RD} k_{Rt-1}^{0.7585} k_{Pt-1}^{0.07585} + \dfrac{1-\omega}{\omega} s_{PF} k_{Pt-1}^{0.7585} k_{Rt-1}^{0.07585} + 0.925 k_{Rt-1} \\ k_{Pt} = s_{PD} k_{Pt-1}^{0.7585} k_{Rt-1}^{0.07585} + \dfrac{\omega}{1-\omega} s_{RF} k_{Rt-1}^{0.7585} k_{Pt-1}^{0.07585} + 0.925 k_{Pt-1} \end{cases}. \quad (6.27)$$

In all simulations described below, we assume that in the year $t = 0$ capital per worker in a rich economy equals 5, and in a poor economy it equals 1. This implies, as per equations (6.26a,b), that in the year $t = 0$ labour productivity in a rich economy equals about 3.3895, and in a poor economy it equals 1.1298.

Let us also use $k_R^* = \lim_{t\to\infty} k_{Rt}$, $k_P^* = \lim_{t\to\infty} k_{Pt}$ to denote long-run capital per worker in both analyzed types of economy, $y_R^* = \lim_{t\to\infty} y_{Rt}$, $y_P^* = \lim_{t\to\infty} y_{Pt}$ to denote long-term labour productivities, and $u^* = k_R^* / k_P^*$ and $v^* = y_R^* / y_P^*$ to denote long-run ratios of capital per worker (u*) and labour productivities (v*) in an R-type economy to those in a P-type economy.[7] Let also $\overline{t}$ represent the year in which the poor economy overtakes the rich economy in terms of labour productivity and capital per worker.

The numerical simulations of growth paths of capital per worker and labour productivity were performed for the following variants:

I there are no investment flows between the economies (this is a base version used as a reference for results obtained in other variants);
II a rich economy absorbs 20% of the total of workers;
III 40% of workers work in a rich economy;
IV the percentage of workers in either economy equals 50%;
V a poor economy absorbs 40% of workers;
VI 20% of the total of workers work in a poor economy;
VII the savings rate equals 25% in a rich economy, and 15% in a poor economy, and ω equals (subsequently) 20%, 40%, 50%, 60% and 80%;
VIII the savings rate reaches the level of 15% in a rich economy, and 15% in a poor economy, at ω developing like in the preceding variant.

We assume in variants I–VI that the savings rates in either analyzed economy equal (in nine various combinations) 17%, 20% or 23%. We also assume in all variants (i.e. in cases I–VIII) that savings achieved in a rich economy are invested in 10% in a poor economy, and savings achieved in a poor economy are allocated in 5% to investment in a rich economy.

Let us begin with the scenario of no investment flows. Complete national savings are allocated to domestic investment. Thus, we have a Solow model extended by the effect of external factors originating from a poor (rich) economy on a rich (poor) economy. Selected results of those numerical simulations are contained in Table 6.1. It follows from those simulations that:

- At the same savings rates achieved in both analyzed types of economy, complete convergence occurs both in labour productivity and in investment rates. The reason is if savings rates in both analyzed economies reach a level of $s \in (0,1)$, the rates of decline in capital per worker equal $\mu > 0$, and the elasticities in labour productivity functions (6.1ab) equal α and β (where $\alpha, \beta, (\alpha+\beta) \in (0,1)$ and $\alpha > \beta$), then system of differential equations (6.27) can be written as:

$$\begin{cases} \Delta k_{Rt} = s k_{Rt-1}^{\alpha} k_{Pt-1}^{\beta} - \mu k_{Rt-1} \\ \Delta k_{Pt} = s k_{Pt-1}^{\alpha} k_{Rt-1}^{\beta} - \mu k_{Pt-1} \end{cases}.$$

Performing some simple transformations, it can be demonstrated that the non-trivial steady state of the above system of differential equations represents a solution of the following system of equations:

$$\begin{bmatrix} 1-\alpha & -\beta \\ -\beta & 1-\alpha \end{bmatrix} \cdot \begin{bmatrix} \ln k_R^* \\ \ln k_P^* \end{bmatrix} = \ln \frac{s}{\mu} \begin{bmatrix} 1 \\ 1 \end{bmatrix} \tag{6.28}$$

Table 6.1 Selected simulation results in Variant I (no investment flows)

s_R (%)	s_P (%)	k_R^*	k_P^*	y_R^*	y_P^*	u^* (%)	v^* (%)	$\bar{t}$
17	17	139.5	139.5	61.6	61.6	100.0	100.0	+∞
	20	176.4	294.4	77.8	110.4	59.9	70.5	35
	23	215.8	559.3	95.2	182.4	38.6	52.2	22
20	17	294.4	176.4	110.4	77.8	166.9	141.8	Never
	20	372.1	372.1	139.5	139.5	100.0	100.0	+∞
	23	455.2	707.0	170.7	230.6	64.4	74.0	34
23	17	559.3	215.8	182.4	95.2	259.2	191.6	Never
	20	707.0	455.2	230.6	170.7	155.3	135.1	Never
	23	864.9	864.9	282.0	282.0	100.0	100.0	+∞

Source: Own calculations.

The solution of system of equations (6.28) is given by stocks k_R^* and k_P^* that satisfy the relation: $\ln k_R^* = \ln k_P^* = \dfrac{1-\alpha-\beta}{(1-\alpha)^2-\beta^2}\ln\dfrac{s}{\mu}$, which leads to $k_R^* = k_P^*$.

- If the savings rate in a rich economy is less by 3% points than in a poor economy, then the *P*-type economy will overtake the *R*-type economy after 34–35 years in terms of capital per worker and labour productivity. In a long run, capital per worker in an initially richer economy will amount to about 60%–65% of capital per worker in an initially poorer economy. Regarding output per worker, the proportion will drop to about 70%–75%.
- If the rich economy had a savings rate equal 17% and the poor economy by a savings rate greater by 6% points, capital per worker and labour productivity in the latter economy would be greater than in the former economy as soon as after 22 years. In a long-run, capital per worker in the initially richer economy would be by more than 60% less than in the initially poorer economy and consequently labour productivity in the latter economy would be almost twice as great as in the former economy.
- At savings rates greater by three points in an *R* economy, partial convergence[8] of the poor economy with the rich economy takes place. The ratio of capitals per worker drops then from 5:1 (in the year $t = 0$) to 1.669:1 or 1.553:1 (at $t \to \infty$), and the ratio of labour productivities drops from 3:1 to 1.418:1 or 1.351:1.
- Also a difference in savings rates amounting to 6% points (in favour of the rich economy) leads to partial convergence of the poor economy with the rich economy. The reason is that under those circumstances (as per the quantities stated in Table 6.1) at $t \to \infty$: $u \to 2.592$ and $v \to 1.916$. Partial convergence of a poorer economy with a richer economy at higher savings rates in the rich economy results from two reasons indicated below. First, due to the Cobb-Douglas production function used in the Solow model, there are diminishing marginal productivities of both physical capital and capital per worker, and this naturally leads to convergence of major macroeconomic variables analyzed in the Solow model. Second, due to an extension of the labour productivity function (6.1a,b) by external effects, an increase in labour productivity in a poor economy is also driven by an increase in capital per worker in a rich economy (this correlation is ignored in the original Solow model).
- The simulation exercises summarized in Table 6.1 also confirm the hypothesis theoretically confirmed in Section 6.2 and predicting that the higher savings rate is characteristic of one of the analyzed economies the higher values are assumed by capital per worker and labour productivity in both economies in a long-run equilibrium of the economic growth model proposed here.

Table 6.2 contains numerical simulation results of capital per worker and labour productivity (in both types of economy) in Variant II described above. The quantities given in that table lead to the following conclusions:

- Assuming the same savings rates in a rich economy and in a poor economy, capital per worker and labour productivity partly converge in the poor economy with those variables in the rich economy. The reason is that under the analyzed circumstances the relationship between capital-labour ratios drops from 5:1 (in the year $t = 0$) to 1.306:1 (at $t \to +\infty$) while the ratio of labour productivities drops from 3:1 to 1.2:1.
- At a savings rate equal 17% in a rich economy and equal 20% in a poor economy, the *P*-type economy will overtake (considering capital per worker and output per worker) the *R*-type economy after 91 years. Under conditions of long-run equilibrium, capital per worker will be by about 1.4% less, and the labour productivity will be less by 0.9% in an *R*-type economy than in a *P*-type economy. Hence, capital per worker and labour productivity partly converge in this scenario.
- A similar process will also take place if the savings rate equals 20% in a rich economy and 23% in a poor economy it equals. The only difference lies in the fact that under these conditions $u^* \approx 1.024$ and $v^* \approx 1.016$.
- If the savings rate in a poor economy was by 6% points greater than in a rich economy, the poor economy would overtake the rich economy after 31 years. Under conditions of long-run equilibrium, capital per worker will be by about 20.3% greater and labour productivity will be by 14.3% greater in a *P*-type economy than in an *R*-type economy.
- Considering the scenarios wherein the savings rate in a rich economy is by 3% points greater than in a poor economy, we conclude that capital per worker will be greater by about 70%–80% and labour productivity will be greater by about 44%–49% in the rich economy than in the poor economy in a long-run equilibrium.

Table 6.2 Selected simulation results in Variant II ($\omega = 20\%$)

s_R (%)	s_P (%)	k_R^*	k_P^*	y_R^*	y_P^*	u^* (%)	v^* (%)	$\bar{t}$
17	17	182.3	139.6	75.4	62.8	130.6	120.0	Never
	20	305.5	309.7	118.5	119.6	98.6	99.1	91
	23	503.7	632.0	182.8	213.4	79.7	85.7	31
20	17	311.7	174.9	115.2	77.7	178.2	148.4	Never
	20	486.1	372.2	170.9	142.4	130.6	120.0	Never
	23	754.6	737.0	251.3	247.2	102.4	101.6	Never
23	17	522.9	221.0	173.6	96.4	236.6	180.0	Never
	20	767.8	450.6	245.2	170.5	170.4	143.9	Never
	23	1129.9	865.1	345.4	287.9	130.6	120.0	Never

Source: Own calculations.

Numerical simulation results in Variant III (assuming that the proportion of people working in a rich economy equals 40% of the total number of workers) are given in Table 6.3. The simulations lead to the following conclusions:

- At the same savings rates in both types of economies, the initially poor economy will overtake the rich economy after about 49–60 years. In a long-run equilibrium, the ratios of u^* and v^* will reach about 0.904 and 0.933.
- However, if a poor economy is characterized by a savings rate greater by 3% points than a rich economy, the poor economy will catch up the rich economy in terms of capital per worker and labour productivity after 27–28 years. In a long run, capital per worker in an *R*-type economy will amount to about 65%–68% of capital per worker in the other economy while the ratio of labour productivities will approach about 75%–77%.
- If the savings rate equals 23% in a poor economy and 17% in a rich economy, the poor economy will overtake the rich economy after 20 years. In a long-run equilibrium, capital per worker in an *R*-type economy will equal <50% and labour productivity about 62% of the respective variables in the other analyzed economy.
- If the savings rate in a rich economy was greater than in a poor economy by 3% points, partial convergence would occur, because in a long run the ratio of u would approach about 1.2–1.3, while the ratio of v would approach about 1.14–1.17.
- However, a savings rate greater by 6% points in a rich economy than in a poor economy will lead to $u \to 1.676$ and $v \to 1.423$.

Table 6.4 contains numerical simulation results for Variant IV (wherein each of the analyzed economies absorbs 50% of the total of workers). The numerical simulation results contained in the table lead to the following conclusions:

- At the same savings rates in both types of economy, the *P*-type economy will be characterized by greater values of capital per worker and

Table 6.3 Selected simulation results in Variant III ($\omega = 40\%$)

s_R (%)	s_P (%)	k_R^*	k_P^*	y_R^*	y_P^*	u^* (%)	v^* (%)	$\bar{t}$
17	17	129.6	143.4	58.3	62.5	90.4	93.3	60
	20	189.6	291.6	82.2	110.2	65.0	74.6	28
	23	278.1	558.5	115.4	185.7	49.8	62.1	20
20	17	252.0	199.3	99.0	84.4	1.265	117.4	Never
	20	345.7	382.4	132.2	141.7	90.4	93.3	54
	23	477.5	701.7	176.9	230.1	68.0	76.9	27
23	17	466.9	278.6	162.2	114.0	167.6	142.3	Never
	20	610.1	505.5	207.8	182.8	120.7	113.7	Never
	23	803.5	888.8	267.3	286.3	90.4	93.3	49

Source: Own calculations.

Table 6.4 Selected simulation results in Variant IV ($\omega = 50\%$)

s_R (%)	s_P (%)	k_R^*	k_P^*	y_R^*	y_P^*	u^* (%)	v^* (%)	$\bar{t}$
17	17	120.9	153.8	55.6	65.5	78.6	84.9	40
	20	168.0	298.8	75.1	111.2	56.2	67.5	24
	23	234.9	553.7	101.4	182.2	42.4	55.7	17
20	17	245.9	224.9	98.1	92.3	109.3	106.3	Never
	20	322.4	410.0	126.1	148.6	78.6	84.9	35
	23	426.2	723.4	162.7	233.4	58.9	69.7	22
23	17	471.1	329.9	165.4	129.7	142.8	127.5	Never
	20	591.8	566.3	204.8	198.8	104.5	103.0	Never
	23	749.5	952.9	254.9	300.3	78.6	84.9	32

Source: Own calculations.

labour productivity after 32–40 years. In a long run, the ratio of capital per worker in an *R*-type economy to that variable in a *P*-type economy will reach about 0.786 and the ratio of respective labour productivities should equal about 0.849.

- If the savings rates in a poor economy are greater by 3% points than in a rich economy, the poor economy should catch up the rich economy in 22–24 years. Then, also $u \to 0.562$ (at $s_R = 17\%$ and $s_P = 20\%$) or $u \to 0.589$ (in the case where $s_R = 20\%$ and $s_P = 23\%$), and $v \to 0.675$ or $v \to 0.697$.
- If the savings rate in a poor economy equals 23% while in a rich economy it is less by 6% points, the *P*-type economy will be characterized by greater values of capital per worker and labour productivity than the rich economy as soon as after 17 years. In a long run, the ratio of capitals per worker will approach about 0.424, and the ratio of labour productivities will approach about 0.557.
- If the savings rates are greater by 3% points in a rich economy, long-run capital per worker in that rich economy will be greater by about 4.5%–9.3% than in a poor economy, and the ratio of labour productivities will approach about 1.03–1.063.
- If a rich economy is characterized by a savings rate greater by 6% points than the savings rate in a poor economy, long-run capital per worker in the rich economy will be greater by almost 43% and labour productivity in the rich economy will be greater by more than 27%.

Considering a scenario wherein a rich economy absorbs 60% of workers (Table 6.5), we can conclude that:

- At the same savings rates, a poor economy is characterized by greater values of the macroeconomic variables analyzed here than a rich economy after 23–29 years. In a long run, the ratio of capitals per worker will amount to about 0.681, and the ratio of labour productivities will amount to about 0.77.

Table 6.5 Selected simulation results in Variant V ($\omega = 60\%$)

s_R (%)	s_P (%)	k_R^*	k_P^*	y_R^*	y_P^*	u^* (%)	v^* (%)	$\bar{t}$
17	17	117.0	171.6	54.7	71.1	68.1	77.0	29
	20	155.1	317.2	71.0	115.7	48.9	61.4	20
	23	207.3	565.9	92.4	183.4	36.6	50.4	15
20	17	247.5	265.3	99.8	104.7	93.3	95.4	56
	20	311.9	457.7	124.0	161.1	68.1	77.0	26
	23	396.2	773.2	154.7	244.1	51.2	63.4	18
23	17	488.0	408.8	172.6	153.0	119.4	112.8	Never
	20	592.5	662.8	207.5	224.0	89.4	92.6	43
	23	724.9	1063.8	250.6	325.6	68.1	77.0	23

Source: Own calculations.

- If savings rates in a poor economy were greater by 3% points than in a rich economy, the *P*-type economy would be characterized by greater capital per worker and output per worker than the *R*-type economy after 18–20 years. In the long-run equilibrium, capital per worker in the initially rich economy should amount to about 48.9%–51.2% of capital per worker in the initially poor economy, and this results in a ratio of labour productivities in those economies equal about 0.614–0.634.
- If a poor economy is characterized by a savings rate greater by 6% points (than a rich economy), the poor economy will overtake the *R*-type economy after 15 years. In the long-run equilibrium, $u \to 0.366$, and $v \to 0.504$.
- If the savings rate equalled 20% in a rich economy and 17% in a poor economy, the poor economy would overtake the rich economy in terms of capital per worker and labour productivity after 56 years. In a long run, capital per worker in an *R*-type economy will amount to about 93.3% of capital per worker in the other analyzed economy while the ratio of long-run labour productivities will equal about 0.954.
- However, at savings rates equal 23% in a rich economy and 20% in a poor economy $u \to 1.045$, and $v \to 1.030$.
- If a rich economy is characterized by a savings rate greater by 6% points than a poor economy, the rich economy will be characterized in the long-run equilibrium by capital per worker greater by about 19.4% and labour productivity greater by about 12.8% than the poor economy.

Analyzing a scenario wherein a rich economy absorbs 80% of workers (Table 6.6), we can conclude that:

- At the same savings rates, the initially poor economy reaches greater values of the analyzed macroeconomic variables after 11–14 years.[9] The quotients k_R/k_P and y_R/y_P approach then values of about 0.454 and about 0.584.

Table 6.6 Selected simulation results in Variant VI (ω = 80%)

s_R (%)	s_P (%)	k_R^*	k_P^*	y_R^*	y_P^*	u^* (%)	v^* (%)	$\bar{t}$
17	17	122.2	268.8	58.5	100.2	45.4	58.4	14
	20	148.0	434.1	70.2	146.2	34.1	48.0	11
	23	180.7	694.4	84.6	212.0	26.0	39.9	10
20	17	278.8	476.4	114.2	164.6	58.5	69.4	15
	20	325.8	716.8	132.6	227.1	45.4	58.4	12
	23	383.3	1077.7	154.7	313.3	35.6	49.4	10
23	17	580.3	821.0	207.6	263.0	70.7	78.9	17
	20	661.0	1167.7	235.3	347.0	56.6	67.8	13
	23	757.2	1666.2	268.0	459.1	45.4	58.4	11

Source: Own calculations.

- If the savings rate in a poor economy is greater by 3% points, the poor economy will overtake the rich economy after 10–11 years. The long-run ratio of capitals per worker approaches about 0.341–0.356, and the long-run ratio of labour productivities approaches about 0.480–0.496.
- If the savings rate in a poor economy is greater by 6% points, that economy will be characterised by higher values of capital per worker and labour productivity than an *R*-type economy after 10 years. In a long run, capital per worker will be almost four times greater and labour productivity will be more than 2.5 times greater in the poor economy than in the rich economy.
- If the savings rate is greater by 3% points in a rich economy than in a poor economy, the poor economy will catch up the rich economy after 13–15 years. In a long run, the ratio of capitals per worker will equal about 0.566–0.585, and the ratio of labour productivities will equal about 0.678–0.694.
- However, if a rich economy is characterized by a savings rate greater by 6% points than a poor economy, the poor economy will overtake the rich economy (in terms of capital per worker and labour productivity) after 17 years. The ratio of capitals per worker approaches (in a long run) about 0.707, and the ratio of labour productivities about 0.789.

Let us consider a scenario wherein a rich economy is characterized by a considerably greater savings rate than a poor economy. Let us then assume that the value of that macroeconomic variable equals 25% in a rich economy and 15% in a poor economy. We analyze long-run processes with a rich economy absorbing (subsequently) 20%, 40%, 50%, 60%, and 80% of the total of workers (Table 6.7). Then, it is concluded that:

- In each of the analyzed scenarios, capitals per worker and labour productivities partly converge, but a poor economy overtakes a rich economy (after 27 years), considering the analyzed macroeconomic variables, only at $\omega = 0.8$.

Table 6.7 Selected simulation results in Variant VII (s_R = 25% and s_P = 15%)

ω (%)	k_R^*	k_P^*	y_R^*	y_P^*	u^* (%)	v^* (%)	$\bar{t}$
20	580.2	159.5	183.3	75.9	363.8	241.4	Never
40	587.9	237.9	190.8	102.9	247.1	185.4	Never
50	618.0	303.1	201.8	124.1	203.9	162.6	Never
60	663.1	403.2	217.6	154.9	164.5	140.4	Never
80	841.3	940.3	277.9	299.9	89.5	92.7	27

Source: Own calculations.

- The higher the proportion of people working in a rich economy, the lower the long-run ratios of capitals per worker and labour productivities.
- Moreover, a high proportion of people working in a rich economy also corresponds to high long-run values of capital per worker and labour productivity both in the rich economy and in the poor economy.

Let us also consider a scenario wherein the savings rate in a rich economy (15%) is considerably less than in a poor economy (25%). Numerical simulation results for that scenario are stated in Table 6.8. The simulation results given in that table lead to the following conclusions:

- In each of the scenarios analyzed here, a poor economy will overtake a rich economy (after 9–19 years). Moreover, the greater (considering the number of workers) the rich economy, the sooner it will be overtaken by the poor economy.
- The greater the resource of workers absorbed by an R-type economy, the lower the long-run capital per worker and labour productivity in that economy and the greater the values of those macroeconomic variables in the other analyzed economy.

Table 6.9 contains ratios of average estimated k_R^*, k_P^*, y_R^* and y_P^* in the several variants described above, compared to the base Variant I (a scenario wherein there are no investment flows between the analyzed economies). Analyzing the quantities from Table 6.9, we must remember that the figures resulting from Variants II–VI and those resulting from Variants VII–VIII are not

Table 6.8 Selected simulation results in Variant VIII (s_R = 15% and s_P = 25%)

ω (%)	k_R^*	k_P^*	y_R^*	y_P^*	u^* (%)	v^* (%)	$\bar{t}$
20	544.7	894.8	199.1	279.4	60.9	71.3	19
40	255.5	732.6	110.4	226.7	34.9	48.7	15
50	200.6	697.0	91.6	214.3	28.8	42.7	13
60	164.7	679.3	78.7	207.1	24.2	38.0	12
80	122.7	722.7	63.3	212.2	17.0	29.8	9

Source: Own calculations.

Table 6.9 Ratios of average estimated k_R^*, k_P^*, y_R^* and y_P^* in the several variants relative to Variant I (Variant I = 100)

Variant	*Variable*			
	k_R^*	k_P^*	y_R^*	y_P^*
II	131.2	103.1	124.3	105.0
III	93.9	104.4	96.4	103.5
IV	88.0	111.3	92.1	108.3
V	85.6	123.8	90.9	117.2
VI	90.8	193.5	98.2	165.3
VII	156.5	97.2	142.8	101.0
VIII	61.3	177.2	72.4	151.9

Source: Own calculations.

comparable, due to significantly different assumptions about developments of exogenous variables. It follows from the summary in Table 6.9 that:

- A rich economy benefits from openness to investment flows between it and a poor economy only if the rich economy is small, considering the number of workers. At $\omega = 0.2$, average estimated values of capital per worker and labour productivity in that economy rise by more than 30%, and estimated labour productivity rises by almost 25% (compared to average estimated values without investment flows).
- A poor economy benefits from openness to investment flows from a rich economy in each of the analyzed scenarios. Moreover, the greater (considering the number of workers) the rich economy, the greater the benefits derived by the poor economy.
- If a rich economy is characterized by considerably greater (less) savings rates than a poor economy, the rich (poor) economy benefits while the poor (rich) economy loses from openness to investment flows (Variants VII–VIII relative to the variant with no investment flows).

However, remember that we adopted a fundamental assumption in each analyzed scenario that a rich economy invests in a poor economy a fraction of its savings that is twice as large as the fraction invested by the poor economy in the rich economy. Let us consider what will happen, if either of the analyzed economies invests in the other economy 10% of its savings. Table 6.10 contains similar indices as those given in Table 6.9.

The simulations summarized in Table 6.10 lead to the following conclusions:

- At 20% and 40% proportions of people working in a rich economy, that economy benefits while a poor economy loses from openness to investment flows. If $\omega = 0.5$, both economies benefit to the same extent. However, if the proportion equals 0.6 or 0.8, a rich economy loses while a poor economy benefits from openness to investments.

Table 6.10 Ratios of average estimated k_R^*, k_P^*, y_R^* and y_P^* in the several variants relative to Variant I, assuming that either economy invests 10% of its savings in the other economy (Variant I = 100)

Variant	*Variable*			
	k_R^*	k_P^*	y_R^*	y_P^*
II	178.7	95.6	156.3	101.5
III	112.8	95.2	110.2	98.0
IV	101.3	101.3	102.0	102.0
V	95.2	112.8	98.0	110.2
VI	95.6	178.7	101.5	156.3
VII	165.0	91.1	147.8	96.3
VIII	91.1	165.0	96.3	147.8

Source: Own calculations.

- If the savings rate equals 25% (15%) in a rich economy, and is less (greater) by 10% points in a poor economy, investment flows between those economies will lead to benefits derived by the rich (poor) economy combined with losses suffered by the poor (rich) economy.

6.4.2 *Investment flows depending on capital productivity*

Numerical simulations of the trajectories of capital per worker and labour productivity in a bipolar economic growth model can be conducted following an approximation of system of differential equations (6.18) using the following system of differential equations[10]:

$$
\begin{cases}
\Delta k_{Rt} = s_R \left(1 - \dfrac{\gamma_R}{1+\exp\left(-\dfrac{p_{pt-1}}{p_{Rt-1}}\right)}\right) k_{Rt-1}^{\alpha} k_{Pt-1}^{\beta} \\
\qquad + s_P \dfrac{\gamma_P}{1+\exp\left(-\dfrac{p_{Rt-1}}{p_{pt-1}}\right)} \dfrac{1-\omega}{\omega} k_{Pt-1}^{\alpha} k_{Rt-1}^{\beta} - \mu_R k_{Rt-1} \\
\Delta k_{Pt} = s_P \left(1 - \dfrac{\gamma_P}{1+\exp\left(-\dfrac{p_{Rt-1}}{p_{pt-1}}\right)}\right) k_{Pt-1}^{\alpha} k_{Rt-1}^{\beta} \\
\qquad + s_R \exp\left(-\dfrac{p_{pt-1}}{p_{Rt-1}}\right) \dfrac{\omega}{1-\omega} k_{Rt-1}^{\alpha} k_{Pt-1}^{\beta} - \mu_P k_{Pt-1}
\end{cases},
$$

where $p_{Rt} = \frac{y_{Rt}}{k_{Rt}} = k_{Rt}^{\alpha-1} k_{Pt}^{\beta}$ and $p_{pt} = \frac{y_{Pt}}{k_{Pt}} = k_{Pt}^{\alpha-1} k_{Rt}^{\beta}$ denote capital productivity (respectively) in a rich economy and in a poor economy in the year t. The above system of equations can also be written as:

$$\begin{cases} k_{Rt} = s_R \left(1 - \frac{\gamma_R}{1+\exp\left(-\frac{p_{pt-1}}{p_{Rt-1}}\right)} \right) k_{Rt-1}^{\alpha} k_{Pt-1}^{\beta} \\ \quad + s_P \frac{\gamma_P}{1+\exp\left(-\frac{p_{Rt-1}}{p_{pt-1}}\right)} \frac{1-\omega}{\omega} k_{Pt-1}^{\alpha} k_{Rt-1}^{\beta} + (1-\mu_R) k_{Rt-1} \\ k_{Pt} = s_P \left(1 - \frac{\gamma_P}{1+\exp\left(-\frac{p_{Rt-1}}{p_{pt-1}}\right)} \right) k_{Pt-1}^{\alpha} k_{Rt-1}^{\beta} \\ \quad + s_R \exp\left(-\frac{p_{pt-1}}{p_{Rt-1}}\right) \frac{\omega}{1-\omega} k_{Rt-1}^{\alpha} k_{Pt-1}^{\beta} + (1-\mu_P) k_{Pt-1} \end{cases} . \tag{6.29}$$

The parameters α, β, μ_R, μ_R in system of differential equations (6.29), were calibrated, like previously, at the levels: $\beta = \frac{\ln 3}{9 \ln 5}$, $\alpha = 10\beta$ and $\mu_R = \mu_R = 0.075$. It is assumed about parameters γ_R and γ_P that they equal 0.1. This implies that either of the analyzed economies is ready to invest in the other economy not more (not less) than 10% (5%) of its savings.

Additionally, nine various combinations of savings rates are considered (per each of Variants A-E described below) wherein the rates s_R and s_P can assume the values 17%, 20% or 23%.

The numerical simulation results given below start from the following additional assumptions:

- A a rich economy absorbs 20% of the total of workers;
- B $\omega = 0.4$;
- C 50% of the total of workers work in either of the analyzed economies;
- D $\omega = 0.6$;
- E 80% of the total of workers work in a rich economy;
- F the savings rate equals 25% in a rich economy, 15% in a poor economy, and ω assumes the subsequent values of 0.2, 0.4, 0.5, 0.6 or 0.8;
- G $s_R = 0.15$, $s_P = 0.25$ at ω, like in the preceding variant.

Selected numerical simulation results for Variant A are summarized in Table 6.11. It follows from the table that:

- No combination of the analyzed savings rates gives a poor economy the chance to catch up a rich economy, in terms of capital per worker and output per worker (although the process of partial convergence takes place in each scenario considered).
- At the same savings rates, long-run capital per worker will be greater by about 65.4% in a rich economy than in a poor economy, and labour productivity will be greater by about 41.0% in a rich economy than in a poor economy.
- If a poor economy is characterized by a savings rate greater by three percentage points than a rich economy, the rich economy will be characterized in a long run by capital per worker greater by about 29%.0–33.3% and by labour productivity greater by about 19.0%–21.7% than the poor economy. At a savings rate in a poor economy greater by 6% points $u^* \approx 1.071$ and $v^* \approx 1.048$.
- If the savings rate in a rich economy is greater by 3% points, the rich economy will enjoy in a long run capital per worker greater by about 110.2%–119.0% and labour productivity greater by about 66.0%–70.8%. At a savings rate in a rich economy greater by 6% points $u \to 2.841$, and $v \to 2.040$.

Table 6.12 contains numerical simulation results for a proportion of workers ω equal 40%. The table leads to the following conclusions.

- At the same savings rates in the analyzed economies, the ratio of long-run capitals per worker reaches a value of about 1.145, the ratio of labour productivities equals about 1.097.

- If the savings rate in a poor economy is greater by 3% points, that economy will be characterized by greater capital per worker and greater

Table 6.11 Selected numerical simulation results in Variant A (ω = 20%)

s_R (%)	s_P (%)	k_R^*	k_P^*	y_R^*	y_P^*	u^* (%)	v^* (%)	$\bar{t}$
17	17	222.6	134.6	87.5	62.1	165.4	141.0	Never
	20	389.1	301.6	142.1	119.4	129.0	119.0	Never
	23	664.4	620.5	225.2	214.9	107.1	104.8	Never
20	17	365.7	167.0	129.6	75.9	219.0	170.8	Never
	20	593.7	358.9	198.3	140.7	165.4	141.0	Never
	23	955.3	716.8	299.8	246.4	133.3	121.7	Never
23	17	594.8	209.3	190.7	93.5	284.1	204.0	Never
	20	905.7	430.9	277.0	166.8	210.2	166.0	Never
	23	1379.9	834.2	400.9	284.3	165.4	141.0	Never

Source: Own calculations.

Table 6.12 Selected numerical simulation results in Variant B (ω = 40%)

s_R (%)	s_P (%)	k_R^*	k_P^*	y_R^*	y_P^*	u^* (%)	v^* (%)	$\bar{t}$
17	17	152.1	132.9	65.5	59.7	114.5	109.7	Never
	20	232.0	273.7	95.3	106.6	84.8	89.3	41
	23	354.1	530.1	138.0	181.8	66.8	75.9	25
20	17	285.5	182.4	108.1	79.7	156.5	135.8	Never
	20	405.7	354.3	148.4	135.3	114.5	109.7	Never
	23	580.6	657.5	204.2	222.3	88.3	91.9	42
23	17	516.3	252.8	173.7	106.7	204.2	162.8	Never
	20	694.3	463.6	227.7	172.8	149.8	131.8	Never
	23	943.0	823.6	300.0	273.6	114.5	109.7	Never

Source: Own calculations.

output per worker than a rich economy after 41–42 years. In a long run, capital per worker will amount to about 84.8%–88.3% and labour productivity to about 89.3%–91.9% in an *R*-type economy of the respective values in a *P*-type economy. However, if a poor economy is characterized by a savings rate of 23% and a rich economy by a savings rate of 17%, the poor economy will overtake the rich economy after 25 years. In this case, $u^* \approx 0.668$, and $v^* \approx 0.795$.

- Considering the scenario wherein the savings rate in a rich economy is by 3% points greater than in a poor economy, capital per worker in the rich economy will be greater by about 50%–57% and labour productivity will be greater by about 32%–36% than in the poor economy in a long-run. A six-point difference in savings rates (in favour of a rich economy) leads to the ratio k_R^* / k_P^* exceeding 2, and y_R^* / y_P^* greater than 1.6.

Results of numerical simulation in a variant wherein either economy absorbs 50% of the resource of workers are given in Table 6.13. That summary leads to the following conclusions:

- At the same savings rates, complete convergence of capitals per worker and labour productivities will take place.
- If savings rates in a poor economy are greater by 3% points, the poor economy will overtake a rich economy in terms of capital per worker and labour productivity after about three decades. In a long run, capital per worker in an *R*-type economy will be less by about 23.5%–26.7%, and labour productivity will be less by about 16.7%–19.1% than in a *P*-type economy. If a poor economy is characterized by a savings rate greater by 6% points, the poor economy will overtake the *R*-type economy after 21 years. In a long run, $u \to 0.568$, and $v \to 0.679$.
- At a savings rate in a rich economy greater by 3% points, long-run capital per worker in that rich economy will be greater by about 30%–37% than in a poor economy. Long-run labour productivity will be greater

Table 6.13 Selected numerical simulation results in Variant C (ω = 50%)

s_R (%)	s_P (%)	k_R^*	k_P^*	y_R^*	y_P^*	u^* (%)	v^* (%)	$\bar{t}$
17	17	139.5	139.5	61.6	61.6	100.0	100.0	+∞
	20	201.5	275.1	85.7	105.9	73.3	80.9	31
	23	292.9	515.9	119.3	175.6	56.8	67.9	21
20	17	275.1	201.5	105.9	85.7	136.5	123.7	Never
	20	372.1	372.1	139.5	139.5	100.0	100.0	+∞
	23	508.3	664.6	184.7	221.8	76.5	83.3	30
23	17	515.9	292.9	175.6	119.3	176.2	147.2	Never
	20	664.6	508.3	221.8	184.7	130.7	120.1	Never
	23	864.9	864.9	282.0	282.0	100.0	100.0	+∞

Source: Own calculations.

by about 20%–24%. At a savings rate of 23% in a rich economy, and a savings rate in a poor economy less by 6% points, $u^* \approx 1.762$, and $v^* \approx 1.472$.

Table 6.14 contains results of numerical simulations of long-term levels of capital per worker and labour productivity and their ratios in a scenario wherein a rich economy absorbs 60% of the total number of workers. The results lead to the following conclusions:

- At a savings rate of 17% in an *R*-type economy, a *P*-type economy (characterized by a savings rate of 17%–23%) should overtake the former within 18–47 years. Long-run ratios of capitals per worker u^* should then be contained in the interval from about 0.490 to 0.873, and ratios of labour productivities in the interval from 0.614 to 0.912.
- If the savings rate equals 20% in a rich economy, and 17% in a poor economy, long-run capital per worker will be by about 18.0% greater and labour productivity will be by about 11.9% greater in the rich economy than in the poor economy. If the savings rate equals 20% in an

Table 6.14 Selected simulation results in Variant D (ω = 60%)

s_R (%)	s_P (%)	k_R^*	k_P^*	y_R^*	y_P^*	u^* (%)	v^* (%)	$\bar{t}$
17	17	132.9	152.1	59.7	65.5	87.3	91.2	47
	20	182.4	285.5	79.7	108.1	63.9	73.7	25
	23	252.8	516.3	106.7	173.7	49.0	61.4	18
20	17	273.7	232.0	106.6	95.3	118.0	111.9	Never
	20	354.3	405.7	135.3	148.4	87.3	91.2	42
	23	463.6	694.3	172.8	227.7	66.8	75.9	24
23	17	530.1	354.1	181.8	138.0	149.7	131.7	Never
	20	657.5	580.6	222.3	204.2	113.2	108.9	Never
	23	823.6	943.0	273.6	300.0	87.3	91.2	38

Source: Own calculations.

R-type economy and 20% or 23% in a *P*-type economy, then the *P*-type economy will overtake the other analyzed economy after 24–42 years. In a long run, the quotient k_R/k_P will approach the value of about 0.668–0.873, and the quotient y_R/y_P will approach the value of about 0.759-0.912.

- However, if the savings rate equals 23% in a rich economy and 17% or 20% in a poor economy, $u \to 1.497$ or $u \to 1.132$, and $v \to 1.317$ or $v \to 1.089$. If the savings rates equal 23% in both analyzed types of economy, a poor economy will overtake a rich economy after 38 years, and long-run ratios of capitals per worker and labour productivities will reach the levels of $u^* \approx 0.873$ and $v^* \approx 0.912$.

Table 6.15 contains selected numerical simulation results in the variant, wherein a poor economy absorbs 20% of the total of workers. The summary demonstrates that:

- In each of the analyzed scenarios, a *P*-type economy will be characterized by greater values of capital per worker and output per worker than an *R*-type economy.
- At the same savings rates in both types of economy, a poor economy will overtake a rich economy after 15–19 years. In a long run, capital per worker in an *R*-type economy will amount to about 60.5%, and labour productivity to about 70.9% of the respective values in a *P*-type economy.
- If a *P*-type economy is characterized by a savings rate greater by 3% points than an *R*-type economy, the former economy will reach greater values of capital per worker and labour productivity after 13–14 years. The long-run ratio of capitals per worker will approach then about 0.457–0.476, and the ratio of labour productivities will approach about 0.586–0.602. If the savings rate in a *P*-type economy is greater by 6% points, that economy will overtake an *R*-type economy after 12 years.

Table 6.15 Selected simulation results in Variant E ($\omega = 80\%$)

s_R (%)	s_P (%)	k_R^*	k_P^*	y_R^*	y_P^*	u^* (%)	v^* (%)	$\bar{t}$
17	17	134.6	222.6	62.1	87.5	60.5	70.9	19
	20	167.0	365.7	75.9	129.6	45.7	58.6	14
	23	209.3	594.8	93.5	190.7	35.2	49.0	12
20	17	301.6	389.1	119.4	142.1	77.5	84.1	23
	20	358.9	593.7	140.7	198.3	60.5	70.9	16
	23	430.9	905.7	166.8	277.0	47.6	60.2	13
23	17	620.5	664.4	214.9	225.2	93.4	95.4	36
	20	716.8	955.3	246.4	299.8	75.0	82.2	20
	23	834.3	1379.9	284.3	400.9	60.5	70.9	15

Source: Own calculations.

In this scenario, long-run capital per worker in an *R*-type economy will equal about 35.2% and labour productivity about 49.0% of the respective variables in the other analyzed type of economy.

- If a rich economy is characterized by a savings rate greater by 3% points than the other economy, the *P* economy will be characterized by greater values of capital per worker and output per worker after 16–20 years. In a long run, capital per worker in an *R*-type economy will amount to about 75.0%–77.5%, and labour productivity to about 82.2%–84.1% of the respective values in a *P*-type economy. At a six-point difference in savings rates (in favour of an initially rich economy), it takes 36 years for a poor economy needs to catch up an *R*-type economy, and $u \to 0.934$ and $v \to 0.954$ in a long run.

Let now us consider a scenario, wherein a rich economy is characterized by a considerably greater savings rate (equal 25%) than a poor economy (that is characterized by a value of that macroeconomic variable equal 15%). This variant is analyzed in cases with the proportion ω equal 20%, 40%, 50%, 60% or 80% (Table 6.16). Then, numerical simulations lead to the following conclusions:

- Complete convergence is not possible in any of the analyzed cases, but partial convergence takes place in each case.
- At a proportion of people working in a rich economy equal 20%, partial convergence is very limited, because the ratio of capitals per worker drops from 5:1 (in the year $t = 0$) to about 4.245:1 (at $t \to \infty$). The ratio of labour productivities will drop then from 3:1 to about 2.683:1.
- At a 40% proportion of people working in a rich economy, long-run capital per worker in that economy will be almost three times greater than in a poor economy, and labour productivity will be more than twice as great as in a poor economy.
- If the analyzed economies share the number of workers at a 1:1 proportion, then in a long run $u \to 2.482$ and $v \to 1.860$.
- In a scenario with a rich economy absorbing 60% of the total of workers, long-run capital per worker in that economy will be more than twice

Table 6.16. Selected results of numerical simulations in Variant F (s_R =25% and s_P =15%)

ω (%)	k_R^*	k_P^*	y_R^*	y_P^*	u^* (%)	v^* (%)	$\bar{t}$
20	635.3	149.6	195.4	72.8	424.5	268.3	Never
40	632.4	213.8	200.0	95.4	295.8	209.7	Never
50	661.1	266.4	210.4	113.1	248.2	186.0	Never
60	706.2	345.8	225.6	138.6	204.2	162.8	Never
80	887.9	754.1	284.7	254.7	117.7	111.8	Never

Source: Own calculations.

as great as in a poor economy, and its labour productivity will be by more than 60% greater in a long run.

- However, if a rich economy is considerably bigger considering the number of workers (i.e. when $\omega = 0.8$), its capital per worker and labour productivity will be greater by about 12%–18% than in a poor economy in a long run.

Table 6.17 contains selected numerical simulation results in Variant F, opposite to Variant E (in that the savings rate in a poor economy is greater by 10% points than in a rich economy). The results of numerical simulations contained in the table lead to the following conclusions:

- A P-type economy will overtake an R-type economy considering capital per worker and labour productivity in all analyzed scenarios. The poor economy needs from 10 to 28 years to catch up the rich economy.
- The higher proportion of the total of workers is absorbed by an R-type economy, (first) the faster it will be overtaken by a P-type economy and (second) the lower are long-run ratios of u^* and v^*.

The table contains ratios of average estimated k_R^*, k_P^*, y_R^* and y_P^* in the several variants, relative to Variant I (a scenario wherein there are no investment flows). Table 6.18 leads to similar economic conclusions as Table 6.10.

Table 6.17 Selected results of numerical simulations in Variant F ($s_R = 15\%$ and $s_P = 25\%$)

ω (%)	k_R^*	k_P^*	y_R^*	y_P^*	u^* (%)	v^* (%)	$\bar{t}$
20	754.1	887.9	254.7	284.7	84.9	89.4	28
40	345.8	706.2	138.6	225.6	49.0	61.4	17
50	266.4	661.1	113.1	210.4	40.3	53.8	15
60	213.8	632.4	95.4	200.0	33.8	47.7	14
80	149.6	635.3	72.8	195.4	23.6	37.3	10

Source: Own calculations.

Table 6.18 Ratios of average estimated k_R^*, k_P^*, y_R^* and y_P^* in the several variants relative to Variant I (Variant I = 100)

Variant	Variable			
	k_R^*	k_P^*	y_R^*	y_P^*
A	160.4	99.7	144.5	104.0
B	110.0	97.0	108.2	99.1
C	101.3	101.3	101.9	101.9
D	97.0	110.0	99.1	108.2
E	99.7	160.4	104.0	144.5
F	167.6	82.3	148.8	89.9
G	82.3	167.6	89.9	148.8

Source: Own calculations.

6.5 Conclusions

The analyzes contained in this chapter can be summarized as follows[11]:

I The described bipolar economic growth models are based on the Solow growth model (1956) with elements of the gravity model of economic growth (Mroczek, Tokarski and Trojak, 2014).

II It is assumed in those models that investments can be financed in an economy using both domestic savings and foreign savings. The first growth model discussed in this chapter bases on the assumption about an exogenous structure of (domestic and foreign) investments. In the second discussed model, investment flows are made conditional on capital productivity in the analyzed economies (savings flow principally from an economy characterized by a lower capital productivity to an economy characterized by a higher value of that macroeconomic variable).

III Additionally, it is assumed in those models that the level of labour productivity in either economy (i.e. in a rich and in a poor economy) depends not only on capital per worker in that economy but also in the other analyzed economy.

IV The systems of differential equations derived from the assumptions adopted in the models have exactly one non-trivial steady state each. Those states are characterized by asymptotic stability. As such, they determine conditions for a long-run equilibrium of the analyzed economies.

V The ratios of long-run capitals per worker k_R^*/k_P^* and long-run labour productivities y_R^*/y_P^* in the model characterized by exogenous investment flows (the model from Section 6.2) depend on investment rates, rates of capital decline and on the proportions of workers absorbed by the analyzed economies. The higher the investment rates in a rich economy and the higher the decline rate of capital per worker in a poor economy and the lower the decline rate of capital per worker in a rich economy or investment rates in a rich economy and percentage of people working in a rich economy, the greater are the ratios k_R^*/k_P^* and y_R^*/y_P^*.

VI The trajectories of analyzed macroeconomic variables and long-run equilibrium states can be determined in neither of the two considered models. To illustrate the trajectories of analyzed variables, the authors calibrated model parameters and performed numerical simulations of those trajectories.

VII When calibrating model parameters, the authors sought such elasticities α and β of labour productivity functions that lead (first) to an impact of external factors (measured by the elasticity of domestic labour productivity with respect to capital per worker abroad) that is ten times lower than the elasticity of domestic output per worker with respect to domestic capital per worker and (second) to a ratio of labour productivities of 3:1 at a relationship between capital-labour ratios of 5:1. It was also arbitrarily assumed that e.g. the rate of decline in capital per worker in either economy equals 7.5%, savings rates fluctuate between 17% and 23% and the economies are ready to invest abroad 5%–10% of their savings. The performed numerical simulations are also based on the assumption that initial capital per worker equals five in a rich economy, and one in a poor economy.

VIII The results of numerical simulations given above indicate complete or partial convergence between the analyzed economies (although combinations of model parameters are also possible that lead to divergence).[12] The reason is that the analyzed growth models are characterized by diminishing marginal productivities of capital (resulting from the Cobb-Douglas production function) and that accelerated capital accumulation in one of the economies stimulates production in the other economy.

IX Moreover, the greater proportion of workers is absorbed by a rich economy, the sooner it is caught up by a poor economy. The greater the savings rate in a poor economy relative to the savings rate in a rich economy, the greater the speed of the convergence process.

X The numerical simulations described in this chapter also lead to the following, more general conclusions. First, if a rich economy is smaller (considering the number of workers) than a poor economy, and both have similar savings rates, openness to investment flows between the economies is beneficial to the rich economy, and disadvantageous to the poor economy. Second, if a greater number of workers is absorbed by a poor economy, openness to investment flows is beneficial to that economy and disadvantageous to a rich economy. Third, if a rich (poor) economy is characterized by an investment rate greater by 10% points, investment flows are beneficial to that economy and disadvantageous to the other economy.

Notes

1 Poland could use e.g. German autobahns connecting us with France or Italy, the Germans could not (until recently) use Polish motorways on their way to Ukraine, because Polish motorways (simply) did not exist.

2 The following relation holds: $\forall u > 0 \ \frac{\partial \phi}{\partial u} = -\left((1-\alpha)a_1 u^{\alpha-2} + (1-\beta)a_2 u^{\beta-2} + \beta b_1 u^{\beta-1} + \alpha b_2 u^{\alpha-1}\right) < 0$, so that an analysis of signs of partial derivatives u*, given by formula (6.13), with respect to subsequent independent variables x, leads to:

3 Differential equations (6.14a,b) are interpreted in economic terms like equations (6.5a,b).

4 Certainly, the parameters $\delta_R, \delta_P \in (0,1)$ represent capital depreciation rates in rich economies and poor economies, while $n > 0$ denotes the growth rate of the number of workers in both types of countries.

5 While estimating the signs of the quantity j_{ij} (for $i, j = 1, 2$), we use the relations:

$$\frac{d\ell_R}{d(k_R / k_P)} > 0 \text{ and } \frac{d\ell_P}{d(k_R / k_P)} < 0.$$

6 See also simulations in the study by Filipowicz and Tokarski (2015).
7 In the simulations described below, we adopt an approximated long-run value of any variable x given by the formula: $x^* = \lim_{t \to \infty} x_t \approx x_{1,000}$.
8 The concept of convergence (or complete convergence) is understood below as a process wherein (using the symbols introduced in this study) $u(t) \underset{t \to +\infty}{\rightarrow} 1 \wedge v(t) \underset{t \to +\infty}{\rightarrow} 1$. Partial convergence is understood by the authors as a process wherein the ratios of u and v drop (in time), approaching a value other than 1.
9 The statement is apparently illogical. However, remember that (first) the rich economy invests in the poor economy a fraction of its savings that is twice as large as the fraction invested by the poor economy in the rich economy, and (second) the rich economy is four times bigger (considering the number of workers) than the poor economy.
10 See also numerical simulations in the study by Filipowicz, Wisła and Tokarski (2015).
11 See also Filipowicz and Tokarski (2015) or Filipowicz, Wisła and Tokarski (2015).
12 If we assume in a model with exogenous investment rates that 10% of the total of workers work in a rich economy, either economy invests abroad 10% of its savings, the savings rate equals 40% in a rich economy, and 10% in a poor economy, then at $t \to \infty$, we get: $u \to 26.135$ and $v \to 9.277$. In a model with investment flows conditional on capital productivity, considering the same assumptions and $\gamma_R = \gamma_P = 10\%$, we obtain $u^* \approx 25.277$ and $v^* \approx 9.068$ (quantities strikingly similar to those implied by a model with exogenous investment rates).

7 The gravity model of economic growth

7.1 Introduction

The gravity model of economic growth described in this chapter bases on the Solow growth model. We assume in the gravity model that variation across total productivities of production factors in economies is affected by spatial interactions between them that can be described by what is known as gravitational effects. How those gravitational effects work in the discussed economic growth model can be explained by analogy to Newton's law of universal gravitation. It is assumed that economies attract each other with a specific force that is directly proportional to the product of their economic potentials and inversely proportional to the square of the distance between them. We will also propose golden rules of capital accumulation for the gravity model of economic growth, and those rules will be defined in two ways. We assume that the golden rule of capital accumulation can be defined as either such combination of investment rates in economies covered by the gravitational effects that maximizes the geometric mean of consumption per worker in all economies, or such combination of investment rates that maximizes long-run consumption per worker in each of the economies. The growth models described in this chapter were proposed by Mroczek, Tokarski and Trojak (2014), Filipowicz, Tokarski and Trojak (2015) and Filipowicz (2019).

7.2 Assumptions of the model

The gravity model of economic growth is based on the following assumptions about a finite N number of economies (see e.g. Mroczek, Tokarski, and Trojak, 2014 or Filipowicz, 2019):

1 Labour productivity in each of the economies is described by a Cobb-Douglas function given by the formula:

$$\forall m \quad y_m(t) = a \cdot (g_m(t))^{\beta} \cdot (k_m(t))^{\alpha}, \tag{7.1}$$

where y_m denotes labour productivity in economy m (for $m = 1, 2, \ldots, N$), $a > 0$ is a constant,[1] g_m represents gravitational effects that connect economy m with other economies,[2] k_i represents capital per worker in

DOI: 10.4324/9781003323792-8

economy m, and α and β denote the elasticities of labour productivity with respect to capital per worker and to gravitational effects. It is assumed about the elasticities α and β that $\alpha, \beta, (\alpha+\beta) \in (0,1)$, $\alpha > \beta$ and $\beta < \frac{1-\alpha}{2}$. The assumptions about elasticities lead to the conclusion that the labour productivity function: (first) is characterized by diminishing marginal productivities of gravitational effects and of capital per worker and (second) that gravitational effects are less important as a determinant of labour productivity than capital per worker.

2 Total gravitational effects g_m influencing economy m represent an arithmetic means of individual gravitational effects g_{mn} (for m, n = 1, 2, ..., N at $n \neq m$) connecting that economy with each of the remaining economies. Hence:

$$\forall m \quad g_m(t) = \sqrt[N-1]{\prod_{n \neq m} g_{mn}(t)}. \tag{7.2}$$

3 Individual gravitational effects connecting any pair of economies (like in Newton's law of universal gravitation) are directly proportional to the product of their economic potentials and inversely proportional to the distance between them. The economic potential of each economy is measured by capital per worker. Hence, individual gravitational effects are defined by the relation:

$$\forall m, n \wedge n \neq m \quad g_{mn}(t) = \frac{k_m(t) \cdot k_n(t)}{d_{mn}^2}, \tag{7.3}$$

where $d_{mn} > 0$ represents the distance (in geographic space) between economy m and economy n.

4 An increase in capital per worker in economy m is defined by Solow equation (2.15), hence:

$$\forall m \quad \dot{k}_m(t) = s_m y_m(t) - \mu_m k_m(t), \tag{7.4}$$

where for subsequent m, $s_m \in (0,1)$ denotes the savings/investment rate in economy m, and $\mu_m = \delta_m + n_m > 0$ is the rate of decline in capital per worker in economy m, being the total of capital deprecation rate $\delta_m \in (0,1)$ and the growth rate of the number of workers $n_m > 0$ in that economy.

7.3 A solution of the model

Substituting individual gravitational effects from equation (7.2) into (7.5), we get:

$$\forall m \quad g_m(t) = \frac{k_m(t) \cdot \sqrt[N-1]{\prod_{n \neq m} k_n(t)}}{\sqrt[N-1]{\prod_{n \neq m} d_{mn}^2}}$$

or:

$$\forall m \quad g_m(t) = \frac{k_m(t) \cdot \sqrt[N-1]{\prod_{n \neq m} k_n(t)}}{\bar{d}_m^2}, \tag{7.5}$$

where $\bar{d}_m$ denotes the geometric mean of the distance between economy m and the remaining economies. Equation (7.5) leads to the conclusion that the total of gravitational effects affecting economy m is directly proportional to the value of capital per worker in that economy and to capitals per worker in the remaining economies and the greater the closer to the centre is the location of economy m (i.e. the lower is the value of $\bar{d}_m$).

Substituting the equation of total gravitational effects (7.5) into labour productivity function (7.1), we get:

$$\forall m \quad y_m(t) = a\left(\frac{k_m(t) \cdot \sqrt[N-1]{\prod_{n \neq m} k_n(t)}}{\sqrt[N-1]{\prod_{n \neq m} d_{mn}^2}}\right)^{\beta} \cdot (k_m(t))^{\alpha},$$

which results in:

$$\forall m \quad y_m(t) = a\frac{\left(\prod_{n \neq m} k_n(t)\right)^{\beta/(N-1)} \cdot (k_m(t))^{\alpha+\beta}}{\bar{d}_m^{2\beta}}. \tag{7.6}$$

Equation (7.6) makes labour productivity y_m in economy m conditional on capital per worker k_m in that economy, capitals per worker k_n in the remaining economies and on the geographic location of economy m, described by the distance $\bar{d}_m$.

Substituting labour productivity function (7.6) into equations (7.4), we obtain the following system of differential equations:

$$\forall m \quad \dot{k}_m(t) = as_m\frac{\left(\prod_{n \neq m} k_n(t)\right)^{\frac{\beta}{(N-1)}} \cdot (k_m(t))^{\alpha+\beta}}{\bar{d}_m^{2\beta}} - \mu_m k_m(t). \tag{7.7}$$

System of differential equations (7.7) is analyzed in the phase space $P = [0,+\infty)^N$.

System of equations (7.7) has in the phase space P a trivial steady state (that is ignored as uninteresting for economic and mathematical analyzes) and (as will be demonstrated soon) exactly one non-trivial steady state $\kappa \in (0,+\infty)^N$.

In the non-trivial steady state k, $\forall m \ \dot{k}_m = 0 \wedge k_m > 0$. It follows from equations (7.7) that the following hold in than point:

$$\begin{cases} k_1^{1-\alpha-\beta}\prod_{n\neq 1} k_n^{-\beta/(N-1)} = \dfrac{as_1}{\mu_1 \bar{d}_1^{2\beta}} \\ k_2^{1-\alpha-\beta}\prod_{n\neq 2} k_n^{-\frac{\beta}{(N-1)}} = \dfrac{as_2}{\mu_2 \bar{d}_2^{2\beta}} \\ \vdots \\ k_N^{1-\alpha-\beta}\prod_{n\neq N} k_n^{-\frac{\beta}{(N-1)}} = \dfrac{as_N}{\mu_N \bar{d}_N^{2\beta}} \end{cases}.$$

The above system of equations (considering that $\kappa\epsilon(0,+\infty)^N$) can be written:

$$\begin{cases} (1-\alpha-\beta)\ln k_1 - \dfrac{\beta}{N-1}\sum_{n\neq 1}\ln k_n = \theta_1 \\ (1-\alpha-\beta)\ln k_2 - \dfrac{\beta}{N-1}\sum_{n\neq 2}\ln k_n = \theta_2 \\ \vdots \\ (1-\alpha-\beta)\ln k_N - \dfrac{\beta}{N-1}\sum_{n\neq N}\ln k_n = \theta_N \end{cases}, \tag{7.8}$$

where: $\forall m \;\; \theta_m = \ln\dfrac{as_m}{\mu_m \bar{d}_m^{2\beta}} \in R.$

Adding up the subsequent equations of system (7.8), we obtain:

$$(1-\alpha-2\beta)\sum_m \ln k_m = \sum_m \theta_m,$$

which results in:

$$\sum_m \ln k_m = \frac{\sum_m \theta_m}{1-\alpha-2\beta} = \frac{\sum_m \ln\dfrac{as_m}{\mu_m \bar{d}_m^{2\beta}}}{1-\alpha-2\beta}. \tag{7.9}$$

Each equation in system (7.8) can be written:

$$\forall m \;\; \left(1-\alpha-\frac{N-2}{N-1}\beta\right)\ln k_m - \frac{\beta}{N-1}\sum_n \ln k_n = \theta_m,$$

and this together with equation (7.9) gives:

$$\forall m \;\; \left(1-\alpha-\frac{N-2}{N-1}\beta\right)\ln k_m = \theta_m + \frac{\beta}{N-1}\sum_n \ln k_n$$
$$= \theta_m + \frac{\beta}{(N-1)(1-\alpha-2\beta)}\sum_n \theta_N$$

hence, the following holds in the steady state $\kappa = \left(k_1^*, k_2^*, \ldots, k_N^*\right) \in (0,+\infty)^N$:

$$\forall m \quad \ln k_m^* = \frac{\theta_m + \dfrac{\beta}{(N-1)(1-\alpha-2\beta)}\sum_n \theta_n}{1-\alpha-\dfrac{N-2}{N-1}\beta},$$

or, considering the substitutions $\forall m \quad \theta_m = \ln \frac{as_m}{\mu_m \bar{d}_m^{2\beta}}$, we get:

$$\forall m \quad \ln k_m^* = \frac{\ln \dfrac{as_m}{\mu_m \bar{d}_m^{2\beta}} + \dfrac{\beta}{(N-1)(1-\alpha-2\beta)}\sum_n \ln \dfrac{as_n}{\mu_n \bar{d}_n^{2\beta}}}{1-\alpha-\dfrac{N-2}{N-1}\beta}. \tag{7.10}$$

Equations (7.10) describe the non-trivial steady state of system of differential equations (7.7).

Jacobian matrix J of system of equations (7.7) is described by the formula:

$$J = \begin{bmatrix} (\alpha+\beta)s_1 \dfrac{y_1}{k_1} - \mu_1 & \dfrac{\beta s_1 y_1}{(N-1)k_2} & \cdots & \dfrac{\beta s_1 y_1}{(N-1)k_N} \\ \dfrac{\beta s_2 y_2}{(N-1)k_1} & (\alpha+\beta)s_2 \dfrac{y_2}{k_2} - \mu_2 & \cdots & \dfrac{\beta s_2 y_2}{(N-1)k_N} \\ \vdots & \vdots & \ddots & \vdots \\ \dfrac{\beta s_N y_N}{(N-1)k_1} & \dfrac{\beta s_N y_N}{(N-1)k_2} & \cdots & (\alpha+\beta)s_N \dfrac{y_N}{k_N} - \mu_N \end{bmatrix}. \tag{7.11}$$

In the non-trivial steady state k, the following holds: $\forall j \quad \mu_j = s_j \frac{y_j^*}{k_j^*}$, so that Jacobi matrix (7.11) can be written in that point as:

$$J^* = \begin{bmatrix} \dfrac{-(1-\alpha-\beta)s_1 y_1^*}{k_1^*} & \dfrac{\beta s_1 y_1^*}{(N-1)k_2^*} & \cdots & \dfrac{\beta s_1 y_1^*}{(N-1)k_N^*} \\ \dfrac{\beta s_2 y_2^*}{(N-1)k_1^*} & \dfrac{-(1-\alpha-\beta)s_2 y_2^*}{k_2^*} & \cdots & \dfrac{\beta s_2 y_2^*}{(N-1)k_N^*} \\ \vdots & \vdots & \ddots & \vdots \\ \dfrac{\beta s_N y_N^*}{(N-1)k_1^*} & \dfrac{\beta s_N y_N^*}{(N-1)k_2^*} & \cdots & \dfrac{-(1-\alpha-\beta)s_N y_N^*}{k_N^*} \end{bmatrix}. \tag{7.12}$$

Eigenvalues of matrix (7.12) solve the equation:

$$\begin{vmatrix} \dfrac{-(1-\alpha-\beta)s_1 y_1^*}{k_1^*} - \lambda & \dfrac{\beta s_1 y_1^*}{(N-1)k_2^*} & \cdots & \dfrac{\beta s_1 y_1^*}{(N-1)k_N^*} \\ \dfrac{\beta s_2 y_2^*}{(N-1)k_1^*} & \dfrac{-(1-\alpha-\beta)s_2 y_2^*}{k_2^*} - \lambda & \cdots & \dfrac{\beta s_2 y_2^*}{(N-1)k_N^*} \\ \vdots & \vdots & \ddots & \vdots \\ \dfrac{\beta s_N y_N^*}{(N-1)k_1^*} & \dfrac{\beta s_N y_N^*}{(N-1)k_2^*} & \cdots & \dfrac{-(1-\alpha-\beta)s_N y_N^*}{k_N^*} - \lambda \end{vmatrix} = 0,$$

that can also be written as:

$$\begin{vmatrix} -(1-\alpha-\beta)-\frac{\lambda k_1^*}{s_1 y_1^*} & \frac{\beta}{N-1} & \cdots & \frac{\beta}{N-1} \\ \frac{\beta}{N-1} & -(1-\alpha-\beta)-\frac{\lambda k_2^*}{s_2 y_2^*} & \cdots & \frac{\beta}{N-1} \\ \vdots & \vdots & \ddots & \vdots \\ \frac{\beta}{N-1} & \frac{\beta}{N-1} & \cdots & -(1-\alpha-\beta)-\frac{\lambda k_N^*}{s_N y_N^*} \end{vmatrix} = 0,$$

which results in:

$$\begin{vmatrix} -\frac{(1-\alpha-\beta)(N-1)}{\beta}-\frac{\lambda(N-1)k_1^*}{\beta s_1 y_1^*} & 1 & \cdots & 1 \\ 1 & -\frac{(1-\alpha-\beta)(N-1)}{\beta}-\frac{\lambda(N-1)k_2^*}{\beta s_1 y_2^*} & \cdots & 1 \\ \vdots & \vdots & \ddots & \vdots \\ 1 & 1 & \cdots & -\frac{(1-\alpha-\beta)(N-1)}{\beta}-\frac{\lambda(N-1)k_N^*}{\beta s_1 y_N^*} \end{vmatrix} =$$

or:

$$Q = \begin{vmatrix} -\Omega-\omega_1\lambda & 1 & \cdots & 1 \\ 1 & -\Omega-\omega_1\lambda & \cdots & 1 \\ \vdots & \vdots & \ddots & \vdots \\ 1 & 1 & \cdots & -\Omega-\omega_N\lambda \end{vmatrix} = 0,$$

where $\Omega = \frac{(1-\alpha-\beta)(N-1)}{\beta} > 0$ and $\forall j \;\; \omega_j = \frac{(N-1)k_j^*}{\beta s_j y_j^*} > 0$. Determinant Q, following few elementary transformations, can be written as:

$$Q = (-1)^N \prod_j (\Omega+1+\omega_j\lambda)\left(1-\sum_j \frac{1}{\Omega+1+\omega_j\lambda}\right),$$

hence, eigenvalues of matrix J^* solve the equation:

$$(-1)^N \prod_j (\Omega+1+\omega_j\lambda)\left(1-\sum_j \frac{1}{\Omega+1+\omega_j\lambda}\right) = 0$$

or:

$$1-\sum_j \frac{1}{\Omega+1+\omega_j\lambda} = 0. \tag{7.13}$$

Let us write eigenvalues λ as:

$\lambda = a + bi$, where $a, b \in R$, and $i = \sqrt{-1}$. Then, equation (7.13) can be reduced to the equation:

$$\sum_j \frac{1}{\Omega + 1 + \omega_j \lambda} = 1. \tag{7.14}$$

Since every complex number z satisfies the relation:

$$\frac{1}{z} = \frac{\bar{z}}{|z|^2}$$

Where $\bar{z}$ is a complex conjugate of z, we get as per quotation (7.14):

$$\sum_j \frac{\Omega + 1 + \omega_j a - \omega_j bi}{(\Omega + 1 + \omega_j a)^2 + \omega_j^2 b^2} = 1$$

or:

$$\sum_j \frac{\Omega + 1 + \omega_j a}{(\Omega + 1 + \omega_j a)^2 + \omega_j^2 b^2} - bi \sum_j \frac{\omega_j}{(\Omega + 1 + \omega_j a)^2 + \omega_j^2 b^2} = 1, \tag{7.15}$$

which leads to the conclusion that $b = 0$. Hence, the eigenvalues of the Jacobi matrix (7.12) are real numbers. And equation (7.14) can be written as:

$$\sum_j \frac{1}{\Omega + 1 + \omega_j a} = 1. \tag{7.16}$$

We will now demonstrate that a in equation (7.16) is a negative number. For this purpose, an indirect proof will be given. Let us assume (despite our hypothesis) that $a \geq 0$. Then:

$$\sum_j \frac{1}{\Omega + 1 + \omega_j a} \leq \sum_j \frac{1}{\Omega + 1} = \frac{N}{\Omega + 1} = \frac{N}{(1 - \alpha - \beta)(N - 1) + \beta} < \frac{N\beta}{(N - 1)\beta + \beta} = 1,$$

which is inconsistent with equation (7.16). Hence, all eigenvalues λ of Jacobi matrix J^* are negative real numbers. It follows from the Grobman-Hartman theorem that the Lyapunov asymptotically stable point κ defined by equations (7.10) is the point of long-run equilibrium in the analyzed gravity model of economic growth. It follows from equations (7.10) that:

- Long-run capital per worker k_m^* in economy m depends e.g. on the savings/investment rate s_m in that economy, savings/investment rates s_n (for $n \neq m$) in the remaining economies, the rate of decline in capital per worker μ_m in economy m, rates of decline in capital per worker μ_n in the remaining economies and on the geographic location of economy m (described by geometric means of distances $\bar{d}_1, \bar{d}_2, \ldots, \bar{d}_N$).

- Since $\forall m \ \dfrac{\partial \ln k_m^*}{\partial s_m} = \dfrac{1 + \dfrac{\beta}{(N-1)(1-\alpha-2\beta)}}{\left(1-\alpha-\dfrac{N-2}{N-1}\beta\right)s_m} > 0$, then the higher the savings/investment rate s_m in economy m, the higher the level of capital per worker k_m^* characteristic of that economy in a long run.
- A high rate of decline in capital per worker μ_m in economy m corresponds to a low value of k_m^*. This is because:

$$\forall m \quad \frac{\partial \ln k_m^*}{\partial \mu_m} = -\frac{1 + \dfrac{\beta}{(N-1)(1-\alpha-2\beta)}}{\left(1-\alpha-\dfrac{N-2}{N-1}\beta\right)\mu_m} < 0.$$

- The effect of $\bar{d}_m$ on k_m^* is similar which results from:

$$\forall m \quad \frac{\partial \ln k_m^*}{\partial \bar{d}_m} = -\frac{2\beta\left(1 + \dfrac{\beta}{(N-1)(1-\alpha-2\beta)}\right)}{\left(1-\alpha-\dfrac{N-2}{N-1}\beta\right)\bar{d}_m} < 0.$$

- While $\forall m,n \wedge n \neq m \ \dfrac{\partial \ln k_m^*}{\partial s_n} = \dfrac{\beta}{(N-1)(1-\alpha-2\beta)\left(1-\alpha-\dfrac{N-2}{N-1}\beta\right)s_n} > 0$ implies that (due to gravitational effects) the higher the savings/investment rate s_n in economy n, the higher is capital per worker k_m^* in economy m in a long run.
- Also due to gravitational effects, the higher the values of decline μ_n and geometric means $\bar{d}_n$, the lower the values of capital per worker k_m^*, because:

$$\forall m,n \wedge n \neq m \quad \frac{\partial \ln k_m^*}{\partial \mu_n} = -\frac{\beta}{(N-1)(1-\alpha-2\beta)\left(1-\alpha-\dfrac{N-2}{N-1}\beta\right)\mu_n} < 0$$

and:

$$\forall m,n \wedge n \neq m \quad \frac{\partial \ln k_m^*}{\partial \bar{d}_n} = -\frac{2\beta^2}{(N-1)(1-\alpha-2\beta)\left(1-\alpha-\dfrac{N-2}{N-1}\beta\right)\bar{d}_n} < 0.$$

It follows from equation (7.6) that:

$$\forall m \quad \ln y_m(t) = \ln\frac{a}{\bar{d}_m^{2\beta}} + \frac{\beta}{N-1}\sum_{n \neq m} \ln k_n(t) + (\alpha+\beta)\ln k_m(t),$$

or, in the state of long-run equilibrium:

$$\forall m \quad \ln y_m^* = \ln\frac{a}{\bar{d}_m^{2\beta}} + \frac{\beta}{N-1}\sum_{n \neq m} \ln k_n^* + (\alpha+\beta)\ln k_m^*. \tag{7.17}$$

Equation (7.17) can also be written as:

$$\forall m \quad \ln y_m^* = \ln \frac{a}{\bar{d}_m^{2\beta}} + \frac{\beta}{N-1}\sum_n \ln k_n^* + \left(\alpha + \frac{N-2}{N-1}\beta\right)\ln k_m^*,$$

that, considering (7.9) and (7.10), gives:

$$\forall m \quad \ln y_m^* = \ln \frac{a}{\bar{d}_m^{2\beta}} + \frac{\beta}{(N-1)(1-\alpha-2\beta)}\sum_n \ln \frac{as_n}{\mu_n \bar{d}_n^{2\beta}}$$
$$+\left(\alpha + \frac{N-2}{N-1}\beta\right)\frac{\ln \frac{as_m}{\mu_m \bar{d}_m^{2\beta}} + \frac{\beta}{(N-1)(1-\alpha-2\beta)}\sum_n \ln \frac{as_n}{\mu_n \bar{d}_n^{2\beta}}}{1-\alpha-\frac{N-2}{N-1}\beta}.$$

The above equation can also be written as:

$$\forall m \quad \ln y_m^* = \ln \frac{a}{\bar{d}_m^{2\beta}} + \frac{\beta}{(N-1)(1-\alpha-2\beta)}\sum_n \ln \frac{as_n}{\mu_n \bar{d}_n^{2\beta}} + \frac{\alpha + \frac{N-2}{N-1}\beta}{1-\alpha-\frac{N-2}{N-1}\beta}\ln \frac{as_m}{\mu_m \bar{d}_m^{2\beta}}$$
$$+\frac{\beta}{(N-1)(1-\alpha-2\beta)}\cdot\frac{\alpha(N-1)+(N-2)\beta}{(N-1)(1-\alpha)-(N-2)\beta}\sum_n \ln \frac{as_n}{\mu_n \bar{d}_n^{2\beta}},$$

hence:

$$\forall m \quad \ln y_m^* = \ln \frac{a}{\bar{d}_m^{2\beta}} + \frac{\alpha + \frac{N-2}{N-1}\beta}{1-\alpha-\frac{N-2}{N-1}\beta}\ln \frac{as_m}{\mu_m \bar{d}_m^{2\beta}}$$
$$+\frac{\beta}{(N-1)(1-\alpha-2\beta)\left(1-\alpha-\frac{N-2}{N-1}\beta\right)}\sum_n \ln \frac{as_n}{\mu_n \bar{d}_n^{2\beta}}. \tag{7.18}$$

Since it follows from equations (7.10) and (7.18) that $\forall m \quad \mathrm{sgn}\frac{\partial \ln k_m^*}{\partial x} = \mathrm{sgn}\frac{\partial \ln y_m^*}{\partial x}$ (where x denotes any independent variable determining long-run capital per worker or long-term labour productivity), the higher the savings/investment rates $s1, s2, \ldots, s_N$ or the lower the rates of decline in subsequent capitals per worker $\mu 1, \mu 2, \ldots, \mu_N$ or the lower the average distances $\bar{d}_1, \bar{d}_2, \ldots, \bar{d}_N$, the higher is long-term labour productivity y_m^* in any economy $m = 1, 2, \ldots, N$.

7.4 Golden rules of capital accumulation

The golden rule of capital accumulation[3] in the gravity model of economic growth will be defined using two approaches in the below theoretical analyzes. The golden rule of capital accumulation will be understood either as such combination of savings/investment rates that maximizes the geometric mean of long-run consumption per worker in all economies (the analyzes in Section 7.4.1) or such combination of those rates that in a long run maximizes consumption per worker in each of the economies (Section 7.4.2).

7.4.1 Maximization of the geometric mean of long-run consumption per worker

Let us introduce $s=(s_1,s_2,\ldots,s_N)\in(0,1)^N$ to denote any combination of savings/investment rates in the analyzed economies. Let us also write equation (7.18) as follows:

$$\forall m\ \ \ln \overset{*}{y}_m(s)=\Theta+\frac{\alpha+\frac{N-2}{N-1}\beta}{1-\alpha-\frac{N-2}{N-1}\beta}\ln s_m +\frac{\beta}{(N-1)(1-\alpha-2\beta)\left(1-\alpha-\frac{N-2}{N-1}\beta\right)}\sum_n \ln s_n, \tag{7.19}$$

where:

$$\Theta=\ln\frac{a}{\bar{d}_m^{2\beta}}+\frac{\alpha+\frac{N-2}{N-1}\beta}{1-\alpha-\frac{N-2}{N-1}\beta}\ln\frac{a}{\mu_m\bar{d}_m^{2\beta}} +\frac{\beta}{(N-1)(1-\alpha-2\beta)\left(1-\alpha-\frac{N-2}{N-1}\beta\right)}\sum_n \ln\frac{a}{\mu_n\bar{d}_n^{2\beta}}\in R.$$

Since at each moment t consumption per worker in economy m can be written as:

$$\forall m\ \ c_m(t)=(1-s_m)\,y_m(t),$$

we get in a long run:

$$\forall m\ \ \overset{*}{c}_m(s)=(1-s_m)\,\overset{*}{y}_m(s), \tag{7.20}$$

or:

$$\forall m\ \ v_m(v)=\ln\overset{*}{c}_m(s)=\ln(1-s_m)+\ln\overset{*}{y}_m(s), \tag{7.21}$$

Equations (7.20 and 7.21) make long-run consumption per worker (or its natural logarithm) conditional on savings/investment rates s.

Since at positive values of any property x the natural logarithm of the geometric mean of that property is the arithmetic mean of natural logarithms of the values of that property ($\ln\bar{x}_G=\overline{\ln x}$), we obtain the function $\bar{v}(s)$ in the form:

$$\bar{v}(s)=\frac{\sum_m v_m(s)}{N}, \tag{7.22}$$

that represents the natural logarithm of the geometric mean of long-run consumptions per worker. Consequently, the combination $s \in (0,1)^N$, which maximizes function (7.22), describes the golden rule of capital accumulation in the analyzed case.

It follows from equations (7.21 and 7.22) that the function $\bar{v}(s)$ can be written as:

$$\bar{v}(s) = \frac{\sum_m \ln(1-s_m) + \sum_m \ln y_m^*(s)}{N}. \tag{7.23}$$

From relation (7.17), we obtain:

$$\begin{aligned}\sum_m \ln y_m^*(s) &= \sum_m \ln \frac{a}{\bar{d}_m^{2\beta}} + \beta \sum_m \ln k_m^*(s) + (\alpha+\beta) \sum_m \ln k_m^*(s) \\ &= \sum_m \ln \frac{a}{\bar{d}_m^{2\beta}} + (\alpha+2\beta) \sum_m \ln k_m^*(s),\end{aligned}$$

and it follows from the above relation and from equation (7.9) that:

$$\begin{aligned}\sum_m \ln y_m^*(s) &= \sum_m \ln \frac{a}{\bar{d}_m^{2\beta}} + \frac{\alpha+2\beta}{1-\alpha-2\beta} \sum_m \ln \frac{a s_m}{\mu_m \bar{d}_m^{2\beta}} \\ &= \sum_m \ln \frac{a}{\bar{d}_m^{2\beta}} + \frac{\alpha+2\beta}{1-\alpha-2\beta} \sum_m \ln \frac{a}{\mu_m \bar{d}_m^{2\beta}} + \frac{\alpha+2\beta}{1-\alpha-2\beta} \sum_m \ln s_m\end{aligned}$$

that can also be written as:

$$\sum_m \ln y_m^*(s) = \Phi + \frac{\alpha+2\beta}{1-\alpha-2\beta} \sum_m \ln s_m, \tag{7.24}$$

where: $\Phi = \sum_m \ln \frac{a}{\bar{d}_m^{2\beta}} + \frac{\alpha+2\beta}{1-\alpha-2\beta} \sum_m \ln \frac{a}{\mu_m \bar{d}_m^{2\beta}} \in R$. Substituting relation (7.24) into (7.23), we obtain:

$$\bar{v}(s) = \frac{\sum_m \ln(1-s_m) + \frac{\alpha+2\beta}{1-\alpha-2\beta} \sum_m \ln s_m + \Phi}{N}. \tag{7.25}$$

First-order conditions for the maximization of function (7.25) can be written as:

$$\forall m \quad \frac{\partial \bar{v}}{\partial s_m} = 0, \tag{7.26}$$

and second-order conditions are reduced to the requirement that the Hessian matrix:

$$H = \begin{bmatrix} \partial^2 \bar{v} / \partial s_1^2 & \partial^2 \bar{v} / (\partial s_1 \partial s_2) & \dots & \partial^2 \bar{v} / (\partial s_1 \partial s_N) \\ \partial^2 \bar{v} / (\partial s_2 \partial s_1) & \partial^2 \bar{v} / \partial s_2^2 & \dots & \partial^2 \bar{v} / (\partial s_2 \partial s_N) \\ \vdots & \vdots & \ddots & \vdots \\ \partial^2 \bar{v} / (\partial s_N \partial s_1) & \partial^2 \bar{v} / (\partial s_N \partial s_2) & \dots & \partial^2 \bar{v} / \partial s_N^2 \end{bmatrix} \tag{7.27}$$

be negative-definite. The first- and second-order partial derivatives of the function $\overline{v}(s)$ are given by the formulas:

$$\forall m \ \frac{\partial \overline{v}}{\partial s_m} = \frac{-\frac{1}{1-s_m} + \frac{\alpha+2\beta}{(1-\alpha-2\beta)s_m}}{N}, \tag{7.28}$$

$$\forall m \ \frac{\partial^2 \overline{v}}{\partial s_m^2} = -\frac{\frac{1}{(1-s_m)^2} + \frac{\alpha+2\beta}{(1-\alpha-2\beta)s_m^2}}{N} < 0 \tag{7.29a}$$

and:

$$\forall m,n \wedge m \neq n \ \frac{\partial^2 \overline{v}}{\partial s_m \partial s_n} = 0. \tag{7.29b}$$

It follows from equations (7.29a,b) that Hessian matrix (equation 7.27) can be written as:

$$H = \begin{bmatrix} \partial^2 \overline{v} / \partial s_1^2 & 0 & \cdots & 0 \\ 0 & \partial^2 \overline{v} / \partial s_2^2 & \cdots & 0 \\ \vdots & \vdots & \ddots & \vdots \\ 0 & 0 & \cdots & \partial^2 \overline{v} / \partial s_N^2 \end{bmatrix}.$$

This leads to the conclusion that its principal minors are described by the formulas:

$$\forall m \ m_m = \begin{vmatrix} \partial^2 \overline{v} / \partial s_1^2 & 0 & \cdots & 0 \\ 0 & \partial^2 \overline{v} / \partial s_2^2 & \cdots & 0 \\ \vdots & \vdots & \ddots & \vdots \\ 0 & 0 & \cdots & \partial^2 \overline{v} / \partial s_N^2 \end{vmatrix} = \prod_m \frac{\partial^2 \overline{v}}{\partial s_m^2}.$$

Since, as per equation (7.29a), all second-order partial derivatives $\frac{\partial^2 \overline{v}}{\partial s_m^2}$ are negative, the odd principal minors of Hessian matrix H are negative, and its even principal minors are positive. It follows that Hessian matrix H is negative-definite (i.e. the second-order condition for the maximization of function $\overline{v}(s)$ is met).

It follows from equations (7.26) and (7.28) that the first-order condition for the maximization of function $\overline{v}(s)$ can be reduced to the following equations:

$$\forall m \ \frac{\alpha+\beta}{(1-\alpha-2\beta)s_m} = \frac{1}{1-s_m},$$

which results in:

$$s_1 = s_2 = \ldots = s_N = \alpha+2\beta. \tag{7.30}$$

Since equation (7.30) describes the combination of savings/investment rates s that maximizes the geometric mean of long-run consumptions per worker, that combination defines the golden rule of capital accumulation in the analyzed case. It follows from relation (7.30) that the rule represents a simple generalization of the Phelps golden rule in the Solow model.

7.4.2 Maximization of long-run consumption per worker in each of the economies

The process of determining the golden rule of capital accumulation in the second analyzed case can be reduced to the maximization of function (7.21) with respect to combination s.

Substituting equation (7.19) into (7.21), we obtain:

$$\forall m \ \ v_m(s) = \ln(1-s_m) + \frac{\alpha + \frac{N-2}{N-1}\beta}{1-\alpha-\frac{N-2}{N-1}\beta}\ln s_m + \frac{\beta}{(N-1)(1-\alpha-2\beta)\left(1-\alpha-\frac{N-2}{N-1}2\beta\right)}\sum_n \ln s_n. \quad (7.31)$$

It follows from equation (7.31) that savings/investment rate in economy n (for $n \neq m$) affects long-run labour productivity in economy m, but it has no effect on the proportion $1 - s_m$ of consumption in output in that economy. Therefore, the maximization of functions v_m with respect to combination s can be reduced to the maximization of those functions with respect to rates s_m (hence, it is actually the problem of maximization of a function of one variable).

Functions (7.31) can also be written as:

$$\forall m \ \ v_m(s) = \ln(1-s_m) + \lambda_N \ln s_m + \frac{\beta}{(N-1)(1-\alpha-2\beta)}\sum_{n \neq m} \ln s_n + \Theta, \quad (7.32)$$

where:

$$\lambda_N = \frac{\alpha + \frac{N-2}{N-1}\beta}{1-\alpha-\frac{N-2}{N-1}\beta} + \frac{\beta}{(N-1)(1-\alpha-2\beta)\left(1-\alpha-\frac{N-2}{N-1}\beta\right)},$$

or:

$$\lambda_N = \frac{(N-1)\left(\alpha+\frac{N-2}{N-1}\beta\right) + \frac{\beta}{(1-\alpha-2\beta)}}{(N-1)\left(1-\alpha-\frac{N-2}{N-1}\beta\right)}. \quad (7.33)$$

It follows from equation (7.32) that:

$$\forall m \quad \frac{dv_m}{ds_m} = -\frac{1}{1-s_m} + \frac{\lambda_N}{s_m} \tag{7.34a}$$

and:

$$\forall m \quad \frac{d^2 v_m}{ds_m^2} = -\left(\frac{1}{(1-s_m)^2} + \frac{\lambda_N}{s_m^2}\right). \tag{7.34b}$$

Since it follows from equation (7.34b) that for each m $\frac{d^2 v_m}{ds_m^2} < 0$ holds, the second-order conditions are met for the maximization of function v_m. Setting the derivatives dv_m/ds_m to 0 (in line with the first-order conditions for the maximization of those functions), we get:

$$\forall m \quad \frac{1}{1-s_m} = \frac{\lambda_N}{s_m},$$

which results in:

$$s_1 = s_2 = \ldots = s_N = \frac{\lambda_N}{1+\lambda_N}. \tag{7.35}$$

Equation (7.35) describes the golden rule of capital accumulation in the analyzed case.

Equations (7.33) and (7.35) lead to the following conclusions:

- Golden-rule savings/investment rates s_m depend on the elasticities α and β of labour productivity function (7.1) and on the number of economies that are exposed to gravitational effects (i.e. N).
- Since $\forall m \; \frac{ds_m}{d\lambda_N} = \frac{1}{(1+\lambda_N)^2} > 0$, then $\operatorname{sgn}\frac{\partial s_m}{\partial x} = \operatorname{sgn}\frac{\partial \lambda_N}{\partial x}$, where x denotes any independent variable affecting s_m and l_N.
- If the force of gravitational effects drops to 0 (i.e. $\beta \to 0^+$), then $\lambda_N \to \frac{\alpha}{1-\alpha}$, and thus for each m $s_m \to \alpha$, i.e. we get back to the original golden rule of Phelps.
- However, if $\beta \to \left(\frac{1-\alpha}{2}\right)^-$, or if the gravitational effects are extremely strong, then $\lambda_N \to +\infty$, and thus $\forall m \;\; s_m \to 1^-$.
- Since:

$$\ln \lambda_N = \ln\left((N-1)\left(\alpha + \frac{N-2}{N-1}\right)\beta + \frac{\beta}{1-\alpha-2\beta}\right) - \ln(N-1) - \ln\left(1-\alpha-\frac{N-2}{N-1}\beta\right),$$

then:

$$\frac{\partial \ln \lambda_N}{\partial \beta} = \frac{N-2+(N-1)\alpha + \dfrac{1-\alpha}{(1-\alpha-2\beta)^2}}{(N-1)\left(\alpha+\dfrac{N-2}{N-1}\beta\right) + \dfrac{\beta}{1-\alpha-2\beta}} + \frac{\dfrac{N-2}{N-1}}{1-\alpha-\dfrac{N-2}{N-1}\beta} > 0$$

hence, $\frac{\partial s_m}{\partial \beta}, \frac{\partial \ln \lambda_N}{\partial \beta} > 0$ which implies that the stronger are gravitational effects, the higher are golden-rule savings/investment rates s_m.

- Similarly, it follows from:

$$\frac{\partial \ln \lambda_N}{\partial \beta} = \frac{N-1+\frac{\beta}{(1-\alpha-2\beta)^2}}{(N-1)\left(\alpha+\frac{N-2}{N-1}\beta\right)+\frac{\beta}{1-\alpha-2\beta}} + \frac{1}{1-\alpha-\frac{N-2}{N-1}\beta} > 0$$

that a high elasticity a corresponds to high savings/investment rates s_m.

- For any $N > 2$ the following holds:

$$\lambda_{N+1} - \lambda_N = \frac{N\left(\alpha+\frac{N-1}{N}\beta\right)+\frac{\beta}{(1-\alpha-2\beta)}}{N\left(1-\alpha-\frac{N-1}{N}\beta\right)} - \frac{(N-1)\left(\alpha+\frac{N-2}{N-1}\beta\right)+\frac{\beta}{(1-\alpha-2\beta)}}{(N-1)\left(1-\alpha-\frac{N-2}{N-1}\beta\right)},$$

and this (following a series of complex transformations) leads to:

$$\lambda_{N+1} - \lambda_N = \frac{-\beta^2}{N(N-1)\left(1-\alpha-\frac{N-1}{N}\beta\right)\left(1-\alpha-\frac{N-2}{N-1}\beta\right)(1-\alpha-2\beta)} < 0.$$

It follows that the greater number of economies benefit from gravitational effects (i.e. the greater is N), the lower value is assumed by λ_N and the lower are the savings/investment rates s_m that maximize long-run consumption per worker in each of the analyzed economies.

- $\lim\limits_{N\to\infty} \lambda_N = \lim\limits_{N\to\infty} \frac{\alpha+\frac{N-1}{N-2}\beta+\frac{\beta}{(N-1)(1-\alpha-2\beta)}}{1-\alpha-\frac{N-2}{N-1}\beta} = \frac{\alpha+\beta}{1-\alpha-\beta}$ and thus if $N \to \infty$, then $\forall m \; s_m \to \alpha+\beta$, so that at a very large number of economies benefiting from gravitational effects, the optimum savings/investment rate in each of the analyzed economies is greater than the Phelps rate (equal α), and less than the rate $\alpha+2\beta$ that maximizes the geometric mean of long-run consumptions per worker.

7.5 Conclusions

The discussion contained in this chapter can be summarized as follows:

I The gravity model of economic growth represents an extension of the Solow growth model (1956) by incorporating spatial interactions caused by gravitational effects. Gravitational effects draw upon Newton's law of universal gravitation. It is assumed that economies attract each other with a specific force that is directly proportional to the product of their capitals per worker and inversely proportional to the square of the distance between them. In addition to capital per worker, the total of gravitational effects, understood as the geometric mean of gravitational effects per unit, influences production processes.

II The discussed theoretical model has an asymptotically stable steady state that in terms of macroeconomics is equivalent to the point of long-run equilibrium of the model. Under conditions of long-run equilibrium in the analyzed growth model, capital per worker and labour productivity in an economy depend on the savings/investment rate, the rate of decline in capital per worker, the mean distance of an economy from other economies and on investment rates and capital depreciation rates in the remaining economies.

III The authors give two definitions of the golden rule of capital accumulation in the gravity model of economic growth. The rule is defined as such combination of investment rates in economies subject to the gravitational effect that maximizes the geometric mean of consumptions per worker in all economies. Alternatively, the golden rule of capital accumulation is defined as such combination of investment rates that maximizes long-run consumption per worker in each of the economies.

IV If the golden rule of capital accumulation is identical with the maximization of the geometric mean of long-run consumptions per worker, the savings/investment rates are equal (in each of the economies) to the total of elasticity of output with respect to inputs of physical capital and a double force of the gravitational effect.

V If the golden rule of capital accumulation is defined as such combination of savings/investment rates that maximizes long-run consumption per worker in each of the economies, the optimum investment rates depend on the elasticity of output with respect to capital, on the action force of the gravitational effect and on the number of economies subject to the action of gravitational effect. Additionally, in this case both an increase in the elasticity of output with respect to capital and an increase in the action force of gravitational effects leads to an increase in optimum investment rates. If the number of economies subject to the gravitational effect grows, the investment rates drop that maximize long-run consumption per worker in each of the economies.

Notes

1 The constant a in equation (7.1) can be understood (like total productivity of production factors in the Cobb-Douglas production function) as labour productivity that could be achieved at per-unit gravitational effects and a per-unit level of capital.

2 Those phenomena are referred to below as total gravitational effects.

3 The discussion contained in this section is based on the study by Filipowicz, Tokarski and Trojak (2015).

8 Solow equilibrium at alternative trajectories of the number of workers

8.1 Introduction

It is assumed in the original Solow growth model that the number of workers[1] rises at a constant growth rate, so that the value of that macroeconomic variable increases exponentially to infinity. We modify that assumption in our analyzes contained in this chapter, proposing two alternative versions. We assume in version 1 that an increase in the number of workers forms a logistic curve that approaches an asymptote. On the other hand, it is assumed in version 2 that if labour productivity rises, the growth rate of the number of workers drops from infinity to zero.

Given these modified assumptions about the growth rate of the number of workers, we seek temporal paths of capital per worker and labour productivity, to eventually compare those paths to the curves representing solutions of the original Solow model (described in Chapter 2).

Similar analyzes were made in the study by Guerrini (2006; see also Zawadzki 2007). As demonstrated by Guerrini (2006), if the Solow model assumes a growth rate of the number of workers $\dot{L}(t)/L(t)=\lambda(t)$ such that at any moment $t\in[0,+\infty)$ the following holds:

$$0\le\lambda(t)\le\lambda^{*}\wedge\lim_{t\to+\infty}\lambda(t)=\lambda_{\infty}\in\left[0,\lambda^{*}\right],$$

then the Solow equation $\dot{k}(t)=sf\left(k(t)\right)-\left(\delta+\lambda(t)\right)k(t)$ has an asymptotically stable non-trivial steady state.

Additionally, the study by Guerrini (2010a) contains analyzes of the Ramsay growth model with a logistic growth path of the population size. It is demonstrated there that the analyzed model has exactly one non-trivial steady state. Similar analyzes were made using Mankiw-Romer-Weil models (Guerrini, 2010c).

The structure of this chapter: Section 8.2 describes the economic and mathematical properties of alternative trajectories of the number of workers. Section 8.3 contains analytical solutions of the Solow model at a logistic curve of the number of workers (Section 8.3.1) and at a growth rate of the number of workers falling as labour productivity rises (Section 8.3.2).

DOI: 10.4324/9781003323792-9

The model parameters are calibrated in Section 8.4 to propose numerical simulations of labour productivity growth paths at varying investment rates. The chapter is finalized by Section 8.5, summarizing conclusions drawn from the preceding analyzes.

8.2 Assumptions about alternative trajectories of the number of workers

It is assumed in the analyzes contained in the following sections that the trajectory of the number of workers in a Solow economy is described by a logistic function that can be written as:

$$L(t)=\frac{m}{1+e^{2n(T-t)}} \tag{8.1}$$

or that the trajectory represents a solution of the following differential equation:

$$\frac{\dot{L}(t)}{L(t)}=\frac{n}{y(t)}, \tag{8.2}$$

where: $n > 0$, $m \geq 2$, $T \geq 0$, and $y = Y/L$ denotes labour productivity.

It follows from relation (8.1) that: $L(0)=1 \Leftrightarrow e^{2nT}=m-1$ which leads to:

$$T=\frac{\ln(m-1)}{2n}. \tag{8.3}$$

If condition (8.3) is met, it is certain that the number of workers on the logistic trajectory (8.1) at moment $t = 0$ equals 1. Therefore, we assume further that T is described by formula (8.3) on growth path (8.1).[2]

Equation (8.1) also implies that:

I $L(T)=\frac{m}{2}$;

II $\lim\limits_{t\to+\infty} L(t)=m$;

III $\forall t\geq 0 \quad \dot{L}(t)=2\,nm\dfrac{e^{2n(T-t)}}{\left(1+e^{2n(T-t)}\right)^2}>0$;

IV $\forall t\geq 0 \quad \ddot{L}(t)=4n^2m\dfrac{e^{2n(T-t)}-1}{\left(1+e^{2n(T-t)}\right)^3}$, and consequently $\ddot{L}>0$ $\left(\ddot{L}<0\right)$ if and only if $t < T$ $(T > t)$.

It follows from the above properties of logistic function (8.1) that the number of workers L rises at subsequent moments $t \in [0,+\infty)$ from 1 (at moment $t = 0$) to m (at $t \to +\infty$), so that until the moment $T = \frac{\ln(m-1)}{2n}$ we observe an accelerating growth rate of the number of workers, and a decelerating growth rate of the number of workers thereafter. Additionally, at moment $T = \frac{\ln(m-1)}{2n}$, the number of workers equals $m/2$.

Equation (8.2) describes a growth path of the number of workers known as post-Malthusian.[3] If the number of workers L forms a trajectory described by that equation, then at labour productivity y rising from 0 through 1 to $+\infty$, the growth rate of the number of workers $\dot{L}/L$ drops at an increasing rate from $+\infty$ through n (at $y = 1$) to 0.

Using $\lambda = \dot{L}/L$ to denote the growth rate of the number of workers, we obtain:

$$\lambda(t) = 2n\frac{e^{2n(T-t)}}{1+e^{2n(T-t)}} \tag{8.4a}$$

on a logistic trajectory of the number or workers or:

$$\lambda(t) = \frac{n}{y(t)} \tag{8.4b}$$

on a post-Malthusian trajectory.

8.3 Analytical solutions

We assume in the analyzes made below in this chapter that the production process is described by the Cobb-Douglas production function given by (symbols like in the original Solow model from Chapter 2):

$$Y(t) = (K(t))^{\alpha}(L(t))^{1-\alpha}, \tag{8.5}$$

where $\alpha \in (0,1)$. To simplify notations, we implicitly assume in the production function (8.5) that total productivity of production factors A equals 1 at each moment t. This certainly does not limit the scope of applicability of the below discussion.

Let us also assume that at moment $t = 0$, the capital K, output Y and the number of workers equal 1. This implies that also labour productivity y and capital per worker equal 1.

We also assume that the equation of capital accumulation is given by:

$$\dot{K}(t) = sY(t) - \delta K(t), \quad \text{at } s,\delta \in (0,1) \tag{8.6}$$

Then, the Solow equation resulting from equations (8.5 and 8.6) can be written as:

$$\dot{k}(t)=s\left(k(t)\right)^{\alpha}-\delta k(t)-\lambda(t)k(t). \tag{8.7}$$

If we assume, like in the original Solow model, that at each moment $t\in[0,+\infty)$, the growth rate of the number of workers equals $n>0$, then it follows from equation (8.7) and from the labour productivity function $y(t)=\left(k(t)\right)^{\alpha}$ (corresponding to function (8.5)) that the trajectories of capital per worker k and of labour productivity y can be written as:

$$k(t)=\left(\frac{s}{\delta+n}+\left(1-\frac{s}{\delta+n}\right)e^{-(1-\alpha)(\delta+n)t}\right)^{1/(1-\alpha)}.$$

and:

$$y(t)=\left(\frac{s}{\delta+n}+\left(1-\frac{s}{\delta+n}\right)e^{-(1-\alpha)(\delta+n)t}\right)^{\alpha/(1-\alpha)},$$

and consequently, in a long run:

$$t\to+\infty\Rightarrow\left(k(t)\to k^{*}=\left(\frac{s}{\delta+n}\right)^{1/(1-\alpha)}\wedge y(t)\to y^{*}=\left(\frac{s}{\delta+n}\right)^{\alpha/(1-\alpha)}\right).$$

8.3.1 Growth paths at a logistic trajectory of the number of workers

It follows from equation (8.7) that the following holds[4]:

$$\left(k(t)\right)^{-\alpha}\dot{k}(t)=s-\theta(t)\left(k(t)\right)^{1-\alpha}, \tag{8.8}$$

where $\theta(t)=\delta+\lambda(t)$. Let us now make the Bernoulli substitution in the form:

$$q(t)=\left(k(t)\right)^{1-\alpha}\Rightarrow\frac{\dot{q}(t)}{1-\alpha}=\left(k(t)\right)^{-\alpha}\dot{k}(t), \tag{8.9}$$

so that non-linear differential equation (8.8) is reduced to a linear non-homogeneous equation given by:

$$\dot{q}(t)=(1-\alpha)s-(1-\alpha)\theta(t)q(t). \tag{8.10}$$

Let us write the integral $q(t)$ of equation (8.10) as:

$$q(t)=\exp\left(-(1-\alpha)\int\theta(t)dt\right)\cdot q_{d}(t), \tag{8.11}$$

where $q_d(t)$ is an unknown complementary integral. Then:

$$\dot{q}(t) = -(1-\alpha)\theta(t)\exp\left(-(1-\alpha)\int \theta(t)\,dt\right)\cdot q_d(t) + \exp\left(-(1-\alpha)\int \theta(t)\,dt\right)\cdot \dot{q}_d(t). \tag{8.12}$$

Substituting equations (8.11) and (8.12) into differential equation (8.10), we obtain:

$$\dot{q}_d(t) = (1-\alpha)s\cdot\exp\left((1-\alpha)\int \theta(t)\,dt\right),$$

hence:

$$q_d(t) = (1-\alpha)s\int \exp\left((1-\alpha)\int \theta(t)\,dt\right)dt. \tag{8.13}$$

Calculating the integrals of equations (8.13) and (8.11), given the function (t), we can find the integral $k(t)$ of the Solow equation (8.7). That integral determines the path of capital per worker. From the above conclusion and from the labour productivity function $y(t) = (k(t))^{\alpha}$ (corresponding to the Cobb-Douglas production function (8.5)), we can obtain the temporal path of labour productivity $y(t)$.

The integrals of equations (8.13) and (8.11) will be sought on a logistic growth path of the number of workers. Then, as per equation (8.4a), the trajectory (t) is given by:

$$\theta(t) = \delta + 2n\frac{e^{2n(T-t)}}{1+e^{2n(T-t)}}.$$

One of the integrals of the above equation can be written as:

$$\int \theta(t)\,dt = \delta t + 2n\int \frac{e^{2n(T-t)}}{1+e^{2n(T-t)}}\,dt = \delta t - \ln\left(1+e^{2n(T-t)}\right). \tag{8.14}$$

Substituting the integral of equation (8.14) into equation (8.13):

$$\begin{aligned} q_d(t) &= (1-\alpha)s\int \exp\left((1-\alpha)\left(\delta t - \ln\left(1+e^{2n(T-t)}\right)\right)\right)dt \\ &= (1-\alpha)s\int \frac{e^{\delta t}}{\left(1+e^{2n(T-t)}\right)^{1-\alpha}}\,dt \end{aligned} \tag{8.15}$$

Substituting: $u = e^t \Rightarrow du = e^t dt$, the integral $\int \frac{e^{\delta t}}{\left(1+e^{2n(T-t)}\right)^{1-\alpha}}\,dt$ can be written as:

$$\int \frac{e^{(1-\alpha)\delta t-t}}{\left(1+e^{2n(T-t)}\right)^{1-\alpha}} e^t dt = \int \frac{u^{(1-\alpha)\delta-1}}{\left(1+e^{2nT}u^{-2n}\right)^{1-\alpha}} du.$$

Since:

$$\int \frac{u^{(1-\alpha)\delta-1}}{\left(1+e^{2nT}u^{-2n}\right)^{1-\alpha}} du = \frac{u^{(1-\alpha)\delta}}{(1-\alpha)\delta} {}_2F_1\left(-\frac{(1-\alpha)\delta}{2n}, 1-\alpha, \frac{2n-(1-\alpha)\delta}{2n}, -e^{2nT}u^{-2n}\right) + C,$$

(where ${}_2F_1(a,b,c,z)$ represents the Gaussian hypergeometric function,[5] and $C \in R$ – a constant of integration), then:

$$\int \frac{e^{(1-\alpha)\delta t-t}}{\left(1+e^{2n(T-t)}\right)^{1-\alpha}} e^t dt = \frac{e^{(1-\alpha)\delta t}}{(1-\alpha)\delta} \cdot {}_2F_1\left(-\frac{(1-\alpha)\delta}{2n}, 1-\alpha, \frac{2n-(1-\alpha)\delta}{2n}, -e^{2n(T-t)}\right) + C. \tag{8.16}$$

Substituting the integral of equation (8.16) into equation (8.15), we get a complementary integral q_d given by:

$$q_d(t) = \frac{s}{\delta} e^{(1-\alpha)\delta t} \cdot {}_2F_1\left(-\frac{(1-\alpha)\delta}{2n}, 1-\alpha, \frac{2n-(1-\alpha)\delta}{2n}, -e^{2n(T-t)}\right) + \hat{C},$$

where $\hat{C} = (1-\alpha)sC \in R$. It follows from the above relations and from equations (8.11) and (8.14) that the integral q of differential equation (8.10) is given by:

$$q(t) = e^{-(1-\alpha)\delta t}\left(1+e^{2n(T-t)}\right)^{1-\alpha} \cdot \left(\frac{se^{(1-\alpha)\delta t}}{\delta} \cdot {}_2F_1\left(-\frac{(1-\alpha)\delta}{2n}, 1-\alpha, \frac{2n-(1-\alpha)\delta}{2n}, -e^{2n(T-t)}\right) + \hat{C}\right),$$

that can also be written as:

$$q(t) = \frac{s\left(1+e^{2n(T-t)}\right)^{1-\alpha}}{\delta} \cdot {}_2F_1\left(-\frac{(1-\alpha)\delta}{2n}, 1-\alpha, \frac{2n-(1-\alpha)\delta}{2n}, -e^{2n(T-t)}\right) + e^{-(1-\alpha)\delta t}\left(1+e^{2n(T-t)}\right)^{1-\alpha}\hat{C} \tag{8.17}$$

We get from the Bernoulli substitution (8.9): $k(t)=\left(q(t)\right)^{1/(1-\alpha)}$, and this combined with equation (8.17) gives[6]:

$$k(t)=\left\{\frac{s\left(1+e^{2n(T-t)}\right)^{1-\alpha}}{\delta}\cdot {}_2F_1\left(-\frac{(1-\alpha)\delta}{2n},1-\alpha,\frac{2n-(1-\alpha)\delta}{2n},-e^{2n(T-t)}\right)\right.$$
$$\left.+e^{-(1-\alpha)\delta t}\left(1+e^{2n(T-t)}\right)^{1-\alpha}\hat{C}\right\}^{1/(1-\alpha)} \tag{8.18}$$

Since $y(t)=\left(k(t)\right)^{\alpha}$, then:

$$y(t)=\left\{\frac{s\left(1+e^{2n(T-t)}\right)^{1-\alpha}}{\delta}\cdot {}_2F_1\left(-\frac{(1-\alpha)\delta}{2n},1-\alpha,\frac{2n-(1-\alpha)\delta}{2n},-e^{2n(T-t)}\right)\right.$$
$$\left.+e^{-(1-\alpha)\delta t}\left(1+e^{2n(T-t)}\right)^{1-\alpha}\hat{C}\right\}^{\alpha/(1-\alpha)}. \tag{8.19}$$

Equations (8.18) and (8.19) describe growth paths of capital per worker and labour productivity in the Solow model with a logistic trajectory of the number of workers. Those paths are described by non-elementary functions. Therefore, their graph will be analyzed in the section describing results of numerical simulations (8.4).

However, note that at $t \to +\infty$, the hypergeometric function: ${}_2F_1\left(-\frac{(1-\alpha)\delta}{2n},1-\alpha,\frac{2n-(1-\alpha)\delta}{2n},-e^{2n(T-t)}\right)\to {}_2F_1\left(-\frac{(1-\alpha)\delta}{2n},1-\alpha,\frac{2n-(1-\alpha)\delta}{2n},0\right)$, and (as per equations (8.18) and (8.19)) the following holds:

$$t\to+\infty \Rightarrow \left(k(t)\to\left(\frac{s}{\delta}\right)^{1/(1-\alpha)} \wedge y(t)\to\left(\frac{s}{\delta}\right)^{\alpha/(1-\alpha)}\right).$$

The quantities $\left(\frac{s}{\delta}\right)^{1/(1-\alpha)}$ and $\left(\frac{s}{\delta}\right)^{\alpha/(1-\alpha)}$ describe (respectively) capital per worker and output per worker in the long-run equilibrium of the economic growth model analyzed in this section. Since $\left(\frac{s}{\delta}\right)^{1/(1-\alpha)}>\left(\frac{s}{\delta+n}\right)^{1/(1-\alpha)}$ and $\left(\frac{s}{\delta}\right)^{\alpha/(1-\alpha)}>\left(\frac{s}{\delta+n}\right)^{\alpha/(1-\alpha)}$, the quantities are greater than in the similar original Solow model (with the Cobb-Douglas production function).

8.3.2 Growth paths at a growth rate that drops with rising labour productivity

Analysing the effect of a post-Malthusian trajectory of the number of workers on the long-run equilibrium in a Solow economy, the equation describing the growth rate of the number of workers (equation 8.4b) together with the labour productivity function $y = k^{\alpha}$ can be substituted into the Solow equation (8.7). The following differential equation is then obtained:

$$\dot{k}(t) = s\left(k(t)\right)^{\alpha} - \delta k(t) - \frac{n}{\left(k(t)\right)^{\alpha}} k(t),$$

that can also be written as:

$$\dot{k}(t) = \left(s - \delta\left(k(t)\right)^{1-\alpha} - n\left(k(t)\right)^{1-2\alpha}\right)\left(k(t)\right)^{\alpha}. \tag{8.20}$$

Differential equation (8.20) will be analyzed in the phase space $P = (0, +\infty)$.

Note that $\forall k \in P \ \operatorname{sgn} \dot{k} = \operatorname{sgn} \phi(k)$, where the function $\phi(k)$ is defined as follows:

$$\phi(k) = s - \delta k^{1-\alpha} - nk^{1-2\alpha}. \tag{8.21}$$

The properties of function (8.21) should be considered at $\alpha \in (0, 1/2)$, $\alpha = 1/2$ and $\alpha \in (1/2, 1)$. The reason is that the signs of expressions $1-\alpha$ and $1-2\alpha$ differ in each of the described cases and (consequently) the derivatives $\phi'(k)$ for subsequent $k \in P$ exhibit different behaviours.

In the case of $\alpha \in (0, 1/2)$, we obtain:

i $\phi(0) = s > 0$;
ii $\lim_{k \to +\infty} \phi(k) = -\infty$;
iii $\forall k \in P \ \phi'(k) = \left((2\alpha - 1)nk^{-2\alpha} - (1-\alpha)\delta\right)k^{-\alpha} < 0$,

and hence (as per the Darboux property of a continuous function), there exists exactly one $\bar{k} \in P$ such that:

- first, for any $k \in \left(0, \bar{k}\right)$ $\phi(k) > 0$,
- second, $\phi\left(\bar{k}\right) = 0$
  and
- third, for each $k \in \left(\bar{k}, +\infty\right)$ $\phi(k) < 0$.

Consequently, that $\bar{k}$ represents a non-trivial, stable steady-state point of differential equation (8.20). Moreover, if $s > \delta + n$ ($s < \delta + n$), then $\phi(1) > 0$ ($\phi(1) < 0$), and at each moment $t \in (0, +\infty)$ $\dot{k} > 0$ $\left(\dot{k} < 0\right)$ which leads to the conclusion that the growth path of capital per worker $k(t)$ approaches $\bar{k}$ from the left (right).[7] However, at $s = \delta + n$, the following holds:

$$t \in (0,+\infty)\ \dot{k}(t) = 0$$

which implies that at each moment $t\ k(t) = \bar{k} = 1$.

In the case of $\alpha = 1/2$, the function $\phi(k)$ can be written as:

$$\phi(k) = s - n - \delta\sqrt{k}.$$

Then:

- i $\phi(0) = s - n$;
- ii $\lim_{k \to +\infty} \phi(k) = -\infty$;
- iii $\forall k \in P\ \phi'(k) = -\dfrac{\delta}{2\sqrt{k}} < 0.$

Therefore:

- i If $s \le n$, the value of function $\phi(k)$ at k rising from 0 to $+\infty$ will fall from $s - n \le 0$ to $-\infty$, and differential equation (8.20) has no steady state. Moreover, in this case $\forall k \in P\ \dot{k} < 0$, i.e. the values of capital per worker will fall from 1 to 0.[8]
- ii However, at $s > n$, there exists exactly one non-trivial stable steady-state point $\bar{k} \in P$ and the growth paths of capital per worker and labour productivity behave like at $\alpha = (0,1/2)$.

At $\alpha = (1/2,1)$, we get:

- i $\lim_{k \to 0^+} \phi(k) = -\infty$;
- ii $\lim_{k \to +\infty} \phi(k) = +\infty$;

and:

- iii $\phi'(k) = \left((2\alpha - 1)nk^{-\alpha} - (1-\alpha)\delta\right)k^{-\alpha} < 0$, and consequently (first) at $k \in \left(0, \bar{\bar{k}}\right)$, where:

$$\bar{\bar{k}} = \left(\frac{(2\alpha - 1)n}{(1-\alpha)\delta}\right)^{1/\alpha}, \tag{8.22}$$

the derivative $\phi'(k)$ is positive, (second) at $k = \bar{\bar{k}}$ – it equals 0 and (third) for $k \in \left(\bar{\bar{k}}, +\infty\right)$, the derivative is negative. Therefore, in the interval

$\left(0,\overset{=}{k}\right)$, the function $\phi(k)$ is increasing and in the interval $\left(\overset{=}{k},+\infty\right)$, it is decreasing.

iv If $\phi\left(\overset{=}{k}\right)<0$, for each $k \in P$ $\dot{k}=k^{\alpha}\phi(k)<0$ and then capital per worker and labour productivity will fall (in time) from 1 to 0.

v In the case of $\phi\left(\overset{=}{k}\right)=0$, the point $\overset{=}{k}$ represents a non-trivial steady state of differential equation (8.20). Moreover, (first) if $\overset{=}{k}<1$, then $k(t)$ will fall from 1 to $\overset{=}{k}$ while $y(t)$ will fall from 1 to $\overset{=}{k}^{\alpha}$, (second) for $\overset{=}{k}=1$ at each non-negative moment t $\dot{k}(t)=\dot{y}(t)=0$ and $k(t)=y(t)=1$, and (third) for $\overset{=}{k}>1$, the following holds: $\dot{k}(t),\ \dot{y}(t)>0$, so that the values of capital per worker and labour productivity will fall from 1 to 0.

vi However, at $\phi\left(\overset{=}{k}\right)>0$, differential equation (8.20) has two non-trivial steady states: $\bar{k}_1 \in \left(0,\overset{=}{k}\right)$ and $\bar{k}_2 \in \left(\overset{=}{k},+\infty\right)$. Then, for any $k(t) \in \left(0,\bar{k}_1\right)\bigcup\left(\bar{k}_2,+\infty\right)$ we have $\dot{k}(t),\ \dot{y}(t)<0$, and for each $k(t) \in \left(\bar{k}_1,\bar{k}_2\right)$ $\dot{k}(t),\ \dot{y}(t)>0$. Consequently, the point $\bar{k}_1$ is a non-stable steady state of differential equation (8.20), and the point $\bar{k}_2$ is a stable steady state. Therefore, (first) if $\bar{k}_1>0$, capital per worker and labour productivity will fall from 1 to 0, (second) at $\bar{k}_1=0$, the values of those macroeconomic variables at each moment $t \in [0,+\infty)$ equal 1, (third) if $\bar{k}_1<1<\bar{k}_2$, capital per worker and labour productivity will rise from 1 to (respectively) $\bar{k}_2$ and $\bar{k}_2^{\alpha}$, (fourth) in the case of $\bar{k}_2=1$ at each moment t $k(t) = y(t) = 1$ and (fifth) at $\bar{k}_2<1$, capital per worker and labour productivity will fall from 1 to $\bar{k}_2$ and $\bar{k}_2^{\alpha}$.

It follows from equations (8.21) and (8.22) that:

$$\phi\left(\overset{=}{k}\right)=s-\delta\left(\frac{(2\alpha-1)n}{(1-\alpha)\delta}\right)^{(1-\alpha)/\alpha}-n\left(\frac{(1-\alpha)\delta}{(2\alpha-1)n}\right)^{(2\alpha-1)/\alpha},$$

and consequently, (first) if

$$s>\delta\left(\frac{(2\alpha-1)n}{(1-\alpha)\delta}\right)^{(1-\alpha)/\alpha}+n\left(\frac{(1-\alpha)\delta}{(2\alpha-1)n}\right)^{(2\alpha-1)/\alpha},$$

differential equation (8.20) has two non-trivial steady states, (second) at

$$s=\delta\left(\frac{(2\alpha-1)n}{(1-\alpha)\delta}\right)^{(1-\alpha)/\alpha}+n\left(\frac{(1-\alpha)\delta}{(2\alpha-1)n}\right)^{(2\alpha-1)/\alpha}.$$

the equation has one non-trivial steady state, and (third) for

$$s<\delta\left(\frac{(2\alpha-1)n}{(1-\alpha)\delta}\right)^{(1-\alpha)/\alpha}+n\left(\frac{(1-\alpha)\delta}{(2\alpha-1)n}\right)^{(2\alpha-1)/\alpha},$$

it has no non-trivial steady state.

8.4 Numerical simulations

Like in the studies by Filipowicz and Tokarski (2015), Filipowicz, Wisła and Tokarski (2016) or Filipowicz, Syrek and Tokarski (2017), the elasticity of output with respect to capital (that is α) is calibrated so that the ratio of labour productivities equals 3 at the ratio of capitals per worker in two economies that equals 5. Then, given the labour productivity function $y=k^{\alpha}$, we obtain[9]:

$$\alpha=\frac{\ln(y_1/y_2)}{\ln(k_1/k_2)}=\frac{\ln 3}{\ln 5}\approx 0.68261.$$

It is also arbitrarily assumed that $\delta = 0.07$, $n = 0.01$ and $m = e$, where e is the Euler number. Then, the moment T equals $T=\frac{\ln(e-1)}{0.02}\approx 27.066$ on a logistic growth path. The investment rate s is increased in steps of 10-percentage points from 10% to 40%.

The model is numerically solved in a discrete time, replacing differential equations with equivalent difference equations.

Figure 8.1 shows the trajectories of the number of workers on a logistic growth path and post-Malthusian growth paths, and savings/investment rates equal 10%, 20%, 30% and 40%. The figure demonstrates that:

- On the logistic growth path of the number of workers, that value will rise from 1 to about 2.718.
- On the post-Malthusian growth path, at a savings/investment rate of 10% at infinity (like in the original Solow model), the number or workers will approach infinity.
- A savings/investment rate of 20% leads to a long-run number of workers about 3.489 times greater, of 30% – about 1.757 times greater, and of 40% – about 1.391 times greater than its input value.

Table 8.1 shows results of numerical simulations of labour productivity at standard, logistic and post-Malthusian trajectories of the number of workers. Figures 8.2–8.5 illustrate the trajectories of labour productivity corresponding to standard, logistic and post-Malthusian curves

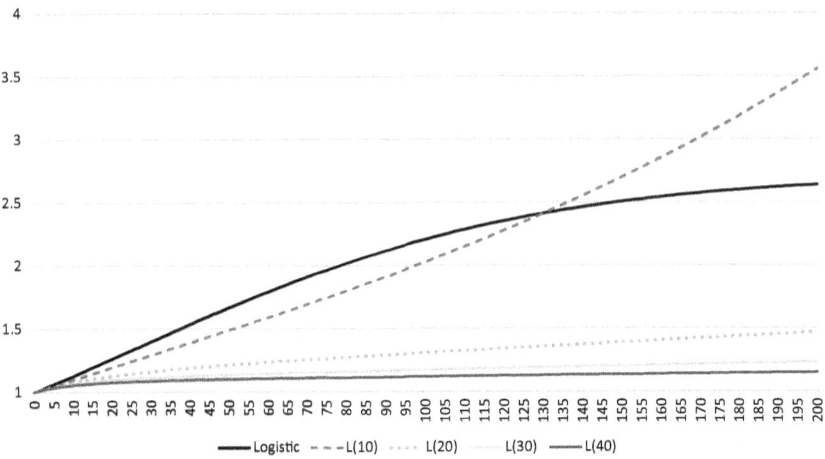

Figure 8.1 Trajectories of the number of workers on a logistic growth path and post-Malthusian growth paths, and investment rates of 10% ($L(10)$), 20% ($L(20)$), 30% ($L(30)$) and 40% ($L(40)$).

Source: Own calculations.

Table 8.1 Simulations of labour productivity at standard (S), logistic (L) and post-Malthusian (PM) trajectories of the number of workers and at $\delta = 0.07$, $n = 0.01$, $\alpha \approx 0.68261$ and $m = e$

Year t	*Investment rate s (%)*											
	10			*20*			*30*			*40*		
	S	*L*	*PM*	*S*	*L*	*PM*	*S*	*L*	*PM*	*S*	*L*	*PM*
10	1.124	1.109	1.128	1.841	1.819	1.868	2.714	2.683	2.772	3.740	3.700	3.836
20	1.226	1.205	1.240	2.700	2.660	2.815	4.752	4.688	5.014	7.387	7.292	7.839
50	1.427	1.435	1.491	4.789	4.826	5.385	10.293	10.380	11.764	18.039	18.198	20.732
75	1.514	1.587	1.622	5.845	6.125	6.876	13.283	13.918	15.893	24.000	25.146	28.870
100	1.562	1.716	1.703	6.452	7.078	7.833	15.040	16.489	18.581	27.545	30.192	34.215
150	1.601	1.913	1.785	6.968	8.311	8.765	16.551	19.726	21.207	30.617	36.477	39.456
200	1.612	2.034	1.815	7.117	8.972	9.089	16.989	21.408	22.112	31.509	39.695	41.259
$+\infty$	1.616	2.153	1.832	7.175	9.562	9.252	17.161	22.870	22.562	31.860	42.459	42.151

Source: Own calculations.

of the number of workers. The table and figures lead to the following conclusions:

- A savings/investment rate of 10% leads to the fastest growth of labour productivity at a post-Malthusian trajectory of the number of workers and the slowest growth of labour productivity at a logistic trajectory of the number of workers over the first 50 years. That macroeconomic

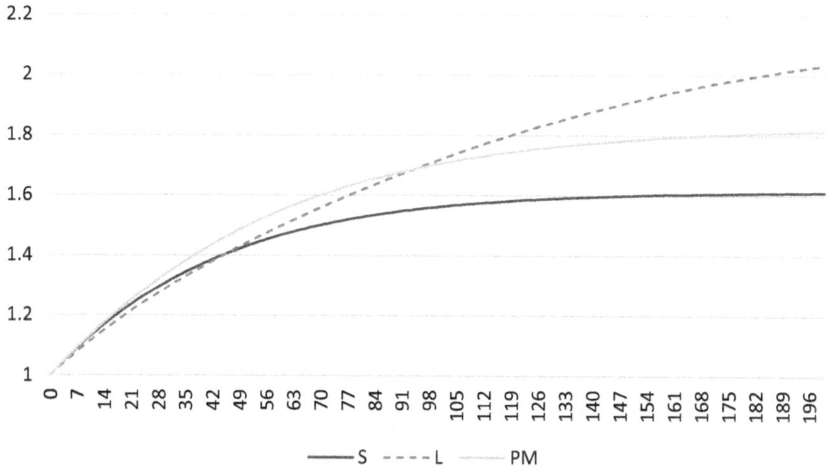

Figure 8.2 Growth paths of labour productivity at standard (*S*), logistic (*L*) and post-Malthusian (*PM*) trajectories of the number of workers and $s = 10\%$.
Source: Own calculations.

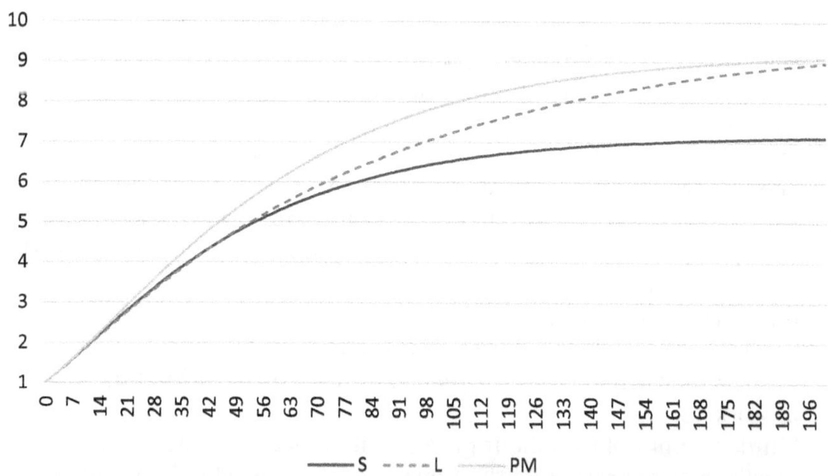

Figure 8.3 Growth paths of labour productivity at standard (*S*), logistic (*L*) and post-Malthusian (*PM*) trajectories of the number of workers and $s = 20\%$.
Source: Own calculations.

variable will reach its highest value also on the post-Malthusian path, and its lowest value on the standard rather than the logistic path after 100 years. In the long-run equilibrium (at $t \rightarrow +\infty$), labour productivity will rise by about 61.6% (compared to its input value) on a standard path, and by about 83.2% on the post-Malthusian path while it will be more than doubled at a logistic trajectory.

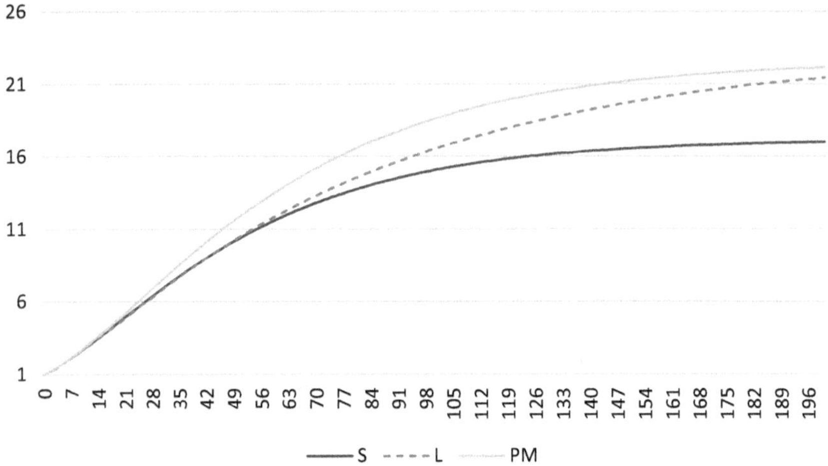

Figure 8.4 Growth paths of labour productivity at standard (*S*), logistic (*L*) and post-Malthusian (*PM*) trajectories of the number of workers and $s = 30\%$.
Source: Own calculations.

- If the savings/investment rate equals 20%, labour productivity initially achieves its fastest growth at a post-Malthusian trajectory of the number of workers, and its slowest growth at a logistic trajectory of the number of workers. However, in the long-run equilibrium, labour productivity will be about 9.5 times greater on the post-Malthusian and logistic growth paths, and slightly more than 7 times greater on the standard growth path.
- At a savings/investment rate of 30%, the fastest growth of output per worker is achieved on a post-Malthusian growth path, and the slowest – on a standard growth path. In the long-run equilibrium, the value of that variable (compared to year $t = 0$) will be slightly more than 17 times greater at a standard trajectory of the number of workers and about 22.5–23 times greater on the other analyzed growth paths of the number of workers.
- Similar graphs of the labour productivity function are generated at savings/investment rates of 40%. Long-run labour productivity values will then be about 31.9 times greater on a standard growth path, 42.4 times greater on a post-Malthusian growth path and 42.5 times greater on a logistic growth path compared to year $t = 0$ (Figure 8.6).

8.5 Conclusions

The analyzes contained in this chapter can be summarized as follows:

I The assumption underlying the original Solow model about a constant growth rate of the number of workers is modified in this chapter. That

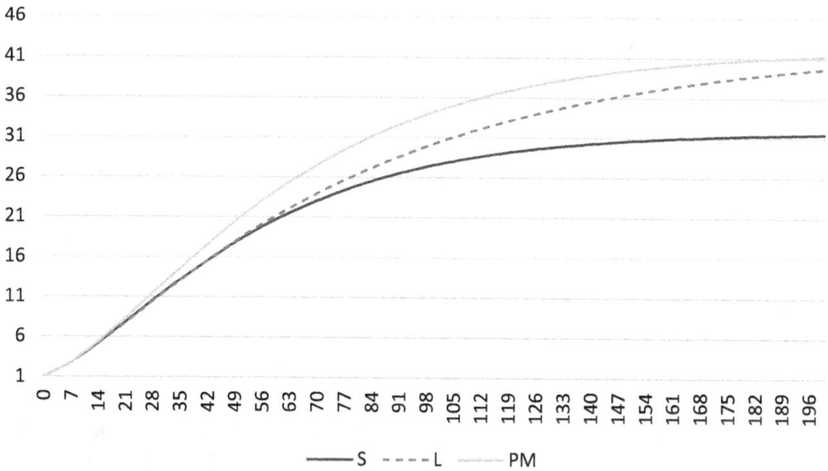

Figure 8.5 Growth paths of labour productivity at standard (*S*), logistic (*L*) and post-Malthusian (*PM*) trajectories of the number of workers and *s* = 40%.

Source: Own calculations.

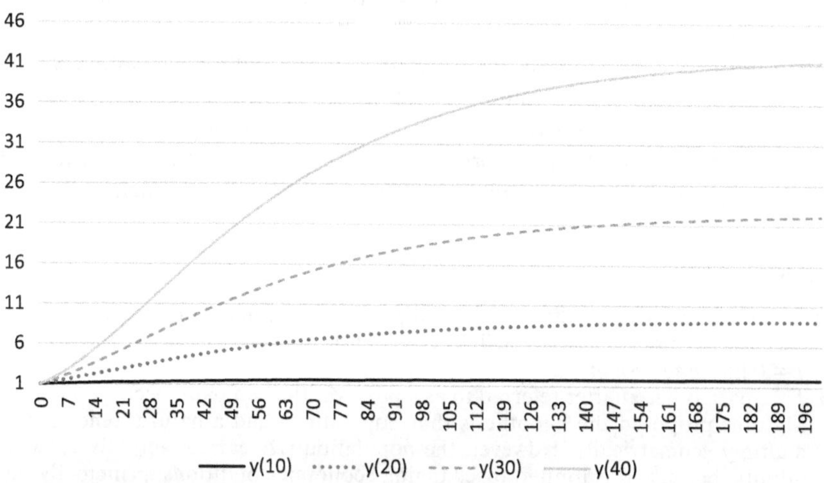

Figure 8.6 Growth paths of labour productivity at a post-Malthusian trajectory of the number of workers and *s* = 10% (*y*(10)), *s* = 20% (*y*(20)), *s* = 30% (*y*(30)) and *s* = 40% (*y*(40)).

Source: Own calculations.

assumption is modified in two ways. First, it is assumed that the number of workers changes forming a trajectory defined by a logistic function; second, it is assumed that the growth rate of the number of workers represents a decreasing function of labour productivity.

II On a logistic growth path of the number of workers, the trajectories of capital per worker and labour productivity represent certain composed functions with the Gaussian hypergeometric function. On a post-Malthusian temporal path of the number of workers, the solution of Solow equation depends on the elasticity of output with respect to capital inputs. The equation may have no steady state and have one non-trivial steady state or two non-trivial steady states.

III In the numerical simulations described in this chapter, the elasticity of output with respect to capital inputs was calibrated at 0.68216, and investment rates were modified in steps of 10 percentage points from 10% to 40%.

IV At all simulated values of saving/investment rates and standard, logistic or post-Malthusian trajectories of the number of workers, labour productivity rises up to an asymptote. The dynamics of labour productivity at a standard and a logistic trajectory of the number of workers are very similar over the first 50 years. Then, the growth rate of labour productivity dramatically drops in the model with a standard trajectory of the number of workers (due to the convergence effect). Finally, labour productivity stabilizes in the original Solow model on a distinctly lower level than in the two other models. Long-run labour productivities are very similar in the logistic and post-Malthusian models (except at a savings/investment rate of 10%).

V In addition to the analyzed trajectory of the number of workers, the described numerical simulations led to the conclusion that an increase in savings/investment rates causes an increase in long-run labour productivity and capital per worker. That conclusion is consistent with the corresponding output of analysing the original Solow model.

Notes

1 This chapter bases on the study by Filipowicz, Grodzicki and Tokarski (2016). See also Filipowicz, Syrek and Tokarski (2017).

2 $T = 0$ in the case of $m = 2$.

3 That path is hereinafter referred to as a post-Malthusian path, because Thomas Malthus proposed the hypothesis that populations had a natural tendency to multiply geometrically. However, the population size cannot actually grow to infinity, because it is limited by changing economic conditions, principally the wage level and foodstuff supply. More on the subject e.g. in Filipowicz, Grodzicki and Tokarski (2016).

4 We ignore a trivial solution of that differential equation.

5 The Gaussian hypergeometric function ${}_2F_1(a,b,c,z)$ is a non-elementary function that represents a solution of the following second-order differential equation:

$$z(1-z)\frac{d^2w}{dz^2}+\left(c-(a+b+1)z\right)\frac{dw}{dz}=abw(z),$$

where $a,b \in R$, and $c \neq 0$. The function can be written as:

$$ {}_2F_1(a,b,c,z) = 1 + \sum_{n=1}^{\infty} \gamma_n z_n, $$

where:

$$ \gamma_n = \frac{\left(\prod_{j=1}^{n}(a+j-1)\right)\left(\prod_{j=1}^{n}(b+j-1)\right)}{n!\left(\prod_{j=1}^{n}(c+j-1)\right)}. $$

The mathematical properties of those functions are characterized e.g. in the studies by Korn and Korn (1983, p. 269 ff.) or Cattani (2006). Applications of Gaussian hypergeometric functions in the modelling of economic growth processes are discussed in the studies by Boucekkine and Ruiz-Tamarit (2004, 2008) or Zawadzki (2015) for the Uzawa-Lucas model, by Guerrini (2006) for the Solow model and by Krawiec and Szydłowski (2002) for the Mankiw-Romer-Weil model.

6 The constant of integration $\hat{C}$ in equations (8.18) and (8.19) should be purposefully selected to meet the condition $k(0) = k0 > 0$, where $k0$ denotes capital per worker at moment $t = 0$. That constant is selected in the numerical simulations described in Section 8.4 so that the equality holds $k(0) = y(0) = 1$.

7 It follows from the labour productivity function analyzed in this chapter that $\operatorname{sgn}\dot{k} = \operatorname{sgn}\dot{y}$, and thus the growth path of labour productivity $y(t)$ exhibits similar behaviour as the path of capital per worker, provided that at $t \to +\infty$ $y(t) \to \bar{k}^{\alpha}$.

8 Analogous values are assumed then by labour productivity $y(t)$.

9 If we assumed, in line with the Solow's 1957 decomposition, that $\alpha = 1/3$, then at $k_1 / k_2 = 5$, we would get: $\frac{y_1}{y_2} = \sqrt[3]{\frac{k_1}{k_2}} = \sqrt[3]{5} \approx 1.70998$, a value that seems to be strongly underestimated.

9 The Solow equilibrium at sine-wave investment rates

9.1 Introduction

Investment belongs to key factors of long-term economic growth and is highly sensitive to business cycles.[1] In the original Solow model, investments represent a constant fraction of output. In this chapter, we question that assumption and introduce fluctuations on the investment side, with an investment rate changing along a sine wave in time. The sine function is adopted to describe changes in the investment rate because investment depends to a great extent on business cycles that are characterized by periodic fluctuations.

Similar analyzes are contained in the studies by Bolińska, Dykas, Mentel and Misiak (2019), where the authors, in addition to fluctuations on the investment side, consider a growth rate of the number of workers that changes in time and in a long run determine the exponential growth path of the number of workers approaching a constant asymptote.

The structure of this chapter is as follows. Section 9.2 describes assumptions of the model, including that about the investment rate. Section 9.3 proposes a solution of the model based on cyclical growth paths of capital per worker and labour productivity. Section 9.4 proposes calibrations of growth paths of labour productivity and summarizes numerical simulations of those paths for various cycle lengths of fluctuations in investment rates and various levels of average investment rate. Section 9.5 contains conclusions drawn from the discussed model and closes this chapter.

9.2 Assumptions of the model

The assumptions listed below underlie the growth model described in this chapter.

I The production process is described by the Cobb-Douglas production function given by the formula:

$$Y(t) = \left(K(t)\right)^{\alpha}\left(L(t)\right)^{1-\alpha}, \tag{9.1}$$

DOI: 10.4324/9781003323792-10

where the symbols have the same meanings as in Chapter 2, and $Y, K, L > 0$ and $\alpha \in (0,1)$.

II The capital accumulation process is described by the differential equation:

$$\dot{K}(t) = s(t)Y(t) - \delta K(t), \tag{9.2}$$

where $s(t) \in (0,1)$ is the investment rate at moment t, and $\delta \in (0,1)$ denotes the capital depreciation rate (that is constant in time).

III The investment rate at each moment t is described by the sine wave:

$$s(t) = \bar{s} + \theta \sin\left(\frac{2\pi}{\omega}t\right), \tag{9.3}$$

where $\bar{s}$, $\bar{s} \pm \theta \in (0,1)$, and $\omega > 0$. $\bar{s}$ denotes the average investment rate in a business cycle, θ is the amplitude of cyclical fluctuations in investment, and ω denotes the period of those fluctuations.

IV The trajectory of the number of workers is described by the exponential function:

$$L(t) = e^{nt}. \tag{9.4}$$

It follows from equation (9.4) that at moment $t = 0$, the number of workers amounted to 1 and rose at the growth rate $n > 0$.

9.3 Equilibrium in the model

Equations (9.1–9.4), like in the original Solow model, lead to the differential equation:

$$\dot{k}(t) = \left(\bar{s} + \theta \sin\left(\frac{2\pi}{\omega}t\right)\right)(k(t))^{\alpha} - \mu k(t), \tag{9.5}$$

where $k = K/L$ denotes capital per worker, and $\mu = \delta + n > 0$ is the rate of capital decline per worker. Equation (9.5), naturally, describes rises in capital per worker. That equation (ignoring its trivial solution $k(t) = 0$) is written as:

$$(k(t))^{-\alpha}\dot{k}(t) = \bar{s} + \theta \sin\left(\frac{2\pi}{\omega}t\right) - \mu (k(t))^{1-\alpha}$$

and after the Bernoulli substitution:

$$z(t) = (k(t))^{1-\alpha} \Rightarrow \frac{\dot{z}(t)}{1-\alpha} = (k(t))^{-\alpha}\dot{k}(t) \tag{9.6}$$

is reduced to the following linear non-homogeneous differential equation:

$$\dot{z}(t) = (1-\alpha)\bar{s} + (1-\alpha)\theta \sin\left(\frac{2\pi}{\omega}t\right) - (1-\alpha)\mu z(t). \tag{9.7}$$

Let us write the integral of equation (9.7) as:

$$z(t) = e^{-(1-\alpha)\mu t} z_d(t) \Rightarrow \dot{z}(t) = -(1-\alpha)\mu e^{-(1-\alpha)\mu t} z_d(t) + e^{-(1-\alpha)\mu t} \dot{z}_d(t), \tag{9.8}$$

where z_d denotes an unknown complementary integral. Substituting equations (9.8) into (9.7) and making a few elementary transformations, we get:

$$\dot{z}_d(t) = (1-\alpha)\overline{s}e^{(1-\alpha)\mu t} + (1-\alpha)\theta\Phi(t) \tag{9.9}$$

where:

$$\Phi(t) = \sin\left(\frac{2\pi}{\omega}t\right)e^{(1-\alpha)\mu t}.$$

It follows from equation (9.9) that:

$$z_d(t) = \frac{\overline{s}}{\mu}e^{(1-\alpha)\mu t} + (1-\alpha)\theta\int\Phi(t)dt. \tag{9.10}$$

Moreover, because the following holds for any $a, b \neq 0$:

$$\int e^{at}\sin(bt)\,dt = \frac{a\sin(bt) - b\cos(bt)}{a^2+b^2} + F,$$

where $F \in R$ is the constant of integration, hence we obtain from equation (9.10):

$$z_d(t) = \frac{\overline{s}}{\mu}e^{(1-\alpha)\mu t} + (1-\alpha)\theta\frac{(1-\alpha)\mu\sin\left(\frac{2\pi}{\omega}t\right) - \frac{2\pi}{\omega}\cos\left(\frac{2\pi}{\omega}t\right)}{(1-\alpha)^2\mu^2 + \frac{4\pi^2}{\omega^2}} + F. \tag{9.11}$$

Substituting the complementary integral equation (9.11) into equation (9.8):

$$z(t) = \frac{\overline{s}}{\mu} + (1-\alpha)\theta\frac{(1-\alpha)\mu\sin\left(\frac{2\pi}{\omega}t\right) - \frac{2\pi}{\omega}\cos\left(\frac{2\pi}{\omega}t\right)}{(1-\alpha)^2\mu^2 + \frac{4\pi^2}{\omega^2}}e^{-(1-\alpha)\mu t} + Fe^{-(1-\alpha)\mu t}$$

and from that relation and from Bernoulli substitution (9.6), we get[2]:

$$k(t) = \left(\frac{\overline{s}}{\mu} + (1-\alpha)\theta\frac{(1-\alpha)\mu\sin\left(\frac{2\pi}{\omega}t\right) - \frac{2\pi}{\omega}\cos\left(\frac{2\pi}{\omega}t\right)}{(1-\alpha)^2\mu^2 + \frac{4\pi^2}{\omega^2}}e^{-(1-\alpha)\mu t} + Fe^{-(1-\alpha)\mu t}\right)^{1/(1-\alpha)}. \tag{9.12a}$$

From the Cobb-Douglas production function (9.1), we obtain the labour productivity function $y = k^\alpha$ that together with equation (9.12a) gives:

$$y(t) = \left(\frac{\overline{s}}{\mu} + (1-\alpha)\theta\frac{(1-\alpha)\mu\sin\left(\frac{2\pi}{\omega}t\right) - \frac{2\pi}{\omega}\cos\left(\frac{2\pi}{\omega}t\right)}{(1-\alpha)^2\mu^2 + \frac{4\pi^2}{\omega^2}}e^{-(1-\alpha)\mu t} + Fe^{-(1-\alpha)\mu t}\right)^{\alpha/(1-\alpha)}. \tag{9.12b}$$

Equations (9.12a,b) describe the growth paths of capital per worker and output per worker in the ninth growth model analyzed in this chapter.

9.4 Calibration of parameters and numerical simulations

Like in Chapter 8, the elasticity of the Cobb-Douglas production function is calibrated in the following numerical simulation results at the level of $\alpha = \frac{\ln 3}{\ln 5} \approx 0.68261$, the capital depreciation rate at $\delta = 0.07$, and the growth rate of working population at $n = 0.01$.

It is also assumed that the amplitude of sine-wave fluctuations in the investment rate reaches 10% of its average value, i.e.: $\theta = 0.1\bar{s}$ which leads to the form of investment rate equation:

$$s(t) = \bar{s} \cdot \left(1 + 0.1 \sin\left(\frac{2\pi}{\omega} t\right)\right).$$

Numerical simulations were run for investment cycles characterized (consecutively) by periods of 3, 5, 10, 25 and 50 years. In those simulations, like in Chapter 8, the investment rate was modified between 10% and 40%, in steps of ten percentage points.

The model is numerically solved in a discrete time, by replacing differential equations with equivalent difference equation. The initial values of capital and labour inputs equal 1.

Table 9.1 and Figure 9.1 summarize numerical simulation results of labour productivity[3] in investment cycles characterized by a period of three years. The following tables and figures summarize simulation results for sine-wave fluctuation periods of (respectively) 5, 10, 25 and 50 years. The last value ω can be identified with the Kondratiev wave (see Korotayev and Tsirel, 2010).

The simulation results contained in Tables 9.1–9.4 and Figures 9.1–9.5 lead to the following conclusions:

- Labour productivity, regardless of the period of cyclical fluctuations in the investment rate, will oscillate in a long run (at $t \to +\infty$) about the

Table 9.1 Simulation of labour productivity at $\omega = 3$

Year t	*Investment rate (%)*			
	10	*20*	*30*	*40*
10	1.123	1.839	2.710	3.734
20	1.231	2.715	4.782	7.437
50	1.430	4.804	10.327	18.099
75	1.510	5.828	13.244	23.929
100	1.557	6.433	14.995	27.463
150	1.596	6.946	16.499	30.519
200	1.614	7.128	17.016	31.558
Oscillations at $t \to +\infty$[a]	1.611	7.152	17.106	31.758
In the original Solow model at $t \to +\infty$	1.616	7.175	17.161	31.860

[a] Tables 9.1–9.4 give the level of labour productivity in the year $t = 1{,}000$.
Source: Own calculations.

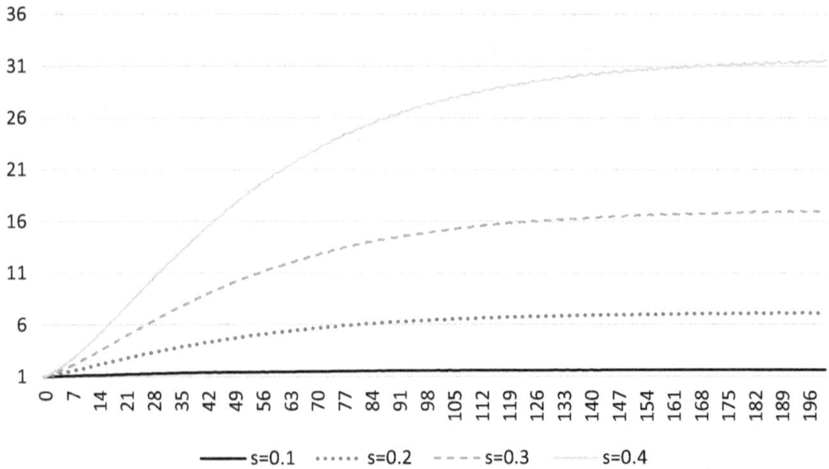

Figure 9.1 Trajectories of labour productivity at $\omega = 3$ and varying investment rates s.

Source: Own calculations.

Table 9.2 Simulation of labour productivity at $\omega = 5$

Year t	*Investment rate (%)*			
	10	*20*	*30*	*40*
10	1.123	1.837	2.707	3.729
20	1.223	2.692	4.735	7.358
50	1.421	4.767	10.245	17.951
75	1.507	5.816	13.216	23.878
100	1.554	6.419	14.961	27.401
150	1.592	6.931	16.462	30.452
200	1.603	7.078	16.897	31.338
Oscillations at$t \to +\infty$	1.607	7.136	17.067	31.686
In the original Solow model at $t \to +\infty$	1.616	7.175	17.161	31.860

Source: Own calculations.

Table 9.3 Simulation of labour productivity at $\omega = 10$

Year t	*Investment rate (%)*			
	10	*20*	*30*	*40*
10	1.121	1.833	2.700	3.718
20	1.220	2.684	4.719	7.330
50	1.416	4.748	10.201	17.872
75	1.527	5.900	13.410	24.231
100	1.547	6.390	14.892	27.274
150	1.585	6.899	16.385	30.309
200	1.595	7.045	16.818	31.191
Oscillations at$t \to +\infty$	1.600	7.102	16.987	31.537
In the original Solow model at $t \to +\infty$	1.616	7.175	17.161	31.860

Source: Own calculations.

Table 9.4 Simulation of labour productivity at $\omega = 25$

Year t	*Investment rate (%)*			
	10	*20*	*30*	*40*
10	1.169	1.954	2.918	4.057
20	1.235	2.726	4.802	7.468
50	1.402	4.694	10.079	17.651
75	1.483	5.719	12.990	23.464
100	1.528	6.308	14.700	26.919
150	1.564	6.808	16.170	29.910
200	1.574	6.952	16.596	30.779
Oscillations at $t \to +\infty$	1.578	7.009	16.763	31.120
In the original Solow model at $t \to +\infty$	1.616	7.175	17.161	31.860

Source: Own calculations.

Table 9.5 Simulation of labour productivity at $\omega = 50$

Year t	*Investment rate (%)*			
	10	*20*	*30*	*40*
10	1.157	1.924	2.865	3.974
20	1.314	2.964	5.282	8.275
50	1.380	4.610	9.890	17.312
75	1.589	6.152	13.995	25.301
100	1.498	6.182	14.402	26.371
150	1.532	6.669	15.837	29.294
200	1.542	6.809	16.253	30.143
Oscillations at $t \to +\infty$	1.546	6.863	16.416	30.476
In the original Solow model at $t \to +\infty$	1.616	7.175	17.161	31.860

Source: Own calculations.

value that emerges in the long-run equilibrium of the original Solow model (without technological progress). Therefore, an increase in the average investment rate $\bar{s}$ leads to a situation wherein capital per worker and labour productivity reach, like in the original Solow model, growth paths placed higher (see also Figures 9.1–9.5).

- The absolute amplitudes of fluctuations in labour productivity increase as economies approach the state of oscillation around the long-run equilibrium in the original Solow model. Moreover, the longer the periods of cyclical fluctuations in investment rates, the greater are those long-term absolute amplitudes of fluctuations in labour productivity.
- Additionally, whatever periods of cyclical fluctuations in investment rates are adopted, it is demonstrated in a long run that an average investment rate reaching 40% in the investment cycle will result in labour productivity that is almost 20 times greater than at average investment rates of 10%.

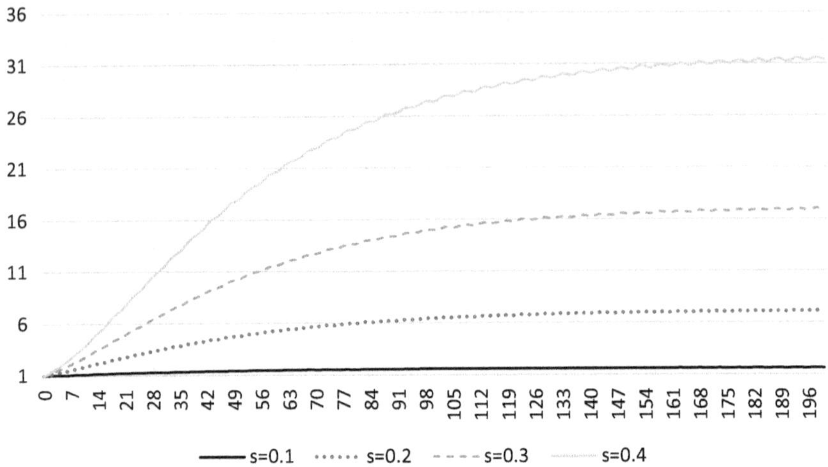

Figure 9.2 Trajectories of labour productivity at ω = 5 and varying investment rates *s*.

Source: Own calculations.

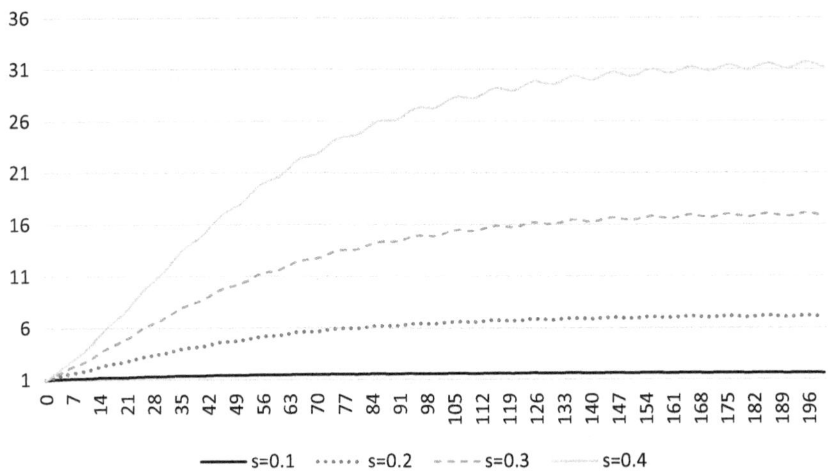

Figure 9.3 Trajectories of labour productivity at ω = 10 and varying investment rates *s*.

Source: Own calculations.

- Comparing long-run labour productivity for periods of fluctuations in investment rates of varying lengths, we obtain greater values of that variable for shorter periods of cyclical fluctuations in investment rates.
- At average investment rates of 10% in the investment cycle, cyclical periods of three and five years will result in an increase in labour productivity

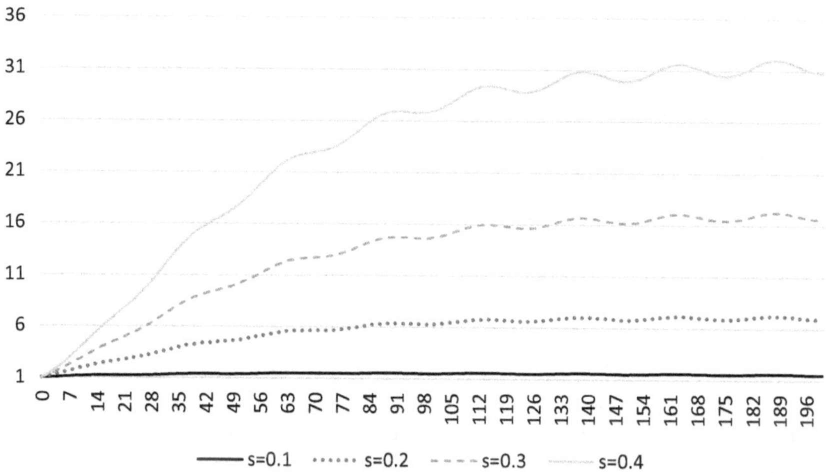

Figure 9.4 Trajectories of labour productivity at ω = 25 and varying investment rates *s*.

Source: Own calculations.

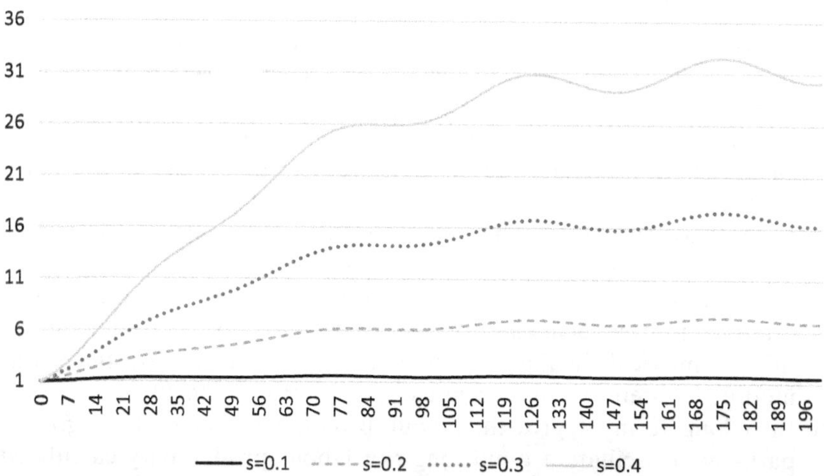

Figure 9.5 Trajectories of labour productivity at ω = 50 and varying investment rates *s*.

Source: Own calculations.

by about 61% in a long run. A period of fluctuations in investment rates lasting ten years will lead to an increase in long-run labour productivity by about 60%, and periods of fluctuations in investment rates lasting 25 and 50 years will lead to an increase in long-run labour productivity by (respectively) 58% and 55%.

- The trajectories of labour productivity at average investment rates of 20% are situated higher than at investment rates of 10%, regardless of fluctuation period lengths. An average investment rate at the level of 20% results in an increase in long-run labour productivity by more than 7 times for each period of fluctuations in investment rates, except the period of 50 years corresponding to an increase by 6.86 times.

- The fluctuation periods lasting three and five years, at an average investment rate of 30%, result in an increase in long-run labour productivity by more than 17 times. An average investment rate at the level of 30%, for other periods of fluctuations in investment rates, results in an increase in long-run labour productivity by 16.42–16.99 times compared to its initial value.
- If the economy is characterized by average investment rates of 40%, then for fluctuation periods lasting three to ten years, labour productivity will increase by about 32 times compared to the initial period. For periods of fluctuations in investment rates lasting 25 and 50 years, investment rates of 40% will lead to an increase in long-run labour productivity by (respectively) 31.12 and 30.48 times.

9.5 Conclusions

The analyzes made in this chapter can be summarized as follows:

I In this chapter, we modified the fairly restrictive assumption adopted in the original Solow model saying that investment in physical capital is constant in time. The authors assume an investment rate that changes in time and deviates from its average level, undergoing cyclical fluctuations.

II In the theoretical part of the study, the adopted assumptions about fluctuations in investment rates led to the determination of growth paths of capital per worker and of labour productivity. The periods of fluctuations in investment rates of 3, 5, 10, 25 and 50 years were assumed in the numerical simulations, and the average value of investment was modified in steps of ten percentage points from 10% to 40%.

III In a long term of growth, labour productivity, at cyclical growth paths, will oscillate around long-run labour productivity calculated in the original growth model. This leads to the conclusion that labour productivity will reach growth paths situated higher when average investment rates are greater. Additionally, the amplitudes of cyclical fluctuations in labour productivity increase as economies approach the state of oscillation around the long-run equilibrium in the original Solow model.

IV Whatever periods of cyclical fluctuations in investment rates are adopted, it is demonstrated in a long run that an average investment rate reaching 40% in the investment cycle will result in labour productivity that is almost 20 times greater than at average investment rates of 10%. In addition, long-run labour productivity assumes greater values at shorter cycles of investment rate fluctuations.

Notes

1 This chapter bases on the studies by Dykas and Misiak (2016ab).

2 The constant of integration F in equations (9.12a) should be purposefully selected to meet the condition $k(0) = k0 > 0$, where $k0$ denotes capital per worker at moment $t = 0$.

3 The trajectories of capital per worker are similar to the trajectories of labour productivity.

10 SIR-Solow model

10.1 Introduction

The epidemiological-economic model described in this chapter represents a compilation of the SIR (Susceptible –Infectious/Infected – Removed/Recovered) epidemiological model proposed by Kermack and McKendrick (1927) and the neoclassical model of economic growth proposed by Solow (1956).

The methods of analytical description of the spread of contagious diseases has been widely discussed in the scientific literature (see Murray, 2003; Ruan, 2007; Xiao and Ruan, 2007; Fei-Ying, Wan-Tong and Zhi-Cheng, 2015; Jardón-Kojakhmetov, Kuehn, Pugliese and Sensi, 2021) that adopts the epidemiological model known as SIR, proposed by Kermack and McKendrick (1927). The original SIR model ignores restrictions imposed on social and economic life to contain the spread of an epidemic, and economic consequences of the epidemic and of those restrictions imposed to contain its spread. Bärwolff (2020) expanded the SIR model to include analyzes of epidemic spread and subsidence. Bärwolff assumes in his study that the government imposes severe restrictions on social and economic life when the proportion of infected people reaches a threshold defined by the government. Bärwolff also assumes that the more restrictive lockdown is introduced, the slower is the pace of epidemic spread. However, he argues that a lockdown leads only to a displacement of the climax of the pandemic, but not really to an efficient flattening of the curve representing the number of infected people.

The effects of a rapid spread of a pandemic on economic growth were not analyzed in mainstream economic research in the past. The economic effects of HIV/AIDS in Asia (Bloom and Lyons, 1993) and in selected countries of Europe, Africa, North America and South America (Bloom and Mahal, 1995; Kambou, Devarajan and Over, 1992) were analyzed in the last two decades of the 20th century. For example, Bloom, Mahal in their studies published in 1995 and 1997 argue that the HIV/AIDS epidemic had no material effect on the rate of growth of income per capita in 51 developed and industrialized countries of the world in the years 1980–1992. After two decades, Cuesta (2010) came to a similar conclusion about Honduras,

DOI: 10.4324/9781003323792-11

the country most severely affected by the HIV/AIDS epidemic in South America.

The current scale and rate of spread of the COVID-19 pandemic caused by a coronavirus entails serious disturbances in social and economic life. The pandemic of 2020 represents the worst global health crisis since the times of Spanish flu that struck in 1918. In response to the chain of events observed, several measures are being presently considered. Alvarez, Argente and Lippi (2020) and Atkeson (2020) address the problem of optimization of the severity level of a lockdown. They use the SIR model under conditions of changing economic activity of the population and enterprises. The importance of social distance is emphasized by Lik Ng (2020) who indicates adverse effects of a lockdown policy treated as the principal method preventing the spread of pandemic. Research into trade-off in public choices was also initiated in 2020. Aum, Lee and Shin (2020) analyze a trade-off between GDP and public health under pandemic conditions. They argue that a lockdown not only limits the spread of pandemic but also mitigates the accumulated GDP loss in the long run. If no lockdown measures are taken during a pandemic, mass quarantining is necessary, leading to adverse economic effects. The self-employed who achieve relatively low income form the group exposed to the most severe consequences of a lockdown. Brock and Xepapadeas (2020) adopt an even wider perspective. They argue that continuous growth of consumption activities, capital accumulation and climate change could increase the exposure of society to the risk of infection. In their opinion, a policy preventing the spread of epidemic should consist of two components. The first component includes short-term measures. The second component includes economic policies aimed at changing consumption patterns and addressing climate change.

Research projects described in the scientific literature also include studies into the effects of an epidemic on economic growth, employing neoclassical growth models. Cuddington (1993) used the Solow model to analyze the growth path of per-capita GDP in the context of HIV/AIDS epidemics and its demographic consequences. The model used by him indicated a material risk of reduction in the GDP growth rate in Tanzania by the year 2010. Cuddington and Hancock (1994) adopted the same methodological approach to assess the effect of HIV/AIDS on the economy of Malawi. Delfino and Simmons (2005) identify significant empirical links between the health structure of the population and the productive system of an economy that is subject to infectious disease, in particular tuberculosis. Another neoclassical model of economic growth used in research into the effects of spread of the HIV virus on economic growth was proposed by Mankiw, Romer and Weil (1992). Lovasz and Schipp (2009) used that model to assess the effects of educational and health capital, and of the pace of epidemic spread on aggregate macroeconomic indicators. The effect of the HIV virus is not the same in all countries, and even within individual countries. The economies characterized by developed healthcare infrastructures are capable of providing means aimed to prevent a rapid spread of an epidemic in its early phase. Additionally, Lovasz and Schipp, when analyzing the problem of accumulation of human capital under epidemic conditions, argue that a loss of human capital due to an epidemic does not always entail the same consequences. The education level and number of skilled workers and their outflow from production processes due to an epidemic affects the GDP growth rate to a varying extent. Similarly, the social capital stock is interrelated with economic growth under epidemic conditions.

The above outline of main topics of research into the impact of an epidemic on economic growth provides foundations to the epidemiological-economic model proposed in this chapter. The proposed model incorporates restrictions imposed by the government on social and economic life in two alternative versions: in a gradual, continual manner as a function of the proportion of infected people in the population and as a strict lockdown adopted abruptly by the government. The value of aggregate production is affected by: the capital stocks, the rising percentage of infectious people that reduces investment and the rate of capital accumulation, and the scale of lockdown restrictions. The model proposed in this chapter is not strictly related or limited to the COVID-19 pandemic, as it is useful in analyzing the effects of any epidemic that leads to material social damage (a high percentage of infected and dead people, limited interpersonal contacts due to lockdown measures implemented) and economic losses (a drop in production caused by a collapse of aggregate demand and a reduction in supply capacity of the economy, and consequently in the rate of capital accumulation).

10.2 An epidemiological-economic model

The original SIR model does not include restrictions imposed on social and economic activity in response to the spread of an epidemic.[1] For this reason, an analysis of the process of spread and subsidence of an epidemic was made using the SIR model as modified by Bärwolff (2020). Bärwolff assumes that governments impose restrictions on social and economic life when an epidemic begins to spread out of control (the percentage of infected people exceeds certain critical level defined in an arbitrary manner by the government). Bärwolff also assumes that the more restrictive lockdown is introduced, the slower is the pace of epidemic spread.

Bärwolff's study is based on the assumption that the state introduces lockdown measures rapidly in an arbitrary manner (within a period or at certain time intervals). In our epidemiological-economic model, we assume that the level of lockdown severity is defined using a specific functional rule. Namely, we assume that the severity index of a lockdown is an analytical function of the percentage of the infected. If the percentage grows, the government does not use arbitrary criteria but follows the rule described by the function when imposing restrictions on social and economic life.

10.2.1 The epidemiological module

We consider two scenarios when analyzing the spread and subsidence of an epidemic. Like in the original SIR model, we consider a scenario wherein the government has no access to a vaccine (preventing the disease spread) and a scenario wherein the government has a vaccine.

In the scenario with the government having no access to a vaccine, we assume that the spread of epidemic is described by the following differential equations:

$$\begin{cases} \Delta S_t = -\beta\kappa_t S_{t-1} I_{t-1} \\ \Delta I_t = \beta\kappa_t S_{t-1} I_{t-1} - \gamma I_{t-1} \\ \Delta H_t = \gamma h I_{t-1} \\ \Delta D_t = \gamma(1-h) I_{t-1} \end{cases}, \tag{10.1}$$

where $S_t \in (0,1)$ represents the percentage of susceptible people on day t (for t = 1, 2, …), $I_t \in (0,1)$ – the percentage of the infected, $H_t \in (0,1)$ – the percentage of the recovered (the recovered are not eventually included in the group of the susceptible), $D_t \in (0,1)$ – the percentage of the dead.[2] We also assume that $\beta, h \in (0,1)$, $\gamma \in (0,\beta)$ and $\kappa_t \in [0,1]$ in consecutive days t = 1, 2, …. The parameter β in the system of equations (10.1) describes the pace of epidemic spread, γ represents the percentage of infected people who either recover or die, and h represents the mortality rate among the infected. The parameter κ_t that can vary in its value in time (like in the original study of Bärwolff from 2020) represents an indicator of restrictions imposed on social and economic life on consecutive days of epidemic duration. If the parameter equals 1, the government does not impose any restriction on social and economic life in response to the epidemic. If $\kappa_t = 0$, a full lockdown is imposed. The lower is the value of the κ_t indicator, the stricter lockdown is imposed. Additionally, the lower is the value of that indicator, the slower is the spread of epidemic.

It follows from the first equation in the system (equation 10.1) that a reduction in the percentage of the susceptible (that is $-\Delta S_t$) is directly proportional to the indicator of restrictions imposed on social and economic life (κ_t), the percentage of the susceptible (S_{t-1}) and the percentage of the infected (I_{t-1}). The second equation in the system (10.1) is interpreted so that an increase in the percentage of the infected (that is ΔI_t) equals the difference between a reduction in the percentage of the susceptible (that is $-\Delta S_t$) and the percentage of the infected who recover or die (γI_{t-1}). Equations three and four in the system of differential equations (10.1) imply that h part of the infected recover and $1-h$ part of them die.

Additionally, it follows from the second equation in the above system of differential equations that the percentage of the infected I_t rises as long as the percentage of the susceptible S_t is greater than the expression $\frac{\beta\kappa_t}{\gamma}$.

Hence, restrictions imposed on social and economic life by the government (and described by a dropping value of the parameter κ_t) lead to a postponement of the initial day of a fall in the percentage of the infected.

In the vaccination scenario, the SIR model is reduced to the following system of differential equations that represents an extension of the system of equations (10.1):

$$\begin{cases} \Delta S_t = \begin{cases} -\beta\kappa_t S_{t-1} I_{t-1} & \text{for} \quad t < \tau + 21 \\ -\beta\kappa_t S_{t-1} I_{t-1} - \varepsilon\rho\pi_{t-21} S_{t-21} & \text{for} \quad t \geq \tau + 21 \end{cases} \\ \Delta I_t = \beta\kappa_t S_{t-1} I_{t-1} - \gamma I_{t-1} \\ \Delta H_t = \gamma h I_{t-1} \\ \Delta D_t = \gamma(1-h) I_{t-1} \\ \Delta P_t = \begin{cases} 0 & \text{for } t < \tau + 21 \\ \varepsilon\rho\pi_{t-21} S_{t-21} & \text{for} \quad t \geq \tau + 21 \end{cases} \end{cases} . \tag{10.2}$$

$P_t \in (0,1)$ in the system of equations (10.2) represents the percentage of effectively vaccinated people (that is people who are no longer susceptible to infection after their vaccination), τ – the first day of vaccination, $\varepsilon \in (0,1)$ – an indicator of vaccine effectiveness (that is the percentage of vaccinated population that will not contract the disease), $\rho \in (0,1)$ – the percentage of those who wish to receive the vaccine, and $\pi_t \in (0,1)$ (for consecutive days $t = \tau, \tau + 1 \ldots$) – the percentage of those who wish to receive the vaccine and are vaccinated until day t. We also assume that people effectively vaccinated develop immunity to the disease in 21 days after vaccination.

A modification in the system of differential equations (10.2) compared to the system of equations (10.1) can be reduced to the conclusion that beginning on day 21 after the first day of vaccination, the percentage of the susceptible is reduced by the percentage of effectively vaccinated people (that is by $\varepsilon\rho\pi_{t-21} S_{t-21}$).

When analyzing models without vaccination and with vaccination, we adopt two alternative scenarios of changes in the severity indicator of restrictions imposed on social and economic life κ_t. We assume that:

$$\kappa_t = 1 - I_{t-1}^{\sigma} \tag{10.3}$$

or:

$$\kappa_t = \begin{cases} 1 & \text{for} \quad \overline{I}_{Gt} < \iota \\ \theta & \text{for} \quad \overline{I}_{Gt} \geq \iota \end{cases} , \tag{10.4}$$

where $\bar{I}_{Gt} = \prod_{i=1}^{14} I_{t-i}$ represents a geometric moving average of the percentage of the infected in the most recent two weeks. Regarding the parameters θ, σ and ι in the equations (10.3 and 10.4), we assume that: $\theta, \iota \in (0,1)$, and $\sigma > 0$.

We assume in equation (10.3) that if the percentage of the infected I_t rises from 0 to 1, the restriction severity indicator κ_t drops from 1 to 0, and if $\sigma \in (0,1)$ $(\sigma > 1)$, subsequent falls in the indicator κ_t, corresponding to identical rises in the percentage of the infected I_t, are increasingly bigger (smaller).[3] Equation (10.4) implies that we consider a scenario wherein the government does not impose any restriction on social and economic life, if the geometric moving average of the percentage of the infected over the most recent two weeks does not exceed the percentage ι. When that percentage is exceeded, the government imposes a lockdown and the indicator κ_t drops abruptly from 1 to θ.

The indicator of immunization coverage π_t is described by the following equation:

$$\pi_t = \frac{at}{b+t},$$

where $a,b > 0$, and t represents consecutive days of vaccination. That indicator of vaccination coverage (at t increasing from 0 to $+\infty$) rises with a decreasing pace from 0 to a.[4]

10.2.2 The economic module

We adopt the following assumptions about developments of basic macroeconomic variables in our economic module[5]:

1 The value of production on day t (that is Y_t) is described by a modified Cobb-Douglas production function (1928) expressed by the formula:

$$Y_t = \kappa_t K_t^{\alpha} L_t^{1-\alpha}, \tag{10.5}$$

where $\alpha \in (0;1)$ represents output elasticity Y_t of capital input K_t. In function (10.5), we take into account both supply and demand factors affecting the value of production. The supply component (like in the original Cobb-Douglas production function) is described by the expression $K_t^{\alpha} L_t^{1-\alpha}$, hence if the epidemic did not strike, the value of production (like in the Solow model) would amount to[6] $K_t^{\alpha} L_t^{1-\alpha}$. We also assume that if the government imposes a lockdown and reduces the indicator of social and economic activity from 1 to $\kappa_t \in (0;1)$, the value of aggregate demand falls and (due to Keynesian multiplier effects) the volume of production also falls from a level of $K_t^{\alpha} L_t^{1-\alpha}$ to $\kappa_t K_t^{\alpha} L_t^{1-\alpha}$.

Hence, a relative reduction in the volume of production caused by a fall in δ like in the original model proposed by Solow, capital accumulation (daily, in a discrete time) is described by a differential equation in the following form:

$$\Delta K_t = s\frac{Y_{t-1}}{365} - \delta\frac{K_{t-1}}{365}, \quad (10.6)$$

Where $s \in (0;1)$ represents the savings-investment rate, and $\delta \in (0;1)$ – capital depreciation rate.

2 The value of demand for labour (and the number of currently employed people) is described by:

$$L_t = \omega(1 - I_t - D_t)\left(\frac{Y_t}{Y^*}\right), \quad (10.7)$$

Where $\omega, \phi \in (0;1)$, and $Y^* > 0$ represents the value of production in the Solow long-run equilibrium (that is at $\Delta K_t = 0$). The parameter ϕ represents elasticity of demand for labour relative to the volume of production. I_t and D_t in equation (10.7) represent (like in the epidemiological module of the proposed model) percentages of the infected and those who died of the epidemic.

It follows from equation (10.7) that in our model, if the epidemic did not strike, at production rising from $Y_t < Y^*$ to Y^*, the percentage of the employed would rise from a level of $\omega\left(\frac{Y_t}{Y^*}\right)^{\phi}$ to ω. In the time of epidemic, the percentage of the employed represents $(1 - I_t - D_t)$ part of the demand for labour, because the infected and dead (certainly) do not work.

3 The unemployment rate u_t is (by definition) described by the formula:

$$u_t = 1 - \frac{L_t}{w}, \quad (10.8)$$

where $w \in (0;1)$ represents the percentage of the professionally active. We assume implicitly that on day $t = 1$ the population amounted to 1, and on consecutive days equalled $1 - D_t$ while the number of professionally active people amounted to $w(1 - D_t)$.

It follows from equations (10.5–10.8) that in the Solow long-run equilibrium (i.e. at $\Delta K_t = 0$): $L^* = \omega$, $K^* = \omega\left(\frac{s}{\delta}\right)^{\frac{1}{1-\alpha}}$, $Y^* = \omega\left(\frac{s}{\delta}\right)^{\frac{\alpha}{1-\alpha}}$, and $u^* = \frac{w - \omega}{w}$, where asterisks next to consecutive variables indicate their values in the long-run equilibrium of the economic growth model analyzed here.

The following system of differential equations is obtained from equation (10.5–10.8):

$$\begin{cases} Y_t = \kappa_t K_t^{\alpha} L_t^{1-\alpha} \\ \Delta K_t = s\dfrac{Y_{t-1}}{365} - \delta\dfrac{K_{t-1}}{365} \\ L_t = \omega(1 - I_t - D_t)\left(\dfrac{Y_t}{Y^*}\right), \\ u_t = 1 - \dfrac{L_t}{w} \\ U_t = \sqrt[4]{(1-I_t)\kappa_t \dfrac{u_{Nt}}{u_t}\dfrac{Y_t}{Y_{Nt}}} \end{cases} \tag{10.9}$$

where u_{Nt} and Y_{Nt} represent (respectively) an unemployment rate and a production value that would be recorded if the epidemic did not strike (that is in a scenario wherein on each day $t = 1, 2, \ldots$ the percentage of the susceptible S_t would equal 1).

The last equation in system (10.9) describes the social utility function U_t. The function represents a geometric average of the indicator of social and economic activity κ, the percentage of the susceptible $1-I_t$, the ratio of the unemployment rate under non-epidemic to that rate under epidemic conditions (u_{Nt}/u_t) and the ratio of production under non-epidemic conditions to production under epidemic conditions (Y_t/Y_{Nt}). The function of social utility:

$$U_t = \sqrt[4]{(1-I_t)\kappa_t \frac{u_{Nt}}{u_t}\frac{Y_t}{Y_{Nt}}}.$$

takes into account both social (described by the indicator κ_t) and health $(1-I_t)$, and economic (u_{Nt}/u_t and Y_t/Y_{Nt}) consequences of the epidemic.

Additionally, the social utility function U_t assumes values from the interval [0;1]. If the epidemic did not strike, $\kappa_t = 1 - I_t = \frac{u_{Nt}}{u_t} = \frac{Y_t}{Y_{Nt}}$, and hence $U_t = 1$. The lower values are assumed by function U_t, the higher are aggregate social, health and economic costs of the epidemic. During a full lockdown (that is at $\kappa_t = 0$), the value of social utility function falls to 0.

10.3 Calibrated model parameters

10.3.1 Parameters of the epidemiological module

We assume that the infection lasts for 14 days on average. Hence, the parameter γ in the epidemiological module is selected at the level of $\gamma = 1/14 \approx 0.071429$.

The parameter β is calibrated so that peak incidence, if the government does not impose any lockdown, falls on day 365 of the epidemic. Hence the parameter equals 0.1066 in consecutive versions of numerical simulations.

We also assume that the mortality rate among the infected amounts to 2%, hence $h = 0.98$. We assume than 1 person per million was infected on day one of the epidemic, that is $I_1 = 10^{-6}$.

When analyzing the equation of social and economic activity indicator $\kappa_t = 1 - I_t^{\sigma}$, we assume σ equal 0.5 (if the government imposes severe restrictions to contain the epidemic) or 1 (if a liberal approach is adopted). When we use the function $\kappa_t = \begin{cases} 1 & \text{for } \bar{I}_{Gt} < \iota \\ \theta 1 & \text{for } \bar{I}_{Gt} \geq \iota \end{cases}$ to describe restrictions imposed by the government to contain the epidemics, we assume that the government adopts a lockdown when the geometric moving average of the percentage of the infected $\bar{I}_{Gt}$ exceeds $\iota = 0.5\%$ and then social and economic activity will be reduced by 15% (that is $\theta = 0.85$). If the government adopts a liberal approach to the epidemic, we assume $\iota = 1\%$ and $\theta = 0.95$.

When analyzing the models with vaccination, we assume that vaccines are administered as of day 300 of the pandemic. We also assume that a percentage $\rho = 48\%$ of the population wish to receive the vaccine and the effectiveness of vaccination ε equals 95%.

We make two alternative assumptions about the dynamics of daily immunization coverage in the population π_t:

- First, we assume that the parameters a and b in the indicator of immunization coverage are such that the indicator equals 1% on day 7 of vaccination and 2% on day 100. Hence, we obtain: $\frac{7a}{b+7} = 0.001$ and $\frac{100a}{b+100} = 0.002$ which gives (in line with the Cramer's rule): $a \approx 0.00216$ and $b \approx 8.140$. The scenarios are referred to below as scenarios with slow progress in immunization coverage of the population.
- Second, we assume that $\pi 7 = 0.001$ and $\pi 100 = 0.006$. In this case, the Cramer's formula produces: $a \approx 0.00962$ and $b \approx 60.345$. The scenarios are referred to below as scenarios with rapid progress in immunization coverage.

10.3.2 Parameters of the economic module

The elasticity α of Cobb-Douglas production function (10.5) is calibrated at the level of 0.5. We also assume a 20% savings-investment rate s and a 5% capital depreciation rate δ. The long-run capital output ratio K^*/Y^* at the values of those parameters set as above equals 4.

We assume the indicator of economic activity of the population $w = 46\%$, that is similar to the value recorded in the EU states.

The parameter ω in the function of demand for labour (10.7) is calibrated at the level of 0.44, and consequently the long-run unemployment rate equals about 4.35% at $w = 0.46$. The parameter ϕ is selected so that under non-epidemic conditions, in an economy with an initial capital input $K1$ representing 40% of capital in the Solow long-run equilibrium (that is K^*), the unemployment rate equals 10%. Then, the elasticity of demand for labour L_t relative to production Y_t equals about 0.106.

10.4 Scenarios and numerical simulation results

The numerical simulations discussed below include 12 scenarios of epidemic development. The first four of those scenarios give the government no access to a vaccine, and a vaccine is available in the remaining 8 scenarios (see the statement in Table 10.1).

Table 10.1 Scenarios of epidemic development

Scenario	κt	*Vaccine*	*Notes*
I	$1-\sqrt{I_t}$	None	-
II	$1-I_t$		
III	$\kappa_t = \begin{cases} 1 & \text{for } \bar{I}_{Gt} < 0.0005 \\ 0.85 & \text{for } \bar{I}_{Gt} \geq 0.0005 \end{cases}$		
IV	$\kappa_t = \begin{cases} 1 & \text{for } \bar{I}_{Gt} < 0.001 \\ 0.95 & \text{for } \bar{I}_{Gt} \geq 0.001 \end{cases}$		
V	$1-\sqrt{I_t}$	First vaccinations on day 300 of the epidemic following the formula: $\pi_t = \dfrac{0.00216t}{8.14+t}$ where t is the consecutive day of vaccination	Slow progress in immunization coverage. About 17.2% of those wishing to receive the vaccine are immunized within 100 days
VI	$1-I_t$		
VII	$\kappa_t = \begin{cases} 1 & \text{for } \bar{I}_{Gt} < 0.0005 \\ 0.85 & \text{for } \bar{I}_{Gt} \geq 0.0005 \end{cases}$		
VIII	$\kappa_t = \begin{cases} 1 & \textit{for } \bar{I}_{Gt} < 0.001 \\ 0.95 & \textit{for } \bar{I}_{Gt} \geq 0.001 \end{cases}$		
IX	$1-\sqrt{I_t}$	First vaccinations on day 300 of the epidemic following the formula: $\pi_t = \dfrac{0.00962t}{60.345+t}$	Rapid progress in immunization coverage. About 39.8% of those wishing to receive the vaccine are immunized within 100 days
X	$1-I_t$		
XI	$\kappa_t = \begin{cases} 1 & \text{for } \bar{I}_{Gt} < 0.0005 \\ 0.85 & \text{for } \bar{I}_{Gt} \geq 0.0005 \end{cases}$		
XII	$\kappa_t = \begin{cases} 1 & \text{for } \bar{I}_{Gt} < 0.001 \\ 0.95 & \text{for } \bar{I}_{Gt} \geq 0.001 \end{cases}$		

Source: Own assumptions.

In the scenarios wherein the government has no access to a vaccine (scenarios I–IV), we assume that the government reduces the intensity of social and economic activity gradually, in line with a functional formula (10.3) (scenarios I and II) or that activity is restricted abruptly (scenarios III and IV). In scenarios I and III, the government imposes severe restrictions to contain the spread of epidemic; in scenarios II and IV, the government adopts a liberal approach.

The scenarios with vaccination (V–XII) can be divided into those with slow progress (scenarios V–VIII) and those with rapid progress (IX–XII) in immunization coverage of the population. Scenarios V and IX assume that the government adopts a lockdown like in scenario I; scenarios VI and X assume a lockdown as in scenario II, etc.

The results of numerical simulations of epidemiological indicators in the extended SIR model (systems of equations (10.1 and 10.2)) in consecutive scenarios are contained in Table 10.2. Figures 10.1–10.4 represent curves of analyzed epidemiological variables.[7]

The simulation results contained in Table 10.2, and Figures 10.1–10.4 lead to the following conclusions:

- If the government did not adopt any lockdown measures and had no access to a vaccine, the greatest percentage of the infected would be recorded (as already indicated) on day 365 of the epidemic. If the government has no access to a vaccine and imposes a severe lockdown, the peak will be postponed to day 391 (scenario I) or 456 (scenario II) of the epidemic. If a mild lockdown is imposed, the greatest number of the infected will be recorded on day 365 (scenario II) or 383 (scenario IV).

Table 10.2 Epidemiological indicators in consecutive scenarios

Scenario	*Variable*						
	κ_m	S_m	I_M	H_M	D_M	P_M	T
I	0.8347	0.5762	0.0273	0.4153	0.0085	-	391
II	0.9475	0.4566	0.0525	0.5326	0.0109	-	365
III	0.85	0.6043	0.0246	0.3878	0.0079	-	456
IV	0.95	0.4728	0.0490	0.5167	0.0105	-	383
V	0.8380	0.1485	0.0263	0.3374	0.0069	0.5072	381
VI	0.9480	0.1122	0.0520	0.4927	0.0101	0.3850	363
VII	0.85	0.1650	0.0189	0.2650	0.0054	0.5646	428
VIII	0.95	0.1181	0.0473	0.4649	0.0095	0.4075	378
IX	0.8389	0.0014	0.0260	0.2885	0.0059	0.7042	377
X	0.9481	0.0010	0.0519	0.4632	0.0095	0.5264	363
XI	0.85	0.0016	0.0167	0.1939	0.0040	0.8006	408
XII	0.95	0.0011	0.0468	0.4259	0.0087	0.5643	376

Note: The subscript m indicates the minimum value of a variable, M indicates its maximum value. T indicates the day of the greatest percentage of the infected.
Source: Own calculations.

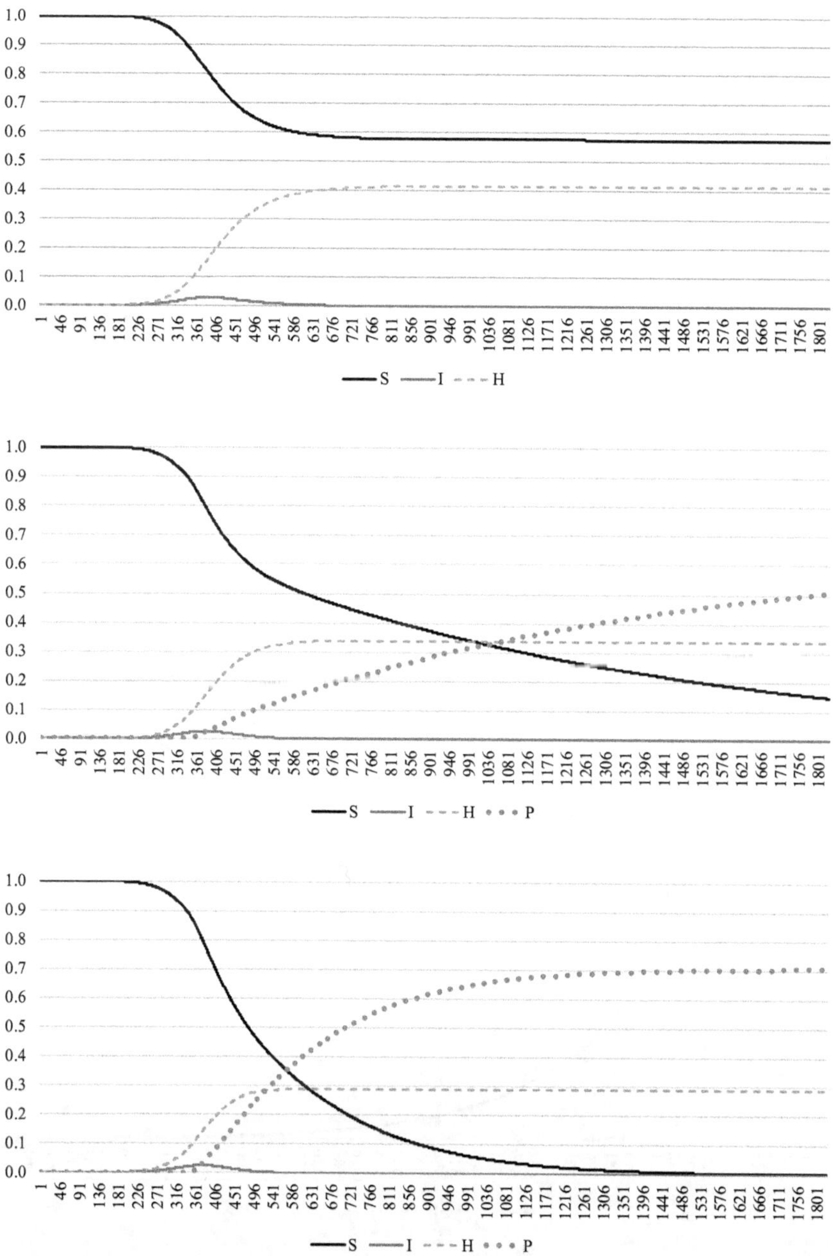

Figure 10.1 Curves of S, I, H and P in scenarios I, V and IX (at $\kappa_t = 1 - \sqrt{I_t}$). (a) Scenario I, (b) scenario V, and (c) scenario IX.

Source: Own calculations

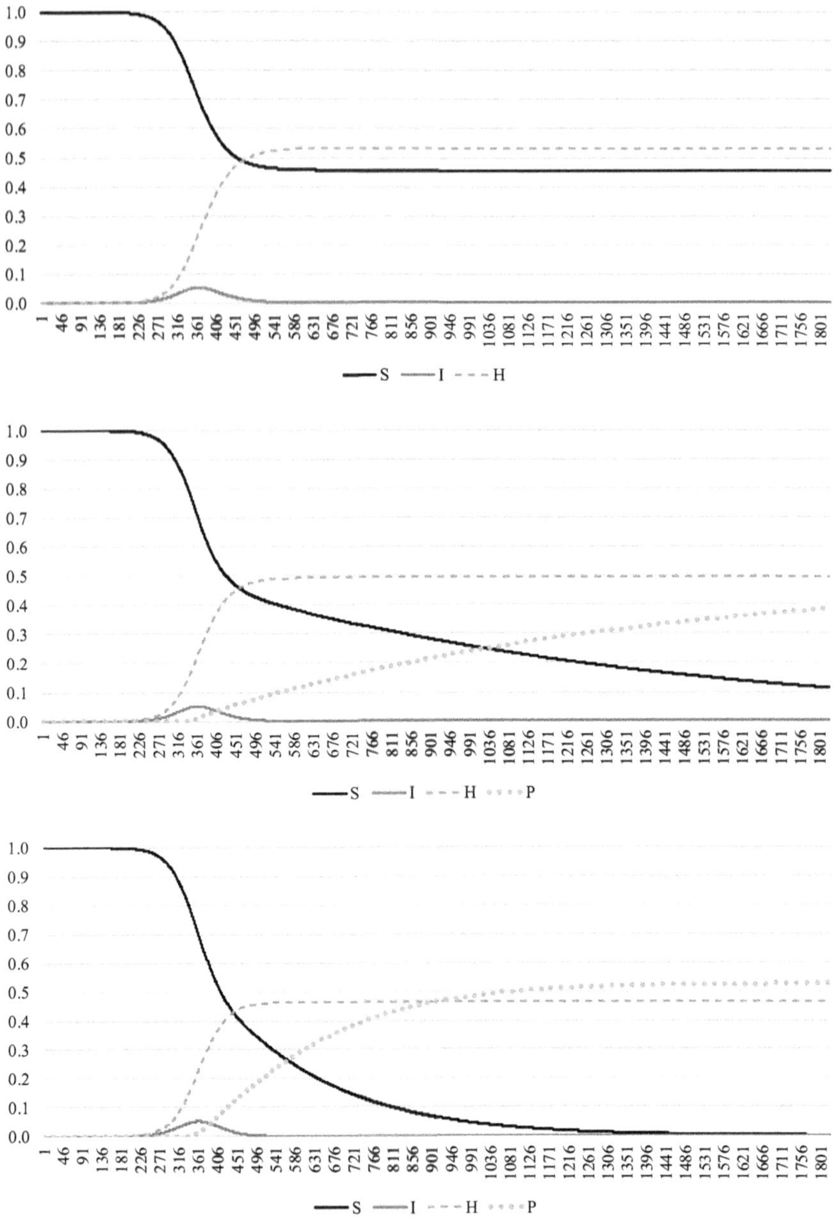

Figure 10.2 Curves of *S*, *I*, *H* and *P* in scenarios II, VI and X (at $\kappa_t = 1 - I_t$). (a) Scenario II, (b) scenario VI, and (c) scenario X.

Source: Own calculations.

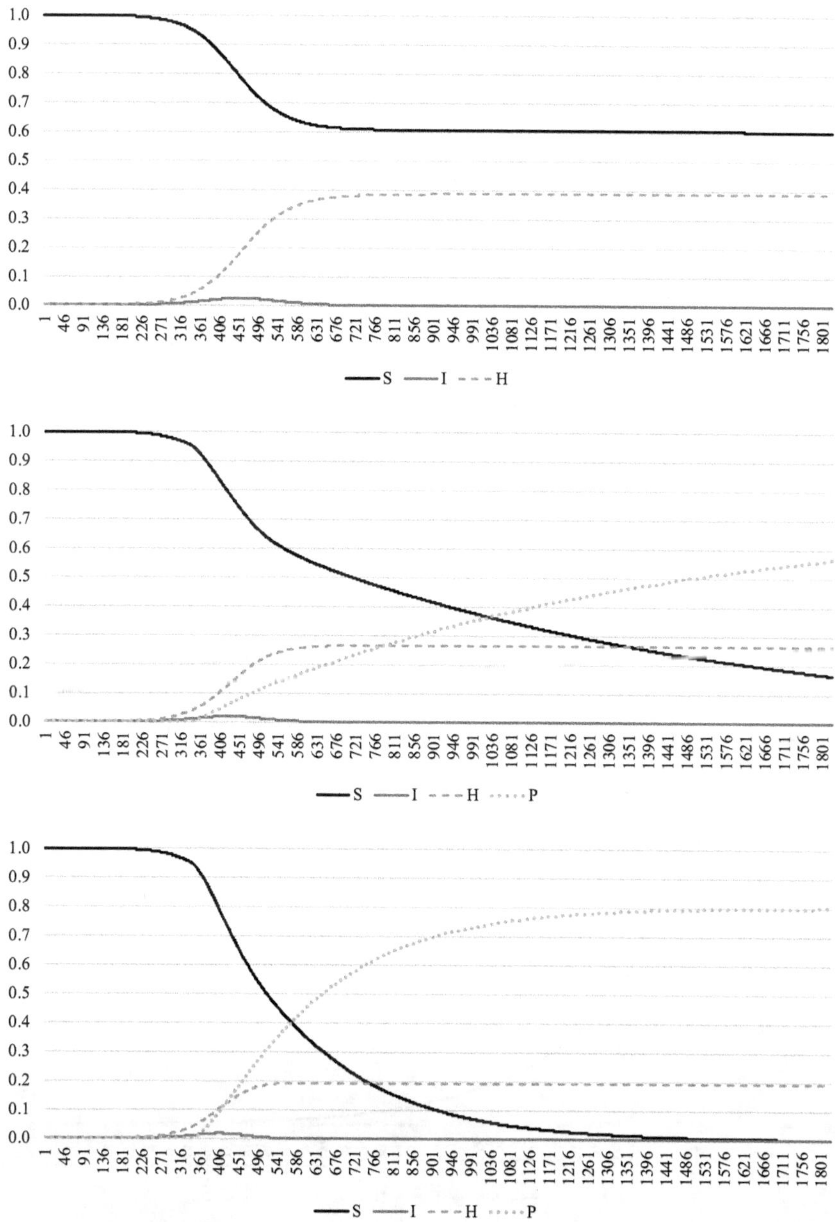

Figure 10.3 Curves of S, I, H and P in scenarios III, VII and XI, at $\kappa_t = \begin{cases} 1 & \text{for } \bar{I}_{Gt} < 0.0005 \\ 0.85 & \text{for } \bar{I}_{Gt} \geq 0.0005 \end{cases}$. (a) Scenario III, (b) scenario VII, and (c) scenario XI.

Source: Own calculations.

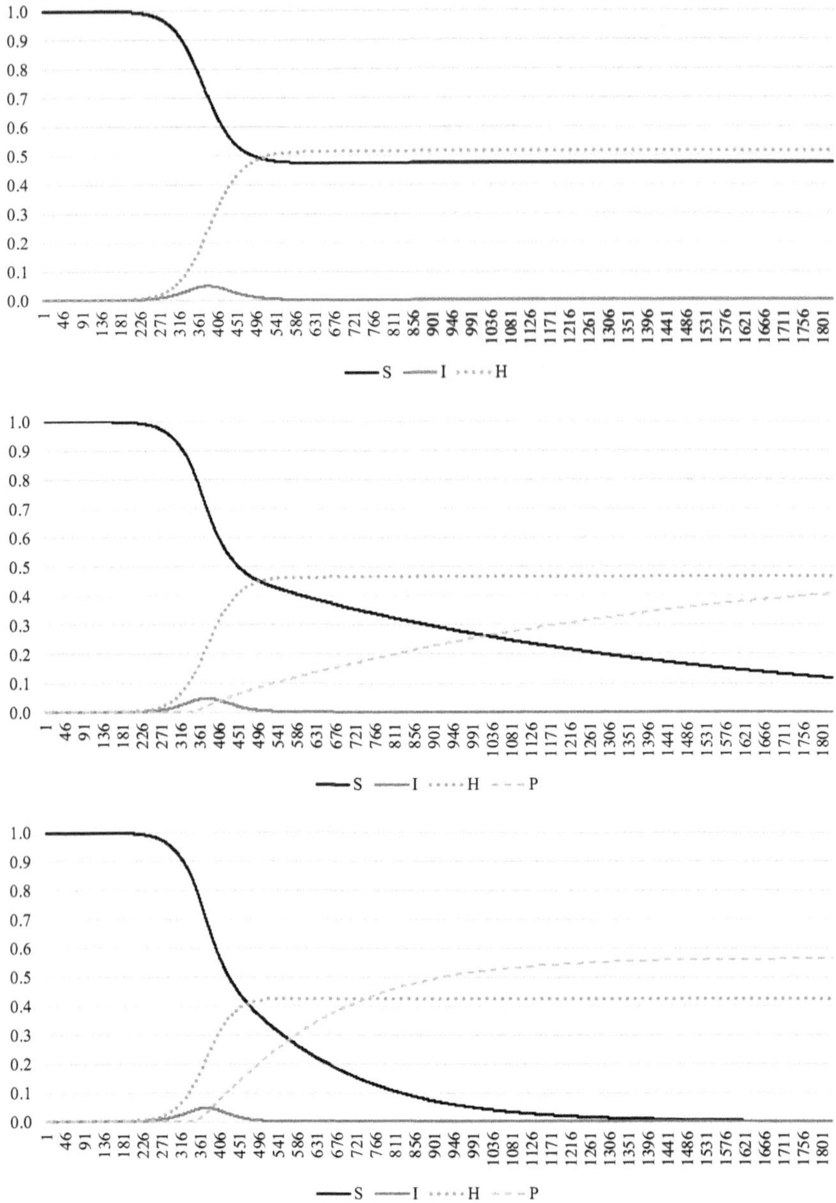

Figure 10.4 Curves of S, I, H and P in scenarios IV, VIII and XII, at $\kappa_t = \begin{cases} 1 & \text{for } \bar{I}_{Gt} < 0.001 \\ 0.95 & \text{for } \bar{I}_{Gt} \geq 0.001 \end{cases}$. (a) Scenario IV, (b) scenario VIII, and (c) scenario XII.

Source: Own calculations.

- At slow progress in immunization coverage of the population (scenarios V–VIII), the greatest number of the infected is recorded between days 381 and 428 of the epidemic (if severe restrictions are imposed in response to the epidemic) or between days 363 and 378 (if a liberal approach to the epidemic is adopted). On the other hand, rapid progress in immunization coverage results in a postponement of epidemic peak to a date between days 377 and 408 of the epidemic (if severe restrictions are imposed in response to the epidemic), or between days 363 and 376 (if a liberal approach to the epidemic is adopted).
- In the scenarios wherein the government has no access to a vaccine, a maximum limitation of social and economic activity (at the peak of epidemic) can reach 15%–16.5% under conditions of a severe lockdown or 5%–6.5% under conditions of a mild lockdown. The scenarios wherein the government uses vaccination (i.e. scenarios V–XII) have no significant effect on that parameter.
- If no vaccine is administered, the maximum percentage of infected people will reach 2.5%–2.7% (severe restrictions in scenarios I and III) or 4.9%–5.3% (liberal scenarios II and IV). In the case of slow progress in immunization coverage, that percentage will drop to about 1.9%–2.6% under conditions of a severe lockdown or to 4.7%–5.2% if a liberal approach is adopted. In the case of rapid progress in immunization coverage, that percentage will slightly fall.
- In the scenarios without vaccination, the percentage of the susceptible (uninfected) will reach after the epidemic about 57.6%–60.4% under conditions of a severe lockdown or 45.7%–47.3% under conditions of a mild lockdown.
- If the government has access to a vaccine but progress in immunization coverage is slow, the percentage of uninfected population (understood then as $S_m + P_M$) will reach 65.6%–73.0% under conditions of a severe lockdown or 49.7%–52.6% if a liberal approach is adopted.
- Rapid progress in immunization coverage leads to an increase in those indicators to 70.6%–80.2% (a severe lockdown) or 52.7%–56.5% (a mild lockdown).
- If no vaccine is administered, 7.9%–8.5% of the population will die of the epidemic under conditions of a severe lockdown imposed by the government or 10.5%–10.9%‰%under conditions of a mild lockdown. Slow progress in immunization coverage will reduce those indicators to 5.4%–6.9% (a severe lockdown) or 9.5%–10.1% (a liberal approach). Rapid progress in immunization coverage will reduce the rate of mortality caused by the epidemic to 4.0%–5.9% of the population (a severe lockdown) or 8.7%–9.5% (a mild lockdown).

An analysis of the epidemic effect on the values of principal macroeconomic indicators (in the real economy sector) includes the scenarios described above in 2 versions. We consider values of those indicators in an economy

Table 10.3 Economic indicators in consecutive scenarios at $K1/K^* = 0.4$ (a poorly developed economy)

Scenario	*Variable*							
	$\min_t \frac{Y_t}{Y_{Nt}}$	$\frac{\sum_t Y_t}{\sum_t Y_{Nt}}$	$\min_t \frac{K_t}{K_{Nt}}$	$\frac{\sum_t K_t}{\sum_t K_{Nt}}$	$\max_t \frac{u_t}{u_{Nt}}$	$\frac{\bar{u}_G}{\bar{u}_{GN}}$	$\min_t U_t$	$\bar{U}_G$
	From monthly data						*From daily data*	
I	0.801	0.932	0.987	0.993	1.212	1.068	0.855	0.951
II	0.891	0.977	0.996	0.998	1.112	1.023	0.901	0.974
III	0.814	0.902	0.982	0.990	1.197	1.100	0.866	0.936
IV	0.893	0.965	0.994	0.996	1.109	1.034	0.903	0.969
V	0.805	0.945	0.990	0.994	1.208	1.055	0.858	0.961
VI	0.894	0.979	0.996	0.998	1.108	1.021	0.902	0.978
VII	0.821	0.919	0.985	0.991	1.190	1.082	0.869	0.947
VIII	0.895	0.968	0.994	0.996	1.107	1.031	0.905	0.973
IX	0.806	0.953	0.991	0.994	1.206	1.046	0.859	0.967
X	0.895	0.980	0.996	0.998	1.107	1.020	0.902	0.981
XI	0.824	0.934	0.988	0.992	1.186	1.066	0.870	0.956
XII	0.896	0.971	0.995	0.997	1.106	1.029	0.905	0.976

Note: The subscript N indicates non-epidemic conditions, and G indicates the geometric average.
Source: Own calculations.

conventionally termed "poorly developed" (with capital input $K1$ representing 40% of the value of that variable in the Solow long-run equilibrium) and in a strongly developed economy (with $K1 = 0.9K^*$).[8]

Selected results of numerical simulations are contained in Table 10.3 (a poorly developed economy) and Table 10.4 (a strongly developed economy). Figures 10.5–10.7 depict curves of the social utility function U_t in consecutive scenarios both in a poorly developed and in a strongly developed economy.

The simulation results contained in Tables 10.3 and 10.4 lead to the following conclusions:

- In a poorly developed economy that has no access to a vaccine, falls in production at peak incidence (measured by the indicator $\min_t \frac{Y_t}{Y_{Nt}}$, where Y_{Nt} represents the value of production that could be achieved if the epidemic did not strike) will reach 18.6%–19.9% under conditions of a severe lockdown or 10.7%–10.9% if a liberal approach is adopted. In a strongly developed economy, the falls are slightly smaller and reach (respectively) 18.3%–19.7% or 10.4%–10.6%.
- Slow progress in immunization coverage of the population combined with severe restrictions imposed in response to the epidemic will reduce falls in production to 17.9%–19.5% in a poor economy or 17.7%–19.3% in

a wealthy economy. If a liberal approach to the epidemic is adopted, falls in production will reach (respectively) 10.5%–10.6% or 10.2%–10.3%.

- Rapid progress in immunization coverage has no material effect on falls in production at peak incidence.
- If severe restrictions are imposed in response to the epidemic, without vaccination, accumulated falls in the value of production will reach over three years about 6.8%–9.8% in a poorly developed economy or 6.7%–9.6% in a strongly developed economy. If a liberal approach to the epidemic is adopted, the falls will reach 2.3%–3.5% in a poor economy and 2.2%–3.3% in a wealthy economy.
- Slow progress in immunization coverage of the population combined with severe restrictions imposed in response to the epidemic will lead to accumulated falls in production by 5.5%–8.1% in a poorly developed economy or by 5.4%–7.9% in a strongly developed economy. A liberal approach to the epidemic will lead to accumulated falls in production by 2.1%–3.2% in a poor economy or 2.0%–3.1% in a wealthy economy.
- A rapid pace of progress in immunization coverage of the population will reduce falls in production in a poor economy to 4.7%–6.6% (severe restrictions imposed) or 2.0%–2.9% (a liberal approach), and in a wealthy economy to 4.6%–6.5% or 1.9%–2.8%.
- A more general conclusion can be reached: the introduction and rapid administration of a vaccine will have a stronger effect on accumulated

Table 10.4 Economic indicators in consecutive scenarios at $K1/K^* = 0.9$ (a strongly developed economy)

Scenario	*Variable*							
	$\min_t \frac{Y_t}{Y_{Nt}}$	$\frac{\sum_t Y_t}{\sum_t Y_{Nt}}$	$\min_t \frac{K_t}{K_{Nt}}$	$\frac{\sum_t K_t}{\sum_t K_{Nt}}$	$\max_t \frac{u_t}{u_{Nt}}$	$\frac{\bar{u}_G}{\bar{u}_{GN}}$	$\min_t U_t$	$\bar{U}_G$
	From monthly data						*From daily data*	
I	0.803	0.933	0.990	0.995	1.436	1.135	0.819	0.938
II	0.894	0.978	0.997	0.998	1.225	1.044	0.865	0.960
III	0.817	0.904	0.986	0.992	1.404	1.198	0.831	0.922
IV	0.896	0.967	0.995	0.997	1.219	1.067	0.866	0.954
V	0.807	0.946	0.992	0.995	1.428	1.108	0.823	0.950
VI	0.897	0.980	0.997	0.998	1.218	1.041	0.866	0.967
VII	0.823	0.921	0.989	0.993	1.389	1.160	0.834	0.936
VIII	0.898	0.969	0.996	0.997	1.215	1.061	0.868	0.962
IX	0.808	0.954	0.994	0.996	1.425	1.091	0.824	0.957
X	0.898	0.981	0.997	0.998	1.215	1.038	0.867	0.971
XI	0.826	0.935	0.991	0.994	1.382	1.129	0.835	0.947
XII	0.899	0.972	0.996	0.998	1.213	1.056	0.869	0.966

Note: The subscript N indicates non-epidemic conditions, and G indicates the geometric average.

Source: Own calculations.

falls in production than on the depth of recession. In addition, both accumulated falls in production and the depth of recession will be slightly greater in a poorly developed economy than in a strongly developed economy.

- Both one-off (at the epidemic peak) and accumulated falls in capital stock are significantly smaller than falls in production. Whether the government has access to a vaccine or not, whether severe restrictions are imposed or a liberal approach to the epidemic is adopted, accumulated falls in capital stock in both analyzed types of economy, that is $\frac{\sum_t K_t}{\sum_t K_{Nt}}$, will not exceed 1%.
- Relative increases in the unemployment rate (understood as $\max_t \frac{u_t}{u_{Nt}}$) at peak incidence in a poor economy without vaccination will reach about 20%, if severe restrictions are imposed in response to the epidemic or about 10%–11%, if a liberal approach is adopted. In a wealthy economy the indicators will reach 40%–44% or 22%–23%.[9]
- The indicators only slightly fall with slow or rapid progress in immunization coverage.
- The average unemployment rates over a three-year period (and more precisely the products $\frac{\bar{u}_G}{\bar{u}_{GN}}$) will be higher in the scenarios of severe restrictions imposed by the government in response to the epidemic and will decrease with an increase in the pace of immunization coverage of the population. Those products will also be higher in a wealthy economy. However, it must be emphasized that the geometric average of the unemployment rate $\bar{u}_{GN}$ is significantly lower in a wealthy economy than in a poor economy due to the model design.
- Figures 10.5–10.7 (depicting curves of the social utility function in consecutive scenarios in a poor and in a wealthy economy) lead to the following conclusions. First, falls in social utility U in both types of economy, in scenarios of severe restrictions imposed in response to the epidemic (the scenarios marked with odd Roman numerals), are significantly greater than in scenarios of a liberal approach (the scenarios marked with even numbers). Second, the sooner a vaccine is administered, the smaller are falls in social utility. Third, falls in social utility are slightly smaller in a poor economy, because expressions $\frac{u_{Nt}}{u_t} \cdot \frac{Y_t}{Y_{Nt}}$ are higher in that type of economy.

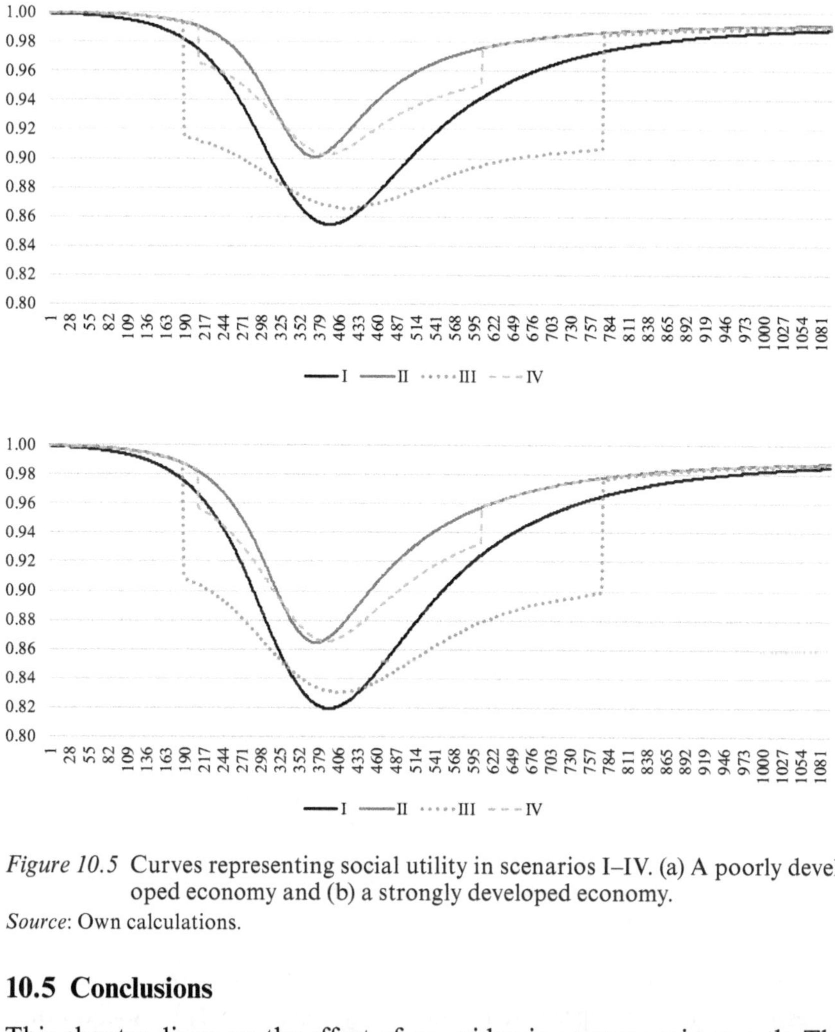

Figure 10.5 Curves representing social utility in scenarios I–IV. (a) A poorly developed economy and (b) a strongly developed economy.

Source: Own calculations.

10.5 Conclusions

This chapter discusses the effect of an epidemic on economic growth. The analysis is conducted using a model of economic growth under epidemic conditions. The epidemiological module introduces an indicator that shows restrictions imposed on social and economic life during the epidemic. The indicator is defined in two versions; in the first version, it changes continually on consecutive days of the epidemic as a function of the percentage of infections, and in the second version, it changes discretely when the government abruptly imposes a lockdown. The epidemiological section also includes a scenario wherein a vaccine (against the spreading disease) is available to the government and a population vaccination programme is implemented. In the section of the model discussion that is dedicated to economy, it is assumed that the production process is described by a neoclassical Cobb-Douglas production function; accumulation of fixed capital,

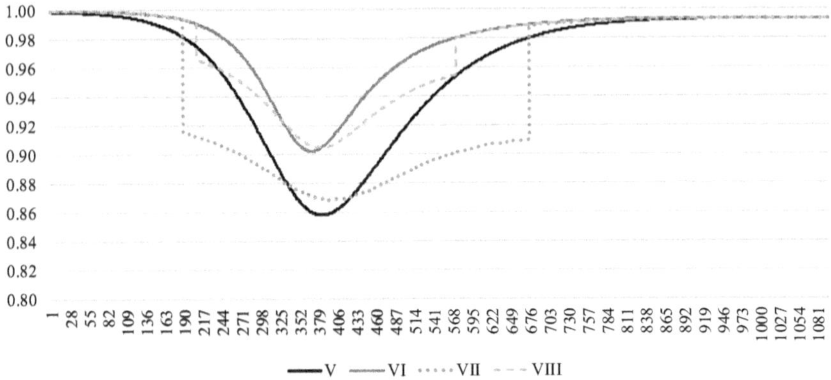

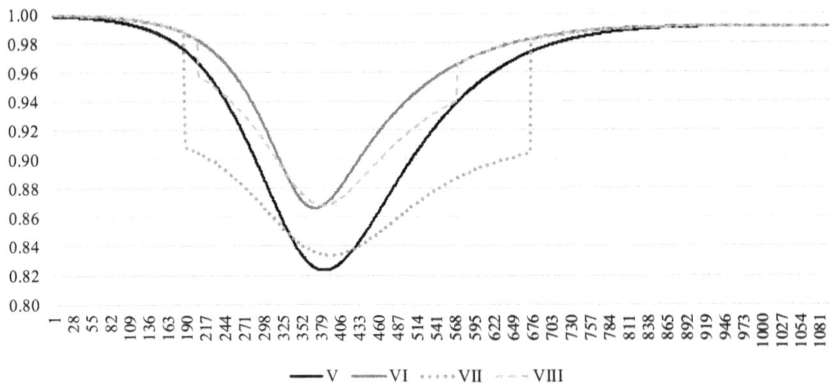

Figure 10.6 Curves representing social utility in scenarios V–VIII. (a) A poorly developed economy and (b) a strongly developed economy.

Source: Own calculations.

like in the original Solow model of 1956, is defined as the difference between investment and the depreciated value of that capital. Also a social utility function is introduced, defined as a geometrical average of the indicator of social and economic activity, the percentage of the uninfected, the ratio of unemployment rate under non-epidemic conditions to that rate under epidemic conditions and the ratio of production during the epidemic to production under non-epidemic conditions.

The chapter also discusses scenarios of epidemic development depending on the availability of a vaccine to the government. In the scenarios wherein the government has no access to a vaccine, it was assumed that the government imposes restrictions on social and economic activity following certain functional relation or abruptly. The scenarios with vaccination are divided into those with slow and those with rapid progress in immunization coverage of the population. Those scenarios also include a lockdown imposed by the government, like in the scenarios without vaccination.

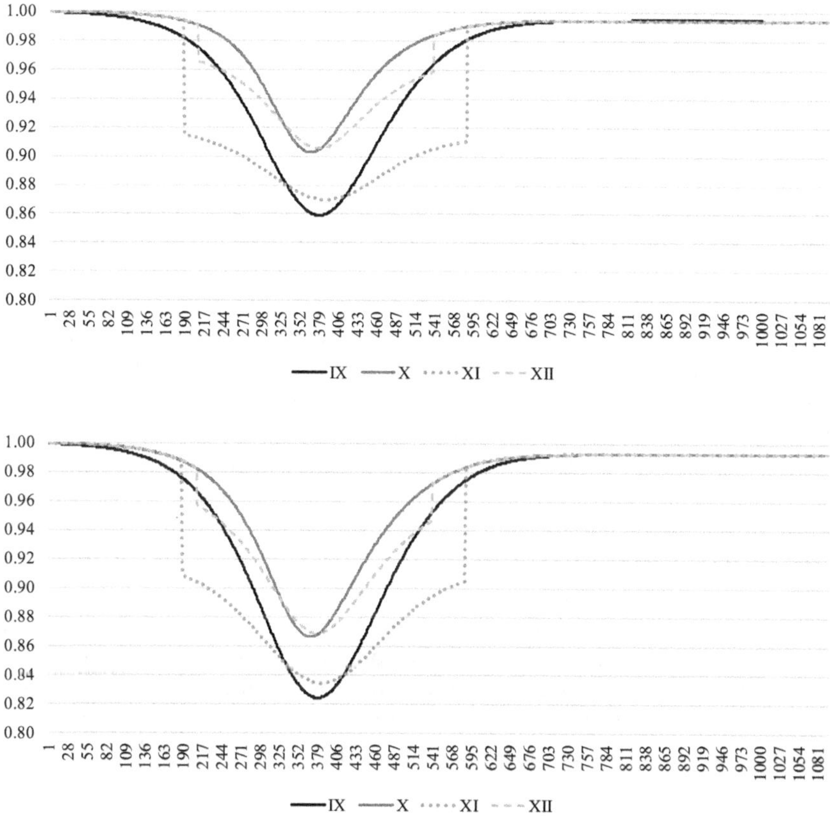

Figure 10.7 Curves representing social utility in scenarios IX–XII. (a) A poorly developed economy and (b) a strongly developed economy.

Source: Own calculations.

Falls in production in an economy without access to a vaccine reach at peak incidence 18.3%–19.9%, if severe restrictions are imposed in response to the epidemic or 10.4%–10.9%, if a liberal approach is adopted. Slow progress in immunization coverage of the population combined with severe restrictions imposed in response to the epidemic will reduce falls in production by 17.7%–19.5%. If a liberal approach to the epidemic is adopted, falls in production will reach (respectively) 10.2%–10.6%. Additionally, rapid progress in immunization coverage has no material effect on falls in production at peak incidence.

If the government imposes severe restrictions in response to the pandemic and has no access to a vaccine, accumulated falls in the value of production will reach over three years about 6.7%–9.8%, and if a liberal approach to the epidemic is adopted, the falls will reach 2.2%–3.5%. Slow progress in immunization coverage of the population combined with severe restrictions imposed in response to the pandemic will lead to accumulated falls in production by 5.4%–8.1% while a liberal approach to the pandemic will lead to accumulated falls in production by 2.0%–3.2%. A rapid pace of progress in immunization coverage of the population reduces accumulated drops in production to about 4.6%–6.6%, if severe restrictions are imposed or to 1.9%–2.9%. Consequently, the introduction of vaccination and rapid progress in immunization coverage will have a stronger effect on accumulated falls in production than on the depth of recession. Additionally, whether the government has access to a vaccine or not, falls in the capital stock will be significantly smaller than falls in production and will not exceed 1%.

Relative increases in the unemployment rate at peak incidence in a poor economy without vaccination will reach about 20%–44%, if severe restrictions are imposed in response to the epidemic or about 10%–23%, if a liberal approach is adopted. The introduction and acceleration of vaccination entails a minor reduction in relative rises in the unemployment rate at peak incidence. Additionally, average unemployment rates over a three-year period will be higher in the scenarios of severe restrictions imposed by the government in response to the epidemic and will decrease with an increase in the pace of immunization coverage of the population.

Falls in social utility will be significantly greater in scenarios of severe restrictions imposed in response to the epidemic than in scenarios of a liberal approach. Implementation of a vaccination programme will result in a reduced depth of fall in social utility, and the faster is progress in immunization coverage of the population, the relatively smaller are falls in social utility.

Notes

1 This model is based on the model proposed in Dykas and Wisła (2022).

2 Certainly, on each day t the equation is true: $S_t + I_t + H_t + D_t = 1$.

3 This is because we obtain from a continuous function $f(x)=1-x^{\sigma}$: $f'(x)=-\sigma x^{\sigma-1}$ and $f''(x)=(1-\sigma)\sigma x^{\sigma-2}$, and consequently for $\sigma > 0$: $\forall x \in (0,1)$ $f'(x)<0$, $\sigma \in (0,1) \Rightarrow f''(x)>0 \wedge \sigma>1 \Rightarrow f''(x)<0$.

4 This is because we obtain from a continuous function $f(t)=\frac{at}{b+t}$:

$$f(0)=0,$$

$$\lim_{t\to+\infty} f(t)=a,$$

$$f'(t)=\frac{ab}{(b+t)^2}>0 \wedge \forall t>-b \quad f''(t)=-\frac{2ab}{(b+t)^3}<0.$$

5 Assumptions 1) and 2) refer directly to the Solow model, and assumptions 3) and 4) extend that model to include basic variables describing the functions of the labour market.

6 To simplify notation, we assume that the total factor productivity on each day t, described by the formula $\frac{Y_t}{K_t^{\alpha} L_t^{1-\alpha}}$, equals 1. This has no effect on the scope of applicability of the below discussion.
7 All epidemiological simulations are carried out for a five-year period while macroeconomic simulations for a three-year period. This is because curves of macroeconomic variables stabilize after three years.
8 Those economies are also termed below "poor" and "wealthy".
9 The parameters of the macroeconomic module of the proposed model are calibrated so that the initial unemployment rate in a poorly developed economy amounts to about 5%, and in a strongly developed economy to about 10%. Hence, the value of indicator $\max_t \frac{u_t}{u_{Nt}}$ amounting e.g. to 1.1 means that the unemployment rate rises from 5% to 5.5% in a wealthy economy of from 10% to 11% in a poor economy. The indicator $\overline{u}_G / \overline{u}_{GN}$ is to be similarly interpreted.

References

Aghion, P., Howitt, P., (1998). *Endogenous Growth Theory*. The MIT Press: Cambridge, MA, London.

Aghion, P., Howitt, P., (2009). *The Economics of Growth*. The MIT Press: Cambridge, MA, London.

Aizenman, J, Jinjarak, Y., Park, D., (2011). Capital flows and economic growth in Era of financial integration and crisis, *NBER Working Paper*, No. 17502, October 2011.

Alfaro, L., (2003). Foreign direct investment and growth: does the sector matter? *Harvard Business School*, April 2003.

Alfaro, L., Chanda, A., Kalemli-Ozcan, S., Sayek, S., (2003). FDI spillovers, financial markets, and economic development, *IMF Working Paper*, WP/03/186, September 2003.

Allen, R.G.D., (1975). *Teoria makroekonomiczna*. Ujęcie matematyczne. Wydawnictwo Naukowe PWN: Warszawa.

Alvarez, F., Argente, D., Lippi, F. (2020). A simple planning problem for COVID-19 lockdown, *NBER Working Paper*, No. 26981.

Arrow, K.J., Chenery, H.B., Minhas, B.S., Solow, R.M., (1961). Capital-labor substitution and economic efficiency, *Review of Economics and Statistics*, 43(3), 225–250.

Atkeson, A. (2020). What will be the economic impact of COVID-19 in the US? Rough estimates of disease scenarios, *NBER Working Paper*, No. 26867.

Aum, S., Lee, S., Shin, Y. (2020). Inequality of fear and self-quarantine: is there a trade-off between GDP and public health? *NBER Working Paper*, No. 27100.

Barro, R.J., (1989). A cross country study of growth, saving, and government, *NBER Working Paper*, No. 2855.

Barro, R.J., (1990). Government spending in a simple model of endogenous growth, *Journal of Political Economy*, 98(S5), 103–125.

Barro, R.J., (1991). Economic growth in cross-section of countries, *Quarterly Journal of Economics*, 106(2), 407–443.

Barro, R.J., Sala-i-Martin, X., (1995). *Economic Growth*, McGraw-Hill Inc.: New York.

Barro, R.J., Mankiw, M.G., Sala-i-Martin, X., (1995). Capital mobility in neoclassical models of growth, *American Economic Review*, 85, 103–115.

Bärwolff, G. (2020). Mathematical modeling and simulation of the COVID-19 pandemic. *Systems*, 8(3), 1–12.

Becker, G.S., (1975). *Human Capital: A Theoretical and Empirical Analysis, with Special References to Education*, University of Chicago Press: Chicago, IL.

Blaug, M., (1990). *Economic Theories, True or False? Essays in the History and Methodology of Economics*. Edward Elgar Publishing Limited: Hants, England.

Bloom, D., Lyons, J. (Eds.) (1993). *Economic Implications of AIDS in Asia*, United Nations Development Programme: New York.

Bloom, D., Mahal, A. (1995). Does the AIDS epidemic really threaten economic growth? *National Bureau of Economic Research Working Paper, No.* 5148, NBER, Cambridge, MA.

Bloom, D., Mahal, A. (1997). Does the AIDS epidemic really threaten economic growth? *Journal of Econometrics*, 77(1), 105–124.

Blume, L.E., Sargent, T.J., (2015). Harrod 1939. *The Economic Journal*, 125(583), 350–377.

Bolińska, M., Dykas, P., Mentel, G., Misiak, T. (2019). Demographic forecasts and volatility of investment rates vs. labor productivity trajectories, *Journal of Business Economics and Management*, 20(6), 1045–1063.

Borensztein, E., De Georgio, J., Lee, J.-W., (1995). How does foreign direct investment affect economic growth? *NBER Working Paper*, No. 5057, March.

Boucekkine, R., Riuz-Tamarit, J.R., (2004). Special functions for the study of economic dynamics: the case of Lucas-Uzawa Model, *CORE Discussion Paper*, No. 84.

Boucekkine, R., Riuz-Tamarit, J.R., (2008). Special function for the study of economic development: The case of Lucas-Uzawa Model, *Journal of Mathematical Economics*, 44, 33–54.

Brock, W., Xepapadeas, A. (2020). The economy, climate change and infectious diseases: Links and policy implications. *Environmental and Resource Economics*, (76), 811–824.

Carkovic, M., Levine, R., (2002). Does foreign direct investment accelerate economic growth? *University of Minnesota Working Paper.*

Cattani, E. (2006). Three lectures on hypergeometric functions, Department of Mathematics and Statistics, University of Massachusetts, http://people.math.umass.edu/~cattani/hypergeom_lectures.pdf.

Chiang, A.C., (1994). *Podstawy ekonomii matematycznej*, Polskie Wydawnictwo Ekonomiczne: Warszawa.

Cichy, K., (2008). *Kapitał ludzki i postęp techniczny jako determinanty wzrostu gospodarczego*, Instytut Wiedzy i Innowacji: Warszawa.

Cichy, K., Malaga, K., (2007). Kapitał ludzki w modelach i teorii wzrostu gospodarczego, in: M. Herbst (Ed.) *Kapitał ludzki i kapitał społeczny a rozwój regionalny*, Wydawnictwo Naukowe SCHOLAR: Kraków, 18–53.

Cobb, C.W., Douglas, P.H., (1928). A theory of production, *American Economic Review*, 18, 139–165.

Coccia, M. (2021). The relation between length of lockdown, numbers of infected people and deaths of Covid-19, and economic growth of countries: Lessons learned to cope with future pandemics similar to Covid-19 and to constrain the deterioration of economic system, *Science of The Total Environment*, 775, 145801.

Cuddington, J. (1993). Modeling the macroeconomic effects of AIDS, with an application to Tanzania, *The World Bank Economic Review*, 7, 173–789.

Cuddington, J., Hancock, J. (1994). Assessing the impact of aids on the growth path of the Malawian economy. *Journal of Development Economics*, 43(2), 363–368.

Cuesta, J. (2010). How much of a threat to economic growth is a mature AIDS epidemic? *Applied Economics*. 42(24), 3077–3089.

Delfino, D., Simmons, P. (2005). Dynamics of tuberculosis and economic growth. *Environment and Development Economics*, 10(6), 719–743.

Dinh, T.-H., Vo, D.H., Vo A.T., Nguyen, T.C. (2019) Foreign direct investment and economic growth in the short run and long run: empirical evidence from developing countries, *Journal of Risk and Financial Management,* 12(4), 176.

Domar, E.D., (1946). Capital expansion, rate of growth, and employment. *Econometrica*, 14, 137–147.

Domar, E.D., (1957). *Essays in the Theory of Economic Growth*. Oxford University Press: Oxford and New York.

Dykas, P., Tokarski, T., (2013). Podażowe czynniki wzrostu gospodarczego – podstawowe modele teoretyczne, *Acta Universitatis Lodziensis, Folia Oeconomica*, tom 294.

Dykas, P., Misiak, T., (2016a). Neoklasyczny model wzrostu gospodarczego z sinusoidalnymi inwestycjami, *Przegląd Statystyczny,* 63(1), 46–66.

Dykas, P., Misiak, T., (2016b). Cykliczność inwestycji w modelu wzrostu gospodarczego – ujęcie teoretyczne oraz symulacje numeryczne, *Studia Prawno-ekonomiczne*, tom C, s. 197–209.

Dykas, P., Wisła, R. (Eds.) (2022). *The Socioeconomic Impact of COVID-19 on Eastern European Countries*, Routledge: London. doi: 10.4324/9781003211891.

Dykas, P., Sulima, A., Tokarski, T., (2008). Złote reguły akumulacji w N-kapitałowym modelu wzrostu gospodarczego, *Gospodarka Narodowa*, nr 11–12.

Dykas, P., Edigarian, A., Tokarski, T., (2011). Uogólnienie N-kapitałowego modelu wzrostu gospodarczego Nonnemana-Vanhoudta, *Zeszyty Naukowe Uniwersytetu Ekonomicznego w Poznaniu*, No 176. pp. 161–177.

Engen, E., Skinder, J., (1992). Fiscal policy and economic growth, *NBER Working Paper,* No. 4223.

Fei-Ying, Y., Wan-Tong, L., Zhi-Cheng, W. (2015). Traveling waves in a nonlocal dispersal SIR epidemic model. *Nonlinear Analysis: Real World Applications*, 23, 129–147.

Filipowicz, K., (2019). *Wpływ interakcji przestrzennych na zróżnicowanie rozwoju gospodarczego Polski*, Wydawnictwo Uniwersytetu Jagiellońskiego: Kraków.

Filipowicz, K., Tokarski, T. (2015). Dwubiegunowy model wzrostu gospodarczego z przepływami inwestycyjnymi, *Studia Prawno-Ekonomiczne*, No 96.

Filipowicz, K., Tokarski, T., Trojak, M., (2015). Złote reguły akumulacji kapitału w grawitacyjnym modelu wzrostu gospodarczego, *Gospodarka Narodowa*, No 3.

Filipowicz, K., Wisła, R., Tokarski, T., (2016). Produktywność kapitału a inwestycje zagraniczne w dwubiegunowym modelu wzrostu gospodarczego: analiza konwergencji, *Przegląd Statystyczny*, No 1.

Filipowicz, K., Grodzicki, M., Tokarski, T., (2016). Równowaga Solowa przy alternatywnych trajektoriach liczby pracujących, *Acta Universitatis Lodziensis, Folia Oeconomica*, tom 326.

Filipowicz, K., Syrek, R., Tokarski, T., (2017). Ścieżki wzrostu w modelu Solowa przy alternatywnych trajektoriach liczby pracujących, *Przegląd Statystyczny,* No 1.

Folster, S., Henrekson, M., (2001). Growth effects of government expenditure and taxation in rich countries, *European Economic Review*, 45(8), 1501–1520.

Gandolfo, G., (1971). *Mathematical Methods and Models in Economic Dynamics*, North- Holland Publishing Company: Amsterdam, London.

Grossman, G.M., Helpman, E., (1991). *Innovation and Growth in the Global Economy*, The MIT Press: Cambridge, MA.

Guerrini, L., (2006). The Solow-Swan model with the bounded population growth rate, *Journal of Mathematical Economics*, 42, 14–21.

Guerrini, L., (2010a). The Ramsey model with a bounded population growth rate, *Journal of Macroeconomics*, 32(3), 872–878.

Guerrini, L., (2010c). A closed-form solution to the Ramsey model with logistic population growth, *Economic Modelling*, 27(5), 1178–1182.

Harrod, R., (1936). *The Trade Cycle: An Essay.* Oxford University Press: Oxford.

Harrod, R.F., (1939). An essay in dynamic theory. *Economic Journal*, 49(193), 14–33.

Jardón-Kojakhmetov, H., Kuehn, Ch., Pugliese, A., Sensi, M. (2021). A geometric analysis of the SIR, SIRS and SIRWS epidemiological models. *Nonlinear Analysis: Real World Applications*, 58, 103220.

Kaldor, N., (1963). *Essays on Economic Stability and Growth.* G. Duckworth & Co., Ltd: London.

Kalecki, M., (1963). *Zarys teorii wzrostu gospodarki socjalistycznej*, PWN: Warszawa.

Kalecki, M., (1996). *Collected Works of Michal Kalecki*, Clarendon Press Oxford: Oxford.

Kambou, G., Devarajan, S., Over, M. (1992). The economic impact of AIDS in an African country: simulations with a computable general equilibrium model of Cameroon, *Journal of African Economies*, 1, 109–130.

Kelly, T., (1997). Public expenditures and growth, *Journal of Development Studies*, 34, 60–84.

Kermack, W.O., McKendrick, A.G. (1927). A contribution to the mathematical theory of epidemics, *Proceedings of the Royal Society, Series A*, 115, 700–721.

Klump, R., Preissler, H., (2000). CES production function and economic growth, *Scandinavian Journal of Economics*, 102(1), 41–54.

Klump, R., McAdam, P., Willman, A. (2011). The normalized CES production function: Theory and empirics, *European Central Bank Working Paper Series*, No. 1294, February 2011.

Kneller, R., Bleaney, M.F., Gemmell, N., (1999). Fiscal policy and growth: evidence from OECD countries, *Journal of Public Economic*, 74, 171–190.

Konopczyński, M., (2004). Model wzrostu gospodarczego małej gospodarki w unii monetarnej. Ujęcie neoklasyczne, *Studia Oeconomica Posnaniensia*, No 41.

Konopczyński, M., (2005). Znaczenie kapitału ludzkiego w unii monetarnej w świetle neoklasycznego modelu wzrostu gospodarczego, *Studia Oeconomica Posnaniensia*, No 64.

Konopczyński, M., (2006). Polityka budżetowa w warunkach unii monetarnej w świetle neoklasycznego modelu wzrostu gospodarczego, *Studia Oeconomica Posnaniensia*, No 78.

Konopczyński, M., (2009). Optimal investment in immobile human capital in an economic and monetary union, *International Journal of Computational Economics and Econometrics*, 2, 126–147.

Konopczyński, M., (2014). Wpływ podatków i kapitału ludzkiego na wzrost gospodarczy na przykładzie Polski, *Ekonomista*, No 6.

Konopczyński, M., (2015). *Optymalna polityka fiskalna w gospodarce otwartej w świetle teorii endogenicznego wzrostu gospodarczego,* Wydawnictwo Uniwersytetu Ekonomicznego w Poznaniu: Poznań.

Korn, G.A., Korn, T.M. (1983). *Matematyka dla pracowników naukowych i inżynierów*, część 1, Polskie Wydawnictwo Naukowe: Warszawa.

Korotayev, A.V., Tsirel, S., (2010). A spectral analysis of world GDP dynamics: Kondratieff Waves, Kuznets Swings, Juglar and Kitchin Cycles in Global Economic Development, and the 2008–2009 Economic Crisis, *Structure and Dynamics: eJournal of Anthropological and Related Sciences*, 4, 1–57.

Krajewski, S. (2000), *Wzrost gospodarczy, restrukturyzacja i bezrobocie w Polsce: Ujęcie teoretyczne i praktyczne,* Katedra Ekonomii Uniwersytetu Łódzkiego: Łódź.

Krawiec, A., (2005). A note on optimized growth model with public sector, *Acta Universitatis Lodziensis, FoliaOeconomica*, tom 190.

Krawiec, A., Szydłowski, M., (2002). Własności dynamiki modeli nowej teorii wzrostu, *Przegląd Statystyczny*, No 1.

Latocha, T., (2005). Bezpośrednie inwestycje zagraniczne w Unii Europejskiej w świetle teorii rozwoju regionalnego i teorii lokalizacji, *Studia Europejskie,* No 2/2005.

Lik Ng, W. (2020). To lockdown? When to peak? Will there be an end? A macroeconomic analysis on COVID-19 epidemic in the United States. *Journal of Macroeconomics*, 65, 103230.

Lovasz, E., Schipp, B. (2009). The impact of HIV/AIDS on economic growth in Sub-Saharan Africa. *South African Journal of Economics*, 77(2), 245–256.

Lucas, R.E., (1988). On the mechanics of economic development, *Journal of Monetary Economics*, 22, 3–42.

Lucas, R.E., (1990). Why doesn't capital flow from rich to poor countries, *American Economic Review*, 80(2), 92–96.

Lucas, R.E., (2010). *Wykłady z teorii wzrostu gospodarczego*, Wydawnictwo C.H. Beck: Warszawa.

Malaga, K., (2004). *Konwergencja gospodarcza w krajach OECD w świetle zagregowanych modeli wzrostu*, Akademia Ekonomiczna w Poznaniu: Poznań.

Malaga, K., (2013). *Jednolita teoria wzrostu gospodarczego – stan obecny i nowe wyzwania*, wystąpienie na IX Kongresie Ekonomistów Polskich: Warszawa.

Malaga, K., Kliber, P., (2007). *Konwergencja i nierówności regionalne w Polsce w świetle neoklasycznych modeli wzrostu,* Akademia Ekonomiczna w Poznaniu: Poznań.

Mankiw, N.G., Romer, D., Weil, D.N. (1992). A contribution to the empirics of economic growth. *Quarterly Journal of Economics*, 107(2), 407–437.

Markusen J.R., Venables A.J. (1999). Foreign direct investment as a catalyst for industrial development, *European Economic Review*, 43(2), 335–356.

Milo, W., Malaczewski, M., (2005). Stabilność punktu równowagi modelu Solowa, in: *Dynamiczne modele ekonometryczne,* Uniwersytet Mikołaja Kopernika w Toruniu: Toruń, 15–24.

Moudatsou, A., (2003). Foreign direct investment and economic growth in European Union, *Journal of Economic Integration*, 18(4), 689–707.

Mroczek, K., Tokarski, T., (2013). Regionalne zróżnicowanie kapitału ludzkiego w Polsce, *Studia Prawno-Ekonomiczne,* tom 89.

Mroczek, K., Tokarski, T., Trojak, M., (2014). Grawitacyjny model zróżnicowania ekonomicznego województw, *Gospodarka Narodowa*, No 3.

Murray, J.D. (2003). *Mathematical Biology, II, Spatial Models and Biomedical Applications*, third ed., Bressloff, P.C. et al. (Eds.) Interdisciplinary Applied Mathematics Series, vol. 18, Springer-Verlag: New York.

Nonneman, W., Vanhoudt, P., (1996). A further augmentation of the Solow model and the empirics of economic growth, *Quarterly Journal of Economics*, 111, 943–953.

Nowosad, A., Wisła, R., (2016, red.). *Zróżnicowanie rozwoju współczesnej Europy*, Wydawnictwo Uniwersytetu Jagiellońskiego: Kraków.

Ombach, J., (1999). *Wykłady z równań różniczkowych wspomagane komputerowo – Maple*, Wydawnictwo Uniwersytetu Jagiellońskiego: Kraków.

Phelps, E.S., (1961). The golden rule of accumulation: a fable for growthmen, *American Economic Review*, 51(4), 638–643.

Pietraszewski, P., (2009). Analiza możliwości oddziaływania państwa na wzrost gospodarczy w kontekście maksymalizacji dobrobytu, *Ruch Prawny, Ekonomiczny i Socjologiczny*, No 4.

Ptaszyńska, B., (2015). Inwestycje zagraniczne czynnikiem wzrostu gospodarczego w Polsce, *Wiadomości Statystyczne,* No 2/2015.

Roman, M.D., Padureanu, A., (2012). Models of foreign direct influence on economic growth, evidence from Romania, *International Journal of Trade, Economics and Finance*, 3(1), 25–29.

Romer, D., (2012). *Advanced Macroeconomics*, Fourth Edition, The McGraw-Hill Companies, Inc: New York.

Romer, P.M., (1986). Increasing returns and long-run growth, *Journal of Political Economy*, 94(5), 1002–1037.

Romer, P.M., (1990). Endogenous technological change, *Journal of Political Economy*, 98, S71–S102.

Roszkowska, S., (2005). Kapitał ludzki a wzrost gospodarczy w ujęciu wojewódzkim, *Wiadomości Statystyczne*, No 10.

Roszkowska, S., (2013). Wpływ kapitału ludzkiego na wzrost w gospodarce polskiej – oszacowania wieloczynnikowej funkcji produkcji, *Acta Universitatis Lodziensis, Folia Oeconomica*, tom 281.

Roszkowska, S., (2014). *Kapitał ludzki a wzrost gospodarczy w Polsce*, Wydawnictwo Uniwersytetu Łódzkiego: Łódź.

Ruan, S. (2007). Spatial–temporal dynamics in nonlocal epidemiological models, in: Y. Takeuchi, K. Sato, Y. Iwasa (Eds.), *Mathematics for Life Science and Medicine*, Springer-Verlag: Berlin, pp. 99–122.

Sasaki, H., (2017). A note on the Solow Growth Model with a CES Production Function, *Munich Personal RePec Archive*, No. 80062.

Snowdon, B., Vane, H.R., (2000). *Conversations with Leading Economists: Interpreting Modern Macroeconomics*, Edward Elgar Publishing: Cheltenham.

Solow, R.M., (1956). A contribution to the theory of economic growth. *The Quarterly Journal of Economics*, 70(1), 65–94.

Solow, R.M., (1957). Technical change and the aggregate production function. *The Review of Economics and Statistics*, 39(3), 312–320.

Solow, R.M., (1988). Growth theory and after. *The American Economic Review*, 78(3), 307–317.

Sulima A. (2011) Równowaga w modelu Nonnemana-Vanhoudta z funkcją produkcji CES, *Gospodarka Narodowa,* No 11–12.

Tokarski, T., (2000). Polityka fiskalna a wzrost gospodarczy [w:] *Wzrost gospodarczy, restrukturyzacja i bezrobocie w Polsce. Ujęcie teoretyczne i praktyczne.*

Tokarski, T., (2005). Wybrane modele podażowych czynników wzrostu gospodarczego, Wydawnictwo Uniwersytetu Jagiellońskiego, Kraków.

Tokarski, T., (2007). Efekty skali a wzrost gospodarczy, *Gospodarka Narodowa,* No 1–2.

Tokarski, T., (2008a). Równowaga neoklasycznych modeli wzrostu gospodarczego przy funkcji produkcji CES, *Studia Prawno-Ekonomiczne*, No 77.

Tokarski, T., (2008b). *Efekty skali a wzrost gospodarczy*, Wydawnictwo Uniwersytetu Jagiellońskiego: Kraków.

Tokarski, T., (2009). *Matematyczne modele wzrostu gospodarczego (ujęcie neoklasyczne)*, Wydawnictwo Uniwersytetu Jagiellońskiego: Kraków.

Tokarski, T., (2011). *Ekonomia matematyczna*, Modele makroekonomiczne, Polskie Wydawnictwo Ekonomiczne: Warszawa.

Tokarski, T., Zachorowska-Mazurkiewicz, A., (2016). Kłopoty z marginalną teorią podziału Clarka, *Gospodarka Narodowa*, 6(286), 23–42.

Welfe, W., (2000). Empiryczne modele wzrostu [w:] *Wzrost gospodarczy, restrukturyzacja i bezrobocie w Polsce, Ujęcie teoretyczne i praktyczne.*

Welfe, W., (2009, red.). *Knowledge-Based Economies,* Frankfurt am Main: Peter Lang.

Witkowska, J., (1997). Przepływy bezpośrednich inwestycji zagranicznych w gospodarce światowej a procesy integracji gospodarczej (ze szczególnym uwzględnieniem Unii Europejskiej i Polski), *Studia Europejskie*, No 1/1997.

Xiao, D., Ruan, S. (2007), Global analysis of an epidemic model with nonmonotone incidence rate, *Mathematical Bioscience,* 208, 419–429.

Zawadzki, H., (2007). Model Solowa-Swana ze zmienną stopą wzrostu populacji, [w:] *Modelowanie i prognozowanie gospodarki narodowej, Prace i materiały Uniwersytetu Gdańskiego*, tom 5, Gdańsk.

Zawadzki, H., (2012). Analiza dynamiki modelu Mankiwa-Romera-Weila za pomocą programu Mathematica, *Zeszyty Naukowe Uniwersytetu Ekonomicznego w Poznaniu*, No 239.

Zawadzki, H., (2015). Analiza dynamiki modelu wzrostu gospodarczego za pomocą środowiska obliczeniowego Mathematica, *Zeszyty Naukowe (Cracow Review of Economics and Management)*, No 4.

Zienkowski, L., (2003, red.). *Wiedza a wzrost gospodarczy*, Wydawnictwo Scholar: Warszawa.

Żółtowska, E., (1997). *Funkcja produkcji. Teoria, estymacja, zastosowania*, Wydawnictwo Uniwersytetu Łódzkiego: Łódź.

Index

Note: Page numbers followed by "n" denote endnotes.

For Product Safety Concerns and Information please contact our EU representative GPSR@taylorandfrancis.com
Taylor & Francis Verlag GmbH, Kaufingerstraße 24, 80331 München, Germany

www.ingramcontent.com/pod-product-compliance
Lightning Source LLC
LaVergne TN
LVHW021122300926
849160LV00010B/826
* 9 7 8 1 0 3 2 3 4 7 7 7 6 *